MW01123552

Shadow Banking
Within and Across
National Borders

World Scientific Studies in International Economics

(ISSN: 1793-3641)

Vol. 32 Asian Free Trade Agreements and WTO Compatibility: Goods, Services, Trade Facilitation and Economic Cooperation
by Shintaro Hamanaka (Asian Development Bank, Philippines)

Vol. 33 Economics and Politics of Trade Policy
by Douglas R Nelson (Tulane University, USA)

Vol. 34 Applied Trade Policy Modeling in 16 Countries: Insights and Impacts from World Bank CGE Based Projects
by David G Tarr (Consultant and Former Lead Economist, The World Bank, USA)

Vol. 35 The Floating World: Issues in International Trade Theory
by Wilfred J Ethier (University of Pennsylvania, USA)

Vol. 36 Trade Policy in Asia: Higher Education and Media Services
edited by Christopher Findlay (University of Adelaide, Australia), Hildegunn Kyvik Nordas (Organisation for Economic Co-operation and Development, France) & Gloria Pasadilla (APEC Secretariat, Singapore)

Vol. 37 The Path of World Trade Law in the 21st Century
by Steve Charnovitz (The George Washington University, USA)

Vol. 38 International Trade, Distribution and Development: Empirical Studies of Trade Policies
by Paul Brenton (The World Bank, USA)

Vol. 39 Evolving Patterns in Global Trade and Finance
by Sven W Arndt (Claremont McKenna College, USA)

Vol. 40 Shadow Banking Within and Across National Borders
edited by Stijn Claessens (International Monetary Fund, USA), Douglas Evanoff (Federal Reserve Bank of Chicago, USA), George Kaufman (Loyola University Chicago, USA) & Luc Laeven (International Monetary Fund, USA)

The complete list of the published volumes in the series can be found at
http://www.worldscientific.com/series/wssie

40 World Scientific Studies in International Economics

Shadow Banking Within and Across National Borders

Editors

Stijn Claessens
International Monetary Fund, USA

Douglas Evanoff
Federal Reserve Bank of Chicago, USA

George Kaufman
Loyola University Chicago, USA

Luc Laeven
International Monetary Fund, USA

World Scientific

NEW JERSEY • LONDON • SINGAPORE • BEIJING • SHANGHAI • HONG KONG • TAIPEI • CHENNAI

Published by

World Scientific Publishing Co. Pte. Ltd.
5 Toh Tuck Link, Singapore 596224
USA office: 27 Warren Street, Suite 401-402, Hackensack, NJ 07601
UK office: 57 Shelton Street, Covent Garden, London WC2H 9HE

Library of Congress Cataloging-in-Publication Data
International Banking Conference (16th : 2013 : Chicago, Ill.)
Shadow banking within and across national borders / [edited] by Stijn Claessens (International Monetary Fund, USA), Douglas Evanoff (Federal Reserve Bank of Chicago, USA), George Kaufman (Loyola University Chicago, USA) & Luc Laeven (International Monetary Fund, USA).
pages cm. -- (World scientific studies in international economics, ISSN 1793-3641 ; v. 40)
Papers and keynote speeches presented at the sixteenth annual International Banking Conference in Chicago, held on November 7–8, 2013.
Includes bibliographical references.
ISBN 978-9814602709
1. Banks and banking--Developing countries--Congresses. 2. Informal sector (Economics)--Developing countries--Congresses. 3. Financial crises--Congresses. 4. International finance--Congresses. I. Claessens, Stijn. II. Title.
HG3550.I58 2013
332.1--dc23

2014014635

British Library Cataloguing-in-Publication Data
A catalogue record for this book is available from the British Library.

Cover Illustration by Ping Homeric

In-house Editors: Dipasri Sardar/Chye Shu Wen/Rajni Gamage

Typeset by Stallion Press
Email: enquiries@stallionpress.com

Preface

In recent years, activities generally regarded as banking in nature have been conducted outside of traditional banking institutions, in what have been labeled "shadow banks". The shadow banking system has garnered increased attention as a rapidly growing, lightly regulated complex of financial markets and institutions that operates in parallel with the formal banking sector and has grown to match or exceed it in size in some markets. It also has been identified as having had a significant role in the recent financial crisis, both in the United States and abroad. Yet, surprisingly little is known about the shadow system's scope and operations. Nevertheless, many regulatory proposals have been developed for "taming" the shadow system and are currently under consideration.

On November 7–8, 2013, the Federal Reserve Bank of Chicago and the International Monetary Fund cosponsored the 16th annual International Banking Conference in Chicago to address issues associated with the shadow banking system. Why has this alternative financial system developed? Who are the key players? How large is the system? What are its implications for financial stability? Is it, or should it be, regulated? Why? What benefits and costs does the sector accrue for society?

Some 175 financial policymakers, regulators, researchers, scholars, and practitioners from more than 20 countries attended the conference. This volume includes papers and keynote speeches presented at the conference. The publication is intended to disseminate the conference ideas, analyses, and conclusions to a wider audience, in hope that the broader distribution will generate additional discussion, serve as the basis for further analyses, and be helpful in guiding future public policy.

Acknowledgments

Both the conference held at the Federal Reserve Bank of Chicago, November 7–8, 2013, and this book represent a joint effort of the Federal Reserve Bank of Chicago and the International Monetary Fund. Various people at each institution contributed to the effort. The editors served as the principal organizers of the conference program and would like to thank all the people from both organizations who contributed their time and energy to the effort. At the risk of omitting someone, we would also like to thank Julia Baker, Bob Dlotkowski, John Dixon, Ella Dukes, Ping Homeric, and Rita Molloy. Special mention should be accorded Kathryn Moran, who managed the Chicago Fed's web effort; Sandy Schneider, who expertly managed the conference administration; as well as Helen O'D. Koshy and Sheila Mangler, who had responsibility for preparing the manuscripts for this volume.

Contents

I
Special Addresses

The Fire-Sales Problem and Securities Financing Transactions

Jeremy C. Stein*

Board of Governors of the Federal Reserve System

Thank you. I thought I would focus my remarks today on one piece of the shadow banking system, namely the market for securities financing transactions (SFTs). In so doing, I want to call attention to the fire-sales problem associated with SFTs, and consider potential policy remedies. I will do so in three parts. First, I will briefly discuss the welfare economics of fire-sales. That is, I will try to make clear when a forced sale of an asset is not just an event that leads to prices being driven below long-run fundamental values, but also one that involves a market failure, or externality, of the sort that might justify a regulatory response. Second, I will argue that SFTs are a leading example of the kind of arrangement that can give rise to such externalities, and hence are particularly deserving of policy attention. And third, I will survey some of the recently enhanced tools in our regulatory arsenal (e.g., capital, liquidity, and leverage requirements) and ask to what extent they are suited to tackling the specific externalities associated with fire sales and SFTs.

To preview, a general theme is that while many of these tools are likely to be helpful in fortifying individual regulated institutions — in reducing the

*At the time of this speech, Jeremy Stein was a Member of the Board of Governors of the Federal Reserve System. In May 2014 he returned to his professorship in the Department of Economics at Harvard University.

probability that, say, a given bank or broker-dealer will run into solvency or liquidity problems — they fall short as a comprehensive, market-wide approach to the fire-sales problem associated with SFTs. In this regard, some of what I have to say will echo a recent speech by my Board colleague, Daniel Tarullo.[1]

Positive and Normative Economics of Fire-Sales

In a recent survey paper, Andrei Shleifer and Robert Vishny write that: "… [A] fire sale is essentially a forced sale of an asset at a dislocated price. The asset sale is forced in the sense that the seller cannot pay creditors without selling assets.… Assets sold in fire-sales can trade at prices far below value in best use, causing severe losses to sellers".[2] Shleifer and Vishny go on to discuss the roles of investor specialization and limited arbitrage as factors that drive the magnitude of observed price discounts in fire-sales, and there is, by now, a large body of empirical research that supports the importance of these factors.

However, by itself, the existence of substantial price discounts in distressed sales speaks only to the positive economics of fire sales, not the normative economics, and hence is not sufficient to make a case for regulatory intervention. To see why, consider the following example: An airline buys a 737 and finances the purchase largely with collateralized borrowing. During an industry downturn, the airline finds itself in distress and is forced to sell the 737 to avoid defaulting on its debt. Other airlines also are not faring well at this time and are not interested in expanding their fleets. So the only two bidders for the 737 are a movie star, who plans to reconfigure it for his personal use, and a private-equity firm, which plans to lease out the plane temporarily and wait for the market to recover so the firm can resell it at a profit. In the end, the private-equity firm winds up buying the plane at half its original price. Two years later, it does indeed resell it, having earned a 60% return.

This is clearly a fire sale in the positive-economics sense, but is there a market failure here that calls for regulation? Intuition suggests not. The airline arguably caused the fire sale by using a lot of leverage in its purchase

[1] Tarullo (2013).
[2] Shleifer and Vishny (2011).

of the 737, but it also seems to bear most of the cost by being forced to liquidate at a large loss. The movie star and the private-equity firm are, if anything, made better off by the appearance of a buying opportunity, and there are no other innocent bystanders. So the airline's *ex-ante* capital structure choice would seem to internalize things properly; the fire sale here is just like any other bankruptcy cost that a firm has to weigh in choosing the right mix of debt and equity.

For a fire-sale to have the sort of welfare effects that create a role for regulation, the reduced price in the fire-sale has to hurt somebody other than the original party making the leverage decision, and this adverse impact of price has to run through something like a collateral constraint, whereby a lowered price actually reduces, rather than increases, the third party's demand for the asset.[3] So if hedge fund A buys an asset-backed security and finances it largely with collateralized borrowing, A's fire selling of the security will create an externality in the conventional sense only if the reduced price and impaired collateral value lower the ability of hedge funds B and C to borrow against the same security, and therefore force them to involuntarily liquidate their positions in it as well.[4] The market failure in this case is not simply the fact that this downward spiral causes a large price decline; it is that when hedge fund A makes its initial leverage choice, it does not take into account the potential harm — in the form of tightened financing constraints — that this may cause to hedge funds B and C.[5]

Another key point is that the fire-sales problem is not necessarily caused by a lack of appropriate conservatism on the part of whoever lends to

[3]An alternative mechanism that works similarly is when the third party is a regulated intermediary and mark-to-market losses reduce its capital ratios and again force it to involuntarily sell assets in the face of falling prices.

[4]The fundamental welfare economics at work here is developed in Geanakoplos and Polemarchakis (1986). A discussion of the connection of this work to specific aspects of macroprudential regulation is in Hanson, Kashyap, and Stein (2011).

[5]This is the first-round externality. Adverse spillovers from a fire sale of this sort may also take the form of a credit crunch that affects borrowers more generally. Such a credit crunch may arise as other financial intermediaries (e.g., banks) withdraw capital from lending, so as to exploit the now-more-attractive returns to buying up fire-sold assets. Ultimately, it is the risk of this credit contraction, and its implications for economic activity more broadly, that may be the most compelling basis for regulatory intervention.

hedge fund A in this example — let us call it dealer firm D. By lending on an overnight basis to A, and with an appropriate haircut, D can virtually assure itself of being able to terminate its loan and get out whole by forcing a sale of the underlying collateral. So D's interests may be very well protected here. But precisely in the pursuit of this protection, A and D have set up a financing arrangement that serves them well, but that creates a negative spillover onto other market participants, like B and C. It follows that even if policies aimed at curbing too-big-to-fail (TBTF) problems are entirely successful in aligning D's interests with those of taxpayers, this is not sufficient to deal with fire-sales externalities. They are a fundamentally different problem, and one that arises even absent any individually systemic institutions or any TBTF issues.

Fire-Sale Externalities in SFTs

The preceding discussion makes clear why SFTs, such as those done via repurchase (repo) agreements, are a natural object of concern for policymakers. This market is one where a large number of borrowers finance the same securities on a short-term collateralized basis, with very high leverage — often in the range of twenty-to-one, fifty-to-one, or even higher. Hence, there is a strong potential for any one borrower's distress — and the associated downward pressure on prices — to cause a tightening of collateral or regulatory constraints on other borrowers.

I will not go into much detail about the institutional aspects of SFTs and the repo market. Instead, I will just lay out two stylized examples of SFTs that I can then use to illustrate the properties of various regulatory tools.

Example 1: Broker-dealer as principal

In this first example, a large broker-dealer firm borrows in the triparty repo market — from, say, a money market fund — in order to finance its own holdings of a particular security. Perhaps the broker-dealer is acting as a market-maker in the corporate bond market and uses repo borrowing to finance its ongoing inventory of investment-grade and high-yield bonds. In this case, the asset on the dealer's balance sheet is the corporate bond, and the liability is the repo borrowing from the money fund.

Example 2: Broker-dealer as SFT intermediary

In this second example, the ultimate demand to own the corporate bond comes not from the dealer firm, but from one of its prime brokerage customers — say, a hedge fund. Moreover, the hedge fund cannot borrow directly from the money market fund sector in the triparty repo market, because the money funds are not sufficiently knowledgeable about the hedge fund to be comfortable taking it on as a counterparty. So instead, the hedge fund borrows on a collateralized basis from the dealer firm in the bilateral repo market, and the dealer then turns around and, as before, uses the same collateral to borrow from a money fund in the triparty market. In this case, the asset on the dealer's balance sheet is the repo loan it makes to the hedge fund.

Clearly, there is the potential for fire-sale risk in both of these examples. One source of risk would be an initial shock either to the expected value of the underlying collateral or to its volatility that leads to an increase in required repo-market haircuts (e.g., the default probability of the corporate bond goes up). Another source of risk would be concerns about the creditworthiness of the broker-dealer firm that causes lenders in the triparty market to step away from it.

In either case, if the associated externalities are deemed to create significant social costs, the goal of regulatory policy should be to get private actors to internalize these costs. At an abstract level, this means looking for a way to impose an appropriate Pigouvian (i.e., corrective) tax on the transactions.[6] Of course, the tax must balance the social costs against the benefits that accompany SFTs; these benefits include both "money-like" services from the increased stock of near-riskless private assets, as well as enhanced liquidity in the market for the underlying collateral — the corporate bond market, in my examples.[7] So in the absence of further work on calibrating costs and benefits, there is no presumption that the optimal tax

[6]Of course, the Pigouvian taxation approach by itself cannot completely eliminate the *ex post* costs associated with fire-sales. This would require a broad and active lender-of-last resort function, which I do not discuss here. The best that any form of *ex ante* regulation can hope to do is to reduce the incidence and magnitude of *ex post* fire-sales damage.

[7]Further discussion on the money-like benefits that are created by near-riskless private assets such as repo can be found in the following: Gorton and Metrick (2012); Krishnamurthy and Vissing-Jørgensen (2012); and Stein (2012).

should be large, only that it may be non-zero, and that it may make sense for it to differ across asset classes.

Can Existing Regulatory Tools be Used to Tax SFTs Efficiently?

With this last observation in mind, my next step is to run through a number of our existing regulatory instruments, and in each case ask: To what extent can the instrument at hand be used efficiently to impose a Pigouvian tax on an SFT, either one of the dealer-as-principal type or one of the dealer-as-intermediary type? As will become clear, the answer can depend crucially on both the structure of the transaction as well as the nature of the underlying collateral involved. Also, I should emphasize that nothing in this exercise amounts to a judgment on the overall desirability of any given regulatory tool. Obviously, even if risk-based capital requirements are not particularly helpful in taxing SFTs, they can be very valuable for other reasons. I am asking a different question: To what extent can the existing toolkit be used — or be adapted — to deal with the specific problem of fire-sale externalities in SFTs?

1. *Risk-based capital requirements*

Current risk-based capital requirements are of little relevance for many types of SFTs. In my Example 1, where the dealer firm holds a corporate bond as a principal and finances it with repo borrowing, there would be a capital charge on the corporate bond, but this capital charge is approximately independent of whether the corporate bond is financed with repo or with some other, more stable, form of funding. So there is no tax on the incremental fire-sale risk created by the more fragile funding structure.[8]

In Example 2, in which the dealer is an intermediary with a matched book of repo borrowing and lending, there is, in principle, a capital requirement on its asset-side repo loan to the hedge fund. However, the

[8] To be more precise, under Basel III capital rules, there is a small risk-based capital requirement on the repo liability. This requirement is driven by counterparty credit risk, not liquidity risk, and is independent of the term of the repo borrowing. The basic idea is that the repo borrower has to hold a little bit of capital because it has sent $102 in Treasury securities over to its counterparty lender and only received $100 cash. If the repo lender defaults, the borrower could be out $2.

Basel III risk-based capital rules allow banks and bank holding companies to use internal models to compute this capital charge for repo lending, and the resulting numbers are typically very small — for all practical purposes, close to zero — for overcollateralized lending transactions, with repo being the canonical example.

I'm not arguing that the very low risk-based charges on repo lending in Basel III are "wrong" in any microprudential sense. After all, they are designed to solve a different problem — that of ensuring bank solvency. And if a bank holding company's broker-dealer sub makes a repo loan of short maturity that is sufficiently well-collateralized, it may be at minimal risk of bearing any losses — precisely because it operates on the premise that it can dump the collateral and get out of town before things get too ugly. The risk-averse lenders in the triparty market — who, in turn, provide financing to the dealer — operate under the same premise. As I noted earlier, these defensive reactions by providers of repo finance mean that the costs of fire sales are likely to be felt elsewhere in the financial system.

2. *Liquidity requirements*

Liquidity requirements, such as those embodied in the Basel III Liquidity Coverage Ratio (LCR), can impose a meaningful tax on certain SFTs in which the dealer acts as a principal. If the dealer holds a corporate bond and finances it with repo borrowing of less than 30 days' maturity, the LCR kicks in and requires the dealer to hold high-quality liquid assets (HQLA) against the risk that it is unable to roll the repo over. In this particular case, there can be said to be a direct form of regulatory attack on the fire-sales problem. However, this conclusion is sensitive to the details of the example. If, instead of holding a corporate bond, the dealer holds a Treasury security that is deemed to count as Level 1 HQLA, there is no impact of the LCR.

Moreover, the LCR plays no role in mitigating fire-sales externalities in the important matched-book case in which the dealer acts as an intermediary.[9] If a dealer borrows on a collateralized basis with repo and

---

[9]A similar comment applies to the Net Stable Funding Ratio (NSFR), which requires regulated firms to fund illiquid exposures with some amount of long-term debt or other form of stable funding. Like the LCR, the NSFR effectively treats matched-book repo as creating no net liquidity exposure, and hence imposes no requirement on it.

then turns around and lends the proceeds to a hedge fund in a similar fashion, the LCR deems the dealer to have no net liquidity exposure — and hence imposes no incremental liquidity requirement — so long as the lending side of the transaction has a maturity of less than 30 days. The implicit logic is that as long as the dealer can generate the necessary cash by not rolling over its loan to the hedge fund, it will always be able to handle any outflows of funding that come from being unable to roll over its own borrowing. This logic is not incorrect *per se*, but it is very micro-focused in nature, and does not attend to fire-sales externalities. It worries about the ability of the dealer firm to survive a liquidity stress event, but does not take into account the fact that the dealer's survival may come at the cost of forcing its hedge fund client to engage in fire-sales.[10]

3. *Leverage ratio*

If a broker-dealer firm faces a binding leverage ratio, this constraint can act as a significant tax on two types of SFTs that are largely untouched either by risk-based capital requirements or by liquidity regulations. The first is when the dealer, acting as a principal, uses repo to finance its holdings of Treasury securities or agency mortgage-backed securities, assets that generally have only modest risk weights when held as trading positions. The second is when the dealer acts as an intermediary and has a matched repo book. In both cases, the SFTs blow up the firm's balance sheet and, hence, the denominator of the leverage ratio, even while having little impact on risk-based capital or LCR calculations.

The crucial issue here, however, is whether the leverage ratio does, in fact, bind. A traditional view among regulators has been that the leverage ratio should be calibrated so as to serve as a meaningful "backstop" for risk-based capital requirements, but that under ordinary circumstances it should not actually be the binding constraint on firms. For if it were to bind, this would put us in a regime of completely un-risk-weighted capital requirements, where the effective capital charge for holding short-term Treasury securities

---

[10]Even from a microprudential perspective, the LCR can be said to have a flaw in that it is blind to maturity mismatches within the 30-day window. For example, if a dealer borrows on an overnight basis from a money fund, and then makes a 29-day loan to a hedge fund, the LCR deems it to be fully matched, and to have no incremental liquidity exposure.

would be the same as that for holding, say, risky corporate debt securities or loans.

Recently, US regulators have issued a proposed rulemaking that seeks to raise the Basel III supplementary leverage ratio requirement to 5% for the largest US bank holding companies, and to 6% for their affiliated depository institutions. While this increase might be considered a parallel shift that preserves the backstop philosophy in light of the fact that risk-based requirements have also gone up significantly, it does increase the likelihood that the leverage ratio may bind for some of these firms at some times — particularly for those firms with a broker-dealer-intensive business model in which the ratio of total assets to risk-weighted assets tends to be higher. In this event, there would indeed be a significant tax on SFTs undertaken in the affected firms. However, because it is unlikely that the leverage constraint would bind symmetrically across all of the largest firms, my guess is that the effect would be less to deter SFT activity in the aggregate than to cause it to migrate in such a way as to be predominantly located in those firms that — because they have, say, a larger lending business and, hence, more risk-weighted assets — have more headroom under the leverage ratio constraint.

Other Possible Approaches

To summarize the discussion thus far, the mainstays of our existing regulatory toolkit — risk-based capital, liquidity and leverage requirements — have a variety of other virtues, but none seem well suited to lean in a comprehensive way against the specific fire-sale externalities created by SFTs. The LCR affects a subset of SFTs in which a dealer firm acts as a principal to fund its own inventory of securities positions, but does not meaningfully touch those in which it acts as an intermediary. By contrast, an aggressively calibrated leverage ratio could potentially impose a significant tax on a wider range of SFTs, but the tax would by its nature be blunt and highly asymmetric, falling entirely on those firms for whom the leverage ratio constraint was more binding than the risk-based capital constraint. As such, it would be more likely to induce regulatory arbitrage than to rein in overall SFT activity.

These observations raise the question of whether there are other tools that might be better suited to dealing with SFT-related fire-sales externalities. I will touch briefly on three of these.

Capital surcharges

In his May speech, Governor Tarullo alluded to the possibility of liquidity-linked capital surcharges that would effectively augment the existing regime of risk-based capital requirements.[11] Depending on how these surcharges are structured, they could act in part as a tax on both the dealer-as-principal and dealer-as-intermediary types of SFTs. Accomplishing the latter would require a capital surcharge based on something like the aggregate size of the dealer's matched repo book; this comes quite close to the Pigouvian notion of directly taxing this specific activity. As compared to relying on the leverage ratio to implement the tax, this approach has the advantage that it is more likely to treat institutions uniformly: The tax on SFTs would not be a function of the overall business model of a given firm, but rather just the characteristics of its SFT book. This is because the surcharge is embedded into the existing risk-based capital regime, which should in principle be the constraint that binds for most firms.

There are a couple of important qualifications, however. First, going this route would involve a significant conceptual departure from the notion of capital as a prudential requirement at the firm level. As noted previously, a large matched repo book may entail relatively little solvency or liquidity risk for the broker-dealer firm that intermediates this market. So, to the extent that one imposes a capital surcharge on the broker-dealer, one would be doing so with the express intention of creating a tax that is passed on to the downstream borrower (i.e., to the hedge fund, in my example).

Second, and a direct corollary of the first, imposing the tax at the level of the intermediary naturally raises the question of disintermediation. In other words, might the SFT market respond to the tax by evolving so that large hedge funds are more readily able to borrow via repo directly from money market funds and securities lenders, without having to go through broker-dealers? I can't say that I have a good understanding of the institutional factors that might facilitate or impede such an evolution. But if the market ultimately does evolve in this way, it would be hard to argue that the underlying fire-sales problem has been addressed.

[11]Tarullo (2013).

Modified liquidity regulation

A conceptually similar way to get at matched-book repo would be to modify liquidity regulation so as to introduce an asymmetry between the assumed liquidity properties of repo loans made by a broker-dealer, and its own repo borrowing. For example, in the context of the Net Stable Funding Ratio (NSFR), one could assume that a dealer's repo loans to a hedge fund roll off more slowly than do its own repo borrowings from the triparty market. This assumption would create a net liquidity exposure for a matched repo book, and would thereby force the dealer to hold some long-term debt or other stable funding against it. Although the implementation is different, the end result is quite close to that obtained with the capital-surcharge approach I just described: in one case, there is a broad stable funding requirement for intermediaries against a matched repo book; in the other case, there is an equity requirement. It follows that, whatever its other advantages, going the modified-NSFR route does not eliminate concerns about disintermediation and regulatory arbitrage.

Universal margin requirements

These sorts of regulatory-arbitrage concerns have motivated some academics and policymakers to think about a system of universal margin requirements for SFTs.[12] In its simplest form, the idea would be to impose a minimum haircut, or down payment requirement, on any party — be it a hedge fund or a broker-dealer — that uses short-term collateralized funding to finance its securities holdings. Because the requirement now lives at the security level, rather than at the level of an intermediary in the SFT market, it cannot be as easily evaded by, say, a hedge fund going outside the broker-dealer sector to obtain its repo funding.[13] This is the strong

[12]A closely related motivation for universal margin requirements is that they might be able to limit procyclicality by leaning against increases in leverage during boom times.

[13]Of course, there is always the potential for other forms of regulatory arbitrage. For example, a hedge fund that faces a minimum margin requirement when it uses repo borrowing to fund a corporate-bond position may instead seek to take a leveraged position in the corporate-bond through other means by, for example, engaging in a total-return swap with its prime broker. This is the growing business of "synthetic" prime brokerage. Properly harmonized initial margin requirements on uncleared derivatives may help to level the playing field between traditional and synthetic prime brokerage activities.

conceptual appeal of universal margin from the perspective of a fire-sales framework.

In this regard, it is worth noting that the Financial Stability Board (FSB) has recently released a proposal to establish minimum haircut requirements for certain SFTs.[14] However, the FSB proposal stops well short of being a universal margin requirement. Rather, the minimum haircuts envisioned by the FSB would apply only to SFTs in which entities not subject to capital and liquidity regulation (e.g., hedge funds) receive financing from entities that are subject to regulation (i.e., banks and broker-dealers), and only to transactions in which the collateral is something other than government or agency securities. In this sense, there is a close relationship between the FSB minimum-haircut proposal and the specific variant of the capital-surcharge idea that I mentioned a moment ago. Both have the potential to act as a restraint on those SFTs that are intermediated by regulated broker-dealer firms, but both are vulnerable to an evolution of the business away from this intermediated mode. The minimum margin levels in the FSB proposal are also quite small, so it is unclear how much of an effect, if any, they will have on market behavior. For example, the minimums for long-term corporate bonds, securitized products, and equities are 2%, 4%, and 4% respectively.

Conclusions

Let me wrap up. My aim here has been to survey the landscape — to give a sense of the possible tools that can be used to address the fire-sales problem in SFTs — without making any particularly pointed recommendations. I would guess that a sensible path forward might involve drawing on some mix of the latter set of instruments that I discussed: namely, capital surcharges, modifications to the liquidity regulation framework, and universal margin requirements. As we go down this path, conceptual purity may have to be sacrificed in some places to deliver pragmatic and institutionally feasible results. It is unlikely that we will find singular and completely satisfactory fixes.

[14] Financial Stability Board (2013).

With this observation in mind, I would be remiss if I did not remind you of another, highly complementary area where reform is necessary: the money market fund sector. Money funds are among the most significant repo lenders to broker-dealer firms, and an important source of fire-sale risk comes from the fragility of the current money fund model. This fragility stems in part from their capital structures — the fact that they issue stable-value demandable liabilities with no capital buffer or other explicit loss-absorption capacity — which make them highly vulnerable to runs by their depositors. I welcome the work of the Securities and Exchange Commission on this front, particularly its focus on floating net asset values, and look forward to concrete action. Another source of fragility arises from money funds investing in repo loans collateralized by assets that they are unwilling or unable to hold if things go bad. This feature creates an incentive for them to withdraw repo financing from broker-dealers at the first sign of counterparty risk, even if the underlying collateral is in good shape.

In closing, I just want to acknowledge how much my own thinking about these complicated issues has benefited from the work of so many of you on the program at this conference. I look forward to continuing the conversation. Thank you.

References

Financial Stability Board (2013). *Strengthening Oversight and Regulation of Shadow Banking: Policy Framework for Addressing Shadow Banking Risks in Securities Lending and Repos*, August 29. Available at www.financialstabilityboard.org/publications/r_130829b.pdf.

Gorton, G.B. and A. Metrick (2012). Securitized Banking and the Run on Repo. *Journal of Financial Economics*, Vol. 103, pp. 425–451.

Geanakoplos, J. and H.M. Polemarchakis (1986). Existence, Regularity, and Constrained Suboptimality of Competitive Allocations When the Asset Market is Incomplete. In *Essays in Honor of Kenneth Arrow: Vol. 3: Uncertainty, Information, and Communication*, W.P. Heller, R.M. Starr and D.A. Starrett (eds.), New York: Cambridge University Press, pp. 65–95.

Hanson, S.G., A.K. Kashyap and J.C. Stein (2011). A Macroprudential Approach to Financial Regulation. *Journal of Economic Perspectives*, Vol. 25, Winter, pp. 3–28. Available at scholar.harvard.edu/files/stein/files/a-macropurdenital-final.pdf.

Krishnamurthy, A. and A. Vissing-Jørgensen (2012). The Aggregate Demand for Treasury Debt. *Journal of Political Economy*, Vol. 120, No. 2, pp. 233–267. Available at www.jstor.org/stable/10.1086/666526?origin=JSTOR-pdf.

Shleifer, A. and R. Vishny (2011). Fire Sales in Finance and Macroeconomics. *Journal of Economic Perspectives*, Vol. 25, Winter, p. 30. Available at scholar.harvard.edu/files/shleifer/files/fire_sales_jep_final.pdf.

Stein, J.C. (2012). Monetary Policy as Financial-Stability Regulation. *Quarterly Journal of Economics*, Vol. 127, pp. 57–95. Available at http://intl-qje.oxfordjournals.org/content/127/1/57.full.

Tarullo, D.K. (2013). Evaluating Progress in Regulatory Reforms to Promote Financial Stability. Speech at the Peterson Institute for International Economics, Washington, DC, May 3. Available at www.federalreserve.gov/newsevents/speech/tarullo20130503a.htm.

Too Much Debt, Financial System Stability, and Wider Economic Impacts

Adair Turner*

Institute for New Economic Thinking

It's a great pleasure to be here in Chicago for this conference on shadow banking. Shadow banking can mean many specific things. In essence, it entails credit intermediation outside or partially outside the formal banking system, but with the leverage and maturity transformation which are the defining characteristics of banks. Shadow banking enables credit creation additional to what the formal banking system alone delivers. In my comments this evening I want to focus on the broad issue of credit creation and resulting leverage, commenting on shadow banking's crucial role within that wider context.

I will set out a comprehensive argument and propose specific policy implications. To do that without undue length, I will make many of the arguments in summary form, referring for background support to previous two lectures:

- To one I delivered at the Stockholm School of Economics in September this year (Turner, 2013b). In that lecture, I considered the economic function of debt contracts and the danger that a free market banking system might create credit in sub-optimally large quantities.
- And to one given at the School of Advanced International Studies in Washington, DC, in April 2012 (Turner, 2012a). That lecture analyzed

*Adair Turner is a senior fellow of the Institute for New Economic Thinking. He previously was chairman of the UK Financial Services Authority. This is a speech presented at the Federal Reserve Bank of Chicago during its International Banking Conference, November 7, 2013.

the impact on the credit intermediation system of securitization, credit structuring and the complex combination of activities which we label shadow banking. It argued that these innovations had increased the inherent fragility of the credit intermediation system.

My comments tonight seek to integrate those two analyses.

But I am also very aware that the key argument I will make is not original, but draws heavily on the work of, in particular, Steve Cecchetti and Claudio Borio. I am concerned, however, that the global regulatory reform agenda and macro prudential approaches at national level, still do not adequately respond to their key finding — that the credit cycle is fundamental to macro-economic performance as well as to narrowly defined financial stability and that free market financial systems can generate too much debt. I want to consider what policy implications should follow from those findings.

I will propose the following conclusions:

1. Financial deepening is not necessarily and in all respects beneficial. In particular if what we mean by "financial deepening" is an increase in total private sector credit to GDP, or of banking (and shadow banking) assets as a percent of GDP, it is almost certain that beyond some level further "financial deepening" can be negative for long-term growth and human welfare. Free markets can produce too much debt.
2. Different types of credit perform different economic functions of different social value. Both economics textbooks and academic literature predominantly assume that credit flows from households to "entrepreneurs/businesses" to fund new capital investment: But in modern banking (and shadow banking) systems, only a small proportion of credit expansion performs that function. And free markets can be biased towards other categories of credit creation which do not contribute in the same way to growth.
3. Both aggregate levels of private sector leverage and the balance between different categories of credit are therefore issues of primary importance to macro-economic stability, and not just to more narrowly defined "financial stability".
4. The innovations of securitization, credit tranching, derivatives, mark-to-market accounting, secured short-term financing, and VAR-based risk-management systems had two consequences: They facilitated the

creation of additional credit, and they increased the potential fragility of the financial system and its susceptibility to runs.

5. Financial regulation reform needs to address issues of financial system stability, reducing the probability of major systemic shocks and of disorderly firm failure. Reforms introduced to date have focused on those objectives and have made significant progress, but further strengthening is required, particularly in the shadow banking arena.
6. But central banks/macro prudential regulators must also be able to deploy policy levers in pursuit of wider macro-economic stability, leaning against credit and asset price cycles, and constraining levels of leverage, overall and by specific category of credit. Both pre-emptive interest rate policies and the use of macro prudential policy levers are likely to be appropriate. Those latter levers should include direct borrower constraints (e.g., maximum LTV or LTI limits) as well as levers working via bank capital requirements.
7. This has major implications for central bank roles, and for the balance between rules and discretion. It implies that "monetary stability" and "financial stability" cannot be considered as entirely separate activities, each with their quite distinct set of policy objectives and tools.

The first three conclusions also carry implications for the policies needed to navigate our way out of our current post-crisis travails. Increased private sector leverage in the pre-crisis period, followed now by attempted deleveraging, is the main reason why we face anaemic growth and deflationary threats. Faced with those threats, the full range of policy responses, including some previously considered taboo, should be considered (Turner, 2013a). And it is vital to avoid facile assumptions of symmetry: The fact that excessive debt created the problems does not mean that rapidly reducing public or private borrowing will now solve them. But this evening I will not comment on the policies required to manage out of the post-crisis predicament. Instead, my focus this evening is on how we should manage the future financial system to ensure that we do not repeat our pre-crisis errors.

One final comment before I turn to my argument. My implications for policy may seem remarkably interventionist to propose here in Chicago, in the home of Chicago school-free market economics. But it is striking that one historic figure of Chicago economics — Henry Simons — argued for a more radical intervention than I am suggesting: He proposed the abolition of fractional reserve banks (Simons, 1936). And John Cochrane of today's Chicago school has recently argued that private credit creation imposes a negative externality and that we should consider imposing a tax on credit intermediation (Cochrane, 2013).

Both Simons and Cochrane thus treat the markets for credit and money as very special cases. And rightly so, for the principles in favor of free markets, strong in so many other sectors of the economy, are far weaker in credit and money markets. In these, for inherent reasons, private and social optimality can dramatically diverge.

Rising Financial Intensity in the Pre-Crisis Era

The 2008 crisis was preceded by several decades of rising financial intensity — of "financial deepening" in many advanced economies (Exhibit 1). Financial system assets grew relative to GDP. Trading activity grew relative to underlying real economic activity. Financial innovation brought us structured credit securities and derivatives. The measured value added of financial services grew as a percent of GDP.

Within this rising financial intensity, changes in the provision of credit were particularly important. Two different dimensions of change can be distinguished.

- First, the growth of real economy private sector leverage, with either household or corporate debt (or both) growing significantly as a percentage of GDP in many countries. Exhibit 2 provides just one of many possible illustrations — the growth of UK household debt from 15% of GDP in 1964 to over 90% by 2008.
- Second, the increasing complexity of the credit intermediation process. This complexity reflected the development of securitization and shadow banking, with credit intermediation between real economy savers and borrowers passing through multiple steps along complex intermediation chains. As a result, intra-financial system assets and liabilities exploded in size relative to GDP. Banks themselves became more leveraged. And wholesale short-term funding became more important. Exhibits 3 and 4 provide some illustration of these effects. In Exhibit 3, we can see

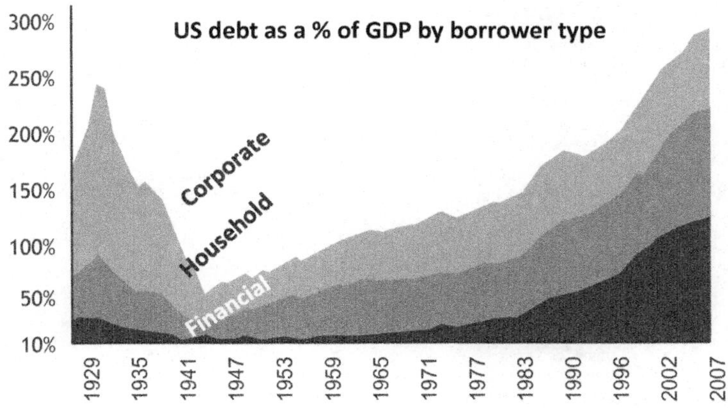

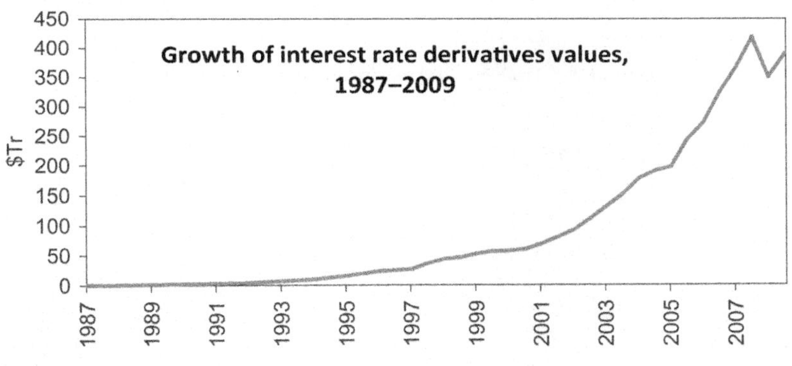

Exhibit 1. Measures of increasing financial intensity.

rising real economy leverage, but also the even more rapid growth of intra-financial system leverage. Exhibit 4 illustrates the increasing complexity of the US intermediation process, as various categories of shadow banking-related assets grew far more rapidly than traditional bank balance sheets.

Ahead of the crisis, the predominant view of economists and policymakers was that both of these dimensions of change were either neutral or benign. Modern macro-economics and central bank monetary models to

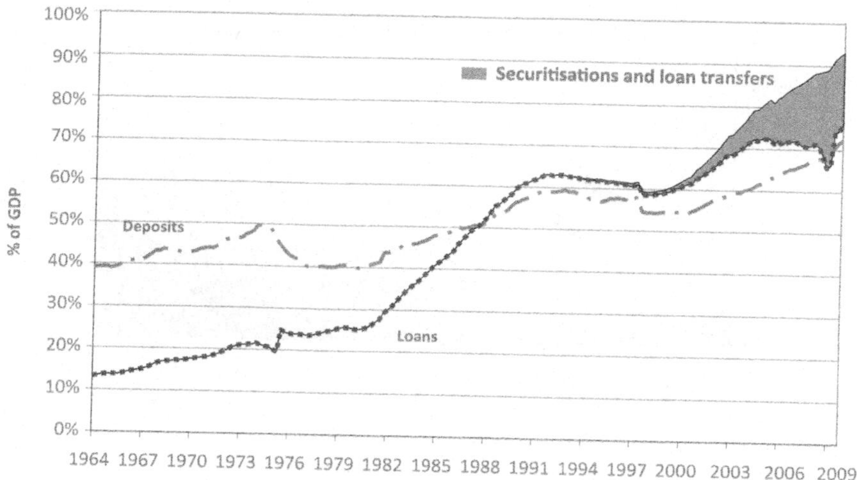

Exhibit 2. Household deposits and loans, 1964–2009.

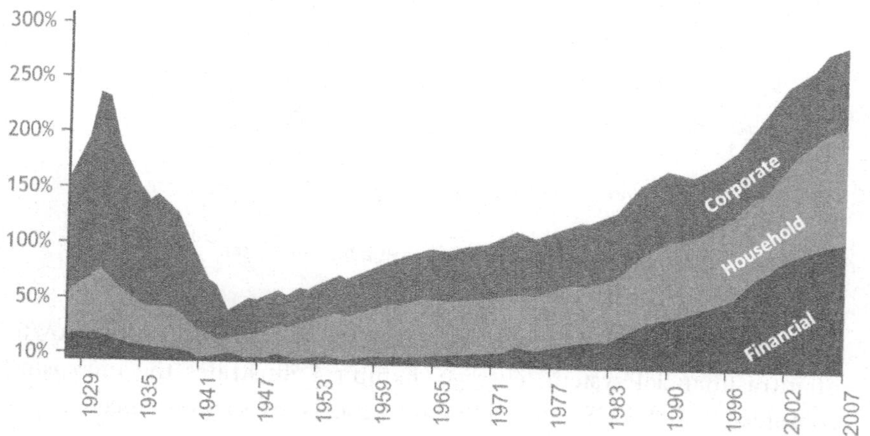

Exhibit 3. Evidence of increasing financial intensity.

a large extent ignored the trends, treating the financial system as a neutral veil. Financial regulators, and global authorities such as the IMF, largely welcomed them, assuming that increased financial intensity was positive for allocative efficiency and effective risk management, since it completed

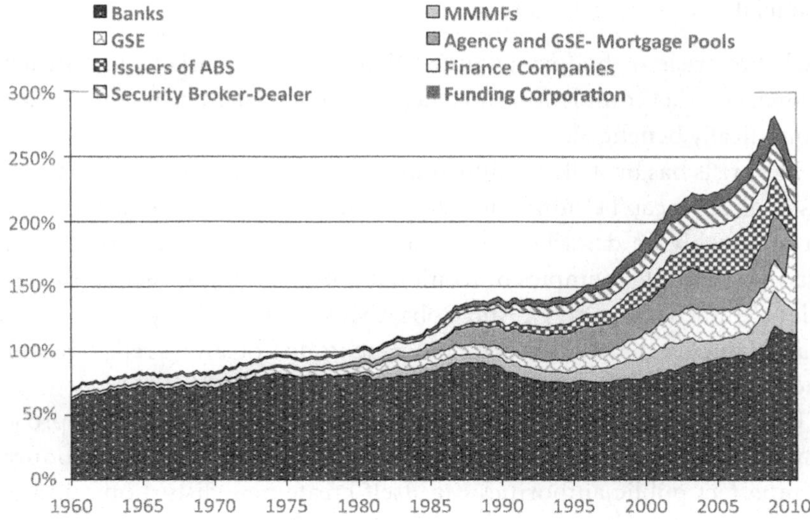

Exhibit 4. US financial sector assets.

more markets, facilitated price discovery, and made possible the dispersion of risks into the most appropriate hands (IMF, 2006).

That conventional wisdom collapsed in 2008: A financial system which had been ignored or lauded produced a massive crisis and severe post-crisis recession. It is crucial we learn the lessons. To do so, a crucial question we must answer is whether both of those two pre-crisis trends were important, or only those developments which made the financial system itself more fragile.

- Did the crisis occur because we allowed the credit intermediation system to become dangerously complex and risky, with overleveraged banks too reliant on short-term funding, and with the innovations of securitization, derivatives, and shadow banking, making the system more fragile?
- Or was it also a crisis produced or exacerbated by too much leverage and by particular categories of credit creation within the real economy?

I will suggest that both dimensions of change were vitally important. And that our policy response cannot focus solely on issues of financial system risk and stability narrowly defined, but must also address the wider issue of the credit cycle and macro-economic stability.

Financial Markets are Different

Much pre-crisis orthodoxy assumed that financial markets are efficient. Financial market completion and increasing financial intensity thus seemed axiomatically beneficial.

The crisis has brutally reminded us that this is not true. Financial markets of all sorts can be subject to self-reinforcing momentum effects which can reasonably be described as "irrational". Charles Kindleberger's work describes multiple examples of irrational booms and busts across the centuries (Kindleberger, 2011). And Robert Shiller's work has provided compelling evidence that market price movements do not always reflect rational fundamentals (Shiller, 2000).

But that might still leave the case for a broadly free market approach compelling in many areas of finance. Any policy intervention introduced by imperfect public authorities can itself create new distortions; and the case for a market economy is not that it is perfect, but simply better than the alternative.

And when market irrationality is confined to equity markets, the adverse consequences may be limited and acceptable. Exhibit 5 shows the movement of the NASDAQ index during the Internet boom and bust of 1997 to 2002, first soaring from 1,500 to over 5,000 before falling back again to 1,500. I think it is clear that the upswing owed a lot to irrational exuberance. And some misallocation of real resources undoubtedly resulted. But the rapid fall from the exuberant peak did not produce a major

Exhibit 5. NASDAQ index, 1990–2003.

macro-economic recession: And as Bill Janeway has argued, the process of innovation involves and indeed may require surges of overoptimistic exuberance and resulting Schumpeterian waste (Janeway, 2012).

As long as financial market irrationality is confined to equity markets, a broadly benign attitude may remain justified.

It is when the inherent potential imperfections of financial markets infect the market for credit creation and debt contracts that major adverse macro-economic consequences can result.

Debt can be Dangerous: Free Markets May Create too Much

The distinctive character of debt contracts means that free markets left to themselves can produce "too much" debt relative to the size of income flows, and thus relative to GDP. They can also produce too much of particular categories of debt. And high private sector leverage can wreak serious economic harm.

Debt contracts, inefficient markets, and cycles of credit creation

Debt contracts can perform important and beneficial economic functions. In my Stockholm lecture I explored the extensive academic literature which has described those functions and benefits. Debt contracts overcome, or at least respond to, the difficulties of "costly state verification" (either *ex-ante* the project assessment or *ex-post* the project realization), which make a pure equity economy infeasible (See, e.g., Townsend, 1979). Without debt as well as equity contracts, it would have been far more difficult and perhaps impossible to achieve the mobilization of the capital required for the initial industrial revolution, for subsequent advanced economy growth at the frontier of technology, or for economic catch-up by emerging economies towards advanced economy living standards.

But there are also strong arguments for believing that free financial markets and banking systems can create debt contracts in excessive, sub-optimally large quantities. This reflects both investor myopia and imperfections of information and incentives along chains of principal/agent relationships.

- The myopia argument has been set out by Gennaioli, Shleifer, and Vishny (2010). It derives from the asymmetric character of the frequency

distribution of debt contract pay-outs, which creates the potential for "local thinking". Investors in the good times may focus solely on the part of the distribution in which contracts pay out 100%, ignoring the currently unobserved possibility of losses. As a result, many credit securities may be issued which "owe their very existence to neglected risk".
- The role of imperfect incentive alignments between principals and agents was explored earlier this year by Jeremy Stein (2013a). As he demonstrates, such misalignments, deriving in particular from the put options inherent in debt contracts, could drive credit creation cycles even in the absence of more "behavioral" factors.

These imperfections could produce sub-optimally excessive debt creation even if all debt contracts took a direct form — linking savers with borrowers without bank intermediation. But the danger of excessive credit creation is greatly increased if we have fractional reserve banks, able to create credit and money *de novo*, rather than simply intermediate the flow of already existing money. And it is still further increased once we recognize different categories of credit and the different economic functions that they perform.

Economic theory has tended to concentrate on one particular category of credit performing one particular economic function. In undergraduate and advanced textbooks, and in most academic papers, to the extent that the banking system is present at all, it is assumed that banks take deposits from households and lend the money on to "entrepreneurs/businesses", allocating available funds between alternative capital investment projects.

In the real world, however, bank credit creation can also serve other purposes (Exhibit 6).

- It might indeed fund new capital investment projects or fund human capital investment (e.g., through student loans).
- But it can instead fund the purchase by businesses or investors of already existing assets.
- And it can fund household mortgages, in some cases stimulating new residential construction, but in many cases financing competition for the ownership of already existing houses.

Loans to businesses/ "entrepreneurs"	... to finance real investment projects
Loans to businesses/ speculators/investors	... to finance purchase of existing assets
Mortgage loans to households	... to finance residential houses
Loans to "impatient"/ temporarily cash limited/ poorer households	... to bring forward consumption

Exhibit 6. Categories of credit.

- And in the form of consumer credit, it may fund consumption by impatient, or in some cases simply poorer, households.

The balance between these different categories of credit varies by country. But in advanced economies, the categories which do not finance new capital investment tend to dominate. In the UK, in 2009 only about 15% of total credit was clearly devoted to the capital investment projects on which economic theory has tended to focus (Exhibit 7).[1]

Conversely, the majority of credit in most advanced economies finances commercial and residential real estate purchase. That fact greatly increases the danger that free market banking systems will be susceptible to self-reinforcing cycles of credit creation and subsequent destruction.

- Credit extension will appear least risky to lenders when it can be secured against assets which have alternative use value: Lending against real estate meets this criterion; lending to finance specific-use equipment, training, or research and development does not.

[1] The other categories of credit provision — in particular household debt which facilitates life cycle consumption smoothing — may also deliver welfare benefits, but these benefits are different in nature from the growth-enhancing benefits typically ascribed to the efficient funding of capital investment projects.

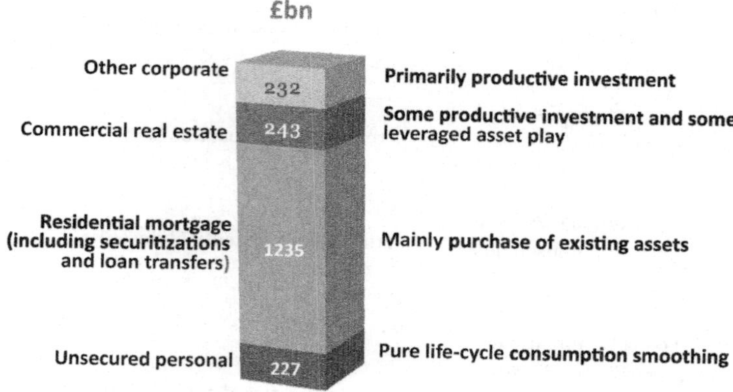

Exhibit 7. Categories of debt, UK 2009.

- And if real estate assets are location-specific, their new supply will be highly inelastic in the face of price increase, with real estate values primarily driven by the value of irreproducible land, rather than by construction costs.
- As a result, a free market credit creation system can have a sub-optimal bias toward the financing of existing assets, in particular real estate.
- And it can be susceptible to strong self-reinforcing cycles, in which credit extension drives asset prices, which in turn stimulates both credit supply and demand, as a consequence of changes in the net worth and expectations of both borrowers and lenders (Exhibit 8).

Adverse effects of too much — and the wrong sort of — debt

Free market banking and shadow banking systems may generate suboptimally high levels of debt, overall and particularly in specific sectors. That might cause economic harm even in the upswing of the credit cycle, but it is in the periods of post-crisis deleveraging that the harm becomes most significant.

In the upswing of the cycle, an adverse impact might result from the bias towards lending against collateral which has an alternative uses value. Real estate lending might be preferred at the expense of other business projects. A recent paper by Chakraborty *et al.* presents evidence of such a

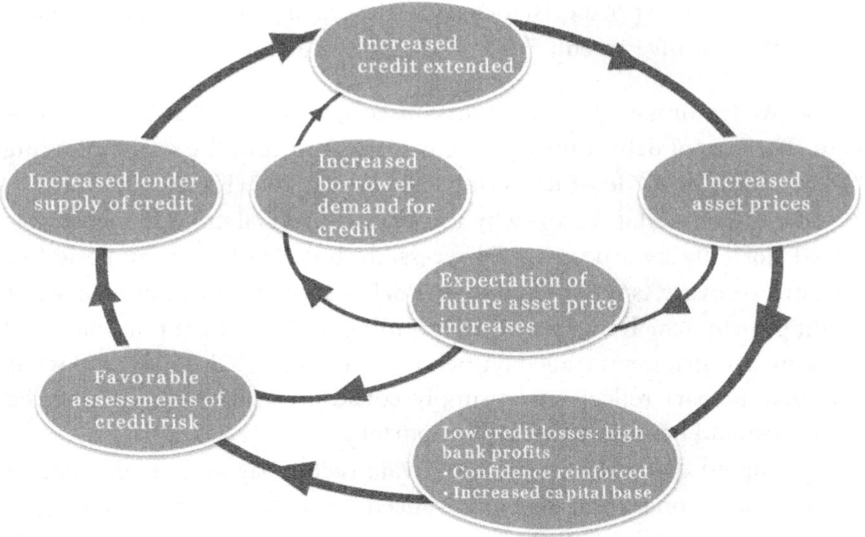

Exhibit 8. Credit and asset price cycles.

crowding-out effect, suggesting that when house prices rise rapidly (in part as an endogenous consequence of mortgage lending) banks tend to reduce lending to commercial and industrial companies. (Chakraborty, Goldstein, and MacKinlay, 2013). How significant such effects might be merits further research.

The far more serious and more certain impact of excessive leveraged however arises in the aftermath of financial crises, as asset prices, credit demand, and credit supply fall in a reverse of the upswing's self-reinforcing cycle. In the downswing, two aspects of credit market dynamics become drivers of still further deflation.

- First, the rigidities of default and bankruptcy processes, which as Ben Bernanke has noted would never be observed in a world of complete markets, but which in the real world can drive asset fire sales and disruptive business failures (Bernanke, 2004).
- Second, and probably still more important, the impact of "debt overhang" as households and corporates, faced with lower asset prices and

reduced income prospects, focus on deleveraging at the expense of consumption or investment.

These two features — both inherent consequences of the non-state contingent character of debt contracts — create the danger of the self-reinforcing "Debt Deflation" cycle which Irving Fisher described (Fisher, 1933).

The fundamental reason why the global financial crisis has been followed not only by a deep initial recession, but also by a long period of anaemic recovery, is the strength of the debt overhang effect. Private sector credit growth, which was previously running far faster than nominal GDP in many countries, has trailed far behind since 2008 (Exhibit 9), and while this may in part reflect credit supply constraints, dramatically reduced credit demand has been at least as important.

Attempted deleveraging by the private sector has as a result injected a strong deflationary impulse to advanced economies with consequences which we should have anticipated given Japan's experience after its private sector credit boom turned to bust in 1990.

- As Richard Koo (2009) has persuasively described, attempted deleveraging by Japanese corporates produced a corporate sector financial surplus to which government deficits were the naturally arising but also necessary offset, but with the inevitable consequence that public debt to GDP

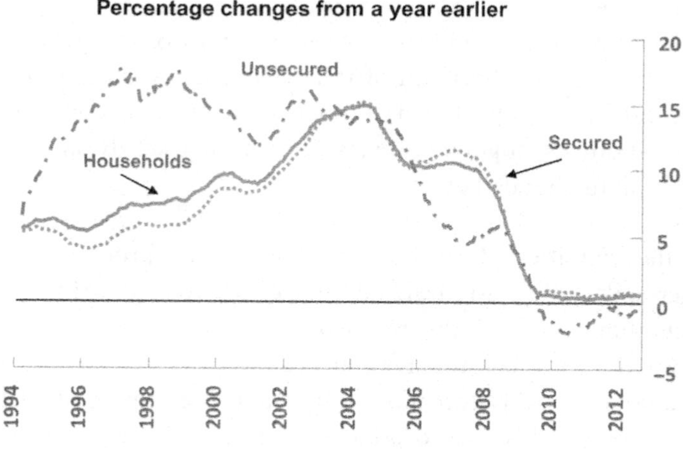

Exhibit 9. Lending to UK households.

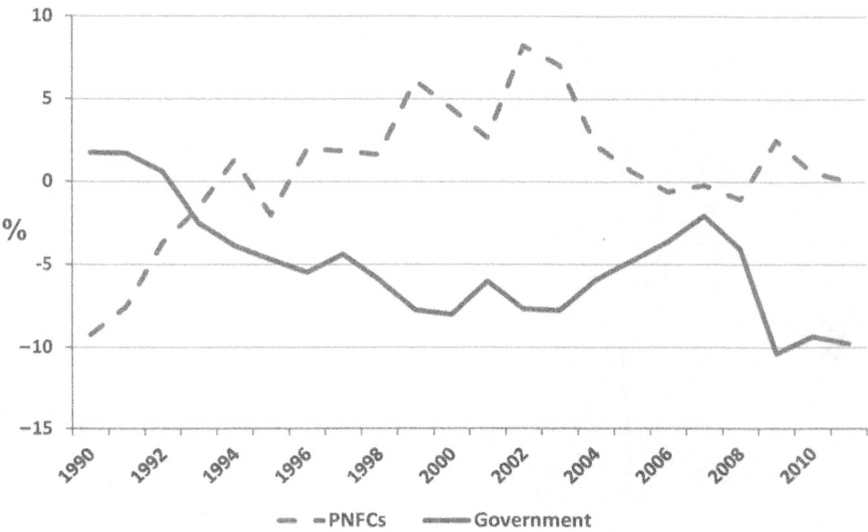

Exhibit 10. Sectoral financial surpluses/deficits as % of GDP Japan, 1990–2012.
Source: IMF, Bank of Japan flow of accounts.

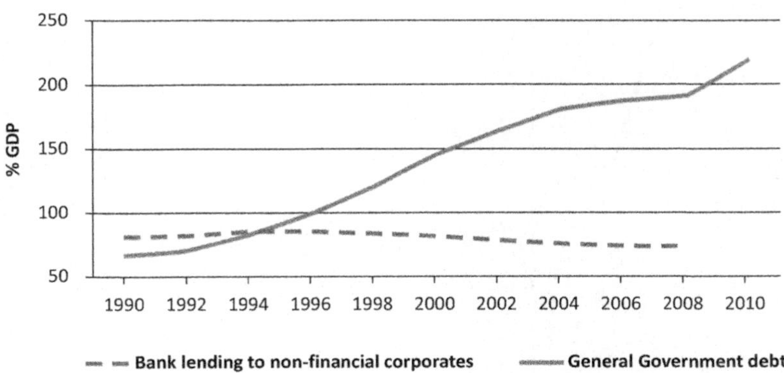

Exhibit 11. Japanese government and corporate debt, 1990–2010.

rose relentlessly (Exhibits 10 and 11). At the total economy level, indeed leverage did not decline, but simply shifted from the private to the public sector. That same pattern has now been repeated in Spain, Ireland, the US, and the UK (Exhibit 12).

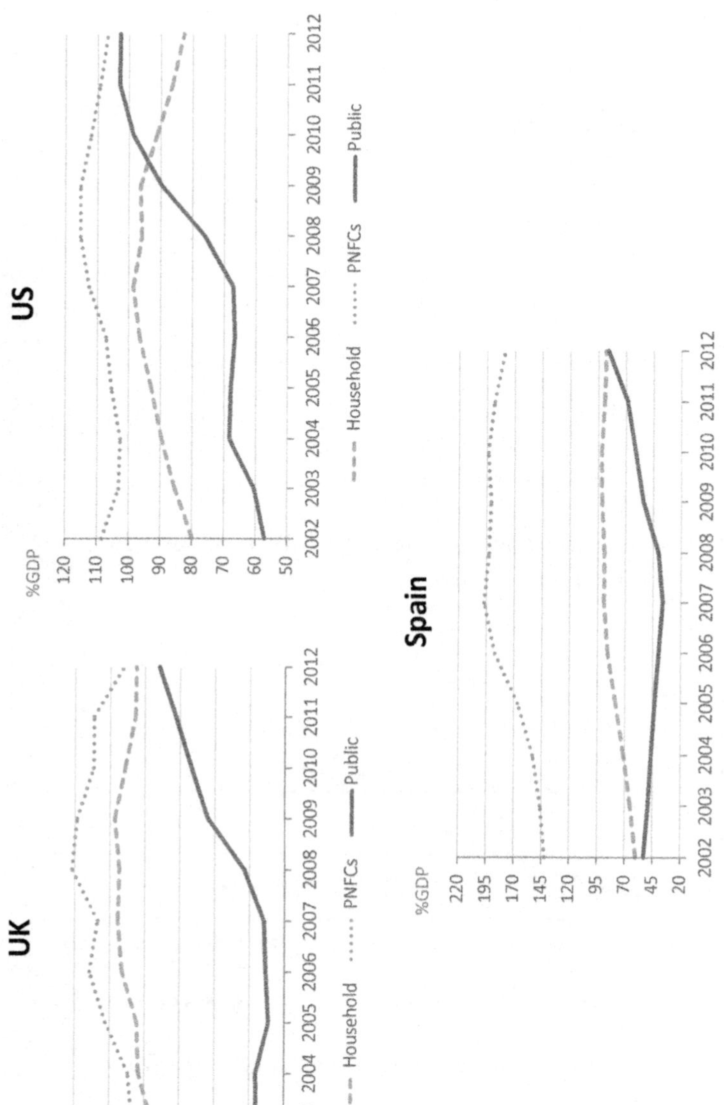

Exhibit 12. Shifting leverage: Private and public debt-to-GDP.

- And just as in Japan, policy makers seem now to have been left with only imperfect policy levers available with which to respond.[2] The potential for fiscal stimulus seems constrained by public debt sustainability concerns; and the effectiveness of monetary policy constrained both by the zero bound and by the inelasticity of some private sector households and corporates to interest rate changes, given their focus on balance sheet improvement.

Real economy private sector leverage matters because it can create a harmful debt overhang problem; the implication is that public policy should aim to prevent the emergence of excessive leverage during the upswing of the cycle.

In the Euro zone today, problems in Greece and Italy may reasonably be ascribed to inadequate control of past public budgets and debt levels. But in Spain, Ireland, and the Netherlands, as also in the UK and the US, public debt levels have risen post crisis because of the pre-crisis growth of private leverage.

And it is the level of private sector leverage that matters and not just its rate of growth, because the level determines the scale of attempted post crisis deleveraging.

These conclusions of course are by no means original. Claudio Borio's work has stressed the centrality of credit-driven cycles to macro-economic fluctuations. And his "core stylised feature Number One" is that the essence of the problem is "credit and property prices" (Borio, 2012). Steve Cecchetti has argued that financial systems can create too much debt, and in his latest work is exploring the specific role of debt secured against tangible assets (Cecchetti, Mohanty, and Zampoli, 2011; Cecchetti and Kharroubi, 2012).

But the conclusion is so important that it bears being repeated and stressed:

- Free market competition can produce too much credit and a suboptimal mix of credit types. Credit creation beyond some level — particularly

[2] In fact, fiscal plus monetary authorities combined never run out of ammunition with which to stimulate nominal demand, as long as they are willing to consider the full range of possible policy options including overt money finance of increased fiscal deficits (see Turner, 2012b). Given the potential disadvantages of such a policy (particularly in terms of the precedent it sets), however, the case remains strong for ensuring that pre-crisis policy restrains excessive leverage growth in order to limit the dangers of a post crisis debt overhang.

when focused in real estate or other existing asset categories — can create a negative social externality.

But What about the Evidence for Beneficial Financial Deepening?

Too much leverage can have harmful economic effects. This conclusion appears to contradict the significant body of economic analysis which has found evidence that financial deepening delivers beneficial effects. Ross Levine's literature survey of 2004, for instance, suggests a broadly favorable impact of financial deepening, not only in general but also if we focus quite specifically on Credit to GDP or Bank Assets to GDP (Levine, 2004). Levine's analysis suggests a positive relationship between these ratios and economic growth.

Recent papers by Steve Cecchetti, however, provide empirical support for the theoretical arguments presented above, with increasing credit to GDP appearing to have a positive impact on growth up to some point but negative beyond it (Exhibit 13). Cecchetti's analysis suggests that we should replace previous assumptions of a limitless and linear relationship between financial deepening and growth, assuming instead an inverse

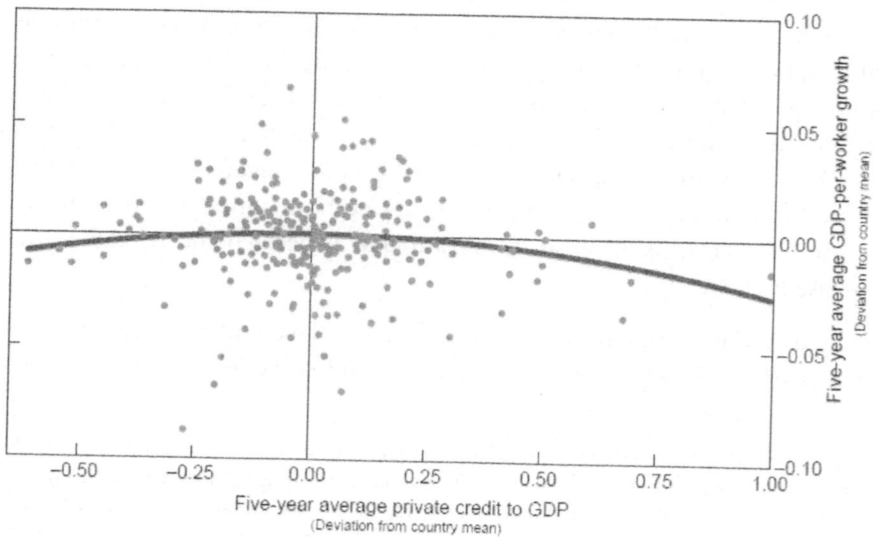

Exhibit 13. Private credit to GDP and growth.

U function. The findings of research by Alan Taylor, Oscar Jordá, and Moritz Schularick are also compatible with this conclusion (Taylor and Schularick, 2009; Jordá, Schularick, and Taylor, 2011; Taylor, 2012).

Further empirical research is clearly desirable. But the theoretical arguments for Ceccheti's inverse U hypothesis are compelling. There are strong reasons for believing that the existence of debt contracts plays a crucial role in facilitating capital mobilization; but an equally strong case that beyond some level increasing debt intensity is likely to cause harm, and that free market finance left to itself will create debt which moves the economy beyond that optimal level.

The specific examples that Levine uses to illustrate his findings are indeed fully compatible with that conclusion. They illustrate the potential benefits of financial deepening starting from very low levels of credit intensity.

- As Levine argues, countries like India, with private credit to GDP averaging 19.5% over the period 1960–1995, would almost certainly have benefited from financial deepening.
- And there are some countries today — such as India and Indonesia — which still have credit to GDP ratios likely to place them on the rising section of Cecchetti's curve.
- But that is wholly compatible with the conclusion that at higher levels of debt to GDP, further financial deepening could have harmful economic reflects. The fact that economics largely ignored that possibility prior to the crisis was a major failure.

Complexity, Shadow Banking, and the Origins of the Crisis

The disadvantages of excessive credit creation considered above could arise even if all credit was extended by traditional banks. There were debt and banking crises long before the development of securitization, credit structuring, and derivatives. The Japanese and Scandinavian banking crises of the early 1990s owed nothing to the increase in credit intermediation complexity which occurred in the decades running up to the 2008 crisis.

But that increase in complexity played a crucial role in precipitating the crisis and increasing its severity. It both facilitated excessive credit extension to the real economy and made the financial system itself more fragile.

This conference is focused on shadow banking. And it is possible to get tied in knots debating what exactly we should include in shadow banking and what not. I will therefore avoid that debate, but focus instead (as did my April 2012 lecture at SAIS) on the wide-ranging sets of changes and innovations, which together contributed to a dramatic increase in the complexity of the global financial system and in particular of the credit intermediation process.

Those changes included:

- The securitization of an increasing proportion of loans, and the resulting increase in credit-trading activities. This established transparent prices for credit risk, set in at least sometimes liquid markets. It made possible, and in some cases unavoidable, the widespread application of mark-to-market accounting.
- The increased use of credit structuring and tranching, creating combinations of risk and return attractive to specific investor groups.
- The development of multistep credit intermediation, delivering through numerous contracts and institutions the intermediation and maturity transformation previously performed within one bank balance sheet. Thus, for instance, investors holding instantly available deposit-like accounts in money market mutual funds, indirectly funded 30-year mortgages, via complex chains involving multiple institutions (e.g., SIVs and hedge funds) and multiple contract markets (e.g., ABCP and repo).
- The application of apparently sophisticated risk-management techniques to control individual agents' risk in this more complex world, and to minimize capital requirements. These techniques included increased use of secured financing contracts, with collateralization and margin calls: mark-to-market accounting to track up-to date exposures, and the use of Value at risk (VAR) models to determine the appropriate level of trading book capital and haircuts.
- The increasing use of derivatives — whether FX, interest rate, or credit related — to hedge risks and to manage regulatory capital.
- An increased role of short-term wholesale funding contracts, both secured and unsecured, as firms became increasingly involved in a complex mesh of intra-financial system assets and liabilities.

These developments and innovations fed upon one another. And crucially, they did not result in the development of a discreet new shadow banking system, parallel to but separate from formally regulated banks, but rather to a complex interrelated system in which commercial banks were deeply involved in and affected by these changes.

The barriers between commercial and investment banks eroded. Commercial banks sponsored off-balance-sheet shadow banking vehicles (e.g., SIVs). Large commercial banks were major traders of credit securities and derivatives. Short-term wholesale funding played an increasing role for banks as well as non-banks. Bank balance sheets ballooned as intra-financial system assets and liabilities proliferated.

The predominant belief ahead of the crisis was that these developments were beneficial.

- Securitization and credit structuring were believed to have enabled the dispersion of risks into the hands of those best placed to manage it.
- Market liquidity and transparent pricing were deemed good for allocative efficiency. The IMF noted with approval that credit derivatives "*enhance the transparency of the markets collective view of credit risks*... [and thus] ... *provide valuable information about broad credit constraints and increasingly set the marginal price of credit*" (IMF, 2006).
- Improved risk-management techniques were believed, again in the words of the IMF to have "*helped make the banking and overall financial system more resilient. The improved resilience may be seen in fewer bank failures and more consistent credit provision*".
- And the fact that the system enabled credit creation outside of bank balance sheets was seen as a positive benefit, ensuring that credit grew fast enough to support economic growth. Indeed even after the crash, in 2012, the *Economist* magazine reported a "senior American regulator" stressing that "*securitisation is a good thing. If everything was on bank balance sheets, there would not be enough credit*".

Clearly, however, something went badly wrong: the financial system suffered its biggest crisis for 70 years. And as the crisis developed over 2007–2008, many of the initial crystallization events involved not plain old-fashioned bank balance sheets, but hedge funds, broker-dealers, money market funds, margin calls on derivatives, and the repo market.

So what went wrong? I think three factors were particularly important.

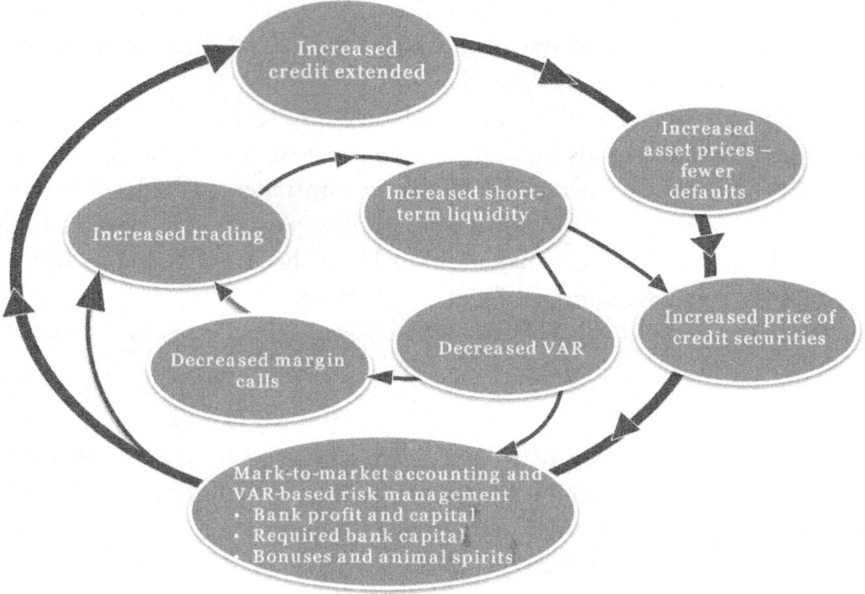

Exhibit 14. Credit and asset prices, with securitised credit and mark-to-market accounting.

- First, the unstable interaction of credit securities trading, transparent pricing, mark-to-market accounting, secured financing, and VAR models. Each of these was seen as a positive factor — improving price discovery and risk control. But as Hyun Shin, Marcus Brunnermeier, and others have explored (Shin, 2010; Brunnermeier and Pedersen, 2009) they can interact in ways which take the potentially self-reinforcing credit and asset price cycle and effectively hardwire and turbocharge it (Exhibit 14). If credit prices were always set in an entirely efficient fashion, rationally and smoothly anticipating future risks, the new credit system might indeed have delivered benefits. But if credit prices can move in the fashion shown on Exhibit 15, with CDS spreads signaling as late as spring 2007 that the financial system had never been less risky, before surging to irrationally high levels, then the same design features can make the overall system more fragile.
- Second, the adverse consequences of multistep credit intermediation. This aggregation dramatically increased the gross value of contracts

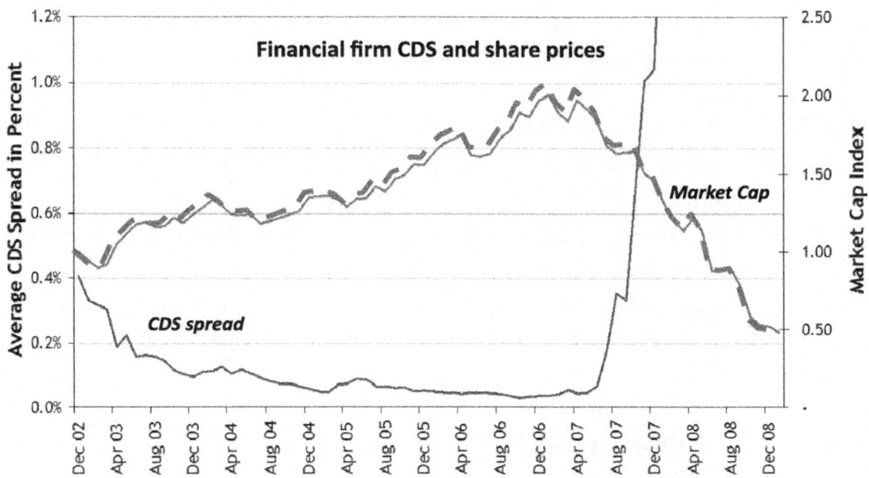

Exhibit 15. Irrational exuberance in equity and debt markets.
Source: Moody's KMV, FSA Calculations.

outstanding and increased the number and complexity of contractual links. It thereby increased the risk of both the "local thinking" described by Gennaioli, Shleifer and Vishny, and of the misaligned principal/agent relationships described by Stein. It undermined incentives for good credit underwriting and increased the potential for the origination and distribution of credit securities, which "owed their very existence to neglected risk".

- Third, the double-edged impact of market completion through innovation of new contract forms. Any new financial contract, which makes possible risk management and reduction, also makes possible increased position-taking, and can thus increase gross risks. Credit derivatives could indeed be used to hedge and manage risks, but they can also be used to take positions unrelated to underlying exposures, inflating still further gross contractual exposures. At the height of the crisis indeed, synthetic credit exposures were created for the sole purpose of providing a match to desired short CDS positions. Financial risk was generated far beyond that inherent in underlying real economy credit exposures.

In several ways therefore, the very features of the pre-crisis credit intermediation system, which had been lauded as delivering market completion, price discovery, and risk management benefits, combined to create a system which was more fragile, more susceptible to sudden equilibria shifts, and with hardwired mechanisms for magnifying the impact of initial shocks. The dramatic wholesale market runs of autumn 2008, in both secured and unsecured funding markets, were the almost inevitable eventual consequence.

In addition, however, it is worth noting that the system did deliver one of its purported stated benefits: It facilitated greater credit creation. But if, as argued before, additional credit creation beyond some threshold can be negative for growth and welfare that too could be a harmful effect.

Addressing Financial System Stability Risks: Necessary but not Sufficient

We earlier argued that the multiple developments and innovations which we might cover under the broad heading "shadow banking" combined to make the credit intermediation system more fragile. That is hardly surprising, since a non-regulated banking system would also be highly unstable. Private incentives encourage maximum leverage, increasing the dangers of insolvency: Run risk is inherent in a system which delivers extensive maturity transformation.

A key objective of prudential regulation is therefore to reduce the fragility of the credit intermediation system itself to pursue the objective of "financial system stability". In this context, I want to use that term to mean:

- A reduced risk of destabilizing runs;
- A reduced risk of a self-reinforcing solvency crisis in which threats to the solvency of one bank result in actual or perceived risks to the solvency of others;
- And a reduced probability of a large bank, or other important credit intermediary, suffering disorderly failure, or near failure only prevented by taxpayer bailout.

Most of our current regulatory reform agenda is essentially focused on achieving these objectives. Much has already been achieved, but some further strengthening is essential.

Reforms focused on the formal banking system have been significant and essential, combining:

- The much higher capital requirements introduced by Basel III. These need to be reinforced by robust reforms to the trading book capital regime, an area where pre-crisis regulatory capital requirements were woefully inadequate to absorb risk.
- Tighter constraints on maturity transformation risks, addressing in particular reliance on short-term wholesale finance, both secured and unsecured. The Liquidity Coverage Ratio (LCR) and the Net Stable Funding Ratio (NSFR) will both be crucial in this regard. In addition, we may need to consider other more direct constraints on wholesale short-term funding.
- The creation of effective resolution regimes, maximizing our ability to resolve major banks without disruptive knock-on effects, but also without relying on tax payer support.

Reforms focused on the shadow banking system have progressed more slowly, essentially because we are not dealing with a clearly defined set of institutions, but with a complex and continually evolving mesh of multiple institutions and markets. Crucial steps here include:

- Measures to ensure that links between the formal and shadow banking systems are transparent and reflected in adequate capital support. The FSB/Basel Committee program of reforms has largely achieved this objective.
- Measures to address clearly crucial nodes in multistep maturity transformation chains. In this context, money market mutual funds are particularly important and it is unfortunate that progress in the most important market, the US, has been slow.
- But also, and crucially I believe, measures to address one of the most fundamental risks of shadow banking widely defined, the danger within a system of securitized and traded credit of the self-reinforcing cycle illustrated on Exhibit 14. Here I believe that the imposition of minimum haircuts on secured finance and securities financing transactions is the way to go, mitigating at least to a degree the dangers of hard-wired procyclicality inherent in secured financing markets. Much good

> preparatory work on the options was done by the Financial Stability Board's Workstream 5, and some measures are edging forward. But I agree with Jeremy Stein in his recent conclusion that while currently planned measures are "*likely to be helpful in fortifying individual regulated institutions ... they fall short of a comprehensive market-wide approach to the fire sales problems associated with securities financing transactions*" (Stein, 2013b).

It is therefore essential that we complete and strengthen further the agenda of bank regulatory reform, and drive forward to effective shadow banking regulation.

But we must also recognize that reforms focused solely on "financial system stability" may be insufficient. For it would be possible to envisage a future scenario in which we managed very significantly to reduce the probability of a large-scale financial system crisis, or of major bank failure, but reverted — once economic recovery is well advanced — to a slow but relentless rise in real economy leverage, which would eventually result in deflationary deleveraging and macroeconomic harm.

We could have banks sufficiently be well capitalized that they could survive the next Minsky turning point without taxpayer subsidy, but with real economy credit and asset price cycles which still caused significant harm.

I want to suggest, therefore, that in the macro prudential arena, we cannot avoid going beyond "financial system stability" narrowly defined, to a wider focus on the macroeconomic impact of increasing and potentially excessive debt levels.

Constraining Credit Creation: Monitoring and Thresholds

The implication of the discussion above is that the level of private sector debt relative to income, and its composition as between different categories of credit, are matters of fundamental economic importance. That is quite contrary to the pre-crisis orthodoxy, which assumed that private sector leverage levels and trends could be either: (i) ignored because financial system balance sheets were neutral veils of no macro importance; or (ii) assumed optimal by definition since private competition was bound to produce a socially optimal result.

We need to reject that pre-crisis orthodoxy. In a perfect world, we would be able to replace it with simple rules, telling us the level of private debt to GDP which is "too much" and seeking to constrain debt below that level. Steve Cechetti's 2011 paper reached a tentative conclusion that "*when corporate debt goes beyond 90% of GDP it becomes a drag on growth. And for household debt, we report a threshold of 85% of GDP, though the impact is very imprecisely estimated*".

If these tentative indicators are broadly right, they mean that several advanced economies have already entered the "too much debt" zone.

We should, however, be careful of believing that we can arrive at any precise or universally applicable rules. Reinhart and Rogoff have made a strong case that higher levels of public debt to GDP can create sustainability concerns, necessitating fiscal consolidation which might be adverse for growth (Reinhart and Rogoff, 2009). But recent debates about the precise empirical evidence have warned us of the dangers of fixing upon one specific figure — such as 90% — and assuming that it is the crucial threshold. For both public and private sector debt, multiple factors make simple and universal rules impossible.

- For both public and private debt, the level at which leverage becomes problematic (or at the limit quite unsustainable), must reflect future nominal income growth potential. The faster that nominal GDP — and as a result household or corporate income levels — can be expected to increase, the more manageable is any given debt stock relative to current income.
- Within private debt, the level of leverage which is concerning needs to be considered separately for household and corporate sectors, but with a potential interdependence. If both sectors are highly leveraged, post-crisis attempts to delever by both sectors simultaneously will have greater deflationary impact.
- And as the recent post-crisis experience demonstrates, the issues of public and private debt sustainability can be closely linked. As the IMF has recently suggested (IMF, 2013), relatively high levels of public debt may only carry severe disadvantages if accompanied by high private debt. The inverse may also apply.

Further empirical analysis may shed more light on these issues. But it seems unlikely that we can ever establish precise "danger thresholds". This has implications for the rules versus discretion debate with which I will conclude.

But the impossibility of precise rules cannot justify a policy of ignoring private leverage levels. The theoretical reasons for believing that there must be a point beyond which higher private leverage causes increasing harm remain strong even if that point cannot be precisely identified.

- In the advanced economies, we should therefore have paid attention to the large increases in leverage underway in many countries even before the explosion of complexity and innovation which triggered the crisis. In the UK, household debt to GDP rose from 15% in 1964 to 95% in 2008 (Exhibit 2); in the US, total private sector leverage rose from around 70% in 1945 to over 200% by 2008 (Exhibit 16). Those increases made those economies greatly more vulnerable to post-crisis deleveraging and deflation.
- And in some emerging economies today, including in particular China, there are dangers that increasing private sector leverage could expose them to similar risks (Exhibits 17 and 18).

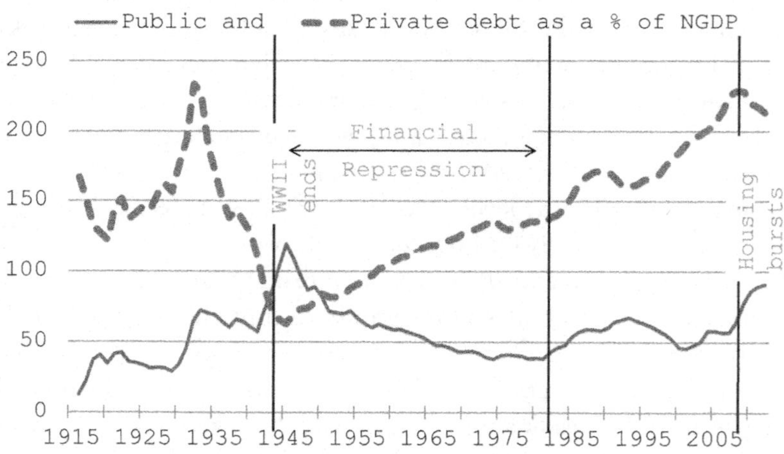

Exhibit 16. Private and public leverage cycles, US.
Source: McCulley and Pozsar (2013).

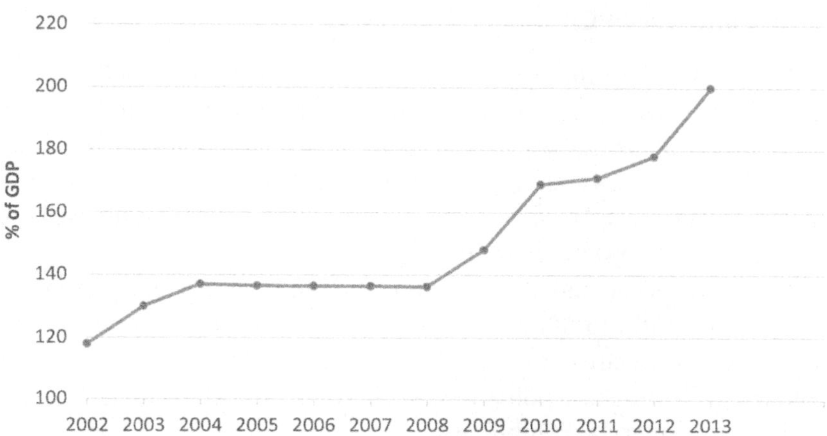

Exhibit 17. Total social finance to GDP, China.

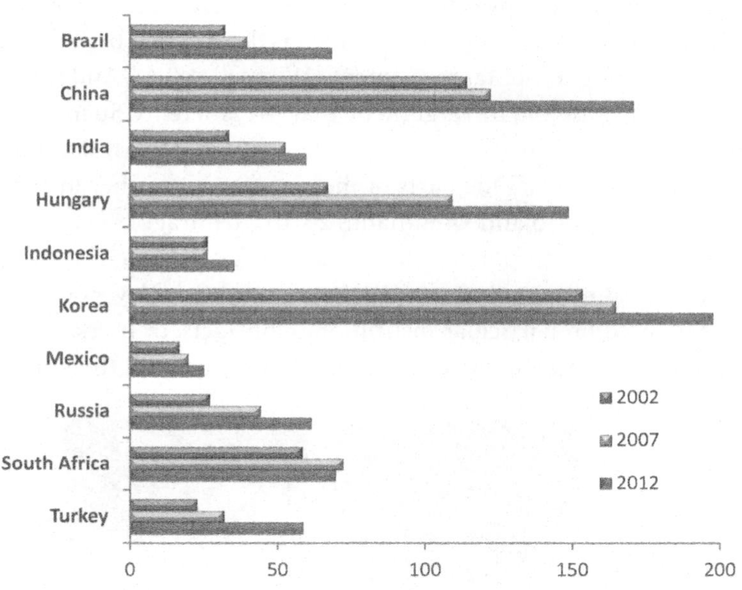

Exhibit 18. Non-financial private sector* credit outstanding, % GDP.

Source: BIS, citi research (*Household + corporates).

Constraining Credit Creation: Policy Levers

We should therefore monitor carefully trends in private as well as public sector leverage and assess their possible implications for future macro-economic stability. But we also need to deploy policy levers which can constrain private sector leverage levels in order to protect macro-economic stability, going beyond those measures which we would take if focused only on financial system stability more narrowly defined.

We could seek to do this by more pre-emptive monetary policy — using interest rates to affect credit creation and asset prices, rather than focusing solely on current price stability; alternatively or as well, we could deploy macro prudential policy levers. There are important advantages and disadvantages of each (Exhibit 19).

- The theoretical case for using interest rates reflects the belief that the essential problem was as described by Knut Wicksell — that credit creation will be excessive if financial interest rates are allowed to fall below the "natural rate of interest", which is determined by the marginal productivity of real capital investment (Wicksell, 1894). And this case is reinforced by a pragmatic argument that — as Jeremy Stein puts it — interest rates "get into all the cracks" (Stein, 2013a), or as Claudio Borio expressed it, "it reaches the parts of the system which other instruments cannot reach" (Borio and Drehmann, 2010). Arbitrage processes ensure that a change in the policy interest rate affects all interest-rate-based contracts in some way. By contrast, macro prudential levers are by their nature focused on particular institutions, contracts, or markets and will inevitably stimulate innovations designed to circumvent their effect.

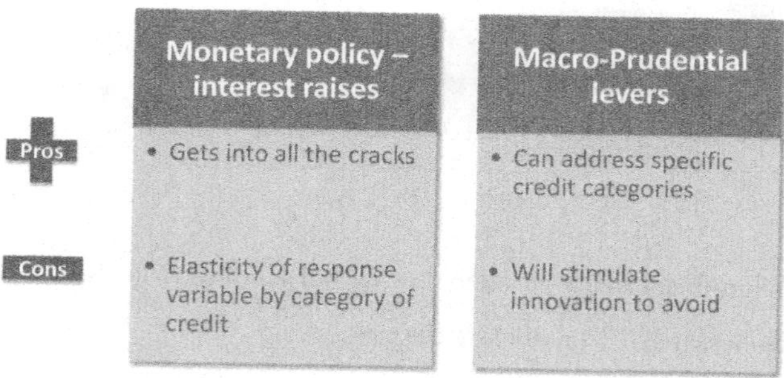

Exhibit 19. Leaning against credit cycles. Monetary or macro-prudential levers?

- Conversely, however, the effectiveness of the interest rate lever can be undermined by significant differences between the interest rate elasticity of response of different sectors of the economy. Once a real estate boom gets going, and both borrowers and lenders develop expectations that asset prices will grow rapidly over the medium term (at, say, 10% per annum), interest rate changes of normal monetary policy magnitude may have little impact; and the increase needed to slow the boom may well constrain other categories of credit growth long before the real estate is constrained. "Too many buildings and not enough machines", as Raghuram Rajan (2013) put it recently, may sometimes be the inevitable consequence of a reliance on interest rates alone.

For these reasons, I believe that the optimal policy response must involve both a greater willingness to use interest rates preemptively, in pursuit of non-price stability-related objectives[3] and the deployment of macro-prudential tools. Those levers, however, need to be more robust and more extensive than those so far agreed within the global regulatory reform program.

- Countercyclical capital buffers (CCB) are clearly important and included within Basel III. But I have two concerns about the current Basel III specification.
  - First, that the 2.5% increase in required capital ratios may prove too small to achieve the desired effects.
  - Second, that as currently written the guideline for CCB deployment focuses solely on the rate of growth of credit relative to its own past trend. This implies that a rate of credit growth permanently faster than nominal GDP might be acceptable just as long as the growth rate was steady. If, as I have argued, levels of leverage matter as well as rates of change, this will prove insufficient.
- We also, I suggest, need to be able to apply macro prudential tools on a credit category-specific basis. As argued above, the negative social

[3]It would of course be possible to argue that monetary policy objective could still be defined as price stability, but simply pursued over a far longer time frame. But note that an uncontrolled credit and asset price boom may never result in a future increase in price inflation, but rather in a future fall in inflation below target as a result of post crisis deleveraging.

externality of credit creation is most likely to arise when credit is extended against specific categories of collateral, in particular real estate. An optimal response would therefore focus on this specific category of credit, seeking to lean against the bias of the system. Logically, we should therefore consider setting risk weights or capital requirements against commercial or residential real estate higher than those which purely private assessments of risks would consider appropriate. Such risk weights or requirements would be applied either continually across the cycle or take the form of sectorally specific countercyclical buffers.
- In addition, however, I believe that central banks as macro prudential regulators should have in the policy toolkit direct borrower constraints such as maximum loan to value (LTV) or loan to income (LTI) ratios. The UK's interim Financial Policy Committee (FPC) on which I sat until March 2013, debated whether we should ask Parliament to include such tools within the FPC's legal powers. The majority was against that at least for now: I was in the minority which favored their inclusion. They are being deployed with some success in several emerging economies. Without them — however imperfect and potentially subject to arbitrage they are — the dangers of harmful credit and asset price bubbles, busts, and post-crisis deleveraging would be significantly increased. That must in particular be the case, given the capacity of shadow banking systems to create credit outside bank balance sheets.

Finally, I think it important to note the implication of the finding that "there can be too much private debt" for the "financial system stability" focused reforms which I discussed earlier.

I noted there that one thing the innovations of the last 30 years almost certainly did achieve, was more credit creation than would otherwise have occurred. And the benefit of increased credit supply was quite overtly cited as a reason to be careful about some stability-focused restraints on risk-taking. I remember even in autumn 2008, when debating arguments for and against constraints on naked CDS contracts, and for and against skin-in-the-game requirements, being told that we had to be wary of anything that interfered with market liquidity and with the resulting ability to support real economy credit creation.

But if real economy credit creation, left to itself, might go beyond optimal levels, constraining it may be beneficial. The implication is that if we believe specific reforms, such as minimum haircuts on a wide range of secured financing contracts, are essential to guard against financial system stability risks, we should not be dissuaded from them by assertions that credit growth will be impaired.

Market Interventions and the Chicago School

Applying such policy measures would certainly amount to a major rejection of a wholly free market approach. It would reflect the conclusion that free market finance can generate too much credit, in particular in specific credit categories.

That may seem a provocative conclusion here in Chicago, home to the Chicago school of rigorous free market economics. But there is a strong strain of historic Chicago school thinking which saw banking and credit creation as special cases, to which the general propositions in favor of free markets did not apply. Indeed Chicago economist Henry Simons, strongly laissez faire in most of his economic thinking, believed that by treating credit creation as an economic activity like any other, we had as it were committed a category error, failing to recognize that credit and money creation is a natural public function, or at the very least a function of vital public interest. Simons indeed, in his famous paper on "Rules and Authorities", argued that the ideal economy would be one in which no debt contracts existed (Simons, 1936). Regretfully conceding that was not practical, he nevertheless argued strongly for the abolition of fractional reserve banks, supporting the Chicago Plan for 100% reserve banking. This would, he hoped, at least dramatically reduce the role of debt contracts within the economy.

And in a striking recent contribution, John Cochrane, a Chicago economist certainly not normally associated with interventionist policies, has argued that we should consider taxing credit intermediation to reflect the negative externality which excessive private credit creation imposes on society (Cochrane, 2013).

Rules, Discretion and Integration

I suspect, however, that Cochrane would still diverge from the conclusions From my conclusions about the appropriateness of constraining credit creation, and on reasonable grounds. For the implications I drew would leave central banks/macro-prudential authorities (and my assumption is that these are one and the same institution) with hugely wide discretion as to both objectives and instruments.

- They would be focused not solely on the attainment of price stability, but also on constraining credit and asset price cycles. They would pay attention not just to the pace of credit growth, but also to levels of leverage, but it would be impossible to set a definitive rule on how much private leverage (overall or by category) was too much.
- And they would be free to use either preemptive interest rate policy (even if this produced some short-term divergence from current price stability objectives) and a fairly wide array of macro-prudential policy tools (covering banks, shadow banks, and borrowers) in pursuit of these objectives.

This would be a dramatic change from the pre-crisis orthodoxy, which had gravitated increasingly to the elegant clarity that central banks should achieve a defined price stability objective using (primarily or entirely) one instrument, the policy interest rate. That pre-crisis orthodoxy allowed clear central bank mandates and accountability: My conclusions about the appropriateness of constraining credit creation would create far muddier waters.

The crucial question is then, whether we can adjust policy objectives and talks to address the central importance of credit cycles and levels of leverage while avoiding carte blanche discretion and achieving reasonable accountability.

I do not have a clear answer to that question, but let me end by suggesting three pointers to the debate:

1. One way to proceed would be to place a significant reliance on permanent measures, applied constantly across the economic cycle, which would lean against the bias of the free market towards excess credit creation, while avoiding too detailed micromanagement of time varying measures. This might involve:
   — Taxes on credit intermediation of the sort which Cochrane has proposed. Or, as he also argued, at very least the removal of the significant bias in favor of debt which most tax systems currently introduce.

— Capital requirements on banks that are set deliberately higher than appears necessary from the point of view of financial system stability narrowly defined. This would indeed be an indirect way of imposing a tax, forcing banks to hold more non-tax-deductible equity and less tax-deductible debt.
— Underwriting standards in mortgage markets, for instance via maximum LTV or LTI limits, which would simultaneously lean against the bias towards real estate lending and which might also serve consumer protection purposes.

Each of these proposals could have merit, and would tend to produce at least a somewhat less credit-intensive economy. But they would still leave the public authorities overall with difficult discretionary decisions — how high should be the tax rates, capital requirements, or underwriting standards. And I suspect that applied on a constant basis across the cycle, they would prove insufficient. Taxes and capital requirements imposed on the formal banking sector would, I think it certain, induce a shift of activity to innovative shadow bank forms; and constant rather than time-varying LTV or LTI limits might be insufficient to offset harmful real estate booms, and tighter than desirable in the downswing.

2. While across-the-board constant policy measures may therefore help to dampen both the credit cycle and resulting levels of leverage, and thus reduce the frequency and severity of more discretionary interventions, I suspect that they cannot be a complete solution. The challenge then becomes how to place discretion within some framework of accountability. Here I can do no better than endorse the approach now taken by the UK which:

— Defines in legislation those macro prudential policy levers which the FPC will be able to deploy.
— Places the use of those policy levers within a clearly defined governance framework, combining a decision-making committee with both internal and external members, and clearly defined procedures for reporting publicly the analysis and logic which has led to the committee's decisions.

3. There remains merit in distinguishing within central banks two somewhat different objectives: (i) the attainment of price stability over the medium term; and (ii) longer term management of both the financial

system stability and the potential wider macro-economic consequences of long trends in credit supply and leverage. Price stability remains an important objective in itself. But if interest rates have a role to play in credit cycle management, because they "get into all the cracks", then the distinction will not be absolute. Mechanisms for coordinating monetary and macro-prudential policy, and for basing them on a somewhat integrated analytical foundation, will be required. Price stability mandates may need amending to recognize that on some occasions central banks may divert from pure price stability objectives for clearly stated and justified macro prudential reasons. Indeed, not only are such developments likely: they are already occurring. The Bank of England now has a forward guidance policy which involves a contingent commitment to a path of interest rates subject to three "knock outs"; and one of those knockouts relates to financial stability.

I am well aware that my three points provide no more than initial stimuli to a difficult and important debate. But we cannot avoid that debate; we cannot stick to the elegant clarity of the pre-crisis world.

In that world, central banks increasingly saw their objective as price stability, defined as a low and stable rate of increase of price indices for the goods and services which enter GDP. And they were highly successful in achieving that objective: in terms of price stability there was (and indeed still largely is) a Great Moderation. But that Great Moderation did not prevent a huge financial crisis, which caused severe economic harm.

The idea that central banks can have one objective (price stability) and one instrument (the policy interest rate) was predicated on the assumption of modern macro-economics that the financial system was a neutral veil and that credit and money aggregates did not matter.

The crisis taught us how wrong that assumption was. Credit cycles and levels of leverage are factors of primary macro-economic importance. Our policy frameworks will have to evolve to reflect that fact.

References

Bernanke, B.S. (2004). Nonmonetary Effects of the Financial Crisis in the Propagation of the Great Depression. In *Essays on the Great Depression*. Princeton, NJ: Princeton University Press.

Borio, C. (2012). The Financial Cycle and Macroeconomics: What Have We Learnt? *Bank for International Settlements Working Paper*, No. 395, December. Available at www.bis.org/publ/work395.htm.

Borio, C. and M. Drehmann (2010). Financial Instability and Macroeconomics: Bridging the Gulf. In *The International Financial Crisis: Have the Rules of Finance Changed?*, A. Demirguc-Kunt, D.D. Evanoff and G.G. Kaufman (eds.), New Jersey, USA: World Scientific Publishing Company.

Brunnermeier, M. and L. Pedersen (2009). Market Liquidity and Funding Liquidity. *Review of Financial Studies*, Vol. 22, No. 6, pp. 2201–2238.

Cecchetti, S. and E. Kharroubi (2012). Reassessing the Impact of Finance on Growth. *Bank for International Settlements Working Paper*, No. 381, July. Available at www.bis.org/publ/work381.htm.

Cecchetti, S., M.S. Mohanty and F. Zampolli (2011). The Real Effects of Debt. *Bank for International Settlements Working Paper*, No. 352, September. Available at www.bis.org/publ/work352.htm.

Chakraborty, I., I. Goldstein and A. MacKinlay (2013). Do Asset Price Bubbles have Negative Real Effects? *University of Pennsylvania, Wharton School Working Paper*, June. Available at http://finance.wharton.upenn.edu.

Cochrane, J. (2013). Financial Reform in 12 Minutes. Remarks Presented at the Conference, *The US Financial System — Five Years After the Crisis*, Brookings Institution and Hoover Institution, Washington, DC, October 1. Available at http://faculty.chicagobooth.edu/john.cochrane/research/papers/cochrane_regulation.pdf.

Fisher, I. (1933). The Debt–Deflation Theory of Great Depressions. *Econometrica*, Vol. 1, No. 4, pp. 337–357.

Gennaioli, N., A. Shleifer and R. Vishny (2010). Neglected Risks, Financial Innovation and Financial Fragility. *National Bureau of Economic Research Working Paper*, No. 16068, March. Available at www.nber.org/papers/w16068.

International Monetary Fund (IMF) (2006). *Global Financial Stability Report: Market Developments and Issues*, April. Available at http://www.imf.org/external/pubs/ft/gfsr/index.htm.

International Monetary Fund (IMF) (2013). European Policies: 2013 Article IV Consultation. *Selected Issues Paper*, July.

Janeway, W. (2012). *Doing Capitalism in the Innovation Economy*. Cambridge, UK: Cambridge University Press.

Jordá, O., M. Schularick and A. Taylor (2011). When Credit Bites Back: Leverage, Business Cycles and the Crisis. *National Bureau of Economic Research Working Paper*, No. 17621, November. Available at www.nber.org/papers/w17621.

Kindleberger, C. (2011). *Manias, Panics and Crashes: A History of Financial Crises*. New York: Palgrave Macmillan. (First edition by Palgrave Macmillan, 1978.)

Koo, R. (2009). *The Holy Grail of Macroeconomics: Lessons from Japan's Great Recession*. Hoboken, NJ: John Wiley & Sons.

Levine, R. (2004). Finance and Growth: Theory and Evidence. *National Bureau of Economic Research Working Paper*, No. 10766, September. Available at www.nber.org/papers/w10766.

McCulley, P. and Z. Pozsar (2013). Helicopter Money: Or How I Stopped Worrying and Love Fiscal-monetary Cooperation. *Global Society of Fellows*, January.

Minsky, H. (2008). *Stabilizing an Unstable Economy.* New York: McGraw-Hill. (First published by Yale University Press, 1986.)

Rajan, R. (2013). A Step in the Dark: Unconventional Monetary Policy After the Crisis. Andrew Crockett Memorial Lecture, Bank for International Settlements, Basel, Switzerland, June 23. Available at www.bis.org/events/agm2013/sp130623.htm.

Reinhart, C. and K. Rogoff (2011). *This Time Is Different: Eight Centuries of Financial Folly.* Princeton, NJ: Princeton University Press.

Shiller, R. (2000). *Irrational Exuberance.* Princeton, NJ: Princeton University Press.

Shin, H.S. (2010). *Risk and Liquidity: Clarendon Lectures in Finance.* Oxford, UK: Oxford University Press.

Simons, H. (1936). Rules versus Authorities in Monetary Policy. *Journal of Political Economy*, Vol. 44, No. 1, pp. 1–30.

Stein, J. (2013a). Overheating in Credit Markets: Origins, Measurements and Policy Responses. Remarks at the Research Symposium, Restoring Household Financial Stability after the Great Recession, Federal Reserve Bank of Saint Louis, February 7.

Stein, J. (2013b). The Fire-sales Problem and Securities Financing Transactions. Remarks at the Federal Reserve Bank of New York Workshop, Fire Sales as a Driver of Systemic Risk in Triparty Repo and Other Secured Funding Markets, October 4.

Taylor, A. (2012). The Great Leveraging. *University of Virginia, NBER, and CEPR, Paper*, July. Available at http://www.bis.org/events/conf120621/taylor.pdf.

Taylor, A. and M. Schularick (2009). Credit Booms Gone Bust: Monetary Policy, Leverage Cycles and Financial Crises, 1870–2008. *National Bureau of Economic Research, Working Paper*, No. 15512, November. Available at www.nber.org/papers/w15512.

Townsend, R.M. (1979). Optimal Contracts and Competitive Markets with Costly State Verification. *Journal of Economic Theory*, Vol. 21, pp. 265–293.

Turner, A. (2012a). Securitisation, Shadow Banking and the Value of Financial Innovation. Remarks at the School of Advanced International Studies, Washington, DC, April. Available at www.fsa.gov.uk/static/pubs/speeches/0419-at.pdf.

Turner, A. (2012b). Monetary and Financial Stability: Lessons from the Crisis and from Some Old Economic Texts. Remarks at the South Africa Reserve Bank Conference, Pretoria, South Africa, November. Available at www.fsa.gov.uk/static/pubs/speeches/1102-at.pdf.

Turner, A. (2013a). Debt, Money and Mephistopheles: How Do We Get Out of This Mess? *Group of Thirty, Occasional Paper*, No. 87, May.

Turner, A. (2013b). Credit, money and leverage: What Wicksell, Hayek and Fisher Knew and Modern Macro-economics Forgot. Remarks at the Stockholm School of Economics Conference, Towards a Sustainable Financial System, Stockholm, Sweden, September. Available at http://ineteconomics.org/blog/institute/adair-turner-credit-money-and-leverage.

Wicksell, K. (1936). *Interest and Prices.* Macmillan. (First published as *Geldzins and Guiterpreise*, 1898.)

II

Description, Measurement, and History of Shadow Banking

Shadow Banking: Challenges for Global Monitoring and Regulation

Nicola Cetorelli*

Federal Reserve Bank of New York

In the years before the financial crisis of 2007–2008, financial intermediation evolved from a system centered on commercial banks as the main brokers between supply and demand for intermediated funds to a decentralized system of specialized financial entities, where the related transactions of funding supply and demand mediate through markets and not within the "walls" of the traditional banking firms. The most relevant aspect of this evolution has been the migration of the systemic externalities typically associated with financial intermediation away from the balance sheet of banks and instead scattered over long "credit intermediation chains" (Pozsar *et al.*, 2010). This transformation in the nature of intermediation is popularized — with the advent of the crisis — as the rise in "shadow banking" activity. In this market-based system of intermediation, the traditional form of banking is less relevant. Intermediation moves away from the regulatory perimeter. Systemic externalities still exist, but with diminished supervisory controls.[1]

Given its emphasized reliance on markets and activities, rather than entities, participation in modern intermediation can more easily take place

*Nicola Cetorelli is an Assistant Vice President in the Research Department of the Federal Reserve Bank of New York. The views expressed in this paper are those of the author and do not necessarily reflect the position of the Federal Reserve Bank of New York or the Federal Reserve System.

[1]Cetorelli, Mandel, and Mollineaux (2012) describe in detail the evolution of financial intermediation from a bank-centered model to a more market-based system.

across borders. Take the financing of mortgage loans originated in, say, the southeastern United States. In a traditional model of intermediation, local banks with a regional presence would likely originate such loans, funding them with local deposits. Now consider the same financing example implemented through a standard, pre-crisis, asset securitization chain: those same mortgage loans originated in the southeastern United States could be warehoused through ABCP conduits sponsored by German banks, funded by the US money market mutual funds funding themselves in Asia, the resulting asset-backed securities in turn marketed by British underwriters, and purchased by South American investors. Shadow banking is consequently a phenomenon that is by nature less constrained by national regulatory boundaries than traditional intermediation. As such, and to identify and contain its systemic externalities, it requires a global approach to monitoring and regulation.

In recent years, the Financial Stability Board (FSB) has spearheaded such an approach, receiving direct mandate from the Group of Twenty in the fall of 2010.[2] The mandate required working on three aspects of the problem. First, defining the scope: what should be included as part of shadow banking, and perhaps just as important, what should fall outside the scope of the exercise? Second, once the perimeter was defined, develop the criteria to conduct global data gathering, and gather the data, this is to be the fundamental pillar for global monitoring. Finally, derive specific regulatory proposals for national regulators and legislative bodies for strengthening the overall system, promoting effective coordination across national jurisdictions, and thus aiming at reducing the potential for cross-border regulatory arbitrage.

As a member of the FSB working groups behind this undertaking, I was asked by the conference organizers to present an overview of the work done to date. Since 2011, the FSB has produced a number of policy reports, all publicly available.[3] This article then, rather than summarizing the work done, offers instead an overview of its basic rationales, of the guiding principles that have been defined and followed throughout, and of the objective

[2] Financial Stability Board (2011), available at http://www.financialstabilityboard.org/publications/r_110412a.pdf.

[3] Full list available at: http://www.financialstabilityboard.org/list/fsb_publications/tid_150/index.htm.

constraints met, and of the challenges for effective global monitoring and regulation going forward.

The first challenge in the FSB undertaking was defining the problem. What are the boundaries of shadow banking? What should be included "in scope", thus implicitly subjecting whatever type of activity or entity to potential future monitoring and regulation, and what should be left out? The FSB embraced the conceptual description of the transition from traditional to modern intermediation described above, thus defining shadow banking broadly as "*the system of credit intermediation that involves entities and activities outside the regular banking system*". Every word in this definition is relevant: The focus is on "the system" of credit intermediation, which acknowledges intermediation's evolution to more complex chains of entities connected through markets and activities. "Credit intermediation", as exemplified earlier, is a way to exclude from scope activities that shadow bank entities may be performing but that do not pertain to credit intermediation (for instance, equity trading or foreign currency transactions). Moreover, it refers to "entities *and* activities", thus recognizing the potential need to take a monitoring and regulatory approach to intermediation that is not entity based (thus evolving from a bank-centered supervisory model). In fact, monitoring of recognized shadow banking activities may be itself a key to identifying entities involved in those activities, which may become in turn the target of enhanced scrutiny. In addition, with a reference to "involvement" of entities and activities, the definition implies that monitoring and regulation should not be just on the actual making of credit intermediation, but also on its *facilitation*. This includes in scope, for instance, the provision of credit and/or liquidity guarantees that are crucial components in the process of intermediation, and consequently staking monitoring and regulatory rights over both *on*-balance sheet and *off*-balance sheet activities. Finally, the definition ends with reference to the "regular banking system", which excludes traditional intermediation services, but at the same time recognizes that those entities that are traditionally subject to prudential regulation, were and still are active participants in the system of shadow banking.[4]

[4]This is the main thesis sustained in a series of NY Fed research contributions that have been published collectively in *Economic Policy Review*, 2012 (available at: http://www.ny.frb.org/research/epr/2012/EPRvol18n2.pdf).

Hence, the FSB definition of shadow banking is flexible enough to encompass credit intermediation activity of both "traditional" and "modern forms". The definition is effective, and practical. Its wide scope has the main purpose of defining common ground across jurisdictions, thus delineating basic principles to conduct consistent monitoring in each country of modern credit intermediation flows, irrespective of whichever entity may be participating, where entity names and types may be just the result of local regulatory environments.

Based on this definition, the FSB has been able to conduct annual global monitoring exercises, tracking its evolution over time and across countries. As shown in the 2013 FSB Global Shadow Banking Monitoring Report,[5] global shadow banking flows followed an upward trend during the last decade and up to 2007, then a not surprising dip, and then a pickup of the upward trend. In terms of GDP share though, the trend has not picked up after the financial crisis, but it still remains at well above 100% (Exhibit 2-2, p. 9 of the 2013 Report). Most shadow banking flows are captured by the US, the UK, and Euro area entities (Exhibit 2-3, p. 10).

The monitoring exercises are an effective tool to detect developments in an ever-evolving industry. The data gathering, however, is just as important, highlighting the degree to which intermediation activity takes place in homogeneous fashion across jurisdictions and to what extent instead heterogeneous national standards may constitute challenges in taking a global perspective on shadow banking. Taking stock of intermediation activities on a regular basis provides national regulators with opportunities to assert, for instance, who and what is subject to prudential regulation, the extent and quality of disclosure requirements, and the scope of allowed activities for banks. Hence, the data's aggregation and comparison within and across jurisdictions is in and of itself a tool to foster international regulatory coordination, thus achieving the goal of minimization of cross-border arbitrage.

The third element of the G20 mandate to the FSB was to offer a framework with specific solutions to strengthen regulation. The approach followed by the FSB has been both backward and forward-looking. First, we

[5]Financial Stability Board (2013a), available at http://www.financialstabilityboard.org/publications/r_131114.htm.

necessarily had to look backward to identify what had been the major weaknesses in the system of intermediation in the years before the crisis, and to suggest appropriate fixes. This lead to the identification of four main areas requiring regulatory reforms: the operations of money market mutual funds, to reduce susceptibility to runs; securitization activity, to cut associated agency problems and enhance transparency, standardization, and risk retention requirements; dealer-based intermediation, to address stability risks of the associated financings (such as repos and securities lending); and the interaction of banks with shadow banking, to mitigate risk exposures of the regulated banking sector in its role along modern intermediation chains.

Second, we recognized that successful reforms could not be limited to just fixing existing weaknesses. Financial intermediation is in constant evolution. Besides adjusting existing markets and activities, effective monitoring also requires building the proper tools to capture future mutations, new market emergences, financial instruments, and activities that could be sources of systemic risk. Financial innovation and technology are likely main factors behind such changes, but so is regulation itself, as existing market participants adapt to new rules and constraints on activities. Regulatory arbitrage is not a new phenomenon, but its detection and anticipation is certainly more challenging with a system spanning geographical borders.

One way to make monitoring and regulation more dynamic and forward-looking is to embrace the recognized roles that regulated bank entities have played and continued to play in the shadow banking system. If there is a new product or activity related to financial intermediation that we are likely to witness in the future, there is a very good chance that a regulated bank entity will be part of it.[6] Hence, the monitoring of banks could offer a preview into newly developed shadow intermediation activities, thus contributing to bridging the gap between regulation and the industry frontier. This principle is explicitly embraced in the FSB recommendations to the G20, produced in the fall of 2011,[7] and used

[6]Cetorelli (2012) elaborates this argument further. Adrian, Ashcraft, and Cetorelli (forthcoming) offer a broader take on the monitoring of shadow banking.

[7]Financial Stability Board (2011, pp. 10, 13) (http://www.financialstabilityboard.org/publications/r_111027a.pdf).

to inform the analysis performed in the annual Global Shadow Banking reports.[8]

Forward-looking monitoring has also been developed as the FSB came to deal with what was initially a backward-looking task: Its first global data mapping showed that while largely it was possible to gather consistent data across countries, a significant part of global financial intermediation flows remained difficult to map into the recognizable entity activity. For instance, the 2011 recommendations report shows that 36% of the global flows of non-bank intermediaries ("other financial intermediaries") had to be categorized as an unspecified "Others". The reasons for the inability to get a complete mapping are the same as mentioned earlier: The high degree of cross-country heterogeneity and diversity in business models and risk profiles, across sectors, but also within the same sector (or entity types). Heterogeneity in legal and regulatory frameworks across jurisdictions also plays a role — in fact, even heterogeneity in the legal definition of certain entities.

In order to define appropriate guidelines for national regulators so that they could gather data in a way to allow a better mapping of shadow banking flows into recognizable entities, the FSB actually had to develop an innovative approach apt to recognizing and assessing the non-bank entity involvement in shadow banking. This approach had to be based on their underlying economic functions, irrespective of legal names and forms, so that any national regulator would be able to properly map out and collect information, assuring a degree of consistency across countries. Five distinct economic functions have been proposed: The management of collective investment vehicles; the provision of loans dependent on short-term funding; the intermediation of market activities with dependence on short-term or secured funding of client assets; the facilitation of credit creation; and credit intermediation based on asset securitization.[9]

These five functions should capture the entire span of credit intermediation activity, but the approach allows for future changes. Such a function-based approach has indeed allowed improving the data gathering and aggregation quality, as reflected in the subsequent data reports,

---

[8]See, e.g., http://www.financialstabilityboard.org/publications/r_131114.pdf, pp. 19–24.

[9]Details are contained in Financial Stability Board (2013b), available at http://www.financialstabilityboard.org/publications/r_130829c.pdf.

but most importantly, it has provided the foundations for an intrinsically dynamic, forward-looking framework to monitor modern financial intermediation activities. National regulators are better able to identify who is involved in credit intermediation activity, and through which channel (economic function), irrespective of entity types and organizational forms, regulation in place and industry innovations.

Since the last financial crisis, there has been significant effort dedicated to enhancing the monitoring and regulation of modern financial intermediation. In particular, the increased complexity of financial intermediation technology perhaps represents the most meaningful challenge. Under a traditional, bank-based system, the locus of intermediation activity is largely the balance sheet of commercial banks. That is also where potential systemic externalities may arise, which justifies a model of prudential monitoring and regulation focused on the health of commercial banking institutions. Modern intermediation, with its transition toward higher reliance on market-mediated transactions, has multiplied the types of entities involved in its process and it has seen its systemic externalities migrating away from bank balance sheets and diffusing "in the shadow" and, just as challenging, extending across national jurisdictions. How should one rate this reform effort? What are the right metrics to assess the work done so far through the FSB? Perhaps the criterion to use should be to see whether the likelihood of a new financial crisis has diminished. However, by that metric and looking back into history, traditional bank-based regulation would have failed miserably. Financial crises may and very likely will occur again, but a way to judge whether there was any lesson learned from this past one is to see to what extent we will meaningfully improve in global coordination of monitoring and regulation.

References

Adrian, T., A. Ashcraft and N. Cetorelli (forthcoming). Shadow bank monitoring. In *The Oxford Handbook of Banking*, A.N. Berger, P. Molyneux and J. Wilson (eds.), Series: Oxford Handbooks in Finance. Oxford: Oxford University Press.

Cetorelli, N. (2012). A Principle for Forward-Looking Monitoring of Financial Intermediation: Follow the Banks*! Federal Reserve Bank of New York Liberty Street Economics Blog.*

Cetorelli, N., B.H. Mandel and L. Mollineaux (2012). The Evolution of Banks and Financial Intermediation: Framing the Analysis. *Federal Reserve Bank of New York Economic Policy Review* 18, No. 2, July 1–12.

Financial Stability Board (2011). FSB Report with Recommendations to Strengthen Oversight and Regulation of Shadow Banking. Available at http://www.financialstabilityboard.org/publications/r_111027a.htm [accessed on 15 June 2014].

Financial Stability Board (2013a). Global Shadow Banking Monitoring Report. Available at http://www.financialstabilityboard.org/publications/r_131114.htm [accessed on 15 June 2014].

Financial Stability Board (2013b). Policy Framework for Strengthening Oversight and Regulation of Shadow Banking Entities. Available at http://www.financialstabilityboard.org/publications/r_130829c.htm [accessed on 15 June 2014].

Pozsar, Z., T. Adrian, A. Ashcraft and H. Boesky (2010). Shadow Banking. Federal Reserve Bank of New York Staff Reports, No. 458, July.

Traditional Banks, Shadow Banks, and Financial Stability

Diana Hancock and Wayne Passmore*

Board of Governors of the Federal Reserve System

We describe a model-based methodology to define shadow banking. Our "traditional banks" originate loans and provide management input that creates wealth for the borrower. In contrast, a "shadow bank" cream skims from these traditional banks and only provides actuarially based financing to seasoned borrowers or to borrowers with easy-to-value collateral. In our framework, the presence of shadow banks means that fewer loans are originated and social welfare declines. We contrast our approach to shadow banking with those of others and also discuss potential government policies that would enhance social welfare by increasing loan originations.

Introduction

Shadow banking has been much in the news since the financial crisis; however, clearly defining shadow banking has proven to be a difficult task.

*Diana Hancock is a Deputy Associate Director and Wayne Passmore is an Associate Director in the Division of Research and Statistics at the Board of Governors of the Federal Reserve System. The views expressed are the authors' and should not be interpreted as representing the views of the FOMC, its principals, the Board of Governors of the Federal Reserve System, or any other person associated with the Federal Reserve System. We thank Anjan Thakor, Matthew Eichner, and participants at an American Economic Association session in San Diego for their useful comments. We also thank Paul Fornia and Frederick Schneider for their research assistance. Wayne Passmor's contact information is: Mail Stop 66, Federal Reserve Board, Washington, DC 20551 (E-mail: Wayne.Passmore@frb.gov). Diana Hancock's contact information is: Mail Stop 153, Federal Reserve Board, Washington, DC 20551 (E-mail: Diana Hancock@frb.gov).

The Financial Stability Board, which is the international entity charged by the leaders of G20 countries to study shadow banking, is the main source of regulatory guidance on shadow banking for many countries (see www.finanicalstability.org). In August 2013, the Financial Stability Board recommended a variety of actions that G20 countries should consider with regard to repurchase agreements (repos), money market funds, and securitization; all these activities are considered by many observers as important components of the shadow banking system (see, for example, Financial Stability Board, 2013a).

The Financial Stability Board describes shadow banking as "credit intermediation involving entities and activities outside of the regular banking system" (Financial Stability Board, 2013b, p. 1). On the one hand, this description encompasses a wide range of entities that engage in credit intermediation (e.g., finance companies, insurance companies, and asset managers) and activities (e.g., repos and securitization). On the other hand, this description seems to preclude banking conglomerates from engaging in shadow banking even though such entities sometimes set up new entities or activities to reduce regulatory burdens or possible intrusions by bank examiners.

The Financial Stability Board has found it difficult to provide more clarity in delineating what shadow banking is and is not. Instead, it argues that "[a]uthorities should have the ability to define the regulatory perimeter" (Financial Stability Board, 2012, p. 9; Financial Stability Board, 2013c, p. 13). Through defining this perimeter, the Financial Stability Board encourages authorities to monitor shadow banking and focus their attention on mitigating the spill-over effect between the regulated banking system and the shadow banking system, particularly by examining large exposures of the banking system to activities outside of banking (Financial Stability Board, 2013d). In essence, this is the "we know it when we see it" approach to defining shadow banking, excluding only credit intermediation performed by the banking system.

Elsewhere, shadow banking is often defined as short-term market-based financing of longer-term loans, usually through collateral-based lending or securitization (see, for example, Pozsar *et al.*, 2012). The scope of shadow banking in such studies is sometimes limited to "financial intermediaries that conduct maturity, credit, and liquidity transformation without access to central bank liquidity, or public sector guarantees" (see, for example,

Pozsar *et al.*, 2012, p. i). But this approach for defining and limiting the scope of shadow banking ignores the possibility that financial institutions may engage in the same transformations with *implicit* access to central bank liquidity and/or *implicit* government backing. Moreover, some non-bank financial institutions (e.g., insurance companies) may have access to other government-backed liquidity programs (e.g., Federal Home Loan Bank advances).

Regardless of definition, shadow banking is estimated to be large. In November 2013, the Financial Stability Board estimated that the assets of the shadow banking system worldwide had reached $71 trillion, although the uncertainty in these estimates of credit intermediation outside the banking system is large (Financial Stability Board, 2013b, p. 2). Claessens *et al.* (2012) provide more detailed information about the shadow banking system and how it finances lending; these authors estimate that the shadow banking system totaled about $64 trillion in 2011, much larger than their estimate of the shadow banking system in 2002, which was just $26 trillion. Together, these estimates suggest that the global shadow banking system is growing rapidly and is currently of comparable size to the global banking system.

The visualization of the distinctions between banking and shadow banking as a battle line that requires regulatory monitoring to protect the financial system is a common description of shadow banking. But neither this description, nor the description where shadow banking is defined as long-term loans financed by short-term funding, are based on more fundamental descriptions of the preferences of economic agents and of the technologies used by such agents when optimizing their utility. We fill this gap by providing a model-based approach for defining shadow banking that focuses on these fundamental economic considerations. Moreover, we argue that both of the foregoing definitions of shadow banking can be derived using the model-based approach.

In particular, we posit there are two fundamental lending technologies: (1) relationship-based lending and (2) actuarially based lending. A relationship loan is defined as a loan that is bundled with management assistance, which allows the borrower to finance a wealth-enhancing project. In contrast, actuarially based funding is where the interest rate offered on a new loan is equal to the risk-free rate plus a mark-up that covers the probability of default multiplied by the (expected) losses given default.

Our model considers the competition between these two lending technologies, and demonstrates that shadow banking systems, which are based on actuarially based lending technologies, can effectively "cream-skim" particular types of loans from the banking system, which employs relationship-based technologies.

Our model suggests that (1) the regulatory perimeter will likely remain ill-defined because traditional banks may embed elements of shadow banks within them, (2) economic function and technology should be considered when discussing whether a financial entity is a "traditional bank" or "shadow bank", and (3) the most important distinction between traditional banking and shadow banking for financial stability purposes is the distinction between relationship-based lending versus actuarially based lending. We will argue that this distinction also has important consequences for loan origination, loan maturity, and social welfare. Finally, because of the social welfare consequences, there are also important implications for the design of subsidies provided by governments to their banking industries.

Although we argue that there is a strong distinction between the social welfare consequences of relationship-based lending and actuarially-based lending, this distinction, by itself, does not determine what entities, activities, or products should be within, or outside of, the government safety net. As Darrell Duffie (2012) has written, "Nothing about the boundaries of the regulated banking system should be taken on principle. Which activities are allowed within this specially protected regulatory environment is a cost–benefit decision that should be based on how dangerous it would be for these activities to be interrupted, what sorts of collateral damage might be caused by their failure, and what risks these activities would pose to financial stability if conducted outside the regulated banking system".

Description of Model-Based Approach to Defining Shadow Banking

In our model, loans are needed by borrowers for two periods. A bank operates in a competitive banking system and provides a relationship loan to a new borrower in the first period. Both the loan and the management assistance associated with this loan are necessary inputs to executing the borrower's project.

We refer to the banks that invest in producing relationship loans as "traditional banks". Most importantly, traditional banks are in the business of originating loans and working with borrowers over time to manage their projects. And in our model, a banking relationship is about finding credible borrowers and providing a management input that creates wealth for the borrower.[1] This process may involve building local bank branches, networking in local communities, meeting repeatedly with borrowers, and creating other modes of borrower interaction for the purpose of handling financial transactions. Because of these opportunities for wealth creation, loan borrowers at traditional banks value the relationship established with their banker.

From the perspective of a formal model, the important aspect of relationship lending is that the bank's upfront investment in establishing the relationship takes two periods to fully recoup. The bank must determine the level of the upfront relationship investment for each borrower at loan origination before knowing the level of the relationship that will be needed by the borrower in the second period. If the borrower no longer needs a bank relationship in the second period, he or she can choose to have the project actuarially financed. As a result, if the borrower does not need the relationship in the second period the bank may have to bear much of the upfront investment cost of the relationship without receiving any benefit in the second period.

Why cannot the traditional bank capture the cost of carrying the relationship technology in the second period using a financial contract? It easily could if any form of prepayment penalty were allowed. However, in many cases, particularly with US mortgages, prepayment penalties are discouraged or the application of such penalties would make it more difficult to sell

[1] In their textbook, Freixas and Rochet (2008) define relationship banking as "the investment in providing financial services that will allow dealing repeatedly with the same customer in a more efficient way". This definition of relationship banking differs from our definition because we argue that the relationship itself may provide a key input into the customer's own production technology, increasing his or her wealth. In addition, our model is distinct from other relationship models, such as Sharpe (1990) and Rajan (1992), where the relationship is viewed as creating better information for the lending bank in a multi-period bargaining game with outside competitors. Thus, in this paper we use the term "traditional banks" rather than "relationship banks".

the mortgage to someone else (say, for securitization). Moreover, borrowers may hesitate to accept contracts with large prepayment penalties, which may attempt to recapture large fixed costs, especially if their perceived odds of needing a relationship with the bank in the future are low. Without the ability to "lock in" borrowers for two periods, the bank risks the possibility of carrying a substantial investment overhead without generating any revenues, and thus would scale back its loan originations.

The social welfare loss of being unable to "lock-in" borrowers may be large. If we examine the optimal *ex ante* contract without the possibility of borrower refinancing, it equates the marginal returns from bank financing and bank relationship investment across both periods and across both the service of financing and the service of providing a management expertise. Without knowledge of its second period relationship type, the borrower chooses a "Rawlsian" contract; covered by the veil of ignorance, that is, the borrower desires a long-term, fixed-rate contact to hedge any downside risk from being a borrower with a high default risk and from having a need for a (large) bank relationship in the second period.

But once shadow banks provide actuarially priced financing in the second period, the borrowers who do not need a bank relationship may opt out of their lending contract and instead use an actuarially priced contract. Shadow banks provide this financing at a low-cost market rate because, unlike banks, they do not invest in relationships; they only evaluate the value of collateral using publicly available sources of information and consider the revealed quality of the borrower. Thus, shadow banks effectively "cream skim" the low-cost borrowers with knowable default risks from the traditional banks in the second period, leaving the traditional banks with an investment overhang. Note that in this context, it does not matter whether shadow banking is either collateral-based (e.g., funded through repurchase agreements) or securitization-based (for a description of this distinction, see Claessens *et al.*, 2012).

With the presence of shadow banks, traditional banks will have to take into account of the possible switching of borrowers to actuarially based lending. In response, traditional banks limit their upfront investment in relationships. With fewer loans originated, fewer positive net-present-value projects are funded; fewer loan originations may mean social welfare declines.

A Discussion of the Literature

We argue that the competition between traditional banks and shadow banks should be recast as a competition between two lending technologies — relationship-based lending and actuarially based lending. We also argue that actuarially based lending effectively "cream skims" the most profitable borrowers from traditional banks. We see our explanation for shadow banking as consistent with four other popular explanations of shadow banking contained in the literature.

One explanation is that shadow banking is the pooling and trenching of cash flows from loans to create safe assets for investors worldwide. Securitization of bank loans overcomes the adverse selection problems associated with banks issuing debt directly and allows banks to increase the liquidity of their balance sheet while earning profits to satisfy investor demand for safe assets (Gorton and Pennacchi, 1990). These "safe assets" can not only perform the role of money for households and businesses but also propagate small shocks into large financial crisis if the small shock is viewed as creating a large change in what was known about the underlying collateral (Gorton and Ordoñez, 2012).

A second explanation is that shadow banking is regulatory arbitrage. Securitization and off-balance sheet collateral-based lending are methods to effectively lower the capital needed to finance relatively safe loans (Acharya and Richardson, 2009; Acharya, Schnabl, and Suarez, 2010).

A third explanation is that shadow banking is maturity transformation. Longer-term loans that are financed by shorter-term market-based funds usually create additional returns because of the slope of the yield curve. However, such a system is vulnerable to runs by short-term debt holders if they perceive that the loans might default (Gorton and Metrick, 2012), or to liquidity or solvency problems at the most critical dealer banks (Krishnamurthy, Nagel, and Orlov, 2012).

Finally, a fourth explanation is that shadow banking is the exploitation of short-sighted investors by the banking industry. Some capital market investors are unable to incorporate "tail risk" into their economic return calculations, and therefore, these investors persistently underprice credit risks. Through securitization, banks are able to effectively expand their balance sheets by selling loans to these short-sighted investors. Of course, once there is a crisis, the system is undercapitalized (Gennaioli, Shleifer, and Vishny, 2013).

All these explanations for shadow banking could be true simultaneously. And each of these explanations depends on the actuarial nature of the loans that are provided through securitization or that are used as the ultimate collateral in repurchase agreements, or asset-backed commercial paper.

What is unique about our approach to defining shadow banking is the focus on the origination of loans by traditional banks, and the characterization of shadow banks as those entities that "cream skim" some of the loans that are originated by these traditional banks to provide the underlying product securitization and other forms of collateral-backed lending. Our focus is on the competition and symbiotic nature between two different technologies: (1) relationship-based lending and (2) actuarially-based loan financing.

Relationship lending has been the focus of many theoretical and empirical studies in economics over the last 30 years. Traditional relationship banking is needed for at least three reasons. First, to provide insurance to some borrowers, who value consistent bank financing across both good and bad economic times. Second, to provide monitoring of borrowers who are opaque to the market and thus cannot raise debt or equity directly. Third, relationship lending is needed to provide loans to borrowers utilizing "soft information". This "soft information" can only be learned by "getting to know" the borrower.

One of the most comprehensive theoretical studies of relationship banking is Boot and Thakor (2000), who compare relationship lending to transaction lending and how the bank's choice between the two technologies is affected by both interbank and capital market competition. They find that greater capital market competition is associated with a reduction in relationship lending (although each relationship loan is more valuable to the bank) and that the highest quality borrowers benefit most from such competition. Both of these results are similar to the results derived from our model that focuses on the competition between traditional banks and shadow banks, even though the modeling framework of Boot and Thakor is different and even though financing through their capital markets — which often involves elements of relationship banking — is not the same as the actuarially based shadow banking system we describe here.

In general, the relationship banking literature establishes that it is difficult for relationship banks to appropriate all the benefits from a borrower relationship (Cetorelli and Peretto, 2012; Thakor, 2012; Dong and Guo, 2011). Our model is consistent with this view, but for different reasons.

An associated empirical literature is focused on whether banks can "lock in" borrowers using banking relationships. The results of these studies are mixed (Fernando, May, and Megginson, 2012; Bharath *et al.*, 2011; Dass and Massa, 2011). Our model suggests that the "lock-in" effect may vary *ex-post* with the quality of the borrower and the quality of collateral, which would make the lock-in effect difficult to estimate.

The Government Response to "Cream Skimming" by Shadow Banks

Our model suggests that loan originations overall are lower, and long-term bank loans are more difficult to sustain, when some borrowers can opt out of their bank relationships and shift to actuarially based financing. Given this outcome, it is not surprising that government-backed loan financing programs often have the goal to increase loan originations to new borrowers and/or to extend the maturities of loan contracts.

One example of this phenomenon in the United States is Fannie Mae and Freddie Mac. The justifications for these government-sponsored enterprises (GSEs) are often stated in terms of helping new borrowers. Moreover, the 30-year fixed-rate mortgage is often argued to exist only because Fannie Mae and Freddie Mac intervene in the secondary mortgage market.

In the context of our model, Fannie Mae and Freddie Mac lower the costs to the banking system of refinancing those borrowers who might otherwise opt out and be refinanced though private sector securitizations. The mortgage borrowers who might opt out are the ones who can be actuarially financed because their default characteristics are well understood by the market. Fannie Mae and Freddie Mac allow banks to have access to a lower-cost actuarially based technology, and thus they can potentially compete with (and perhaps even out-compete) private sector securitizers. By using the Fannie Mae and Freddie Mac underwriting and pricing algorithms and subsequently "selling" the mortgage to the GSEs, the bank is able to capture some of the interest income that is associated with the mortgage in the second period.

However, government actions that allow the bank to capture some of the marginal costs associated with lending to the borrowers who can switch to actuarially based financing in the second period do not resolve the problem that the banking system must carry the costs associated with relationship banking (including the costs of loan originations to new borrowers) across two periods. Loan originations still contract in the presence of actuarially-based financing because the fixed costs of origination are borne by fewer borrowers over the two periods. In contrast, allowing prepayment penalties, for example, would make loan originations to new borrowers more likely because the risks to a bank of originating a loan to a new borrower who can leave the banking system before the bank can recoup its fixed investment are mitigated. More generally, our model suggests that government actions that lower the fixed costs of building banking relationship are more likely to expand credit to new creditworthy borrowers.

Shadow Banking and Financial Stability

Our model suggests that in practice there are three types of entities: (1) traditional banks, (2) shadow banks, which only provide actuarially based loan financing, and "mixed-strategy banks", which combine traditional banking and shadow banking. Traditional banks promote loan originations, provide business assistance or improve financial literacy, and generate wealth through relationship lending. Thus, some traditional banks, as defined by the extent of their borrower relationships, may not be found in the regulated banking industry. Business loan originations to new borrowers might be in the form of private equity or venture capital. Household loan originations to new borrowers might be in the form of financing from non-profit organizations, or finance companies. The key distinction is whether the entity invests in the infrastructure and technologies that are needed to originate loans and forge relationships with new borrowers.

Turning to "shadow banks", actuarially based financing appears to be more financially fragile than traditional banking for at least two reasons. First, actuarially based lending lacks uniqueness. This type of lending is based on expectations of credit loss for large classes of similar loans. As pointed out by Stein (2011), when such calculations do not account for the externality that occurs when a bank (or shadow bank) sells the assets it holds in common with other banks, collateral values can be degraded. In a crisis, the fire sales of such common assets may sharply lower the valuations of all such assets. In contrast, relationship loans that are held by traditional banks are less correlated with each other and may also have longer-term forms of financing.

Second, there is little competitive advantage to be found in large actuarially based financing. As discussed in Hanson, Kashyap, and Stein (2011), narrow margins in actuarially based lending means that slight increases in funding costs yield large decreases in profits. As a result, shadow banks may strongly resist any decline in leverage, even if equity is only slightly more expensive than debt.

Consequently, government policymakers might consider whether government programs are supporting the relationship building aspect of traditional banking, or only lowering the marginal costs associated with actuarially based financing. The activities of traditional banks and shadow banks might be distinguished by examining a lending institution for (1) longer maturity liabilities, (2) longer maturity assets, (3) relationship-based assets, and (4) investments in relationship-building technologies (e.g., management consulting or financial education programs) and credit analyses of new borrowers. To the extent an institution — or a "channel" of non-bank lending — has these characteristics, it might enhance both social welfare and financial stability.

Our model raises many questions about shadow banking and the social welfare of actuarially based financing. Is there any underlying economic value associated with such financing, or is it simply redistributing financial claims on assets? Would more relationship-based lending enhance financial stability, and would less "financial engineering" of cash flows associated with actuarially based lending also enhance financial stability? Should government benefits be more targeted toward traditional relationship banking? And finally, are some types of capital markets activities more like relationship banking, and should these capital markets activities, therefore, be encouraged by public policies?

References

Acharya, V.V. and M. Richardson (2009). How Securitization Concentrated Risk in the Financial Sector. *Critical Review*, Vol. 21, No. 2, pp. 195–210.

Acharya, V.V., P. Schnabl and G.O. Suarez (2010). Securitization Without Risk Transfer. *National Bureau of Economic Research, NBER, Working Paper*, No. 15730, February.

Bharath, S., S. Dahlya, A. Saunders and A. Srinivassan (2011). Lending Relationships and Loan Contract Terms. *Review of Financial Studies*, Vol. 24, No. 4, pp. 1141–1203.

Boot, A. and A. Thakor (2000). Can Relationship Banking Survive Competition? *Journal of Finance*, Vol. 55, No. 2, pp. 679–713.

Cetorelli, N. and P.F. Peretto (2012). Credit Quantity and Credit Quality: Bank Competition and Capital Accumulation. *Journal of Economic Theory*, Vol. 147, No. 3, pp. 967–998.

Claessens, S., Z. Pozsar, L. Ratnovski and M. Singh (2012). Shadow Banking: Economics and Policy. International Monetary Fund, Staff Discussion Note SDN/12/12, December 4. Available at http://www.imf.org/external/pubs/ft/sdn/2012/sdn1212.pdf [accessed on 15 June 2014].

Dass, N. and M. Massa (2011). The Impact of Strong Bank-firm Relationship on the Borrowing Firm. *Review of Financial Studies*, Vol. 24, No. 4, pp. 1204–1260.

Dong, B. and G. Guo (2011). The Relationship Banking Paradox: No Pain No Gain versus Raison D'être. *Economic Modelling*, Vol. 28, September, pp. 2263–2270.

Duffie, D. (2012). Drawing Boundaries Around and Through the Banking System. *World Economic Forum: Financial Development Report*, October 31.

Fernando, C., A.D. May and W.L. Megginson (2012). The Value of Investment Banking Relationships: Evidence from the Collapse of Lehman Brothers. *Journal of Finance*, Vol. 67, No. 1, pp. 235–270.

Financial Stability Board (2012). Consultative Document: Strengthening Oversight and Regulation of Shadow Banking: An Integrated Overview of Policy Recommendations. November 18, Available at http://www.financialstabilityboard.org/ publications/r_121118.pdf [accessed on 15 June 2014].

Financial Stability Board (2013a). Strengthening Oversight and Regulation of Shadow Banking: Policy Framework for Addressing Shadow Banking Risks in Securities Lending and Repos. August 29. Available at http://www.financialstabilityboard.org/publications/r_130829b.htm [accessed on 15 June 2014].

Financial Stability Board (2013b). Global Shadow Banking Monitoring Report 2013. November 14. Available at http://www.financialstabilityboard.org/publications/r_131114.htm [accessed on 15 June 2014].

Financial Stability Board (2013c). Strengthening Oversight and Regulation of Shadow Banking: Policy Framework for Strengthening Oversight and Regulation of Shadow Banking Entities. August 29. Available at http://www.financialstabilityboard.org/publications/r_130829c.pdf [accessed on 15 June 2014].

Financial Stability Board (2013d). Strengthening Oversight and Regulation of Shadow Banking: An Overview of Policy Recommendations. August 29. Available at http://www.financialstabilityboard.org/publications/r_130829a.pdf [accessed on 15 June 2014].

Freixas, X. and J.-C. Rochet (2008). *Microeconomics of Banking*, 2nd Edition. Cambridge, Massachusetts: The MIT Press.

Gennaioli, N., A. Shleifer and R.W. Vishny (2013). A Model of Shadow Banking. *Journal of Finance*, Vol. 68, No. 4, pp. 1331–1363.

Gorton, G. and A. Metrick (2012). Securitized Banking and the Run on Repo. *Journal of Financial Economics*, Vol. 104, No. 3, pp. 425–461.

Gorton, G. and G. Ordoñez (2012). Collateral Crises. *Yale University Working Paper*, March. Available at http://www.econ.yale.edu/~go49/pdfs/CC.pdf [accessed on 15 June 2014].

Gorton, G. and G. Pennacchi (1990). Financial Intermediation and Liquidity Creation. *Journal of Finance*, Vol. 45, No. 1, pp. 49–72.

Hanson, S.G., A.K. Kashyap and J.C. Stein (2011). A Macroprudential Approach to Financial Regulation. *Journal of Economic Perspectives*, Vol. 25, No. 1, pp. 3–28.

Krishnamurthy, A., S. Nagel and D. Orlov (2012). Sizing up Repo. *National Bureau of Economic Research, NBER, Working Paper*, No. 17768, January.

Pozsar, Z., T. Adrian, A. Ashcraft and H. Boesky (2012). Shadow Banking. *Federal Reserve Bank of New York, Staff Report*, No. 458, February.

Rajan, R. (1992). Insiders and Outsiders: The Relationship between Relationship and Arms Length Debt. *Journal of Finance*, Vol. 47, No. 4, pp. 1367–1400.

Sharpe, S.A. (1990). Asymmetric Information, Bank Lending, and Implicit Contracts: A Stylized Model of Customer Relationships. *Journal of Finance*, Vol. 45, No. 4, pp. 1069–1087.

Stein, J.C. (2011). Monetary Policy as Financial-Stability Regulation. *National Bureau of Economic Research, NBER, Working Paper*, No. 16883, March.

Thakor, A. (2012). Incentives to Innovate and Financial Crises. *Journal of Financial Economics*, Vol. 103, No. 1, pp. 130–148.

Bagehot was a Shadow Banker: Shadow Banking, Central Banking, and the Future of Global Finance

Perry Mehrling*

Barnard College, Columbia University

Zoltan Pozsar*

US Treasury

James Sweeney*

Credit Suisse

Daniel H. Neilson*

Institute for New Economic Thinking

The modern shadow banking system, at its core, bears a surprising resemblance to the 19th century world that Walter Bagehot helped us to understand in his magisterial book, *Lombard Street: A Description of the [London] Money Market* (1873). At the heart of both worlds is the wholesale money market, and operating as the crucial liquidity backstop in both worlds is the central bank. At the time Bagehot was writing, this backstop function was not yet fully understood, much less accepted; much the same could be said of the central bank's backstop of the shadow banking system today

*The authors are members of the Shadow Banking Colloquium, a project of the Financial Stability Research Program of the Institute for New Economic Thinking. Thanks to Falk Mazelis for research assistance, and to Phil Prince for searching comments on an earlier draft.

(Capie, 2012). We are living today in a Bagehot moment, when the outlines of the new are just emerging from the ashes of the old.

During crisis, the central banks of Bagehot's time and our own both dutifully employed their balance sheets to stem the downturn. In both his time and ours, they did so without much prior theory about why it would work and with hardly any thought about possible implications for more normal times. The time for all of that would come later, after the crisis. Bagehot's book started the process of necessary rethinking for his own time by bringing out into the open how the Bank of England had acted during previous crises. We start the process of necessary rethinking for our own time by using Bagehot as an entry point for understanding the modern shadow banking system and the Fed's response to the global financial crisis.

In doing so, we are conscious of taking a different approach to the subject than does most of the existing literature. For most authors, the important thing about shadow banking is the "shadow", the distinct whiff of illegitimacy that comes from regulatory evasion in good times combined with unauthorized access to the public purse in bad times. This is the origin of the widespread impulse to frame the question of appropriate oversight and regulation of shadow banking as a matter of how best to extend the existing system of oversight and regulation as it is applied to traditional banking. See, for example, the much-cited paper of Gorton and Metrick (2010), as well as the recent overviews by Adrian and Ashcraft (2012) and the Financial Stability Board (2012).

For us, by contrast, shadow banking is simply "money market funding of capital market lending", sometimes on the balance sheets of entities called banks and sometimes on other balance sheets. As such, shadow banking is not some troubling excrescence on the healthy body of traditional banking. Rather, it is the centrally important channel of credit for our times, which needs to be understood on its own terms. From this vantage point, the question of appropriate oversight and regulation requires us to abstract from what we know about traditional banking, and to start instead by imagining a world in which shadow banking is the only banking system.

The defining role of markets, both money and capital markets, for our understanding of shadow banking directs attention to the central importance of prices, and also to the central importance of market-making institutions, both for price discovery and for continuing secondary market

Capital Funding Bank		Global Money Dealer		Asset Manager	
Assets	Liabilities	Assets	Liabilities	Assets	Liabilities
RMBS CDS IRS FXS	MM funding	MM funding	"Deposits"	"Deposits"	Capital CDS IRS FXS

Derivative Dealer

Assets	Liabilities
CDS IRS FXS	CDS IRS FXS

Fig. 1. A market-based credit system.

liquidity. These institutions, relatively unimportant from the perspective of traditional bank loan-based credit, are both central and essential for modern capital market-based credit. When they are working well, the whole system works well; and when they stumble, the whole system stumbles. In what follows, we place them at the very center of analytical attention.

Figure 1 shows an idealized picture of the shadow banking system, which we might more neutrally call the "market-based credit system". The "capital funding bank" is engaged in money market funding of capital market lending, hence shadow banking, specifically the funding of residential mortgage-backed securities (RMBS). We imagine the risk in these securities being hedged in various swap markets — generically, credit default swaps, interest rate swaps, and foreign exchange swaps — so that the combined CFB asset position is essentially risk-free.[1] We further imagine this asset position being used as security for money market funding.

The "asset manager" is the mirror image of the capital funding bank, holding its capital in (secured) money form and enhancing the return on that capital by selective risk exposure in various swap markets — again

[1] To avoid possible confusion, let it be noted that we adopt an "insurance" convention of booking swaps that strip out risk as contingent assets on their ultimate owner's balance sheet, and hence also as contingent liabilities on the balance sheet of the counterparty to whom the risk is transferred. An alternative "investment" convention is also possible, which would instead book the risk exposure as an asset on the reasoning that it has positive expected return even if zero net present value at inception.

generically credit default swaps, interest rate swaps, and foreign exchange swaps. Standing in between the asset manager and the capital funding bank are two types of market-makers: one the "global money dealer" whose dealing activities establish the price of funding, and the other the "derivative dealer" whose dealing activities establish the price of risk. These dealers will be the central focus of our analysis.

In this stylized model, we abstract from counterparty risk because all funding is secured, and because all derivative positions are matched either by offsetting natural positions (such as RMBS for the CFB) or by reserves sufficient to make good even in the worst-case scenario ("deposits" for the AM). Further, our dealers are matched-book dealers, with no net exposure to price risk, and thus with no need for capital reserves. Because their cash and collateral inflows and outflows are exactly matched, they have no need for liquidity reserves either. The only capital in the system, and the only deposit holding as well, are both on the balance sheet of the asset manager, which is as it should be since the asset manager is the only agent facing any risk. (We will be relaxing these strong assumptions when we consider boom-bust dynamics in the second section.)

The stylized character of this model means that it cannot be expected to line up exactly with the institutional arrangements of current financial markets. Indeed, most large investment banks probably contain within their walls elements of all four functions. The value of the model is in helping us to make conceptual distinctions between these functions, both within given institutions and across institutions. Just so, for example, capital funding bank structures can be found on the balance sheets of most European universal banks, but also in off-balance sheet conduits of various kinds. Money market mutual funds might be considered global money dealers, but they are not the only ones. Pension funds might be considered asset managers, but also non-financial corporate treasurers and even synthetic Exchange-Traded Funds. Central counterparty clearinghouses might be considered derivative dealers, but so also is anyone running a bespoke swap book.

The main purpose of the model is to provide an overarching framework to make conceptual sense of the many moving parts of the market-based credit system. Most important, the model highlights the central importance of the dealers who make prices in money and capital markets. In doing so, we also uncover a link to the older Bagehot-era literature since, in effect, Bagehot's bill brokers were last century's version of the model's Global Money Dealers (Wood, 2000). At the core of the modern-world credit system lies a bill-funding apparatus quite analogous to the one Bagehot and his contemporaries were trying to understand and to manage. For understanding and for managing our own system, we start from Bagehot.

Bagehot and Beyond

Reading Bagehot, we enter a world where securities issued by sovereign states are not yet the focal point of trading and prices, as they would come to be in the 20th century. Instead, the focus of attention is the private bill market, which domestic manufacturers tap as a source of working capital, and which traders worldwide tap to finance the movement of tradable goods. It is a market in short-term private debt, typically collateralized by tradable goods.

Supplying funds to the bill market were, among others, banks that purchased bills at discount from face value using their own deposit liabilities, typically planning to hold to maturity and redeem at par. The institution of "acceptance", by which a bank or some other party guaranteed payment of a bill at maturity, was the way non-prime bills became prime. Backstopping the whole thing was the Bank of England, whose posted "Bank Rate" in effect put a floor on the price of prime bills; bank rate was usually somewhat higher than the market rate of discount. Banks whose immediate cash outflow (from deposit withdrawals) outran their immediate cash inflow (from maturing bills) could take their prime bill assets to the Bank of England for rediscount, and get cash for them. Normally, though, they could get a somewhat higher price by tapping the lively secondary bill market to find a private buyer. In normal times, the central bank backstop operated to support the market; only in crisis times did the central bank backstop become the market.

What has come down to us as the Bagehot Rule for stemming financial crisis — lend freely but at a high rate of interest — was originally about the Bank of England buying bills freely but at a low price. It should be emphasized, however, that the Bank could and did also make loans ("advances") against bill collateral, and the Bank's generous collateral valuations provided further support for market prices. Bagehot famously urged the Bank

Deficit Firm		Bank		Bank of England		Surplus Firm	
Assets	Liabilities	Assets	Liabilities	Assets	Liabilities	Assets	Liabilities
	Bill			Bill	Deposit	Deposit	
			Acceptance	Acceptance			

Fig. 2. Bagehot's lender of last resort.

to accept as collateral "what in ordinary times is reckoned a good security" rather than attending to current market valuation. The point of all these measures was to prevent troubled banks from being forced to liquidate fundamentally sound assets at fire sale prices.

Figure 2 shows a stylized picture of how the discount system worked in Bagehot's day. We show the Bank of England as the ultimate backstop for the system, rediscounting prime bills by using its own liabilities as a source of funds. Note well that the Bank of England takes in as assets both the underlying bill and the acceptance which guarantees par payment at maturity. In principle, the Bank of England's risk exposure was supposed to be about when it would be paid, not about whether it would be paid, thus liquidity risk not solvency risk. The banks writing acceptances were supposed to be taking the solvency risk, so making up with their own capital any losses on the underlying bill.

What would Bagehot make of modern shadow banking?

On the surface, the modern system looks quite different (Pozsar *et al.*, 2010). The closest thing we have to the institution of "acceptance" is the credit default swap (Mehrling, 2010), but that does not so much guarantee eventual par payment as current par valuation. Just so, according to standard financial theory, the price of a "risk-free" security = price of risky security + price of risk insurance. Further, the modern system is fundamentally a world of long-term debt, which connects to the world of short-term bills through the institution of the interest rate swap; in standard financial theory, the price of a short-term security = price of long-term security + price of interest rate swap. Finally, the modern system has dispensed with the gold standard of Bagehot's day, with the consequence that securities contain currency risk which can be stripped out using the institution of the FX swap;

the price of a dollar security = price of foreign currency security + price of FX swap.

These differences from the world of Bagehot are significant but should not distract us from seeing that at the heart of his world, as ours, is the money market, and operating as crucial backstop in both worlds is the central bank. Indeed, it could be said that the whole point of the various swaps is to manufacture prime bills from diverse raw materials. Putting together all the equations in the previous paragraph, we can distinguish the various stages of manufacture:

$$
\begin{aligned}
\text{Price of “risk-free” prime bills} = {} & \text{Price of risky security} \\
& + \text{price of risk insurance} \\
& + \text{price of interest rate swap} \\
& + \text{price of FX swap.}
\end{aligned}
$$

At its core, modern shadow banking is nothing but a bill-funding market, not so different from Bagehot's. The crucial difference between his world and ours is the fact that Bagehot's world was organized as a network of promises to pay in the event that someone else does not pay, whereas our own world is organized as a network of promises to buy in the event that someone else does not buy. (That is what the swaps do, in effect.) Put another way, Bagehot's world was centrally about funding liquidity, whereas our world is centrally about market liquidity (Brunnermeier and Pedersen, 2009), also known as "shiftability" (Moulton, 1918).

What accounts for the shift from Bagehot's time to our own? The key reason seems to be that in today's world, so many promised payments lie in the distant future, or in another currency. As a consequence, mere guarantee of eventual par payment at maturity does not do much good. On any given day, only a very small fraction of outstanding primary debt is coming due, and in a crisis, the need for current cash can easily exceed it. In such a circumstance, the only way to get cash is to sell an asset, or to use the asset as collateral for borrowing. In the private market, the amount of cash you can get for an asset depends on that asset's current market value. By buying a guarantee of the market value of your assets, in effect you are guaranteeing your access to cash as needed; if no one else will give you cash for them, the guarantor will.

That, in effect, is what all the swaps are doing, or at any rate what they are trying to do, because the plain fact of the matter is that all the swaps in the world cannot turn a risky asset into a genuine Treasury bill. What works in standard finance theory works only approximately in actual practice, and the devil is in the details of that approximation. The weird and wonderful world of derivatives at best creates what we might call quasi-Treasury bills, which may well trade nearly at par with genuine Treasury bills during ordinary times, only to gap wide during times of crisis. Here we identify the fundamental problem of liquidity from which standard theory abstracts, as well as the reason that central bank backstop is needed. Promises to buy are no good unless you have the wherewithal to make good on them; the weak link in the modern system is the primitive character of our network of promises to buy.

Just so, consider the situation of a shadow bank that holds both a risky asset and various swaps that reference that risky asset, and then finances the lot in the wholesale money market, as in Fig. 1. In principle the combination of assets and swaps is risk-free (i.e., a quasi-Treasury bill), but the practical question is whether the shadow bank can finance the combination in the same way that it could if it were actually risk-free (i.e., a genuine Treasury bill). Suppose that the market value of the asset falls a bit. Even supposing that the value of the swaps rises pari passu — which it may not, given liquidity issues — there still remains the issue how to use that change in market value to meet the funding gap on the asset itself.

If the terms of the swap contracts are mark-to-market with speedy cash collateral transfer, then the swap value gain produces immediate cash inflow that might possibly be used to fill the funding gap. However, if the terms are otherwise so that the funding gap persists, then the underlying risky asset position may have to be liquidated, so exacerbating downward price pressure as a liquidity spiral gets underway. And even if the swap terms are favorable, there could still be a problem, since what is favorable to one party is unfavorable to its counterparty. Mark-to-market with speedy cash collateral transfer just means that the liquidity troubles of the shadow bank are shifted onto the shoulders of its swap counterparty, which now faces its own funding gap. Even if the shadow bank is fine, its counterparty may be forced to liquidate and so spark its own downward liquidity spiral.

To stem these liquidity spirals, what is clearly needed is some entity that is willing and able to use its own balance sheet to provide the necessary funding. If the funding gap is at the shadow bank, we need an entity that can turn the increased value of swap positions into an actual cash flow. If the gap is at the swap counterparty, we need an entity that can turn whatever assets the counterparty might have into actual cash flow. Ultimately we need a central bank, but that is just the ultimate backstop. Well before this, what we need is a dealer system that offers market liquidity by offering to buy whatever the market is selling. Only in crisis time does the central bank backstop become the market; in normal times, the central bank backstop merely operates to support the market.

Thus, just as in Bagehot's days, the critical infrastructure is an interconnected system of dealers, backstopped by a central bank. Just as in Bagehot's days, the required backstop may involve commitment to outright purchase of some well-defined set of prime securities (such as Treasury securities). But it must also involve commitment to accept as collateral a significantly larger set of securities, in order to indirectly put a floor on their price in times of crisis. In previous work, we have called this commitment "dealer of last resort" rather than "lender of last resort" in order to draw attention to the modern importance of market liquidity, and hence the importance of placing bounds on price fluctuation (Grad, Mehrling, and Neilson, 2011; Mehrling, 2011).[2]

The key issue for financial stability, today as in Bagehot's days, is to find a way to ensure a lower bound on the price of prime bills. The difference is that today, unlike in Bagehot's days, prime bills are manufactured by stripping price risks of various sorts out of risky long-term securities. The consequence is that today, unlike in Bagehot's days, a lower bound on the price of prime bills also requires some kind of liquidity backstop of

[2]The contrast with "lender of last resort" is not meant to be a contrast with Bagehot himself, but rather a contrast with the distorted version of Bagehot that has come to dominate our thinking during the intervening century. Under the bank loan-based credit system, emphasis came to be placed entirely on the lending, i.e., funding liquidity, to the neglect of indirect price support of the underlying accepted collateral, i.e., market liquidity. That happened, so it seems, for two historically contingent reasons. First, most often the underlying accepted collateral was a genuine Treasury security so price support seemed irrelevant. Second, when the underlying collateral was something other than a Treasury, it was typically a collection of illiquid loans that had no real market price that could be supported. Given the rise of the shadow banking system, neither of these historically contingent reasons any longer applies.

the instruments that are used to create the prime bills from riskier raw material.

The Dealer Function, Boom and Bust

Dealers supply market liquidity by quoting a two-sided market and absorbing the resulting order flow on their balance sheets (Harris, 2003). One important kind of idealized dealer is a "matched-book" dealer whose long positions exactly match his short positions, so that the dealer is in principle completely hedged against price risk. This is the kind of idealized dealer we imagined in our basic model of the shadow banking system (Fig. 1). But a dealer who insisted on matched book at every point in time would not, strictly speaking, be supplying market liquidity at all. If customers are able to buy or sell quickly, in volume, and without moving the price, it is because a dealer is willing to take the other side of that trade without taking the time to look for an offsetting customer trade. The consequence is inventories, sometimes long and sometimes short depending on the direction of the imbalance; and the consequence of inventories is exposure to price risk.

For Global Money Dealers, matched book means term funding of quasi-T-bills. Deviations from matched book involve overnight funding of quasi-T-bills (long inventory), or overnight investment of term funding (short inventory). For Derivative Dealers, matched book means offsetting swap positions, and deviations from matched book involve net risk exposures (long or short). In both cases, deviations from matched book involve exposure to risk, so profit-seeking dealers will insist on positive expected profit as the price of bearing that risk. The way that dealers ensure positive expected profit is by shifting the prices they quote in line with the exposures they are bearing.

Figure 3 shows a stylized model, adapted from Treynor (1987), of how inventories affect price quotes in money and capital markets. In money markets, the longer the "inventory" (exposure to liquidity risk) the higher the yield; in risk markets, the longer the "inventory" (exposure to price risk) the higher the risk premium. In both cases, the slope of the quote curve depends on the amount of risk per unit of inventory, and also on the availability of the backstops (which Treynor calls value-based investors), which determine the outside spread. The different slopes in the money and capital markets reflect an assumption that the outside spread is much

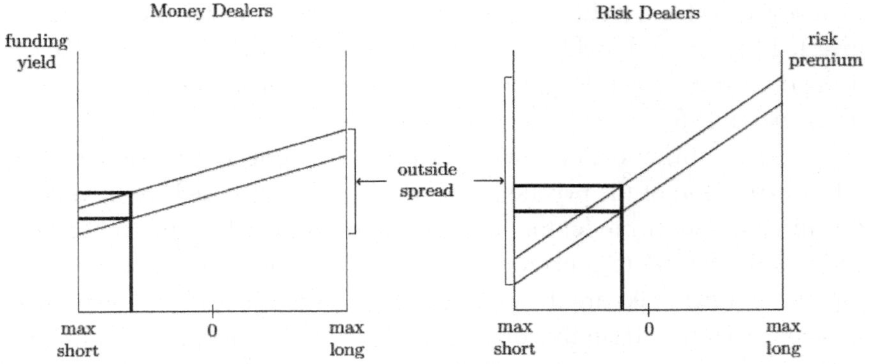

Fig. 3. The dealer system (boom).

tighter in the former than in the latter. In both cases, observe that dealers move their price quotes to bring buy and sell order flows (quantities) closer in line with each other, and in doing so, they move prices farther away from their "fundamental" matched-book reference point.

Because dealer inventory pressure determines prices, the economics of the dealer function interact intimately with the economics of shadow banking. The figure depicts both money dealers and risk dealers as holding net short positions, in effect using their balance sheets to absorb an excess order flow for money and for risk exposure respectively. From a dealer perspective, asset managers are the ultimate buyers of money and risk exposure (see Fig. 1), so the figure can be interpreted as the result of net order flow from asset managers. By absorbing the imbalance, dealers are pushed into short inventory positions, which cause them to quote lower money yields and lower risk premia.

The key point is that this price distortion makes shadow banking more profitable. Responding to the price incentive, shadow banks can be expected to spring up, so creating order flow on the other side of the market, which allows dealers to run off their positions until the next flow imbalance pushes up inventories again with consequent price distortions that stimulate further expansion. From this point of view, it is natural to trace the origins of the market-based credit system to two kinds of net order flow: increased demand for money balances, and increased demand for derivative risk exposure. Pozsar's work on institutional cash pools has emphasized the former (Pozsar, 2011); here we emphasize equally the latter idea, which we treat as arising from techniques of modern portfolio management in which invested capital is all held in money form, and risk exposure is achieved using derivatives (Mehrling, 2012). It is this order flow that created conditions favorable for the expansion of shadow banking.

In expansion mode, the inventory pressure on dealers is readily taken off by expansion of the private profit-seeking market-based credit system. But in contraction mode, the inventory pressure is all on the other side, and it is also harder to get rid of, as we shall see. From a dealer perspective, capital funding banks are the ultimate sellers of money and risk exposure, so when order flow from that direction is high, dealers are pushed into long inventory positions, which causes them to quote higher money yields and higher risk premia. For money market dealers, a shift to a long inventory position means funding term assets in overnight markets. Crucially, inventories of quasi-T-bills serve as collateral for secured funding, but inevitably the price of those quasi-T-bills comes under pressure once there is no longer excess demand for money assets pushing price above fundamental value. And softening price inevitably raises doubts about fundamental value, even if there is no change in actual fundamentals (Sweeney *et al.*, 2012). In such a circumstance, the central bank's willingness to lend against collateral, as also its willingness to buy the underlying, is key to preventing disorderly liquidation. To a generation raised on Jimmy Stewart banking, it looks like an illegitimate extension of lender of last resort from banks to dealers, but Bagehot would have recognized it as a fully legitimate support of the prime bill market.[3]

Less familiar to Bagehot would have been the capital market side of things. For risk dealers, contraction is a situation where everyone wants to sell risk exposure and no one wants to buy, even as the price of risky assets continues to fall. Dealers who dare to accommodate the resulting mismatched order flow find themselves saddled with risk exposure and mark-to-market losses that threaten insolvency. Meanwhile, the prospect of insolvency prevents other dealers from stepping in to buy. Without market-makers there can be no prices, and no prices means no secured borrowing, because there is no way to evaluate the security offered. Even quasi-Treasury

[3]The fact that some of the quasi-T-bills turned out to be less than prime inevitably cast doubt on all of them. Sloppy, or even fraudulent, underwriting during the boom thus exacerbated the downturn when it inevitably came.

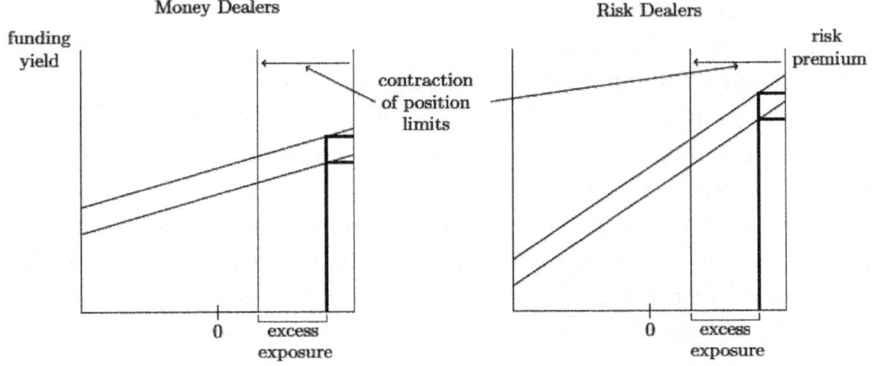

Fig. 4. The dealer system (in crisis).

Assets	Liabilities
Money	Reserves Swaps

Fig. 5. Dealer of last resort.

bills cease to be quasi-Treasury bills since the operative pricing equation — price of "risk-free" security = price of risky security + price of risk insurance — now has unknown values on the right-hand side. In this way, the central bank's classic role in supporting the price of prime bills logically expands during crisis to include supporting the price of the raw material from which prime bills are manufactured.

Figure 4 shows the plight of the dealers during contraction as a matter of position limits that contract beyond realized inventories. If not for central bank support, dealers would be forced to liquidate for whatever price they can get, causing yields to spike and asset prices to plummet. If instead the central bank steps in as dealer of last resort, taking onto its own balance sheet the excess inventories of the strained dealers, the consequence is to place bounds on the disequilibrium price movement. Contraction is not so much halted or reversed as it is contained and allowed to proceed in a more orderly fashion.

Figure 5 shows the balance sheet exposures for a central bank that acts in this way as dealer of last resort. The first line represents the excess inventory of the money dealers (term assets funded with overnight money). The second line represents the excess inventory of the derivative dealers. Comparison with Fig. 1 reveals that the dealer of last resort is in effect filling the gap left by the slowing order flow from asset managers. The key difference, however, is that the asset manager demand was funded by private capital, whereas central bank demand is funded by reserve expansion.

The fact that the central bank can help in this way, by creating money rather than putting up any capital, reflects the maintained assumption of the present paper that the financial crisis is entirely a matter of liquidity and not at all a matter of solvency. Under this strong (and admittedly unrealistic) assumption, no additional capital resources are needed to address the crisis because there are no fundamental losses to be absorbed, only temporary price distortions to be capped. In any real-world crisis, of course, there are both liquidity and solvency elements at play, so liquidity backstop is insufficient. Just so, in the US crisis, there was the Treasury standing in the wings to provide capital as needed (e.g., TARP). In this paper, we have abstracted from such matters in order to draw attention to the liquidity dimension, which remains largely unappreciated.

The Inherent Instability of Credit

The boom-bust expansion and contraction of shadow banking inevitably involves expansion and contraction of the supply of money. Here we find the link between shadow banking and macroeconomic instability (compare Adrian and Shin, 2010). This link exists even though, by maintained assumption, the fluctuation in question does not involve any expansion or contraction of traditional bank deposits, but rather only various kinds of money substitutes. Money market mutual fund shares (invested in ABCP) or outright holding of RP are close substitutes for bank deposits because they can be spent on short notice; Treasury bills and quasi-Treasury bills are close substitutes because they can be used at short notice as collateral to obtain purchasing power. Either way, the growth of shadow banking can be understood as the elastic supply response to increased demand for money balances.

The "boom" character of the resulting expansion is simply the shadow banking version of Hawtrey's famous "inherent instability of credit" (Hawtrey, 1913), and it arises as a direct consequence of the market-making activities of dealers. Simply put, it is easy to make money by making markets when you are standing in between powerful sources of ultimate flow supply and flow demand. As a consequence, during boom times, the supply of market liquidity (i.e., dealer balance sheet capacity) is plentiful, and so the effective supply of money increases even more rapidly than the nominal supply of quasi-Treasury bills (Sweeney *et al.* 2009). Not only the quasi-Treasury bills but also the risky assets they finance become unusually liquid. The consequence is credit inflation, and a boom in the real economy as well.

Of course, even at the peak of the boom, government-issued Treasury bills and Fed-issued cash/reserve balances remain the ultimate form of collateral and the ultimate form of money respectively. But both become decreasingly important quantitatively given the growth of private capital markets and private money markets. Ultimate collateral and ultimate money remain crucial reference points, but the actual instruments are important only in times of crisis when promises to pay are cashed rather than offset with other promises to pay. Just so, during the recent global financial crisis, expansion of Fed reserves, Treasury debt, and contingent Treasury debt (deposit insurance) provided crucial levers to prevent the crisis from spiraling out of control.

Just as the "boom" character of expansion can be understood as a consequence of the dealer balance sheet expansion producing plentiful market liquidity, so too can the "bust" character of contraction be understood as a consequence of dealer balance sheet contraction producing scarce market liquidity. Simply put, it is hard to survive, much less actually to make money, by continuing to make markets when faced with powerful reversal, so the wisest course of action is simply to hold back. As a consequence, the supply of money substitutes that was sufficient to meet demand during the boom no longer proved sufficient once contraction began, simply because quasi-Treasury bills shed their money-like aspect. Even without much actual contraction of the money supply broadly measured, and even with quite aggressive expansion of base money, the effective money supply plummeted, taking with it real economic activity.

Conclusion

The rise of the market-based credit system can be seen as the rise of a (largely) private credit system alongside the existing (largely) public credit system, as well as the rise of a (largely) international credit system alongside the existing (largely) national credit system (Ricks, 2011; Shin, 2011). Increasingly, the dollar has become a private and international currency, and the international dollar money market has become the funding market for all credit needs, private and public, international and national. From this point of view, the rise of the market-based credit system is just part of the broader financial globalization that is such a prominent feature of the last 30 years.

But that new system has yet to show its ability to stand on its own, since it has grown up largely as a parasitical growth on the old system. Money market dealers were and still are typically divisions of traditional banks that enjoy traditional governmental backstops. And risk dealers were and still are typically funded by bank lending of one kind or another, in this way enjoying indirect access to traditional governmental backstops. The regulatory question now facing us is the apparent impossibility of extending these traditional public backstops to a system that is now increasingly private and international.

The way out, we suggest, is to shift our intellectual framework in a fundamental way, back to Bagehot in order to step forward to the 21st century. It is not the shadow bank that requires backstop, but rather the dealer system that makes the markets in which the shadow bank trades. Central banks have the power, and the responsibility, to support these markets both in times of crisis and in normal times. That support, however, must be confined strictly to matters of liquidity. Matters of solvency are for other balance sheets with the capital resources to handle them.

References

Adrian, T. and A. Ashcraft (2012). Shadow Banking: A Review of the Literature. *Federal Reserve Bank of New York Staff Report* No. 580.

Adrian, T. and H.S. Shin (2010). Liquidity and Leverage. *Journal of Financial Intermediation*, Vol. 19, No. 3, pp. 418–437.

Brunnermeier, M.K. and L.H. Pedersen (2009). Market Liquidity and Funding Liquidity. *Review of Financial Studies*, Vol. 22, No. 6, pp. 2201–2238.

Capie, F. (2012). *200 years of Financial Crises: Lessons Learned and Forgotten.* London: Cass Business School, City University.

Financial Stability Board (2012a). Securities Lending and Repos: Market Overview and Financial Stability Issues. Available at http://www.financialstabilityboard.org/publications/r_120427.pdf.

Financial Stability Board (2012b). Strengthening Oversight and Regulation of Shadow Banking; An Integrated Overview of Policy Recommendations. Available at http://www.financialstabilityboard.org/publications/r_121118.pdf.

Gorton, G. and A. Metrick (2010). Regulating the Shadow Banking System. *Brookings Papers on Economic Activity*, Vol. 41, No. 2, pp. 261–312.

Grad, D., P. Mehrling, and D.H. Neilson (2011). The Evolution of Last Resort Operations in the Global Financial Crisis. Available at ssrn.com/abstract=2232348.

Harris, L. (2003). *Trading and Exchanges, Market Microstructure for Practitioners.* New York: Oxford University Press.

Hawtrey, R.G. (1913). *Good and Bad Trade: An Inquiry into the Causes of Trade Fluctuations.* London: Constable and Company.

Mehrling, P. (2010). Credit Default Swaps: The Key to Financial Reform. In *Time for a Visible Hand: Lessons from the 2008 World Financial Crisis*, S. Griffith-Jones, J.A. O'Campo, and J.E. Stiglitz (eds.). New York: Oxford University Press.

Mehrling, P. (2011). *The New Lombard Street, How the Fed became the Dealer of Last Resort.* Princeton, New Jersey: Princeton University Press.

Mehrling, P. (2012). Three Principles for Market-Based Credit Regulation. *American Economic Review Papers and Proceedings* (May 2012).

Moulton, H.G. (1918). Commercial Banking and Capital Formation. *Journal of Political Economy*, Vol. 26, Nos. 5, 6, 7, 9, pp. 484–508, 638–663, 705–731, 849–881.

Pozsar, Z. (2011). Institutional Cash Pools and the Triffin Dilemma of the U.S. Banking System. *IMF Working Paper* 11/190.

Pozsar, Z., T. Adrian, A. Ashcraft and H. Boesky (2010). Shadow Banking. *Federal Reserve Bank of New York Staff Report* No. 458.

Ricks, M. (2011). Regulating Money Creation after the Crisis. *Harvard Business Law Review*, Vol. 1, No. 1, pp. 75–143.

Shin, H.S. (2011). Global Banking Glut and Loan Risk Premium. Mundell–Fleming Lecture, International Monetary Fund. Available at http://www.imf.org/external/np/res/seminars/2011/arc/pdf/hss.pdf.

Sweeney, J. *et al.* (2009). Long Shadows; Collateral Money, Asset Bubbles, and Inflation. *Credit Suisse Fixed Income Research* (May 5).

Sweeney, J. *et al.* (2012). When Collateral is King. *Credit Suisse Global Strategy Research* (March 15).

Treynor, J. (1987). The Economics of the Dealer Function. *Financial Analysts Journal*, Vol. 43, No. 6, pp. 27–34.

Wood, G.E. (2000). Lender of Last Resort Reconsidered. *Journal of Financial Services Research*, Vol. 18, No. 2, pp. 203–227.

III
Causes of the Development of the Shadow Sector

What Drives Shadow Banking? Evidence from Short-Term Business Credit

John V. Duca*

Federal Reserve Bank of Dallas

Introduction

The shadow banking system grew substantially in the years leading up to the recent housing and financial crisis before partially retrenching in the last several years. The literature on the importance of non-bank finance emphasizes several factors behind the rise of shadow banking over the prior decades, mostly a mixture of and interaction between regulatory arbitrage and financial innovation. Some earlier studies stressed the role of reserve and other regulatory requirements that induced shifts from bank loans to other sources of finance (e.g., Berger and Udell, 1994; Bernanke and Lown, 1991; Duca, 1992; Kanatas and Greenbaum, 1982) and the rise of securitization (see Pennacchi (1988), *inter alia*). The earlier literature also mentions declines in information costs along with the rising relative burden of bank capital requirements as factors behind the rise of securitization and the financial innovations supporting it (e.g., Edwards and Mishkin, 1995).

Another strand of the literature emphasizes how credit funded without government-insured deposits may quickly evaporate during flights

*John V. Duca is associate director of research and vice president, Federal Reserve Bank of Dallas, and adjunct professor of economics, Southern Methodist University. The author thanks J.B. Cooke for excellent research assistance; and for their comments, Michael Weiss, Elizabeth Organ, and participants at the 16th Annual International Banking Conference, Shadow Banking: Within and Across National Borders, co-sponsored by the Federal Reserve Bank of Chicago and the International Monetary Fund. The views expressed are those of the author and not necessarily those of the Federal Reserve Bank of Dallas or the Federal Reserve System.

to quality (e.g., Bernanke and Blinder, 1988; Lang and Nakamura, 1995; Stiglitz and Weiss, 1981). Related to these are post-crisis studies stressing the systemic risk aspects of the vulnerability of shadow banking to shifts in liquidity premia (see Adrian and Shin, 2009a, 2009b, 2010; Brunnermeier and Sannikov, 2013; Duca, 2013b; Friewald *et al.*, 2012; Geanakoplos, 2010; Gorton and Metrick, 2012; Schleifer and Vishny, 2010; *inter alia*). Consistent with these theories, the experience of the Great Depression indicates that external finance sources that are funded by securities, such as commercial paper, are vulnerable to the jumps in risk premia typical of financial crises (Duca, 2013b).

In the literature, there has been little formal empirical analysis of the extent to which different factors contributed to the rise of shadow banking in the decades leading up to the recent crisis and its more recent fall-back. Part of this reflects issues about how to measure the shadow banking system. Much of the earlier rise reflected not only the growing use of securitization, particularly of residential mortgages (see Pozsar *et al.* (2010) measurements), but also a greater role of shadow banks in funding business credit. For this reason, a major challenge of empirically analyzing highly aggregated measures of shadow banking is the likely modeling of aggregates that may blend household and business borrowing, as well as credits of varying duration.

To limit such drawbacks, a related study focuses on the relative importance of shadow banks in funding short-run business credit. Using data spanning the last half century, Duca (2014) examines the role of several potential variables — not just the latest fad — and attempts to disentangle short- from long-term factors. In addition, this approach is not limited to the Great Moderation era, but rather draws from experience spanning different regulatory regimes, which may provide more perspective on recent attempts at financial reform.

For example, the importance of shadow banking for business credit can be gauged by the share of short-term debt of non-financial corporations funded by commercial paper and non-bank loans, using data from the Federal Reserve Board's Financial Accounts of the US. The share nearly doubled between the late 1960s and mid-2000s (Fig. 1). Netting out the subset of commercial paper directly issued by non-financial corporations, one can see large shifts in a narrow measure of shadow banking — the share of debt intermediated by non-financial firms and other non-bank

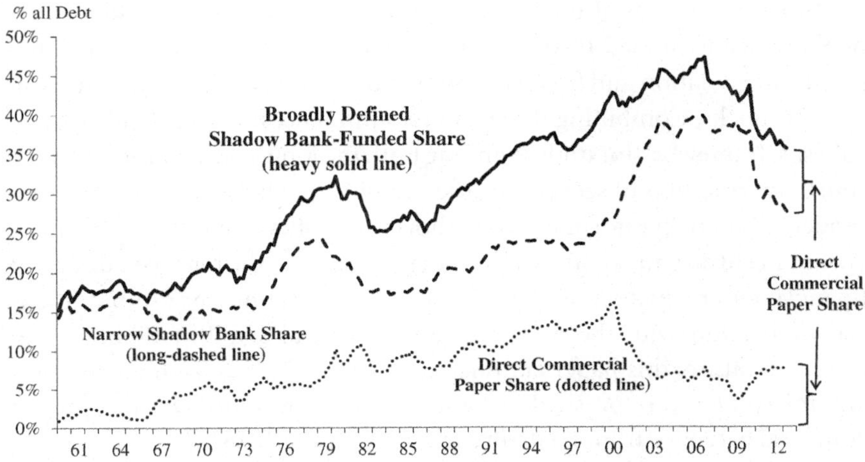

Fig. 1. Narrowly-defined shadow banking share partly reflects substitution with commercial paper directly issued by non-financial corporations.

Source: Financial Accounts of the US, author's calculations, and Duca (2014).

sources.[1] Nevertheless, there is some hard-to-model substitution between this narrow shadow bank share and directly issued commercial paper, which makes modeling the broader shadow banking share for short-term business credit more feasible.

This study briefly reviews theories and the limited evidence of how broad shadow banking reflects short- and long-run factors stemming from regulatory burdens and changes in information costs. The broad shadow bank share is affected positively, on the one hand, by relative advantages of avoiding bank regulations (e.g., reserve and capital requirements, as in Kanatas and Greenbaum (1982)), but negatively, on the other hand, by the informational and transactions cost advantages of banks in lending and funding sources that are less exposed to market risk premia. Insight for analyzing the shadow bank share of short-term business credit can also be drawn from models of the composition of lending (e.g., Adrian and Shin, 2009a, 2009b, 2010; Diamond, 1991; Jaffee and Modigliani, 1969; Kashyap, Wilcox, and Stein, 1993; Oliner and Rudebusch, 1996).

[1]The security-funded share plotted in Fig. 1 internalizes substitution between commercial paper directly issued by non-financial firms and credit to non-financial corporations.

Disparate strands of the literature imply that the extent to which business finance is funded through securities markets has evolved, reflecting trends in regulation and financial innovation, as well as short-run financial market shocks. Combining these different influences could provide a more cohesive framework for understanding both the long-run evolution and the short-run reactions of security market funding. Such financial architecture models could help inform not only short-run policy responses to financial crises by central banks and fiscal authorities, but also the long-run design of financial and regulatory systems that balance the gains from sound financial innovation with the need for some financial stability. Filling a gap in the literature, this paper summarizes various themes in the theoretical and micro literature on shadow banks, and puts into broader perspective empirical evidence from related research by Duca (2014).

To do this, this study is organized as follows. The next section helps frame the later review of theories and empirical evidence by discussing the practical advantages of focusing on the composition of business credit and adopting a market share approach to empirically assess these factors. The paper then selectively reviews the major factors, as suggested by the literature that influence the relative importance of shadow banking over the long run. Next, the paper discusses concerns that shadow banking is vulnerable to short-run financial market disruptions. Against this backdrop, the paper summarizes findings from a study (Duca, 2014) that formally and empirically analyzes shadow banking using a half-century of data. The paper concludes by providing a broader perspective on what has driven the shadow banking sector.

Assessing Shadow Banking using a Market Share View of Short-Term Business Credit

For a number of reasons, the importance of the shadow banking system and what drives it can be formally empirically analyzed from data on the relative share of short-term debt for non-financial corporations funded directly from commercial paper and by non-bank financial intermediaries.[2] First, theories and trends imply that regulatory arbitrage and improved

[2] Despite omitting non-corporate non-financial business, it should be noted that the non-financial corporate sector produces the vast bulk of GDP.

information availability have greatly affected the relative appeal and use of securities market (shadow bank) rather than deposit-funded business credit over recent decades. This suggests that much of what drives shadow banking can be analyzed with a market-share approach, akin to the mix variable of Kashyap, Wilcox, and Stein (1993) that tracks the relative use of commercial paper versus bank loans inspired by Bernanke and Blinder (1988).[3] Second, the relative share variable tracking shadow banking's importance should include commercial paper directly issued by non-financial corporations, much of which is backed by credit lines from commercial banks and is held by a type of shadow bank — money market mutual funds (MMMFs) — whose existence was largely induced by efforts to circumvent the burden of bank regulation (regulatory arbitrage).

Third, the broad shadow market-share variable internalizes shifts between directly issued non-financial corporate commercial paper and credit intermediated by the shadow banking system, much of which is funded by commercial paper issued by financial entities (Fig. 1). Such substitution became notable during the rise and fall of structured finance in the 2000s that first reflected the boost to shadow banking system that emanated from the passage of the Commodity Futures Modernization Act (CFMA) of 2000. By making many derivatives contracts beyond currency and interest-rate swaps enforceable, CFMA fostered the rise of credit enhancements that made many structured financial products used by shadow banks appear sounder than they were. This induced rise in shadow banking was followed by the negative impact of the passage of the Dodd–Frank financial reform act (DFA) that helped level the regulatory playing field between commercial and shadow banks. Interestingly, directly issued commercial paper has risen somewhat in recent years as shown in Fig. 1.

A fourth consideration favoring the relative share approach is that modeling the importance of the shadow banking system is hampered by incomplete data on funding sources, particularly in the financial sector and the unincorporated business sector. Tracking and analyzing the structure of external finance for non-financial corporations is far less hindered by this issue.

[3]In a slight variant, the current study adopts the broad credit channel view of Oliner and Rudebusch (1996) by also considering credit from non-bank intermediaries funded with non-deposit sources.

The substitutability of different maturities of debt, as well as the substitution between debt and equity, poses another empirical challenge. Such complications can be limited and largely circumvented by tracking and analyzing the security market-funded share of short-term non-financial corporate debt, usually used to finance working capital needs. Focusing on short-term debt does not require modeling business fixed investment, which is volatile and externally funded typically by long-term debt or equity.

What Drives Shadow Banking in the Long Run?

The long-run drivers of shadow banking described in the literature generally fall into the two broad categories, information costs and regulatory arbitrage. So far, regulatory arbitrage has received more attention than information costs.

The role of information and transactions costs

The many money and banking textbook depictions of factors affecting the relative importance of banks emphasize not only the burden of regulations, involving capital and reserve requirements, but also how the informational and transactions cost advantages of banks over non-banks have eroded over time owing to improved technology (e.g., Edwards and Mishkin, 1995; Mishkin, 2009). Studies of the rising importance of mutual funds highlight the role played by declining transactions costs at non-banks, which stem from improvements in overall financial sector productivity (Duca, 2005) that have ultimately reduced banks' funding cost advantages over time and induced the rise of deposit alternatives (Duca, 2000). Because these advances involve both hardware and software, one can parsimoniously and consistently track such advances with the ratio of the implicit price deflator for computer equipment and software to that for overall GDP. Such technological improvements — along with regulatory arbitrage incentives — arguably underlie many of the more specific financial innovations that directly fostered the growth of shadow banking. As shown in Fig. 2, declines in this real, relative price measure have been large, but have abated lately. Nevertheless, there has not been much, if any, formal testing of how information costs affect the relative importance of the shadow banking sector (one exception is Duca (2005)).

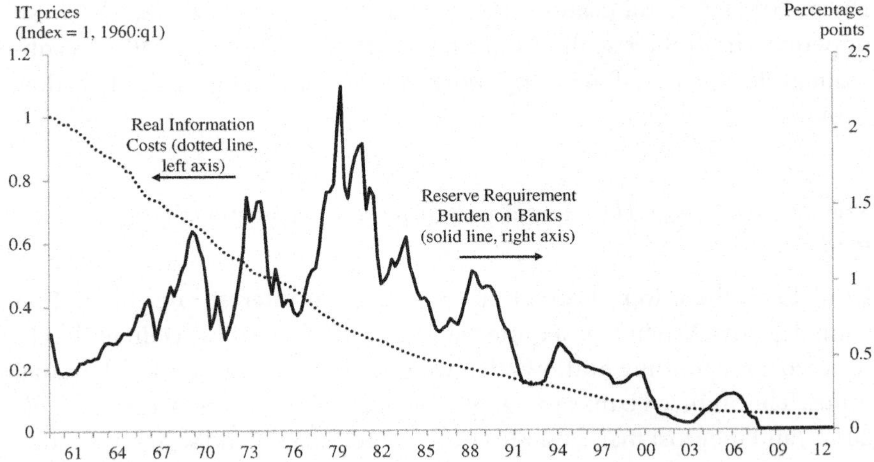

Fig. 2. Information costs and the reserve requirement burden on banks.
Source: Duca (2014).

Despite vague references to information costs, most of the shadow banking literature emphasizes the impact of various incentives for regulatory arbitrage, which can be classified into several categories. These include reserve requirement taxes, deposit regulations, and capital requirements. These regulatory arbitrage factors are discussed in that order.

Regulatory arbitrage: The role of reserve requirements

The disadvantage is that reserve requirements imposes on banks has long been recognized as an impetus for the growth of MMMFs and the adoption of other deposit alternatives (Kanatas and Greenbaum, 1982; Duca, 1992; Rosengren, 2014). The actual burden, or "reserve requirement tax" on banks, reflects not only the level of short-term interest rates and minimum reserve requirement ratios, but also bank efforts to circumvent reserve requirements and the interest rate restrictions on business demand deposits through sweep accounts (see Anderson and Rasche, 2001; Dutkowsky and Cynamon, 2003).

Accounting for all of these factors (see Fig. 2) reveals that the reserve requirement burden was high in the 1970s through early 1980s, but has fallen since then, and to record low levels since the financial crisis (see

Duca, 2014). By implication, the reserve requirement tax had been an impetus behind the rise of shadow banks in the 1970s and 1980s. Its subsequent decline has, if anything, worked to temper the growth of shadow banking.

Regulatory arbitrage: The roles played by deposit and money market fund regulations

Until 1983, there were Regulation Q ceilings on interest rates offered on bank deposits. When market interest rates rose above these ceilings, banks suffered large funding outflows that went to securities markets and mutual funds. This induced banks to tighten their credit standards (see Aron *et al.*, 2012), and they lost market share to commercial paper and security-funded lenders (Duca, 1992). These ceilings became very binding at times (Duca, 1996) and had large macroeconomic effects (Duca and Wu, 2009). In addition to interest rate ceilings on retail deposits, there were ceilings on large time deposits, longer than 90 days, until mid-1974. The Regulation Q effects on shadow banking were partly temporary, partially reversing when market interest rates fell below deposit rate ceilings.

But some of the impact of Regulation Q was longer lasting. It helped spur creation in the US of MMMFs in 1971 that could pay market-determined interest rates. These funds did not grow much until late 1973 and expanded rapidly after MMMF check-writing features were introduced by a major mutual fund family in 1974. By offering investors a more liquid way to own commercial paper, the rise of money market funds lowered the cost of funding commercial paper and other forms of open market paper relative to banks, thereby raising shadow banking's share of credit markets. Partly to limit this substitution, banks were allowed to offer money market deposit accounts (MMDAs) in late 1982. This resulted in inflows into bank deposits from both MMMFs and other assets that were large enough to positively affect money demand (Duca, 2000) and the availability of bank loans (see Aron *et al.*, 2012). Following Duca (2014), one can parsimoniously track these shifts, characterizing the period of 1974q3 to 1982q3 as one in which deposit regulations and financial innovations favored shadow banking to a high degree. This is partially illustrated in Fig. 3, which plots the shadow bank share along with the timing of many major regulatory changes.

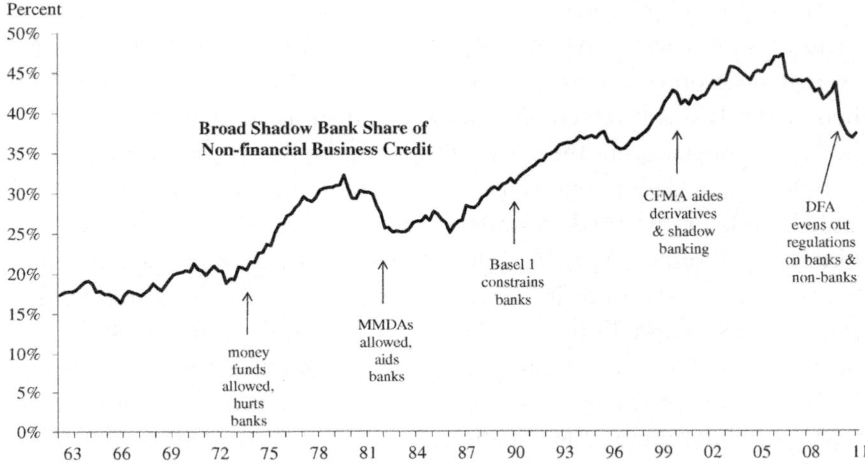

Fig. 3. Broad shadow bank-funded share affected by financial regulation.
Sources: Financial Accounts of the US, author's calculations, and Duca (2014).

Another, albeit short-lived, major short-term regulatory action affecting shadow banking was the imposition and lifting of bank credit controls in 1980:q2 and 1980:q3, respectively, temporarily shifting business finance to security markets in 1980q2, which largely unwound in 1980q3.

Regulatory arbitrage: The roles played by capital requirements and structured finance

The broad shadow bank share reflects substitution between not only banks and direct sources of finance (e.g., directly issued commercial paper), but also between bank and non-bank financial intermediaries. Accordingly, before the adoption of the Basel Accords in 1990s, capital requirements can be viewed as giving banks a mild advantage over both the provision of credit funded by securities markets (which did not have as much protection from the federal safety net as commercial banks) and investment banks, which faced higher capital ratio minimums. From the 1930s through the mid-2000s, the SEC imposed an 8% minimum capital requirement on investment banks and a maximum 15:1 leverage ratio on their brokerage units.

The capital requirements on banks were also relatively stable, but only up until 1990. Beginning in 1981, the FDIC imposed a minimum 5% leverage ratio on commercial banks (see Wall and Peterson, 1987). Before then, a similar, but perceived unofficial ratio was in effect for much of the 1970s. Indeed, from the early 1970s until the Basel Accords took effect in 1990, the aggregate equity capital-to-assets ratio for the commercial banking industry hovered around 6%, providing a cushion over regulatory minimums. From the early 1960s to the early 1970s, this aggregate ratio had fluctuated near 7%, since there were many more small banks that tended to have higher capital ratios (reflecting greater idiosyncratic risk) before the rise of bank holding companies (BHCs) in the late 1960s. Abetted by the Bank Holding Company Act of 1970, which took effect in mid-1971, bank consolidation via the expansion of BHCs accelerated. As Omarova and Tahyar (2011–2012, p. 148) note, even that earlier expansion of BHCs was partly motivated to economize on equity capital held at individual banks owned by a BHC. This resulted in a minor decline in the banking industry's aggregate capital ratio from 7% in the 1960s to about 6% by the early 1970s. Nevertheless, on the whole, the decades of the 1960s through 1980s were generally marked by relatively stable *de facto* and *de jure* bank capital requirements.

That stability ended with the implementation of the Basel Accords in 1990, which effectively raised the capital requirement on most non-home mortgage loans held in portfolio, from 5% to 8%. As discussed in a voluminous literature, starting with the seminal analysis of Pennacchi (1988) and partly spawned by Kanatas and Greenbaum (1982), Basel encouraged the rise of shadow banking by inducing more securitization.[4] Nevertheless, Basel also fostered the rise of business and consumer loan securitization. Such asset-backed securities were either directly held by investors or indirectly held through money market and bond mutual funds, and later by special investment vehicles (SIVs) during the heyday of the structured finance boom of the 2000s. The growth of shadow banks was thus spurred by Basel, both by increasing banks' regulatory burdens relative to direct holdings of securities by investors and by roughly equating the

[4]One motive for this incentive was to promote mortgage securitization as a means of cushioning the availability of US home mortgages following closure of many troubled savings and loan institutions in the late 1980s and early 1990s.

minimum capital requirements across commercial and investment banks, despite fewer other restrictions on investment bank risk taking.

Within the 1990 to mid-2000 period, there was another regulatory change that may have indirectly aided growth of the shadow banking sector. CFMA of 2000 made many derivatives contracts outside of currency and interest-rate swaps enforceable (see Roe, 2011; Stout, 2008). This fostered the development of many credit enhancements that were integral to the increased use of structured financial products by shadow banks to both raise funds and make investments. It is not easy to discern a very clear effect on the shadow bank share of short-term business credit.

One reason was that in 2004 the SEC loosened regulations on the definition of equity capital used by investment banks to meet their overall regulatory leverage ratios. The agency also increased the maximum ceiling on leverage at their brokerage units from 15:1 to 33:1 (arguably lowering the minimum capital ratio from roughly 8 to 3.33% at investment banks). Shortly thereafter, the leverage ratios at most of the large investment banks nearly doubled in the years before the financial crisis. As a result, from mid-2004 until the passage of DFA in mid-2010, commercial banks were very disadvantaged relative to investment banks (Duca, 2014).

This induced rise in shadow banking was followed by DFA, which helped level the regulatory playing field between commercial and shadow banks in several ways. First, DFA made very large bank and non-bank financial firms subject to stress tests and minimum capital requirements established by regulators. By doing so, even though DFA resulted in increasing absolute regulatory requirements on commercial banks, it effectively raised the capital regulatory burdens on shadow banks relative to commercial banks. Second, DFA also imposed new requirements on derivatives to improve the transparency and reduce the risk of structured financial products that had funded much shadow bank lending. Third, DFA also made large systemically important bank and non-bank financial firms subject to minimum liquidity ratios, which help limit the duration risk of both commercial and large shadow banks.

The changing regulation of financial firm capital ratios and structured financial products has had qualitatively different regulatory arbitrage effects on shadow banking over the past half-century. Prior to 1990, the playing field was relatively stable. Then, shadow banking grew in response to incentives for capital regulatory arbitrage from the advent of Basel through the mid-2000s, with enhanced incentives from changes in SEC rules starting in the mid-2000s until the passage of DFA. Not surprisingly, there were very large declines in shadow banking's share of short-term business credit (Fig. 1) that have yet to unwind. For these reasons, the DFA era can be interpreted as an attempt to greatly limit not only absolute levels of risk-taking by financial firms, but also regulatory arbitrage, which had led to high levels of systemic risk stemming from the earlier rapid expansion of the shadow banking sector.

How Shadow Banking is Vulnerable to Short-Run Financial Market Disruptions

A major impetus for financial reform has been to limit the systemic risk posed by both the shadow and commercial banking systems (see Adrian and Shin, 2009a, 2009b; Geanakoplos, 2010; Gorton and Metrick, 2012; McCabe *et al.*, 2013; Rosengren, 2014). Such reforms will likely affect both the long-run level and the short-run volatility of the shadow banking share of credit market activity. Following the earlier discussion of longer-run factors affecting the shadow bank share of activity, it is also useful to review the literature regarding how changing risk premia can give rise to short-term shifts in the shadow banking sector's relative size.

At a fundamental level, short-run volatility arises because the safety net provides greater advantages to commercial banks than shadow banks during periods of economic distress and high risk premia (e.g., Brunnermeier and Sannikov, 2013; Duca, 2013a; Lang and Nakumura, 1995). These sorts of shifts and flights to quality suggest that the shadow bank share should be positively affected by expectations of an improving economy, which empirically can be proxied by lags of the slope of the yield curve, since the term premium is a leading economic indicator of the US business cycle. In addition, spikes in liquidity premia can cause shadow bank funding sources to dry up during financial crises, such as during the Great Depression (see Bernanke (1983) on corporate bond premia and Duca (2013a) on commercial paper) and the Great Recession (see Adrian and Shin, 2009a, 2009b; Duca, 2013b; Duygan-Bump *et al.*, 2013; Geanakoplos, 2010; Gorton and Metrick, 2012; Rosengren, 2014). This implies that the shadow bank share is negatively affected by liquidity premia in the short run, controlling for government interventions intended to cushion such events, e.g., the

Federal Reserve's interventions in commercial paper in 2008 and 2009 as analyzed by Duca (2013b) and Duygan-Bump *et al.* (2013). Candidates for consistently measuring liquidity premia include bond interest rate spreads (Friewald *et al.*, 2012; Jaffee, 1975) and Libor spreads.

In addition to time series measures of liquidity risk, issues concerning nonlinear effects and Knightian uncertainty suggest a role for event risks. These may include episodes such as the stock market crash of 1987 or the Penn Central railroad bankruptcy and subsequent commercial paper default in 1970. More recent events include not only the failure of Lehman Brothers, but also the suspension of redemptions on subprime-exposed hedge funds during August 2007, after which risk premia became elevated (Duca, Muellbauer, and Murphy, 2010).

Recent experience suggests that flights to quality can be countered by central bank asset purchases that cushion the supply of security-funded credit to top-rated borrowers (see Anderson and Gascon (2009), Duca (2013a), and Duygan-Bump *et al.* (2013) on the Fed's commercial paper facility, and Goodhart (1987) on the need for a broad lender of last resort). In contrast to the 1930s — when the real volume of commercial paper fell by 90% over one interval and roughly half of residential mortgages defaulted — the Federal Reserve used new programs in the past few years to limit surges in risk premia on high-grade commercial paper and residential mortgage-backed securities. As a result of these recent efforts among other factors, real commercial paper outstanding fell by relatively half as much (Duca, 2013a) and the recovery in housing markets began sooner than they did in the Great Depression (see Duca, 2014).

Findings about What Drives the Shadow Bank Share of Business Credit

The literature on shadow banking includes many studies focusing on particular incentives for shadow banking and/or the accompanying need for financial reform. The literature lacks empirical analysis that formally assesses the roles of competing factors. Part of this reflects the challenge of modeling financial structure using aggregates that include types of credit that fund different sectors (e.g., housing versus business sectors), or span different maturities (e.g., mortgages, equity, long- to medium-term debt, and money market paper). One strategy to overcome this entails limiting the empirical analysis to a feasibly narrower sector and type of debt, where data are reasonably consistent over long periods of time. As discussed earlier, the shadow bank share of short-term non-financial corporate debt meets this criterion. Other challenges include modeling both the factors that drive long-run trends, as well as important short-run factors. And controlling for long-run factors means dealing with complications from using variables that are non-stationary and that are partially endogenous. These two challenges can be addressed by using cointegration techniques to estimate the impact of factors on the shadow banking share over the long and short run.

Applying cointegration techniques to various measures of such factors in samples extending back to the early 1960s, Duca (2014) finds several robust findings about what drives long-run movements in the shadow bank share. Comprehensive sets of information costs, reserve requirement burdens, and variables tracking the relative impact of other regulations are significantly related to (cointegrated with) the shadow bank share in the long run. Furthermore, statistically significant long-run coefficient estimates confirmed insights from various theoretical models. In particular, the shadow bank share increases as banks become more disadvantaged relative to non-banks with respect to reserve requirements, restrictions on variable deposit interest-rate instruments (money funds and MMDAs), and the burdens of capital requirements. In addition, the results confirm that reductions in information costs are significantly related to higher shares of shadow banks involved in funding non-financial business credit.

However, only the estimated long-run impacts of information and regulatory arbitrage variables are found to be stable and similar in samples that include or exclude the recent financial crisis and its aftermath. In contrast, the estimated impact of the reserve requirement is weaker and sometimes insignificant in pre-crisis sample periods, indicating that the reserve requirement effect on shadow banks should be viewed with caution. It is difficult to identify this effect without the extreme movements in the reserve requirement burden seen during the financial crisis.

Nevertheless, even in samples that include the post-crisis period, the reserve requirement burden has only small estimated effects on the shadow bank share in contrast to the more substantial roles played by gauges of information costs and regulatory arbitrage. This can be seen in Fig. 4, which plots the actual shadow share with the long-run equilibrium implied by a

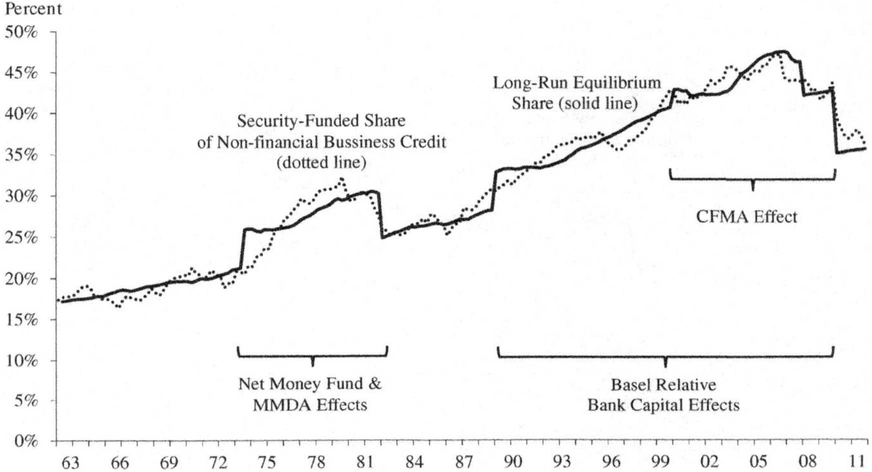

Fig. 4. Shadow share tracked by estimated effects of regulation and information costs over the long run.
Source: Financial Accounts of the US, author's calculations, and Duca (2014).

model that tracks the impact of the Basel capital accords and post-2000 regulatory changes with long-lasting shift dummies. In this figure, the implied long-run estimated equilibrium levels slightly lead and track the shadow bank share over the past half century. As indicated in the chart, movements in the equilibrium share reflect differences across regulatory periods, with shadow bank share elevated during the eras when MMMFs could offer variable interest rate deposits while banks could not, and when regulatory changes either directly disadvantaged banks over shadow banks (i.e., the Basel I and II agreements) or indirectly favored shadow over commercial banks (e.g., the passage of CFMA).

With the virtual disappearance of the reserve requirement tax, the lifting of deposit rate ceilings, and DFA's reversal of many incentives for regulatory arbitrage, one may ask why the shadow bank share did not fall even more than it has in recent years. The answer may come from the often overlooked "usual suspect" of information costs. These plunged dramatically during the 1970s–1990s, and essentially helped undo many of the earlier informational and transaction cost advantages that banks enjoyed over both direct finance via securities issuance and indirect finance by non-bank financial intermediaries. Consistent with this view, the estimated contribution of

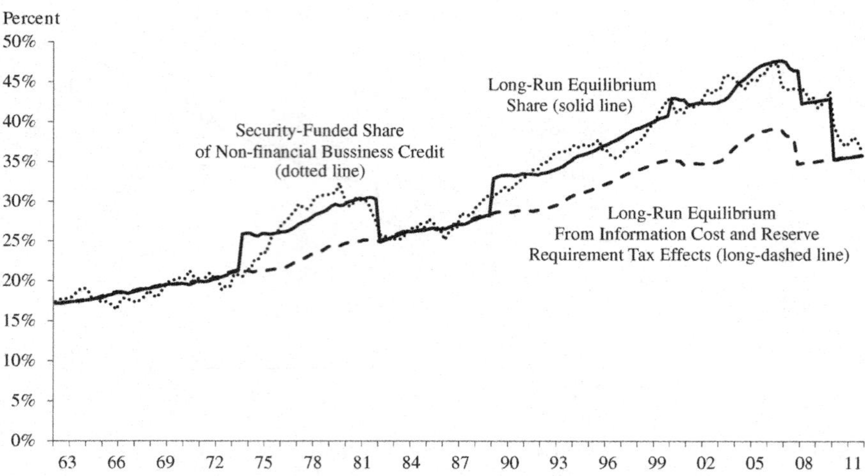

Fig. 5. Shadow share bolstered by falling information costs and reserve requirement burdens over the long run.
Source: Financial Accounts of the US, author's calculations, and Duca (2014).

information costs and the reserve requirement tax to the long-run, equilibrium level of shadow bank share plotted in Fig. 5 suggests that the shadow bank share will likely stabilize near current levels until other structural long-run factors shift or strong short-term shifts in interest rates or financial shocks occur.

Duca (2014) also finds that comprehensive models perform well in tracking short-run changes in the shadow bank share. Also, short-run changes in shadow bank share tend to reduce the prior period's gap between actual and estimated equilibrium levels of shadow bank share — and with a sensible speed of adjustment. Among short-run factors, the bindingness of retail deposit ceilings has a highly significant positive short-run effect, while the deregulation of large time deposits and the imposition of credit controls have temporary negative effects. In addition, regulatory impact variables are significant, indicating that the introduction of MMMFs raised the shadow bank share, while the introduction of MMDAs and the passage of DFA lowered it. Also significant are event risks that temporarily lower the shadow bank share, such as the Penn Central bankruptcy, the stock market crash of 1987, and BNP Paribas's freezing of redemptions involving their subprime-exposed investment funds in August 2007.

These event risk effects are robust to the inclusion of risk premia, about which two patterns emerged. First, money market risk premia (e.g., the Libor-OIS spread) tend to improve models more than measures of risk premia in longer-duration bonds. Second, liquidity premia are only significant when adjusted for the interventions in the money markets during the recent financial crisis period, consistent with the commercial paper market findings of Duca (2013a). Another time-varying risk premia, the lagged yield curve variable, is always highly significant, likely reflecting that an improved economic outlook favors the extension of credit to riskier credits or perhaps that low short-term interest rates that typically accompany steep yield curves induce a "reach for yield" into higher credit or duration risk securities (see Stein, 2013).

Conclusion

The composition of short-term business credit over the last five decades sheds light on what has driven shadow banking in the short and long runs. Consistent with much of the pre- and post-crisis literature, declines in information costs and increased incentives for regulatory arbitrage have raised the importance of shadow banks as a source of credit over the long run. Findings also indicate that recent efforts at leveling the regulatory playing field, for example, DFA requirements that systemically important commercial *and* shadow banks pass stress tests, appear to have induced a retrenchment in the relative importance of shadow banks, both upon impact and ostensibly in the long run.

The size of the shadow banking system has been temporarily affected by event risks (e.g., stock market crashes), as well as by binding deposit rate ceilings, regulatory changes that favor non-bank finance relative to bank finance, and term premia that reflect expectations of an improving economy. The results regarding short-run factors accord with findings by Bernanke (1983) and Duca (2013a, 2013b) that the provision of credit shifted toward debt whose funding sources were less vulnerable to liquidity shocks during the Great Depression.

Evidence also suggests that some government interventions (for example, the Federal Reserve's Commercial Paper Funding Facility) helped make the retrenchment of the shadow banking system somewhat more orderly by cushioning the impact of large-sized liquidity premium shocks

(Duca, 2013a). Alongside other findings that suggest that regulatory arbitrage affects the MMMF industry and that DFA has reduced the ability of the Federal Reserve to stabilize financial markets, these results support arguments favoring reforms of the MMMF industry to make it more resilient against liquidity and other financial shocks (e.g., McCabe *et al.*, 2013; Rosengren, 2014).

Stepping back from particular results, the evidence from a half-century of experience indicates that the importance of shadow banking and its driving factors over the short and long run are best understood using a comprehensive approach. Simply put, there is much to be gained by viewing the evolution of shadow banking as a product of a confluence of factors that reflect information costs, financial regulation, innovation, and risk as suggested by several branches of the money, banking, and finance literature (e.g., Adrian and Shin, 2009a, 2009b; Edwards and Mishkin, 1995; Mishkin, 2009; Kanatas and Greenbaum, 1982; Pennacchi, 1988, *inter alia*).

References

Adrian, T. and H.S. Shin (2009a). Money, Liquidity, and Monetary Policy. *American Economic Review*, Vol. 99, May, pp. 600–609.

Adrian, T. and H.S. Shin (2009b). The Shadow Banking System: Implications for Financial Regulation. Banque de France. *Financial Stability Review*, Vol. 13, September, pp. 1–10.

Adrian, T. and H.S. Shin (2010). Liquidity and Leverage. *Journal of Financial Intermediation*, Vol. 19, July, pp. 418–437.

Anderson, R.B. and C.S. Gascon (2009). The Commercial Paper Market, the Fed, and the 2007–2009 Financial Crisis. *Federal Reserve Bank of St. Louis Review*, Vol. 91, November/December, pp. 589–612.

Anderson, R.B. and R. Rasche (2001). Retail Sweep Programs and Bank Reserves, 1994–1999. *Federal Reserve Bank of St. Louis Review*, Vol. 83, January/February, pp. 51–72.

Aron, J., J. Duca, J. Muellbauer, K. Murata and A. Murphy (2012). Credit, Housing Collateral and Consumption in the UK, US, and Japan. *Review of Income and Wealth*, Vol. 58, September, pp. 397–423.

Berger, A. and G. Udell (1994). Did Risk-based Capital Allocate Credit and Cause a 'Credit Crunch' in the United States? *Journal of Money, Credit and Banking*, Vol. 26, August, pp. 585–628.

Bernanke, B.S. (1983). Non-Monetary Effects of Financial Crises in the Propagation of the Great Depression. *American Economic Review*, Vol. 71, June, pp. 257–276.

Bernanke, B.S. and A.S. Blinder (1988). Credit, Money, and Aggregate Demand. *American Economic Review*, Vol. 78, May, pp. 435–439.

Bernanke, B.S. and C.S. Lown (1991). The Credit Crunch. *Brookings Papers on Economic Activity*, Vol. 1991, No. 2, pp. 205–239.

Brunnermeier, M.K. and Y. Sannikov (2013). The I Theory of Money. Working paper, Princeton University, October.

Diamond, D.W. (1991). Monitoring and Reputation: The Choice Between Bank Loans and Directly Placed Debt. *Journal of Political Economy*, Vol. 91, August, pp. 689–721.

Duca, J.V. (1992). U.S. Business Credit Sources, Demand Deposits, and the 'Missing Money'. *Journal of Banking and Finance*, Vol. 16, June, pp. 567–583.

Duca, J.V. (1996). Deposit Deregulation and the Sensitivity of Housing. *Journal of Housing Economics*, Vol. 3, September, pp. 207–227.

Duca, J.V. (2000). Financial Technology Shocks and the Case of the Missing M2. *Journal of Money, Credit and Banking*, Vol. 32, November, pp. 820–839.

Duca, J.V. (2005). Why Have Households Increasingly Relied on Mutual Fund Loads to Own Equity? *Review of Income and Wealth*, Vol. 51, September, pp. 375–396.

Duca, J.V. (2013a). Did the Commercial Paper Funding Facility Prevent a Great Depression Style Money Market Meltdown? *Journal of Financial Stability*, Vol. 9, December, pp. 747–758.

Duca, J.V. (2013b). The Money Market Meltdown of the Great Depression. *Journal of Money, Credit and Banking*, Vol. 45, March–April, pp. 493–504.

Duca, J.V. (2014). What Drives the Shadow Banking System In the Short and Long-Run? Federal Reserve Bank of Dallas Working Paper No. 1401, January.

Duca, J.V., J. Muellbauer and A. Murphy (2010). Housing Markets and the Financial Crisis of 2007–2009: Lessons for the Future. *Journal of Financial Stability*, Vol. 6, December, pp. 203–217.

Duca, J.V. and T. Wu (2009). Regulation and the Neo-Wicksellian Approach to Monetary Policy. *Journal of Money, Credit and Banking*, Vol. 41, May, pp. 799–807.

Dutkowsky, D.H. and B.Z. Cynamon (2003). Sweep Programs: The Fall of M1 and the Rebirth of the Medium of Exchange. *Journal of Money, Credit and Banking*, Vol. 35, April, pp. 263–279.

Duygan-Bump, B., P.M. Parkinson, E.S. Rosengren, G.A. Suarez and P.S. Willen (2013). How Effective Were the Federal Reserve Emergency Liquidity Facilities? Evidence from the Asset-Backed Commercial Paper Money Market Mutual Fund Liquidity Facility. *Journal of Finance*, Vol. 68, April, pp. 715–737.

Edwards, F.R. and F.S. Mishkin (1995). The Decline of Traditional Banking: Implications for Financial Stability and Regulatory Policy. *New York Federal Reserve Economic Policy Review*, Vol. 1, July, pp. 27–45.

Federal Reserve Bank of St. Louis (2010). Federal Reserve Board Data on M1 Adjusted for Retail Sweeps. Available at http://research.stlouisfed.org/fred2/series/M1ADJ [accessed on 13 June 2014].

Friewald, N., R. Jankowitsch and M. Subrahmanyam (2012). Illiquidity or Credit Deterioration: A Study of Liquidity in the Corporate Bond Market during Financial Crises. *Journal of Financial Economics*, Vol. 105, July, pp. 18–36.

Geanakoplos, J. (2010). The leverage cycle. In *NBER Macroeconomics Annual 2009*, D. Acemoglu, K. Rogoff and M. Woodford (eds.), Vol. 24, pp. 1–65. Chicago: University of Chicago Press, Chicago.

Goodhart, C.I. (1987). Why Banks Need a Central Bank. *Oxford Economic Papers*, Vol. 39, March, pp. 75–89.

Gorton, G.B. and A. Metrick (2012). Securitized Lending and the Run on the Repo. *Journal of Financial Economics*, Vol. 104, June, pp. 425–451.

Jaffee, D.M. and F. Modigliani (1969). A Theory and Test of Credit Rationing. *American Economic Review*, Vol. 59, December, pp. 850–872.

Jaffee, D.M. (1975). Cyclical Variations in the Risk Structure of Interest Rates. *Journal of Monetary Economics*, Vol. 1, January, pp. 309–325.

Kanatas, G. and S.I. Greenbaum (1982). Bank Reserve Requirements and Monetary Aggregates. *Journal of Banking and Finance*, Vol. 6, December, pp. 507–520.

Kashyap, A., D.E. Wilcox and J. Stein (1993). Monetary Policy and Credit Conditions: Evidence from the Composition of External Finance. *American Economic Review*, Vol. 83, March, pp. 78–98.

Lang, W.W. and L.I. Nakamura (1995). 'Flight to Quality' in Bank Lending and Economic Activity. *Journal of Monetary Economics*, Vol. 36, August, pp. 145–164.

McCabe, P.E., M. Cipriani, M. Holsher and A. Martin (2013). Minimum Balance of 5 Percent Could Prevent Future Money Market Fund Runs. *Brookings Papers on Economic Activity*, Spring 2013, pp. 211–278,

Mishkin, F.S. (2009). *The Economics of Money, Banking, and Financial Markets*, 9th Edition. New York: Addison-Wesley.

Oliner, S.D. and G.D. Rudebusch (1996). Monetary Policy and Credit Conditions: Evidence from the Composition of External Finance: Comment. *American Economic Review*, Vol. 86, March, pp. 300–309.

Omarova, S.T. and M.E. Tahyar (2011–2012). That Which We Call a Bank: Revisiting the History of Bank Holding Company Regulation in the United States. *Review of Banking and Financial Law*, Vol. 31, pp. 113–199.

Pennacchi, G.G. (1988). Loan Sales and the Cost of Bank Capital. *Journal of Finance*, Vol. 43, June, pp. 375–396.

Pozsar, Z., T. Adrian, A. Ashcraft and H. Boesky (2010). Shadow Banking. Federal Reserve Bank of New York Staff Report No. 458, February.

Roe, M.J. (2011). The Derivatives Market's Payment Priorities as Financial Crisis Accelerator. *Stanford Law Review*, Vol. 63, March, pp. 539–590.

Rosengren, E.S. (2014). Our Financial Structures — Are They Prepared for Financial Stability. *Journal of Money, Credit and Banking*, Vol. 46, February, pp. 143–156.

Schleifer, A. and R.W. Vishny (2010). Unstable Banking. *Journal of Financial Economics*, Vol. 97, September, pp. 306–318.

Stein, J.C. (2013). Overheating in Credit Markets: Origins, Measurement, and Policy Responses. Speech at the "Restoring Household Financial Stability after the Great Recession: Why Household Balance Sheets Matter", research symposium sponsored by the Federal Reserve Bank of St. Louis, St. Louis, Missouri, February 7, 2013. Available at http://www.federalreserve.gov/newsevents/speech/stein20130207a.htm [accessed on 13 June 2014].

Stiglitz, J.E. and A. Weiss (1981). Credit Rationing in Markets with Imperfect Information. *American Economic Review*, Vol. 71, June, pp. 393–410.

Stout, L.A. (2008). Derivatives and the Legal Origin of the 2008 Credit Crisis. *Harvard Business Law Review*, Vol. 1, January, pp. 1–38.

Wall, L.D. and D.R. Peterson (1987). The Effect of Capital Adequacy Guidelines on Large Bank Holding Companies. *Journal of Banking and Finance*, Vol. 11, December, pp. 581–600.

Leverage, Securitization and Shadow Banking: Theory and Policy*

Ana Fostel†

George Washington University

John Geanakoplos‡

Yale University

Leverage and securitization are at the core of the shadow banking system. We provide a non-technical review of the theory of leverage developed in collateral general equilibrium models with incomplete markets. We explain how leverage can be endogenously determined in equilibrium, and its relation with tail risk, volatility and asset prices. We provide a description of the Leverage Cycle and how it differs from a Credit Cycle. We also describe some cross-sectional implications of multiple leverage cycles, including contagion, flight to collateral, and swings in the issuance volume of the highest quality debt. Finally, we review some ideas on how to measure and manage leverage.

Introduction

Most of the recent post-crisis regulatory reforms concentrate on bank leverage and bank capital requirements. However, leverage and securitization also occur in the shadow banking system, outside traditional banks.

---

*Prepared for the Sixteenth Annual International Banking Conference. IMF and Federal Reserve Bank of Chicago (2013).

†George Washington University, Washington, DC.

‡Yale University, New Haven, CT, Santa Fe Institute, Ellington Capital Management.

Short-term lending (repos) and securitization are indeed at the core of shadow banking activities.

Shadow banks are similar to traditional banks to the extend that they engage into maturity transformation activities. But shadow banks are crucially different from traditional banks since they are subject to a very different regulatory framework and safety nets.

Financial innovation in the form of securitization (like pooling and tranching) increased dramatically in the decade before the financial crisis. There are many forces behind securitization that have been widely analyzed before such as the potential for regulatory arbitrage and increased risk sharing. However collateral is also key to understand securitization. Collateral and securitization are devices to make lending more attractive. In fact, securitization, and financial innovation in general, is a way of stretching the scarce collateral in the economy.

This paper wants to put forward the idea that collateral and leverage are crucial to understand the shadow banking system and its fragility. The goal is to provide a non-technical review of the collateral general equilibrium theory of endogenous leverage and discuss a few policy ideas on how to properly measure and manage leverage.[1]

In classical macroeconomic models with financial frictions like Bernanke-Gertler (1989), Kiyotaki-Moore (1997), Holmstrom-Tirole (1997), the strategy to endogenize leverage is through theoretical foundations coming from the corporate finance tradition. Borrowing limits are set using "skin in the game" type of arguments. On the contrary, the theoretical foundations for endogenous leverage in the collateral general equilibrium models starting with Geanakoplos (1997), are based on the idea that default happens when collateral is worth less than the promise. This situation applies to most of shadow banking where borrowers have no control over the future payoff of the asset.

The main lessons from the collateral general equilibrium theory are the following. First, leverage is endogenous and fluctuates with the fear of default. Second, leverage is therefore related to the degree of uncertainty, volatility or low tail risk of asset markets. Third, increasing leverage on a broad scale can increase asset prices. Fourth, the scarcity of collateral creates a collateral value that can lead to bubbles in which some asset prices are far

[1] For a technical review see Fostel and Geanakoplos (forthcoming).

above their efficient levels, creating leverage cycle. Finally, multiple leverage cycles can explain important phenomena like flight to collateral, contagion and violent swings in volume of trade in high quality assets.

The main policy implication is that managing leverage may be far more important and efficient than managing interest rates. We briefly discuss a few ideas on how to properly measure and manage the leverage cycle.

Theory of Leverage and Collateral

Default and endogenous leverage

Collateral general equilibrium theory not only models the role of leverage on asset prices and economic activity, but it also provides a theory of endogenous determination of collateral requirements. This seems to be a difficult problem, since in standard general equilibrium theory one clearing market condition for the credit market endogenously determines the interest rate. So how can one supply-equals-demand equation for loans determine two variables, interest rate and leverage?

In collateral equilibrium models developed by Geanakoplos (1997) and Geanakoplos and Zame (1997), the problem is solved by considering a whole menu of contracts, each characterized by a collateral level and a promise of repayment. In equilibrium all contracts are priced and hence each contract has a corresponding *LTV*. However because the collateral backing promises is scarce, only a few contracts will be actively traded in equilibrium. In this sense, collateral requirements and leverage are determined endogenously in equilibrium.

But which contracts are traded in equilibrium? Geanakoplos (2003) and Fostel and Geanakoplos (2012a) provide an example in which all agents choose the same contract from the menu. Fostel and Geanakoplos (2013a) provide a complete characterization. They proved that in binomial economies with financial assets serving as collateral, every equilibrium is equivalent (in real allocations and prices) to another equilibrium in which there is no default.[2] Thus in binomial economies with financial assets, actual default is not observable. But potential default has a dramatic effect on equilibrium: it sets a hard limit on borrowing. Agents can promise at

[2]An asset is financial when it does not provide direct utility to its holder and when its payoffs do not depend on ownership. For example, houses and land are not financial assets.

most the worst payoff of the asset in the future. This result shows that agents would like to borrow more at going riskless interest rates but cannot, even when their future endowments are more than enough to cover their debts. The limit on borrowing is caused by the potential of default, despite the absence of default in equilibrium.[3]

Binomial economies and their Brownian motion limit are special cases. But they are extensively used in finance. They are the simplest economies in which one can begin to see the effect of uncertainty on credit markets.[4]

Notice that this strategy of making leverage endogenous is different from the corporate finance approach used in the macro literature such as Kiyotaki and Moore (1997) and Bernanke and Gertler (1989) or more recently in Acharya and Viswanathan (2011) and Adrian and Shin (2010). The corporate finance view relies on "skin on the game" type of arguments. These moral hazard or agency problems are indeed at the core of the corporate world. However, these were not the type of problems that were at the center of the recent crisis and shadow banking: sellers of mortgage backed securities (MBS) did not have any type of control over the MBS future cash flows.

Once we know which contract is traded in equilibrium, we have a well-defined formula for the leverage associated to each asset used as collateral. Loan to value, LTV, is defined as the ratio between what can be borrowed using the asset as collateral and the price of the asset. In binomial economies an asset LTV is given by tail risk as shown by the following[5]:

$$LTV = \frac{\textit{worst case rate of return}}{\textit{riskless rate of interest}}.$$

This formula is simple and easy to calculate. Moreover, it provides interesting insights. First, the formula explains which assets are easier to leverage: those assets with low tail risk. Second, it explains why changes in the

[3]Fostel and Geanakoplos (2013a) provide refinements of the result. They show that under default costs or costs associated to the use of collateral, in every equilibrium only the max–min contract is traded. The max–min contract is the contract that promises to pay the worst payoff of the asset in the future. It is the maximum promise that avoids default.

[4]With multiple states or non-financial assets like houses, default would emerge in equilibrium, but still leverage would be endogenous. For examples, see Fostel and Geanakoplos (2012a), Araujo *et al.* (2011), Simsek (2013), Geanakoplos and Kubler (2013).

[5]See Fostel and Geanakoplos (2013a).

bad tail can have such a big effect on equilibrium even if they hardly change expected asset payoffs: they change leverage. Finally, the formula also explains why, even with rational agents who do not chase yield, high leverage historically correlates with low interest rates.

Leverage and volatility

Many papers have assumed a link between leverage and volatility: low volatility is usually associated with high levels of leverage. It turns out that this is the case in binomial economies with only one financial asset. In this special case the above *LTV* formula expressed in terms of tail risk can be equivalently expressed as[6]:

$$margin = 1 - LTV = k \times Volatility\ of\ collateral\ payoffs.$$

The formula says that the equilibrium margin on an asset is proportional to the volatility of a dollar's worth of the asset. The trouble with this formula is that the risk neutral pricing probabilities used to calculate volatility depend on the asset. If there were two different assets co-existing in the same economy, we might need different risk neutral probabilities to price each of them. In a few words, ranking the leverage of assets by the volatility of their payoffs would fail if we tried to measure the various volatilities with respect to the same probabilities.

This suggests that the link between volatility and leverage is not as robust and that what really matters in general is tail risk.

Leverage and asset prices

Collateral general equilibrium models provide a theory that links collateral and liquidity with asset prices.

When assets can be used as collateral, they are priced above their marginal utility of their payoffs. This pricing premium for collateral is called collateral value, because it stems from the added benefit of enabling borrowing. Fostel and Geanakoplos (2008) showed that the price of an asset that can be used as collateral is given by:

$$p = PV + CV.$$

[6]See Fostel and Geanakoplos (2013a).

The price of any asset has two components. The Payoff Value, *PV*, which reflects the usual discounted marginal utility of future payoffs. The second component, the Collateral Value, *CV*, reflects the value of the asset due to its collateral role. Interestingly, the existence of collateral values create deviations from the efficient markets hypothesis, which in one of its forms asserts that there are risk-adjusted state probabilities that can be used to price all assets.

The collateral value is also related to liquidity. When borrowing is limited by the need to post collateral, some agents would be willing to pay a higher interest for the loan than the market requires, if they did not have to put up the collateral. This extra interest is called the liquidity wedge. Fostel and Geanakoplos (2008) showed that when borrowing constraints are binding, agents discount all the cash flows by the liquidity wedge. As a result, as agents become more liquidity constrained, when liquidity wedge is high, their asset valuation will decline.

On the other hand, the surplus a borrower can gain by taking out a particular loan backed by a particular collateral is called the liquidity value of the loan (or contract). Since one collateral cannot back many competing loans, the borrower will always select the loan that gives the highest liquidity value among all loans with the same collateral. This leads to a theory of endogenous contracts in collateral equilibrium, and in particular, to a theory of endogenous leverage as described above. The liquidity value of a contract depends on the payoff of that contract and on the agents' liquidity need as expressed by the liquidity wedge. Fostel and Geanakoplos (2008) proved that in fact, the collateral value of an asset equals the liquidity value of a contract that uses the asset as collateral. In this way the knot is completely tight: this theory explains the relationship between asset prices, collateral and liquidity.

Finally, as shown in Fostel and Geanakoplos (2012b), collateral values can create bubbles. Harrison and Kreps (1978) defined a bubble as a situation in which an asset trades for a price which is above every agent's payoff value. They showed a bubble could emerge in equilibrium if there were at least three periods, because the buyer in the first period could sell it in the second period to somebody who valued it more than he did from that point on. In collateral equilibrium bubbles can emerge even in a static model due to the presence of collateral values.

The leverage cycle

The theoretical results described in previous sections have interesting time series implications when studied in a dynamic framework. As explained in Geanakoplos (2003), leverage cycles arise in equilibrium. Leverage cycles are characterized by a dynamic feedback between leverage, asset prices and volatility (or tail risk).

First, leverage and asset prices tend to move hand in hand: there is a two-way feedback between leverage and collateral prices. Figures 1 and 2 show

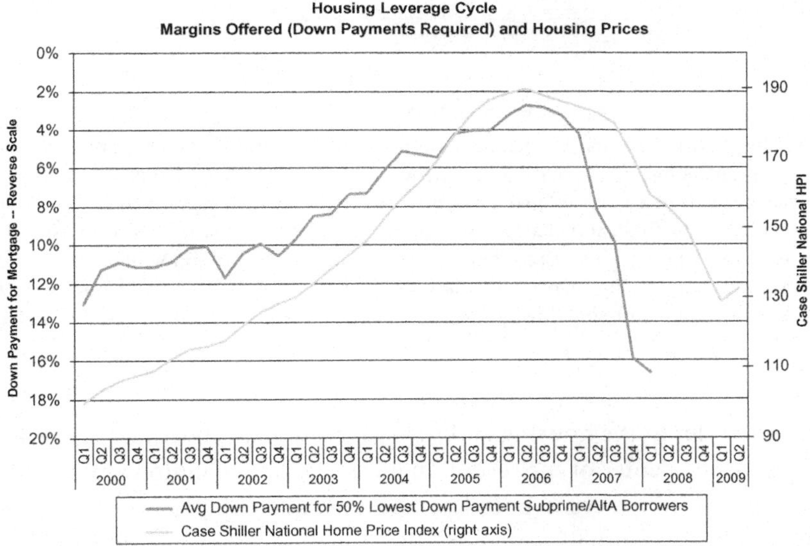

Fig. 1. Housing leverage cycle. From Geanakoplos (2010). Observe that the Down Payment axis has been reversed, because a lower down payment requirements are correlated with higher home prices.

Notes: For every AltA or Subprime first loan originated from Q1 2000 to Q1 2008, down payment percentage was calculated as appraised value (or sale price if available) minus total mortgage debt, divided by appraised value. For each quarter, the down payment percentages were ranked from highest to lowest, and the average of the bottom half of the list is shown in the diagram. This number is an indicator of down payment required: clearly many homeowners put down more than they had to, and that is why the top half is dropped from the average. A 13% down payment in Q1 2000 corresponds to leverage of about 7.7, and 2.7% down payment in Q2 2006 corresponds to leverage of about 37. Subprime/AltA issuance stopped in Q1 2008.

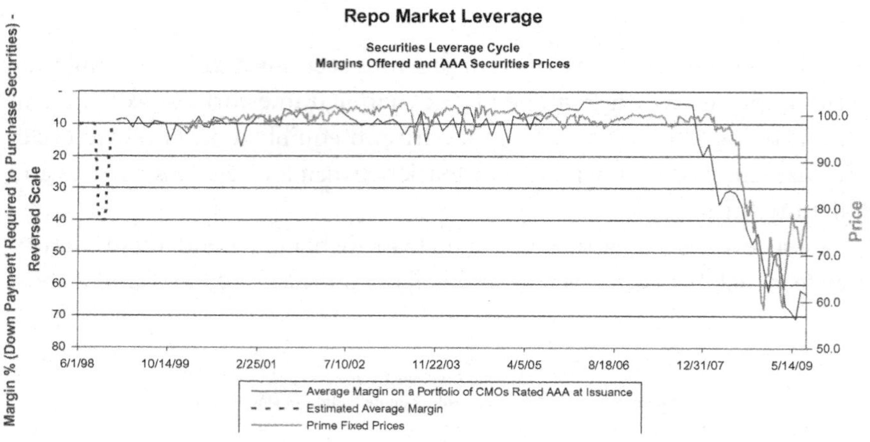

Fig. 2. Security leverage cycle. From Geanakoplos (2010).

Note: The chart represents the average margin required by dealers on a hypothetical portfolio of bonds subject to certain adjustments noted below. Observe that the Margin % axis has been reversed, since lower margins are correlated with higher prices. The portfolio evolved over time, and changes in average margin reflect changes in composition as well as changes in margins of particular securities. In the period following August 2008, a substantial part of the increase in margins is due to bonds that could no longer be used as collateral after being downgraded, or for other reasons, and hence count as 100% margin.

leverage cycles in the housing and repo markets respectively. Both markets were at the epicenter of the recent financial crisis. The figures clearly show how previous to the crisis, both leverage and collateral prices, went up and how they both eventually collapsed after the crisis in the housing and repo markets.

Second, the leverage cycle predicts a two-way feedback between leverage and asset prices with volatility (or more generally with tail risk): when volatility or tail risk is low, leverage and asset prices are high. Figure 3 shows the VIX index, which is considered the "fear factor" in financial markets and widely used as a measure for market volatility. The index is at low levels before the crisis, precisely when leverage and asset prices are at record high levels, and it skyrockets just before the crisis at the moment when leverage and asset prices collapse as seen in Figs. 1 and 2.

As we saw in the previous section, collateral is usually scarce and hence borrowing is usually constrained. But when volatility (or tail risk) is low and stable, the existing scarce collateral can support massive amounts of

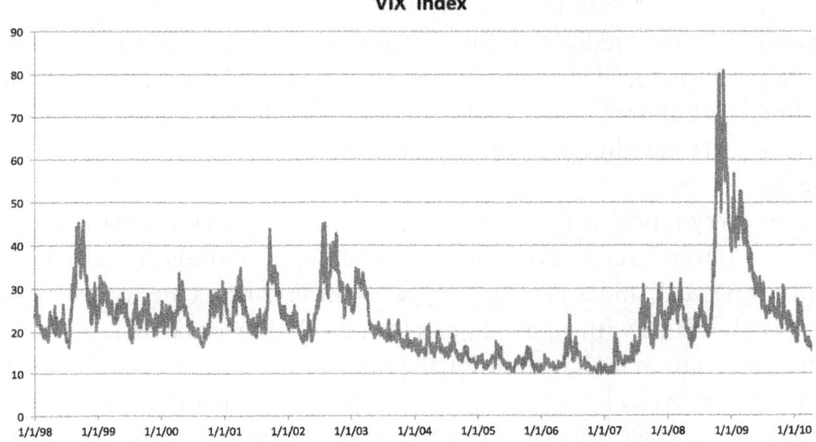

Fig. 3. Volatility.
Source: Fostel and Geanakoplos (2012a).

borrowing, provided there is sufficient agent heterogeneity to generate a need for trading the collateral. In such times a bubble can emerge in which the prices of the assets that can be used as collateral rise to astronomical levels, far above their "Arrow–Debreu" Pareto efficient levels. During this ebullient time, the combination of high prices and low volatility creates an illusion of prosperity. But in fact the seeds of collapse are growing as the assets get more and more concentrated in the hands of the most enthusiastic and leveraged buyers.

When bad news that creates more uncertainty (or that comes with very high low tail risk) occurs, the bubble can burst. The bad news itself lowers the prices. But it also drastically reduces the wealth of the leveraged buyers, forcing them to sell. And most importantly, credit markets tighten and potential new investors cannot find funding. Is the interaction of all these three factors that can reduce the price by much more than the bad news itself.

This evolution from low volatility and rising leverage and asset prices, to high volatility and declining leverage and asset prices is called the leverage cycle.

It is very important to distinguish between a leverage cycle and a credit cycle. They are not the same: leverage cycle is a feedback between asset prices and leverage, whereas a credit cycle is a feedback between asset prices and borrowing. If leverage is constant, then borrowing and asset prices rise and fall together, but leverage is unchanged. Of course a leverage cycle always produces a credit cycle. But the opposite is not true. Macroeconomic models with financial frictions such as Kiyotaki and Moore (1997) produce credit cycles but not leverage cycles. At odds with the empirical evidence, in these models a credit cycles co-exists in equilibrium with counter-cyclical leverage.

Not every model with financial frictions and collateral constraints can generate a leverage cycle. For leverage cycles to appear in equilibrium uncertainty is needed, and a particular type of uncertainty: One in which bad news is associated with an increase in future volatility or tail risk. The literature on credit cycles has traditionally not been concerned with volatility. In a leverage cycle, leverage is the most important quantitative driver of the change in asset prices over the cycle. If *LTV* were held to a constant, or even worse, if it is counter-cyclical, the cycle would be considerably dampened.

Multiple leverage cycles

Many kinds of collateral exist at the same time, and therefore there can be many simultaneous leverage cycles. Collateral equilibrium theory not only explains time series properties like the leverage cycle described earlier, but it also explains some commonly observed cross-sectional differences and linkages between leverage cycles in different asset classes. In particular, multiple co-existing leverage cycles can explain phenomena such as flight to collateral, contagion and drastic swings in the volume of trade of high quality assets.[7]

Flight to collateral

When similar bad news hits different asset classes, some asset classes often preserve their value better than others. This empirical observation is traditionally given the name flight to quality, since it is interpreted as a shift toward safer assets that have less volatile payoff values. Fostel and Geanakoplos (2008) called attention to a new channel which they called flight to collateral: after volatile bad news, collateral values widen more than payoff values.

---

[7] For technical details, see Fostel and Geanakoplos (2008, forthcoming).

More precisely, each asset experiences its own leverage cycle and hence prices for all assets go down after bad news by more than their expected values decline. However, the gap between asset prices widens after bad news by more than the gap in expected payoffs. After bad news, the payoff values of all assets go down. But their collateral values move in different directions: while the collateral value of some assets go down, amplifying their leverage cycle, the collateral value of other assets increase, smoothing their leverage cycle. Hence, the widening spread in prices is almost entirely explained by the widening of collateral values.

Flight to collateral occurs when the liquidity wedge is high (so marginal buyers are liquidity constrained) and the dispersion of *LTV*s is high. During a flight to collateral, investors prefer to buy those assets that enable them to borrow money more easily (higher *LTV*s). The other side of the coin is that investors in need of liquidity get more cash by selling those assets on which they borrowed less money because the sales revenues net of loan repayments are higher.

Flight to collateral is related to what other papers have called flight to liquidity. Flight to liquidity was discussed by Vayanos (2004) in a model where an asset's liquidity is defined by its exogenously given transaction cost. In Brunnermeier and Pedersen (2009), market liquidity is the gap between fundamental value and the transaction price. They show how this market liquidity interacts with funding liquidity (given by trader's capital and margin requirements) generating flight to liquidity. In our model an asset's liquidity is given by its capacity as collateral to raise cash. Hence, our flight to collateral arises from different leverage cycles in equilibrium and their interaction with the liquidity wedge cycle.

Contagion

When bad news hits one asset class, the resulting fall in its price can migrate to other assets classes, even if their payoffs are statistically independent from the original crashing assets.

Fostel and Geanakoplos (2008) showed that a leverage cycle in one asset class can migrate to a different asset class through movements in the liquidity wedge. A leverage cycle in one asset class alone can move the liquidity wedge. As explained above, the liquidity wedge is a universal factor in valuing all assets. So, an increase in the liquidity wedge of marginal buyers after bad news reduces their valuation of all assets. Crucially, contagion does not only happen during extreme episodes through dramatic sell offs. Contagion can occur also during less extreme stages called the anxious phase due to the presence of a portfolio effect: marginal buyers end up buying more after bad news, amplifying the movements of the liquidity wedge.

There is a vast literature on contagion. Despite the range of different approaches, there are mainly three different kinds of models. The first blends financial theories with macroeconomic techniques, and seeks international transmission channels associated with macroeconomic variables. Examples of this approach are Corsetti, Pesenti, and Roubini (1999), and Pavlova and Rigobon (2008). The second kind models contagion as information transmission. In this case the fundamentals of assets are assumed to be correlated. When one asset declines in price because of noise trading, rational traders reduce the prices of all assets since they are unable to distinguish declines due to fundamentals from declines due to noise trading. Examples of this approach are King and Wadhwani (1990), Calvo and Mendoza (2000), and Kodres and Pritsker (2002). Finally, there are theories that model contagion through wealth effects, as in Kyle and Xiong (2001). When some key financial actors suffer losses, they liquidate positions in several markets, and this sell-off generates price comovement. Our model shares with the last two approaches a focus exclusively on contagion as a financial market phenomenon. But our model further shows how leverage cycles can produce contagion in less extreme but more frequent market conditions: the anxious economy, where there is no sell-off. The leverage cycle causes contagion even when trade patterns differ from those observed during acute crises.

Swings in high quality trade volume

When collateral general equilibrium models are extended to include asymmetric information, we can also explain extreme volatility in trade volumes. Importantly, owners of the assets can observe their asset quality, but investors cannot. Following the techniques in Fostel and Geanakoplos (2008) and Dubey and Geanakoplos (2002) we can allow for signaling as well as adverse selection in collateral equilibrium without destroying market anonymity.

Co-existing leverage cycles generate flight to collateral as before. But a new effect comes from the supply side. In order to signal that their assets are high quality (so that investors will pay more for them and be able to borrow more using them as collateral), the owners of the good quality asset always sell less than they would if their types were common knowledge. However, after bad news, the drop in volume of their sales is huge.

Flight to collateral and informational asymmetries generate such a big drop in good issuance, even though the news is almost equally bad for all assets. The explanation is that the bigger price spread between types caused by the flight to collateral requires a smaller good type issuance for a separating equilibrium to exist. Unless the good issuance level becomes onerously low, bad types would be more tempted by the bigger price spread to mimic good types and sell at the high price. The good types are able to separate themselves by choosing low enough quantities since it is more costly for the bad type to rely on the payoff of its own asset for final consumption than it is for the good type.

There is a growing literature that tries to model asymmetric information within general equilibrium, like Gale (1992), Bisin and Gottardi (2006), Rustichini and Siconolfi (2008). Our model combines asymmetric information in a general equilibrium model with a model of endogenous credit constraints and leverage.

Policy: Measuring and Managing Leverage

As we saw in the previous sections, leverage is a crucial variable that affects asset pricing and can generate cycles and cross-market dynamics like contagion and flight to collateral. Asset prices are too high *ex-ante*, compared to Arrow Debreu first best prices, and eventually they crash after bad news, rising and falling in tandem with leverage. If we were to add investment and production of the asset into the model, we would find that there is over-production *ex-ante* as well, and a dramatic drop in production and investment levels during crisis times.[8]

Macroeconomic stability policy has concentrated almost entirely on regulating interest rates. But the interest rate is not the key variable in the

[8]For the effect of collateral on investment and production see Fostel and Geanakoplos (2013b).

leverage cycle, and most of the time, as shown by the theoretical models, they barely move. Hence, collateral equilibrium models and the leverage cycle theory suggest that it might be more effective to stabilize leverage than to stabilize interest rates. This point has be made in several papers such as Geanakoplos (2010), Garleanu and Pedersen (2011), Geanakoplos and Pedersen (2011), and Fostel and Geanakoplos (forthcoming).

Fostel and Geanakoplos (forthcoming) and Geanakoplos and Kubler (2013) show that restricting asset leverage *ex-ante* can be a Pareto improving policy. The main intuitive reason why restricting leverage can lead to pareto improvements is that curtailing credit will lead to relative price changes in the future, which will have redistributive consequences that may be overall beneficial. In particular, restricting leverage *ex-ante* may cause an increase in asset prices in the future and hence can cause a reduction in the number of defaults.

Access to this type of public data of leverage at the institution and security level (properly aggregated) can be very valuable for crisis prevention, detection and post-management. Moreover, leverage has the advantage of being a model-free measure of systemic risk. In what follows we discuss two important ideas regarding measuring and monitoring leverage.[9]

Asset-based leverage versus investor-based leverage

In order to properly monitor leverage it is important to distinguish between investor-based leverage and asset-based leverage.

The balance sheet approach to leverage is an important one. Investor-based leverage data is ultimately a clear indicator of a financial institution's ability to repay the loan. For example, even in the case a bank holds in its balance sheet highly leverage assets, this may not necessarily create default risk if it also holds large liquidity reserves.

Recent policy responses to deal with financial regulation, including Basel III, have focused on imposing leverage caps at the institution level in the form of debt/equity limits. However, as discussed in Geanakoplos (2010) and Geanakoplos and Pedersen (2011), this approach has several problems. First, leverage will migrate from regulated institutions

[9]For a more detailed treatment see Geanakoplos (2010) and Geanakoplos and Pedersen (2011).

to un-regulated ones in the shadow banking system due to regulatory arbitrage. Second, an institution-based cap on leverage will incentivize each institution to shift towards more risky securities. Banks can leverage a lot against say Treasury Bills and much less against risky securities, so a cap on total leverage, without regard to asset type, will induce a balance sheet re-composition towards less leverage and riskier securities. Third, balance sheet leverage poses the question of how to treat some crucial securities such as CDS; should we consider them as debt or equity? Basel III proposes to treat them as debt, in the amount equal to their total payment in case of 100% default; this clearly grossly overstates leverage. Finally, measuring leverage by balance sheet debt to equity ratios could pose measurement problems, since balance sheet data only includes old loans (more of this below).

For these reasons, it is crucial that financial regulation focuses on regulating leverage at the security level (irrespective of borrower or lender) as well. Leverage across all asset classes should be systematically gathered and properly aggregated. Moreover, leverage should be recorded also for those asset classes with 100% margin (those assets that cannot be used as collateral) in order to avoid bias. Tracking leverage is not only about margin levels but also about keeping track of which assets classes are being used as collateral. This also provides relevant information about credit conditions.

Finally, asset-based leverage has the advantage that is agent-independent. Hence, measuring and managing leverage at the security level may be easier to implement and politically more feasible.

Old leverage versus new leverage

Another crucial distinction when measuring and monitoring leverage is that of old loans versus new loans. One of the problems mentioned before with the balance-sheet approach to leverage is that it does not distinguish the leverage of old loans from new loans and thus may not be a timely indicator of increase risk of a crisis.

Leverage of old loans and new loans go in opposite directions: when market conditions deteriorate leverage on old loans goes up whereas on new loans collapses. The old leverage in the balance sheet is backward looking and changes only gradually over time by construction. On the other hand, leverage of new loans provides timely information on the current credit environment. Hence, the average leverage on old loans evolves slowly and reflects the credit environment over the past time period while leverage on new debt can abruptly change.

Incidentally, the lack of measurement on new loans is what drives one of the most important results in Reinhart and Rogoff (2009): de-leveraging on average begins two years after a crisis. It is important to understand that de-leveraging is a key element of a crisis as we discussed before in the theory section, and not a lagged consequence of it.

In short, it is crucial for proper crisis management to keep track not only of leverage on old loans but also of leverage (i.e., down payments or margin requirements) on new loans. Leverage and margins should be recorded every time an asset is used as collateral.

References

Acharya, V. and S. Viswanathan (2011). Leverage, Moral Hazard, and Liquidity. *Journal of Finance*, Vol. 66, No. 1, pp. 99–138.

Adrian, T. and H. Shin (2010). Liquidity and Leverage. *Journal of Financial Intermediation*, Vol. 19, No. 3, pp. 418–437.

Araujo, A., F. Kubler and S. Schommer (2012). Regulating Collateral-Requirements when Markets are Incomplete. *Journal of Economic Theory*, Vol. 147, No. 2, pp. 450–476.

Bernanke, B. and M. Gertler (1989). Agency Costs, Net Worth, and Business Fluctuations. *American Economic Review*, Vol. 79, No. 1, pp. 14–31.

Bisin, A. and P. Gottardi (2006). Efficient Competitive Equilibria with Adverse Selection. *Journal of Political Economy*, Vol. 114, No. 3, pp. 485–516.

Brunnermeier, M. and L. Pedersen (2009). Market Liquidity and Funding Liquidity. *Review of Financial Studies*, Vol. 22, No. 6, pp. 2201–2238.

Calvo, G. and E. Mendoza (2000). Contagion, globalization, and the volatility of capital flows. In *Capital Flows and the Emerging Economies: Theory, Evidence, and Controversies*, S. Edwards (ed.), pp. 15–41. Chicago: University of Chicago Press.

Corsetti, G., P. Pesenti and N. Roubini (1999). Paper Tigers? A Model of the Asian Crisis. *European Economic Review*, Vol. 43, No. 7, pp. 1211–1236.

Dubey, P. and J. Geanakoplos (2002). Competitive Pooling: Rothschild–Stiglitz Reconsidered. *Quarterly Journal of Economics*, Vol. 117, No. 4, pp. 1529–1570.

Fostel, A. and J. Geanakoplos (2008). Leverage Cycles and the Anxious Economy. *American Economic Review*, Vol. 98, No. 4, pp. 1211–1244.

Fostel, A. and J. Geanakoplos (2012a). Why Does Bad News Increase Volatility and Decrease Leverage. *Journal of Economic Theory*, Vol. 147, No. 2, pp. 501–525.

Fostel, A. and J. Geanakoplos (2012b). Tranching, CDS and Asset Prices: How Financial Innovation can Cause Bubbles and Crashes. *American Economic Journal: Macroeconomics*, Vol. 4, No. 1, pp. 190–225.

Fostel, A. and J. Geanakoplos (2013a). Leverage and Default in Binomial Economies: A Complete Characterization. *Cowles Foundation Working Paper*, 1877R.

Fostel, A. and J. Geanakoplos (2013b). Financial Innovation, Collateral and Investment. *Cowles Foundation Working Paper.*

Fostel and Geanakoplos (2014). Endogenous Collateral Constrains and the Leverage Cycle. *Forthcoming Annual Review of Economics.*

Gale, D. (1992). A Walrasian Theory of Markets with Adverse Selection. *Review of Economic Studies*, Vol. 59, No. 2, pp. 229–255.

Garleanu, N. and L. Pedersen (2011). Margin-Based Asset Pricing and the Law of One Price. *Review of Financial Studies*, Vol. 24, No. 6, pp. 1980–2022.

Geanakoplos, J. (1997). Promises, promises. In *The Economy as an Evolving Complex System II*, W. B. Arthur, S. Durlauf and D. Lane (eds.), pp. 285–320. Reading, MA: Addison-Wesley.

Geanakoplos, J. (2003). Liquidity, default, and crashes: Endogenous contracts in general equilibrium. In *Advances in Economics and Econometrics: Theory and Applications, Eighth World Conference*, Econometric Society Monographs, Vol. 2, pp. 170–205.

Geanakoplos, J. (2010). The leverage cycle. In *NBER Macroeconomics Annual 2009*, D. Acemoglu, K. Rogoff and M. Woodford (eds.), pp. 1–65. Chicago: University of Chicago Press.

Geanakoplos and Kubler (2013). Why is too much Leverage Bad for the Economy? *Cowles Foundation Discussion Paper*, Yale University.

Geanakoplos and Pedersen (2011). Monitoring Leverage. *Cowles Foundation Discussion Paper*, Yale University.

Geanakoplos, J. and W. Zame (1997). Collateralized Security Markets. *Working Paper.*

Harrison, M. and D. Kreps (1978). Speculative Investor Behavior in a Stock Market with Heterogenous Expectations. *Quarterly Journal of Economics*, Vol. 92, No. 2, pp. 323–336.

Holmstrom, B. and J. Tirole (1997). Financial Intermediation, Loanable Funds, and the Real Sector. *Quarterly Journal of Economics*, Vol. 112, No. 3, pp. 663–691.

King, M. and S. Wadhwani (1990). Transmission of Volatility between Stock Markets. *Review of Financial Studies*, Vol. 3, No. 1, pp. 5–33.

Kiyotaki, N. and J. Moore (1997). Credit Cycles. *Journal of Political Economy*, Vol. 105, No. 2, pp. 211–248.

Kodres, L. and M. Pritsker (2002). A Rational Expectations Model of Financial Contagion. *Journal of Finance*, Vol. 57, No. 2, pp. 768–799.

Kyle, A. and W. Xiong (2001). Contagion as a Wealth Effect. *Journal of Finance*, Vol. 56, No. 4, pp. 1401–1440.

Pavlova, A. and R. Rigobon (2008). The Role of Portfolio Constraints in the International Propagation of Shocks. *Review of Economic Studies*, Vol. 75, pp. 1215–1256.

Reinhart and Rogoff (2009). *This Time is Different*. Princeton, NJ: Princeton University Press.

Rustichini, A. and P. Siconolfi (2008). General Equilibrium in Economies with Adverse Selection. *Economic Theory*, Vol. 37, pp. 417–437.

Simsek, A. (2013). Belief Disagreements and Collateral Constraints. *Econometrica*, Vol. 81, No. 1, pp. 1–53.

Vayanos, D. (2004). Flight to Quality, Flight to Liquidity, and the Pricing of Risk. Unpublished.

Evolution in Bank Complexity

Nicola Cetorelli, James McAndrews, and James Traina*

Federal Reserve Bank of New York

Introduction

"Entities must not be multiplied beyond necessity". This popular enunciation of Occam's razor extols the virtue of simplicity, whereby "simple" structures should benchmark observation to reality. The principle seems relevant to frame a discussion around the complexity of banks. The banking industry has experienced significant structural transformations over the last 20–30 years that directly affect the complexity of banking firms. Some of these changes are well known. Since the 1980s, for instance, the number of commercial banks operating in the United States fell from approximately 14,000 to 6,000. Most of this reduction was the result of a well-documented process of consolidation, in large part due to geographic deregulation. Along the way, both the average size of banks and the concentration of market share increased remarkably. In the 1980s, the top 10 banking institutions accounted for about 20% of total bank assets; that percentage is now above 50%. Naively viewed through the lens of Occam's razor, the declining number of banks moved the industry toward a simpler structure. However, the remaining organizations grew substantially in size and complexity, incorporating a large and growing number of subsidiaries spanning the entire spectrum of business activities within the financial sector.

*Nicola Cetorelli is an Assistant Vice President, James McAndrews is an executive vice president and research director, and James Traina is a senior research analyst, all in the Research Department of the Federal Reserve Bank of New York. The views expressed in this paper are those of the individual authors and do not necessarily reflect the position of the Federal Reserve Bank of New York or the Federal Reserve System. A version of this article is published as Cetorelli, McAndrews, and Traina, 2014, "Evolution in Bank Complexity", *Federal Reserve Bank of New York Economic Policy Review*.

In particular, the transformation of the banking industry has generated a small number of industry behemoths, and public debate has focused on ways to regulate such super-sized institutions. There are a number of proposed approaches, including break-ups, size caps, or business activity limits. Other suggestions include enhanced regulations in the form of capital and long-term debt requirements, capital surcharges, stress tests, and greatly enhanced resolution planning.

While the discussion around the largest entities is certainly important, we suggest that their emergence is part of a larger process that has transformed the industry more broadly. In this paper, we document and analyze the evolution of the industry over time and pose questions on what might have been the forces that have driven the industry and firm structures we observe today.

Despite the intensity of the debate on bank complexity, there is in fact very little documentation or analysis of the dynamics leading to the current industry configuration. In fact, even the meaning and metrics of complexity are debatable. In both comparative and absolute terms, there is no clear consensus on how to assess the complexity of an entity. This problem is important not only from a positive perspective, as we strive to understand the economics behind the problem, but also from a normative angle, as we decide policy measures exclusively for complex institutions. How do we establish *how complex* entities are? Where do we draw the line across institutions?

These are admittedly difficult questions — indeed, complex ones. In this paper, we focus on *structural* complexity. We look at organizational structure gauged by the number and types of subsidiaries organized under common ownership and control. In fact, we suggest that this definition of complexity offers a framework for analysis, one that allows us to study how industry complexity has evolved, and how complex banks are today. Likewise, it is capable of addressing normative analysis, for example, by assisting in defining effective criteria to designate which entities might be complex.[1] Moreover, the organizational structure of an entity maps into

[1]Alternative metrics focus instead on what an entity does. For instance, the methodology for the designation of global systemically important banks proposes as metrics of complexity the notional value of OTC derivatives, the balance sheet presence of "level 3" assets (assets for which prices cannot be inferred by either markets or models), and the size of the trading

concerns on its resolvability and systemic importance. An institution with a greater number of legally organized affiliates, perhaps engaged in diverse business activities, and may be located across geographic borders, presents enhanced challenges when orchestrating an orderly resolution. Likewise, complex structures are prone to knock-on effects; liquidation events can spread to multiple sub-industries within the financial sector as they propagate across the many affiliates of the organization. Finally, a complex organizational structure is a direct gauge of how complex regulation itself might be and therefore of the challenges to effective oversight of complex organizations.[2]

This paper is the first to provide a rich documentation of the evolution in organizational structure of US financial firms over the past 30 years. Using comprehensive data on the universe of US financial mergers and acquisitions, we track the process of consolidation and cross-industry acquisitions that led to a significant expansion in the complexity of banking institutions. Our study indicates that banks expanded into non-traditional bank business lines through acquisitions of already-formed specialized subsidiaries. Our investigation suggests that this process of organizational transformation is substantial and far-reaching, and not confined simply to the largest entities of today. The massive sequence of transactions was also surprisingly gradual and "hidden in plain sight"; given the regulated nature of BHCs, this process occurred with the explicit authorization of the regulator.

In the next section, we provide a theoretical rationalization for an organizational approach in both positive and normative analysis. In the third section, we present comprehensive panel data on merger and acquisition transactions that occur in the US financial sector over the last 30 years. In the fourth section, we illustrate our method of using transaction-level data to construct metrics of complexity for bank "families", matched to regulated BHCs. The fifth section describes our findings and our interpretation of the

---

and available-for-sale books. This is a more narrow definition of complexity, but it is likely to be captured adequately by metrics of the scope and diversity in business lines of the subsidiaries of an organization.

[2]This applies directly to the regulation of US bank holding companies (BHCs). The Federal Reserve is the regulator of BHCs. However, other agencies are the principal regulators for specific types of subsidiaries.

observable evolution in the complexity of BHCs. The sixth section draws concluding remarks.

A Rationale behind Increasing Bank Complexity

Our structural approach places the evolution of financial intermediaries within the context of the broader evolution of the financial intermediation industry. In a recent special issue of the *Economic Policy Review* (EPR, 2012),[3] Cetorelli, Mandel, and Mollineaux (2012) document that the mode of financial intermediation fundamentally changed over the last three decades. Today's securitization-driven model largely displaced yesterday's bank-centered model. The traditional bank-centered model, familiar from textbooks of banking, puts commercial banks as the central brokers between fund supply and fund demand. In this model of intermediation, the bank's balance sheet defines its organizational boundary by encapsulating all intermediation services and activities that characterize the banking firm. However, the advent of asset securitization changed the technology of intermediation. Pozsar *et al.* (2010) illustrate that the modern system of matching funding supply and demand takes place over longer *credit intermediation chains.* Intermediation services are no longer necessarily centered in a single, one-stop-shop, entity. Instead, highly specialized entities work in parallel and in sequence to fulfill the functions of the traditional intermediary. In this new setting, a traditional commercial bank is not as central. Financial intermediation thus evolves into a much more complex system of entities, markets, and activities, which has become better known as the *shadow banking* system. As we will demonstrate, however, banks have adapted by expanding their organizational boundaries. They have incorporated the newly specialized intermediaries through the holding company corporate form. No longer characterized by the original footprint of commercial banking activity, the nature of the banking firm is now better understood through the more expansive footprint of the BHC.[4] No longer

[3]"The Evolution of Banks and Financial Intermediation". The whole volume is available at http://www.newyorkfed.org/research/epr/2012/EPRvol18n2.pdf.

[4]In 2011, BHCs controlled about 38% of the assets of the largest (top 20) insurance companies, roughly 41% of total money market mutual fund assets, and approximately 93% of the assets of the largest (top 30) brokers and dealers (Cetorelli, 2012).

bundled within the bank, its activities spread across specialized parts of a vertical value-creation chain where each step contributes to the final creation of a security.

Informed by this framework, EPR (2012) recognizes the importance of the evolution of the industry in understanding the evolution of the intermediaries. Its analyses established that very little modern financial intermediation activity truly takes place outside and independently of banks, once one redefines the organizational boundaries of banking firms to include the broader perimeter of the BHC.

These are key insights in the debate around how shadow banking develops and what shadow banking really is. Understanding how and to what extent banks adapt to the changing model of intermediation through the organizational channel is central to developing strategies for effective monitoring and regulation of financial intermediation activity going forward.[5]

This paper builds on EPR (2012) by focusing on the changing banking firm itself. The data suggest that these changes are related to the industrial organization of the banking industry. We find that banking firms expanded within the banking industry in the early and mid-1990s. Subsequently, they expanded beyond banking to purchase other types of intermediaries, such as broker-dealers, insurance underwriters, and insurance brokers. It has long been recognized that the geographical deregulation of banking in the 1980s and 1990s spurred a consolidation wave within US banking. Our findings on the expansion by BHCs into more specialized parts of the financial system are less well documented. These expansions and changes in structure were strikingly widespread.

One hypothesis we would advance is that the *nature of the banking firm* changed in response to a marked evolution in the *technology and industrial organization of intermediation.* The gradual orientation of finance towards the production of marketable securities required a host of specialized services — loan origination, credit enhancements from insurance specialists, underwriting services of dealers, trust services, and others. A traditional bank had a choice: remain a small part of the value-creation chain, perhaps

[5]The Financial Stability Board, which has been heavily engaged in global monitoring and regulation of shadow banking activity, explicitly recognizes the role of BHCs in shadow banking activity (see, e.g., Financial Stability Board, 2013).

only engaged in originating loans, or retain integrated participation in many parts of finance by purchasing specialized firms that play specialized roles in the other parts of the chain. We posit the simple hypothesis that the technology of the value chain changed to favor the conglomerated-specialist model of finance. With a more sequenced chain of intermediation, the links between steps of engaging in finance crossed firm boundaries much more frequently, emphasizing market exchanges over internal bundling. However, these links introduced new informational transaction costs, and other frictions. Adapting to this new industrial environment, banks built large organizational structures that efficiently centralized sources of intermediation information, and could internalize benefits of cross-guarantees and the credit standing of the parent firm, and other efficiencies of the BHC structure. This conglomeration underpins the value-creation component of complexity.

Alternative hypotheses to explain our documented evolution include the hypothesis that financial firms expanded the breadth of their firms via the holding company structure because the passage of the Gramm–Leach–Bliley Financial Modernization Act (GLB Act) in 1999 allowed it. We will examine the timing of many of these changes in the course of our investigation, but even if the timing of the evolution immediately succeeded the passage of the GLB Act, one should ask what private benefits the firms were pursuing once the authority to expand their scope became available. Another potential hypothesis is that firms attempted to evade regulations or supervision. While plausible, this hypothesis strikes us as unlikely given that the acquisitions we observe in the dataset are among firms that are in the regulated sector. Further, many of these firms organize themselves as BHCs, which are supervised at the consolidated level by the Federal Reserve.

Our documentation of the changing structure of banking firms offers potential insights for the comparative evaluation of policy solutions to bank complexity problems. For instance, if much of the complexity build-up is a natural adaptation to a change in the technology and industrial organization of intermediation, then blunt fixes such as caps or break-ups may trade large and complex regulated entities for shadow entities outside the immediate scope of oversight. If, as we suspect, efficiencies of conglomeration in the face of demands for more specialized services drive complexity, then preserving their organizational structure but subjecting them to enhanced regulation may better address the tradeoffs associated with bank operations.

Acquisitions in the Financial Sector

How does the structure of the intermediation industry evolve over time? Which entities undertake significant organizational transformation? How diffuse is this process in the cross-section? When does it take place? We address these questions using SNL Financial's Mergers and Acquisitions (SNL M&A) database.

SNL captures the universe of US financial deals starting in 1983 and continuing to the present using numerous sources, including press releases, public filings, participant surveys, advisor surveys, and news searches. SNL's coverage tracks the emergence of new financial players involved in M&A activity, allowing us to track sector-wide growth in size and complexity.

We start by compiling a panel dataset of acquisitions. For each deal, SNL provides information on the buyer name,[6] the target name, the buyer industry, the target industry, the value, and the completion date. The database lacks a unique entity identifier, so we work with entity names.[7] We use SNL's general industry type variable to bin entities by industry. SNL classifies entities by the SIC code sourced from the SEC or FDIC. When missing or ambiguous, they internally assign an industry code based on major sources of revenue or underwriting operations. When available, SNL reports the nominal value of the deal, defined as the total consideration paid to the seller.

The SNL M&A raw database contains over 37,000 deals. We restrict our analysis to whole entity acquisitions completed before 2013. We drop a small number of observations that we identify as having uninformative participant names, such as "Private Investor", "Management Group", or "Mortgage Banking". We also filter out acquisitions in which

[6] SNL lists the ultimate parent of the actual acquirer as the buyer.

[7] To ensure names are unique within entity and to reduce potential coding errors, we clean all names by removing all special characters and capitalizing all letters.

a participant is not in the financial sector. Ten industry types remain — Bank, Asset Manager, Broker-Dealer, Financial Technology, Insurance Broker, Insurance Underwriter, Investment Company, Real Estate, Savings Bank/Thrift/Mutual,[8] and Specialty Lender. Finally, taking advantage of the fact that one entities appear multiple times, we fill in missing fields of an entity if those fields are unique and available elsewhere in the dataset.

In total, 19,532 deals meet these criteria. The data span 23,451 unique US entities (7,893 unique banks), with a total of 6,507 unique buyers, 18,402 unique targets, and 19,486 unique buyer-target pairs.

Deal value is available whenever disclosed, as is the case with all public acquisitions. These comprise 58% of the acquisitions in our dataset. For calculation purposes, we set the value to zero if missing. We rely on SNL to convert all non-dollar denominated values to USD using exchange rates at the completion date, though this conversion is infrequent due to the US-only nature of the SNL M&A database. We also normalize all deal values to 2012 dollars using the Consumer Price Index (CPI) for All Urban Consumers, All Items, Not Seasonally Adjusted. Since the CPI is only available monthly but our acquisition data is daily, we linearly interpolate to obtain an estimate of the CPI at the deal completion date.

To measure the total acquisition activity of entities, we construct two aggregates across all acquisitions in which the entity acts as the buyer. The first consists of the raw count of deals, while the second consists of the total sum of deal values.

Data Construction

Up until now, we have focused on acquisitions. However, this limits our ability to answer questions on the cumulative effects of acquisition activity. We therefore extend our analysis to studying entire organizations, or families, themselves. We consider a family to be the complete picture of a self-owned entity and all of its subsidiaries.

The term "family" lends itself to a host of other relevant terms for the structure of organizations. Figure 1 illustrates an example of a "family tree".

[8]Note the separation of Banks and Thrifts.

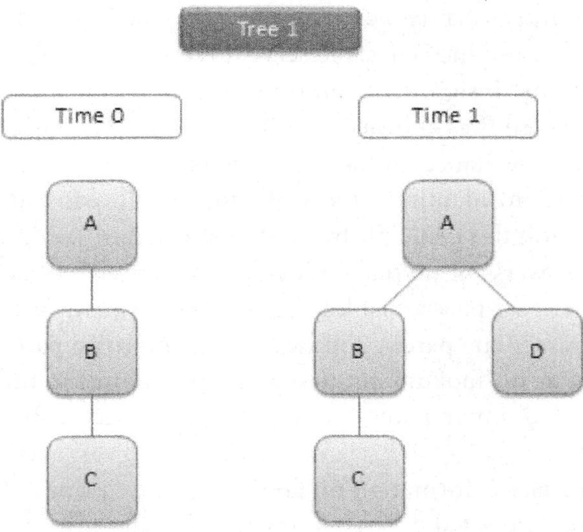

Fig. 1. Example of a family tree.

An entity within a family may have an "immediate parent", the direct owner, and an "ultimate parent", the highest owner in the family tree. For example, in Tree 1 at Time 0, A is the immediate parent of B and the ultimate parent of both B and C.

We use our information on acquisitions to assemble a family-level panel dataset. In our previous dataset, an observation is an acquisition, such as "A buys D". Our family-level dataset looks at an entire tree as an observation, such as "Tree 1 at Time 0".

We start with market data using the Center for Research in Security Prices (CRSP) US Stock Database, provided by Wharton Research Data Services. A key variable from this dataset is the PERMCO, a unique entity identifier that is consistent through time. To bring our previous discussion to the data, we define a family as any group of entities that share a PERMCO, thus restricting our sample to public families. We add in regulatory accounting data (including book value) from the FR Y-9C, the regulatory report filed by BHCs quarterly on a consolidated basis. To match to these databases, we add in four additional linking identifiers available from the SNL M&A dataset: The Ticker of the entity's primary exchange stock, the

CUSIP of the entity's primary exchange security, the Federal Reserve RSSD ID[9] of the entity, and the Federal Reserve RSSD ID of any BHC parent.

A fundamental insight that informed our data construction is that a family tree only requires knowledge of the immediate parent of each entity in the family. For instance, in the above picture, we only need "A owns B" and "B owns C" to identify "Tree 1 at Time 0". To construct our panel dataset, we exploit this principle by creating a separate "dictionary" dataset that lists the universe of unique entities in the cleaned SNL M&A dataset. We then create two new variables that track each entity's ownership — one for the immediate parent and one for the ultimate parent. This new dataset allows us to "lookup" entities at different points in time, using the immediate and ultimate parent variables to construct a snapshot of the family tree.

Because we lack information on family structure prior to SNL's acquisition coverage, we set the baseline owner of each entity to itself at the beginning of our data process. Further, in defining our family structures, we only include entities that are involved in an acquisition at some point in our sample period. In other words, our data limitations anchor our results to changes in complexity *relative to our baseline* and *through the acquisition channel exclusively*; we capture neither the structure before the start of the SNL M&A dataset nor changes through *de novo* entity creation.

Our primary algorithm updates the dictionary dataset by sequentially reading from the acquisition-level dataset described in the third section. As acquisitions occur, we replace the target's parent variables in the dictionary dataset. We first replace the immediate parent with the name of the buyer, reflecting the change in ownership.[10] We assume that whole acquisitions carry all previously acquired entities, so we also replace the immediate parent of all subsidiaries[11] of the target. Finally, we update the ultimate parent variable by tracing up the path of immediate parents.

[9]A unique identifier assigned by the Federal Reserve System to all financial institutions, main offices, and branches. RSSD IDs are the primary identifier for the FR Y-9C.

[10]Note that in replacing the previous immediate parent, we also capture sales.

[11]In all subsidiaries, we include subsidiaries of subsidiaries, subsidiaries of subsidiaries of subsidiaries, and so on.

To illustrate our approach, consider again the picture above. In the dictionary dataset at Time 0, "A owns B", "B owns C", and some entity (perhaps itself) owns D. When we read the deal "A buys D", we change D's immediate parent to A. At Time 1, we have "A owns B", "B owns C", and "A owns D". To identify the ultimate parent, we simply trace all entities back to A.

At each quarter-end, we aggregate the dictionary dataset from entity-level to ultimate parent-level, constructing a profile of variables that count the number of subsidiaries in each industry for each ultimate parent. We append all quarter-specific cross-sections to form the basis of our panel dataset.

Since we only capture changes in organizational structure through the acquisition channel, we may be concerned with important missing links across ultimate parents that do not appear in our data. To resolve this potential issue, we match all owners to their CRSP PERMCO and FR Y-9C RSSD ID at each quarter. This match restricts our sample to public FR Y-9C filers, but ensures a time consistent and regulatory-based definition of a banking family. As noted above, our data from SNL include neither PERMCO identifiers nor RSSD ID identifiers of the top regulatory filer. However, the SNL and CRSP datasets share Ticker and CUSIP variables, allowing a direct match to the PERMCO. Similarly, we use the other SNL-provided RSSD ID variables to match to the top regulatory filer of the FR Y-9C. As a final layer of robustness, we rely on the PERMCO-RSSD ID link dataset provided by the Federal Reserve Bank of New York to ensure proper identification of families.[12] We then aggregate any families with the same PERMCO as before, creating our final panel dataset.

To ensure our algorithm works as intended and correctly captures important acquisitions, we perform a variety of hand inspections using the raw SNL M&A database and the National Information Center (NIC) website.[13] For instance, because of its size and acquisition history, Bank

[12] If any of the identifier matches disagree, we use the link that appears most often. We have confirmed by hand that this reduces error more than throwing away data when links are ambiguous.

[13] For instance, to check for possible conceptual errors in our primary algorithm, we go through a similar exercise as in Fig. 1 with ABN AMRO.

of America offers a rich case study. We examine its history in detail, from NationsBank's buy of C&S/Sovran, Fleet's buy of Shawmut, BankAmerica's buy of Security Pacific, and the consolidation of NationsBank and Bank of America to the name we know today. Our database accurately covers all of these important acquisitions. Among other firms checked are Allco, BNY Mellon, Countrywide, Key, Regions, and Washington Mutual.

Note that the mapping from SNL's bank type industry variable to FR Y-9C filers is not one-to-one. Of the 1,028 unique RSSD IDs in our family-level dataset, approximately 85% are Banks and 15% are Thrifts. Wells Fargo achieves the highest bank consolidation count in 2008q4, totaling 361 Banks. By the end of the sample, Regions Financial Corporation maintains the highest measure at 193.

Our final datasets consists of 1,013 families spanning 1988q1 to 2012q4. This sample captures 22% of all FR Y-9C filers and 79% of all entities with a PERMCO-RSSD ID link. To provide a picture of size, in 2010q4, our sample totals 71% of the BVE from the FR Y-9C.

Analysis

As premised above, we operationalize bank complexity by measuring the extent to which an organization expands its "horizontal" structure, acquiring entities operating in different industries of the financial sector. We must stress that our approach only allows us to capture *incremental* levels of complexity from acquisition dynamics. We cannot capture *organic* growth in complexity (*de novo* entity creations), nor entities acquired before the start of our sample period, nor the purpose of the acquisitions. That said, our checks on the quality of our constructed family-level data establish that we capture a significant extent of the overall evolution in organizational structure of the largest BHCs.

Sector-wide dynamics

We begin by illustrating some of the characteristics of the original SNL Financial M&A database. As mentioned above, we partition the data into 10 industry types within the financial sector.

Table 1. Unique entities in acquisitions.

Industry	Total unique	Unique buyers	Unique targets
Bank	7,893	2,904	5,843
Savings bank/Thrift/Mutual	2,352	676	1,927
Asset manager	1,648	374	1,306
Broker-dealer	1,387	361	1,070
Financial technology	1,989	426	1,621
Insurance broker	3,682	504	3,237
Insurance underwriter	2,193	793	1,514
Investment company	64	40	27
Real estate	229	87	150
Specialty lender	2,014	342	1,707
Total	23,451	6,507	18,402

Source: Authors' calculations, based on data from SNL Financial.

Table 1 presents basic information about the population of acquisitions that take place over the sample period. The leftmost column lists each of the 10 industries within our dataset. The Total unique column presents the total number of unique entities across buyers and targets. The Unique buyers (Unique Targets) column presents the total number of unique buyers (targets).

The database allows us to identify 23,451 unique entities that appear at least once in acquisitions as buyers or targets over our sample period. Amongst industries, commercial banks account for about 34% of the population of unique entities, followed by insurance firms, thrifts, and specialty lenders. Of all these entity types, banks are by far the most involved in buying; 45% of unique buyers are banks and 37% of banks act as buyers at least once in our sample. They are also the largest represented as unique targets, although to a smaller extent. Table 1 gives a flavor of the overall scope in coverage of the database and the related dynamics in acquisitions. However, it cannot offer direct insights into the process of horizontal organizational expansion; in referring to buyers and targets, there is no distinction between whether the underlying participants were from the same or different industries.

Table 2 takes a different look at the same aggregate acquisition activity. It illustrates the extent to which each industry consolidates (same-type

Table 2. Entity Industries in Consolidation and Expansion.

Buyer industry	Target industry										
	Bank	Asset manager	Broker-dealer	Financial technology	Insurance broker	Insurance underwriter	Investment company	Real estate	Savings bank/ Thrift/ Mutual	Specialty lender	Total
Panel A: Types in acquisitions, by number (M USD)											
Bank	6,076	519	292	164	759	38	3	1	1,305	653	9,810
Savings bank/ Thrift/Mutual	359	45	28	8	115	21	—	2	705	138	1,421
Asset manager	2	459	38	110	27	24	6	17	1	51	735
Broker-dealer	6	127	613	78	59	9	4	9	6	42	953
Financial technology	2	13	23	1,123	60	8	—	—	—	13	1,242
Insurance broker	4	31	12	35	1,762	18	—	—	1	6	1,869
Insurance underwriter	14	138	55	126	533	1,451	—	4	18	54	2,393
Investment company	2	19	4	4	4	2	11	4	1	42	93
Real estate	1	3	3	—	—	1	—	111	1	10	130
Specialty lender	19	10	26	20	11	5	3	2	21	769	886
Total	6,485	1,364	1,094	1,668	3,330	1,577	27	150	2,059	1,778	19,532

(*Continued*)

Table 2. (*Continued*)

Buyer industry	Target industry										
	Bank	Asset manager	Broker-dealer	Financial technology	Insurance broker	Insurance underwriter	Investment company	Real estate	Savings bank/ Thrift/ Mutual	Specialty lender	Total
Panel B: Types in acquisitions, by value (M USD)											
Bank	5,983	43,512	173,952	18,083	3,297	16,783	1,127	333	203,243	276,048	2,142,361
Savings bank/ Thrift/Mutual	8,982	3,359	119	74	165	3,409	—	86	54,333	15,165	95,691
Asset manager	0	68,463	7,812	46,776	2,575	1,692	416	70,405	17	29,347	227,504
Broker-dealer	6,099	19,461	106,443	4,302	1,467	970	1,921	15,183	2,665	9,463	167,975
Financial technology	25	3,813	1,784	91,225	437	1,284	—	—	—	733	99,301
Insurance broker	10	41	41	5,346	21,359	244	—	—	11	1	27,054
Insurance underwriter	4,460	28,783	15,605	10,929	8,032	527,592	—	2,284	785	22,354	740,825
Investment company	0	654	18	6	129	5	2,657	4,669	19	4,120	12,276
Real estate	0	599	3	—	—	133	—	136,014	78	93	136,921
Specialty lender	110	1,904	2,006	1,884	62	1,824	393	416	848	73,561	83,008
Total	5,669	170,590	307,784	178,625	37,524	553,935	6,514	229,390	261,999	430,885	3,732,916

Source: Authors' calculations, based on data from SNL Financial.

entity deals) or expands (different-type entity deals). Panel A displays the total number of acquisitions; Panel B displays the aggregate real value of acquisitions. We organize each panel as a two-way matrix. The rows show the industry of the buyer while the columns show the industry of the target. Hence, the on-diagonal numbers represent within-industry consolidation, while the off-diagonal numbers represent cross-industry expansion.

We capture 19,532 acquisition events in our dataset. As indicated by the total number of on-diagonal events (13,070), the financial sector overall experiences a substantial amount of within-industry consolidation. Banks account for almost half of these transactions. Likewise, banks also capture the lion's share of off-diagonal acquisition activity; their 3,742 acquisitions constitute about 60% of the 6,462 total off-diagonal acquisitions. In some instances, banks acquire more entities of a certain type than entities of that same type. For example, banks acquire 519 asset managers, while asset manager entities acquire only 459 other asset managers. Regardless of target industry, the proportion of acquisitions by banks is high. For instance, banks are buyers in about 40% of all asset manager acquisitions, 26% of all broker dealer acquisitions, and 37% of all specialty lender acquisitions.

This summary table suggests the significance of the transformation of bank organizational structure over time. It also hints at how the structure changes with respect to entities in separate but related industries. Our conclusions do not change if we restrict our attention to the dollar value of these transactions (Table 2, Panel B). Indeed, off-diagonal acquisitions performed by banks also account for approximately 60% of the total value in off-diagonal acquisitions.

Who are the top buyers over the whole period? How much are they buying? Tables 3 and 4 exhibit the list of the top 50 buyers by count and value of acquisition, respectively. The top entities by number of acquisitions are three of the currently largest insurance brokers: Arthur J. Gallagher, Brown & Brown, and Hub International. As Table 3 shows, they acquired hundreds of entities, although almost exclusively consolidating within their own industry. Banks follow in the ranking, also displaying very large numbers of acquisitions, but with a more balanced distribution between bank and non-bank targets. Many of the banks at the lower end of the list fell to the mass of acquisition activity after geographic deregulation. Note that unlike the top acquirers in the Insurance Broker industry, those in the Insurance Underwriter industry appear to demonstrate considerable

Table 3. Top fifty buyers, by number.

Rank	Name	Industry	Value			Count		
				Consolidation	Expansion		Consolidation	Expansion
1	Arthur J. Gallagher & Co.	Insurance broker	3,314	3,249	65	249	245	4
2	Brown & Brown	Insurance broker	2,029	2,011	18	236	234	2
3	Hub International	Insurance broker	834	832	2	159	156	3
4	BB&T	Bank	19,989	15,291	4,697	142	23	119
5	Wells Fargo	Bank	50,566	48,577	1,989	138	34	104
6	Norwest	Bank	64,191	55,112	9,079	123	86	37
7	National Financial Partners Corp	Insurance broker	739	731	8	95	62	33
8	Bank of New York	Bank	29,062	22,661	6,401	76	4	72
9	Regions Financial Corporation	Bank	27,951	26,154	1,797	74	50	24
10	Union Planters	Bank	9,564	7,672	1,893	69	53	16
11	First American Corporation	Insurance underwriter	5,738	171	5,566	66	4	62
12	U.S. Bancorp	Bank	12,146	5,151	6,995	64	17	47
13	First Union	Bank	72,837	61,532	11,305	64	29	35
14	Stewart Information Services	Insurance underwriter	40	40	0	63	4	59
15	Goldman Sachs	Broker-dealer	13,725	10,020	3,705	60	10	50
16	SouthTrust	Bank	2,450	1,539	910	60	46	14
17	Marsh & McLennan Companies	Insurance broker	6,757	6,635	122	58	49	9
18	Compass Bancshares	Bank	2,524	2,375	149	55	41	14
19	Bank One Corporation	Bank	70,781	56,069	14,712	55	36	19
20	Citigroup	Bank	100,742	2,530	98,212	54	2	52

(*Continued*)

Table 3. (*Continued*)

Rank	Name	Industry	Value			Count		
				Consolidation	Expansion		Consolidation	Expansion
21	Community First Bankshares	Bank	1,004	983	21	53	26	27
22	Hibernia Corporation	Bank	2,006	1,678	327	51	40	11
23	First American Corporation	Insurance underwriter	178	175	3	50	3	47
24	PNC Financial Services	Bank	34,106	28,577	5,529	47	17	30
25	KeyBank	Bank	12,518	9,648	2,870	46	20	26
26	USI Holdings Corporation	Insurance broker	546	527	19	45	43	2
27	Wachovia	Bank	67,562	23,837	43,726	45	11	34
28	Zions Bancorporation	Bank	5,591	5,463	129	45	35	10
29	First Banks	Bank	1,141	801	340	43	31	12
30	American International Group	Insurance underwriter	59,147	58,330	817	42	22	20
31	Colonial BancGroup	Bank	2,970	2,348	622	42	31	11
32	SunGard	Financial technology	1,942	1,795	148	42	38	4
33	Fifth Third Bank	Bank	18,416	14,189	4,227	41	18	23
34	Synovus	Bank	2,503	1,994	509	41	29	12
35	Old National Bank	Bank	1,641	1,319	322	39	24	15
36	Aon plc	Insurance broker	8,359	3,297	5,063	39	31	8
37	JPMorgan Chase	Bank	85,253	75,001	10,251	38	2	36
38	Marshall & Ilsley	Bank	8,380	4,661	3,720	38	17	21
39	HCC Insurance Holdings	Insurance underwriter	1,339	811	528	37	10	27
40	Comerica	Bank	6,033	5,947	87	36	27	9

(*Continued*)

Table 3. (*Continued*)

Rank	Name	Industry	Value			Count		
				Consolidation	Expansion		Consolidation	Expansion
41	Fidelity National Financial	Insurance underwriter	6,857	2,145	4,712	36	8	28
42	FNB Corporation	Bank	2,135	1,883	252	36	17	19
43	Fiserv	Financial technology	6,533	5,992	541	35	28	7
44	Mercantile Bancorporation	Bank	7,078	4,910	2,169	35	23	12
45	National City Corp	Bank	26,288	20,778	5,509	34	11	23
46	Hilb, Rogal & Hobbs Co.	Insurance broker	380	380	0	34	33	1
47	LandAmerica Financial Group	Insurance underwriter	1,172	971	201	33	2	31
48	Commerce Bancshares	Bank	990	924	67	33	30	3
49	Willis Group	Insurance broker	1,920	1,888	32	33	32	1
50	Royal Bank of Canada	Bank	12,409	5,530	6,879	33	4	29

Source: Authors' calculations, based on data from SNL Financial.
Notes: Consolidation captures acquisitions in which the buyer and target have the same type. Expansion captures acquisitions in which the buyer and target have different types.

Table 4. Top fifty buyers, by value.

Rank	Name	Industry	Value			Count		
				Consolidation	Expansion		Consolidation	Expansion
1	Bank of America	Bank	187,572	87,208	100,364	16	3	13
2	NationsBank	Bank	138,702	135,166	3,535	23	12	11
3	Travelers Group	Insurance underwriter	137,466	5,892	131,573	8	1	7
4	Citigroup	Bank	100,742	2,530	98,212	54	2	52
5	JPMorgan Chase	Bank	85,253	75,001	10,251	38	2	36
6	First Union	Bank	72,837	61,532	11,305	64	29	35
7	Bank One Corporation	Bank	70,781	56,069	14,712	55	36	19
8	Wachovia	Bank	67,562	23,837	43,726	45	11	34
9	Capital One	Bank	66,804	22,434	44,370	12	2	10
10	Norwest	Bank	64,191	55,112	9,079	123	86	37
11	Blackstone Group	Asset manager	61,048	1,271	59,776	19	4	15
12	American International Group	Insurance underwriter	59,147	58,330	817	42	22	20
13	Chase Manhattan	Bank	58,120	45,275	12,845	26	4	22
14	Wells Fargo	Bank	50,566	48,577	1,989	138	34	104
15	Washington Mutual	Bank	50,347	320	50,027	27	4	23
16	Firstar Corporation	Bank	44,430	43,827	602	21	15	6
17	Fleet Financial Group	Bank	43,867	37,165	6,702	26	15	11
18	Berkshire Hathaway	Insurance underwriter	35,792	35,029	763	24	19	5
19	PNC Financial Services	Bank	34,106	28,577	5,529	47	17	30
20	HSBC	Bank	32,703	11,053	21,650	10	2	8

(Continued)

Table 4. (*Continued*)

Rank	Name	Industry	Value			Count		
				Consolidation	Expansion		Consolidation	Expansion
21	MetLife	Insurance underwriter	32,523	31,912	612	17	8	9
22	Toronto-Dominion Bank	Bank	29,866	14,567	15,299	21	5	16
23	Bank of New York	Bank	29,062	22,661	6,401	76	4	72
24	Kohlberg Kravis Roberts	Asset manager	29,002	0	29,002	6	0	6
25	Regions Financial Corporation	Bank	27,951	26,154	1,797	74	50	24
26	BlackRock	Asset manager	26,847	26,847	0	9	7	2
27	Anthem Inc.	Insurance underwriter	26,360	26,360	0	2	2	0
28	National City Corp	Bank	26,288	20,778	5,509	34	11	23
29	St. Paul Companies	Insurance underwriter	25,074	24,063	1,012	12	7	5
30	SunTrust Banks	Bank	24,070	23,019	1,051	32	13	19
31	Chemical Bank	Bank	23,610	23,610	0	13	11	2
32	ING Group	Insurance underwriter	23,270	16,628	6,642	20	4	16
33	UBS	Bank	22,775	0	22,775	17	0	17
34	Morgan Stanley	Broker-dealer	21,216	0	21,216	21	1	20
35	Credit Suisse	Bank	20,110	0	20,110	13	0	13
36	BB&T	Bank	19,989	15,291	4,697	142	23	119
37	UnitedHealth Group	Insurance underwriter	18,476	17,897	579	23	16	7
38	Fifth Third Bank	Bank	18,416	14,189	4,227	41	18	23
39	Deutsche Bank	Bank	18,398	13,055	5,342	13	1	12
40	Aegon	Insurance underwriter	18,274	17,923	352	10	7	3

(*Continued*)

Table 4. (*Continued*)

Rank	Name	Industry	Value			Count		
				Consolidation	Expansion		Consolidation	Expansion
41	First Bank System	Bank	17,646	16,123	1,523	22	14	8
42	Swiss Re	Insurance underwriter	17,108	16,967	140	16	14	2
43	Merrill Lynch	Broker-dealer	16,182	4,761	11,422	25	17	8
44	Conseco	Insurance underwriter	15,583	4,253	11,331	16	7	9
45	Banco Bilbao Vizcaya Argentaria	Bank	15,499	15,499	0	9	7	2
46	Dean Witter Discover	Broker-dealer	15,390	15,390	0	2	2	0
47	Household International	Specialty lender	14,610	14,421	189	13	6	7
48	Monte dei Paschi di Siena	Bank	13,898	13,898	0	1	1	0
49	Equity Office	Real estate	13,813	13,813	0	3	3	0
50	Goldman Sachs	Broker-dealer	13,725	10,020	3,705	60	10	50

Source: Authors' calculations, based on data from SNL Financial.
Notes: Consolidation captures acquisitions in which the buyer and target have the same type. Expansion captures acquisitions in which the buyer and target have different types.

diversification. Though not presented in the table, we examine these cases more carefully to find significant diversification into the Insurance Broker industry.

Interestingly, banks dominate the ranking by value. Table 4 captures the most active firms over time, irrespective of when the activity took place and whether the entities are still in operation. This time-independence is the reason NationsBank is second on the list, despite its current incarnation as Bank of America. The artifacts of bank acquisition activity indicate a compounding and progressive industry build-up. For instance, though Bank of America is highly diverse today, it inherited the previous evolution of NationsBank and Merrill Lynch. Likewise, Citigroup inherited part of its diversity from the previous activity of Travelers Group. The same holds for Wells Fargo from Wachovia (originally First Union) and Norwest; JPMorgan Chase from Bank One, Chase Manhattan, and Washington Mutual.

It is important to remark that the phenomenon of horizontal expansion is not confined to a small handful of entities. As the tables show, below the top-ranked acquirers, we observe significant off-diagonal acquisition counts.

Next, we provide documentation on the dynamics of acquisitions. Figure 2 shows pie charts of the composition of buyers by industry in four-year periods within our sample. Although the database shows mainly banks (and thrifts) as buyers in the late 1980s, the variation of buyer types steadily increases over time. By the second half of the 1990s, all industry types perform acquisitions. Likewise, the variety in target types increases gradually over time, with non-bank targets already representing the large majority in the second half of the 1990s (Fig. 3).

Figures 4 and 5 illustrate that the share in dollar value of acquisitions reflects the gradual process of expansion in industry types, although the relative prevalence of each industry by value differs somewhat from prevalence by count. For instance, there is a relatively large number of insurance broker entities that are either buyers or targets of acquisitions, but they account for a much smaller share of the overall value. Conversely, there are relatively fewer insurance underwriters involved in acquisitions, but they account for a larger share.

Figures 6–8 combine the count of acquisitions within and across industries. While the process of within-industry consolidation is important

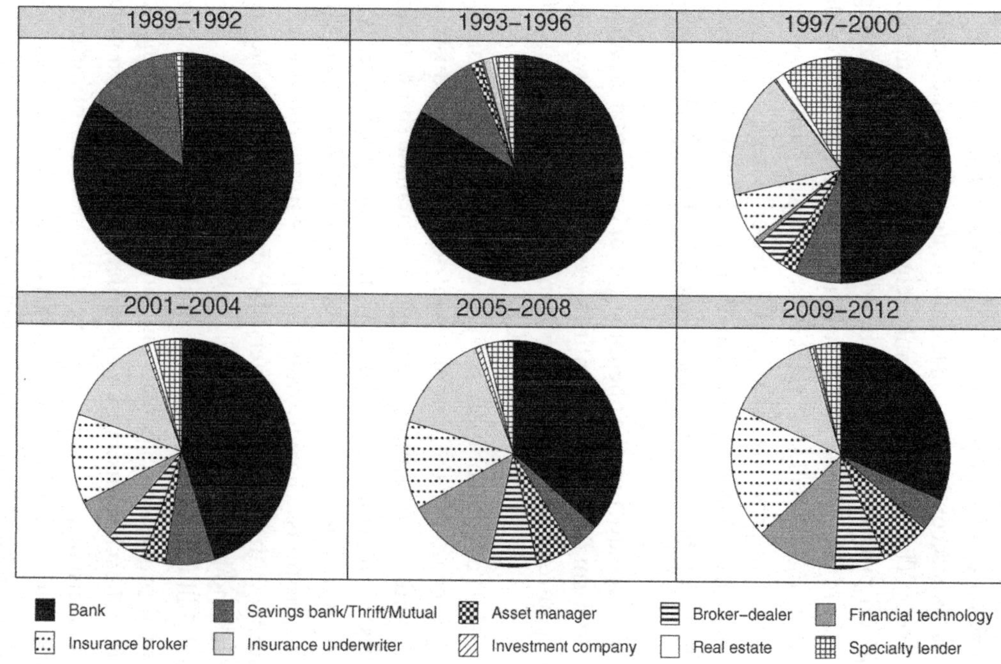

Fig. 2. Buyers in all acquisitions, by number.

Note: Figure 2 presents results on the composition of buyers by industry through time. Slices illustrate the proportional observation count of buyer types for all sample deals in each four-year period.

Source: Authors' calculations, based on data from SNL financial.

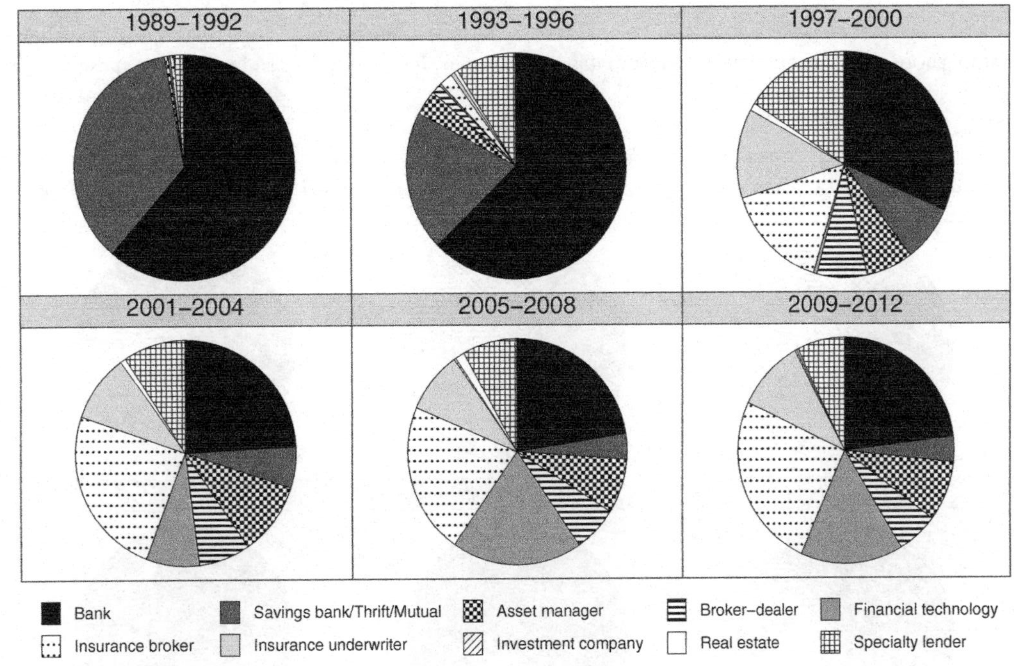

Fig. 3. Targets in all acquisitions, by number.
Note: Figure 3 presents results on the composition of targets by industry through time. Slices illustrate the proportional observation count of target types for all sample deals in each four-year period.

Source: Authors' calculations, based on data from SNL financial.

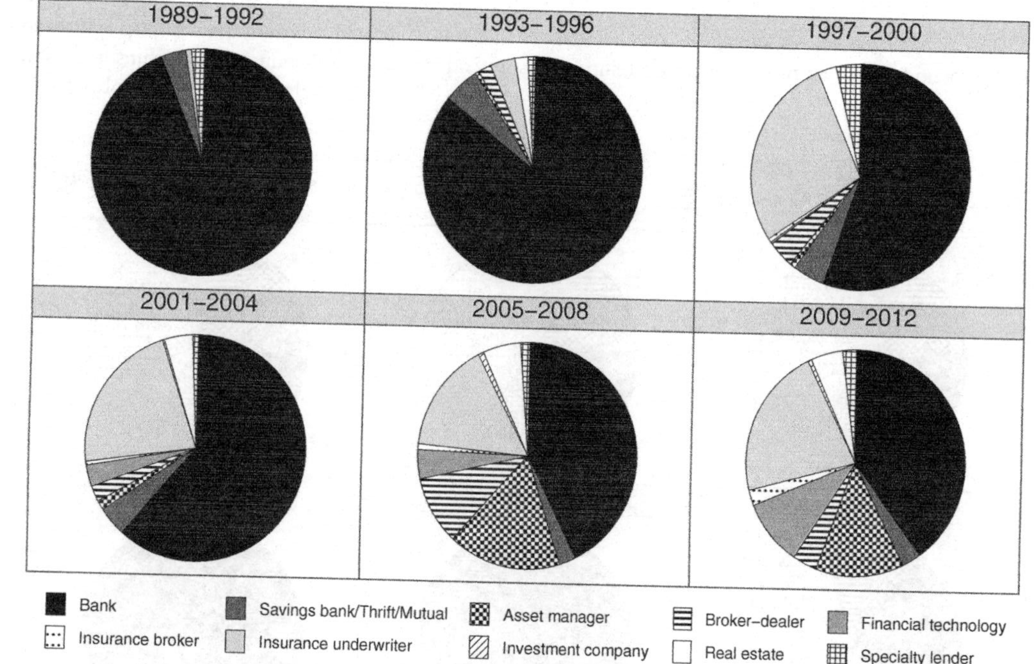

Fig. 4. Buyers in all acquisitions, by value.
Note: Figure 4 presents results on the composition of buyers by industry through time. Slices illustrate the proportional deal value (if available) of buyer types for all sample deals in each four-year period.

Source: Authors' calculations, based on data from SNL financial.

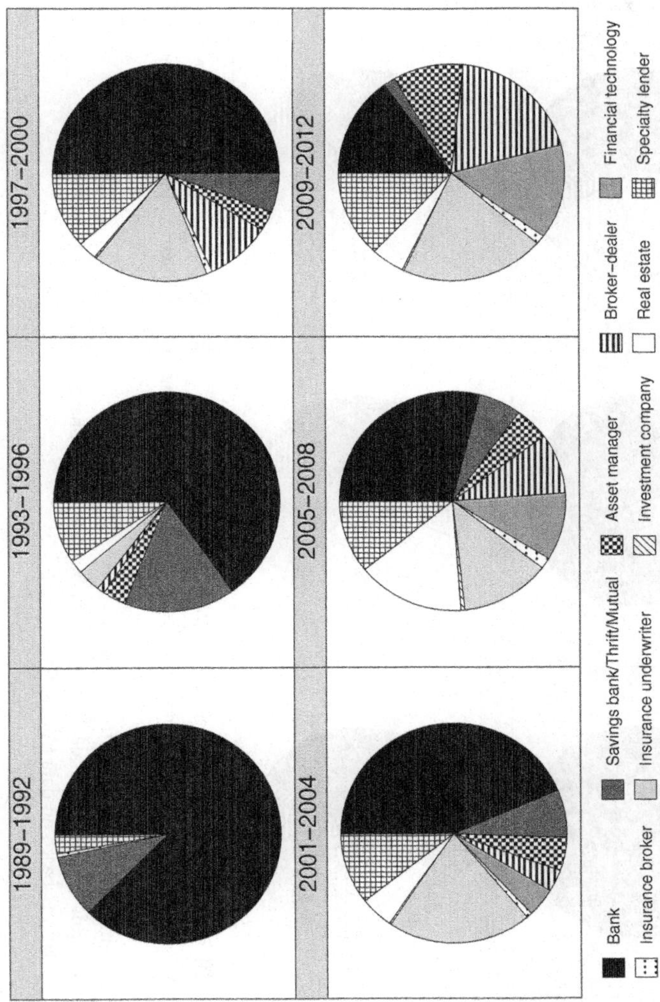

Fig. 5. Targets in all acquisitions, by value.

Note: Figure 5 presents results on the composition of targets by industry through time. Slices illustrate the proportional deal value (if available) of target types for all sample deals in each four-year period.

Source: Authors' calculations, based on data from SNL financial.

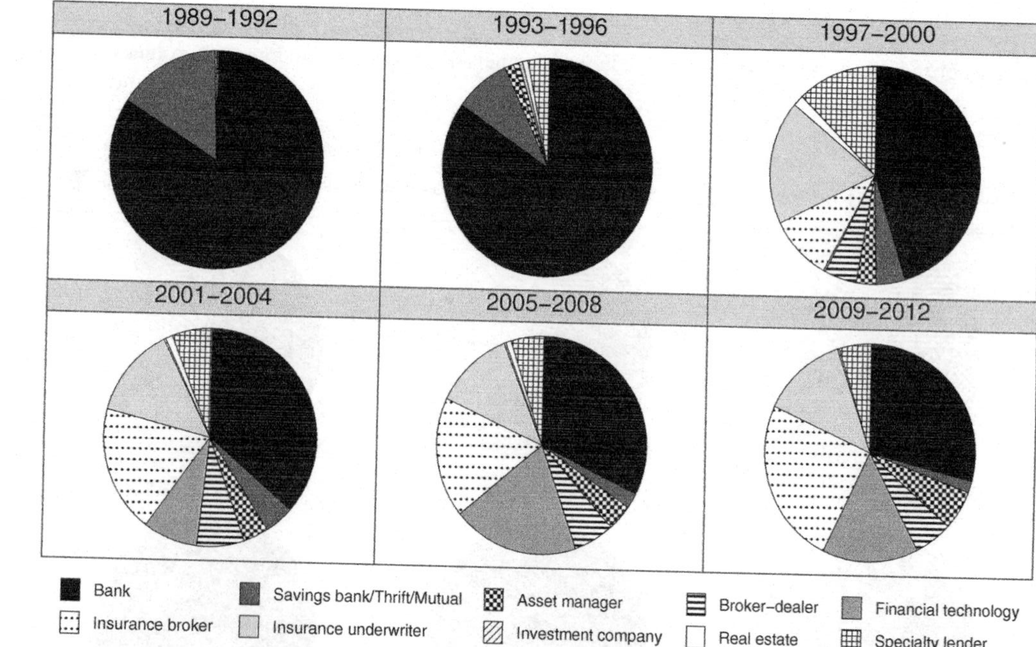

Fig. 6. Types in same-industry acquisitions, by number.
Note: Same-industry acquisitions represent deals in which the buyer and target have the same type (on-diagonal).
Source: Authors' calculations, based on data from SNL financial.

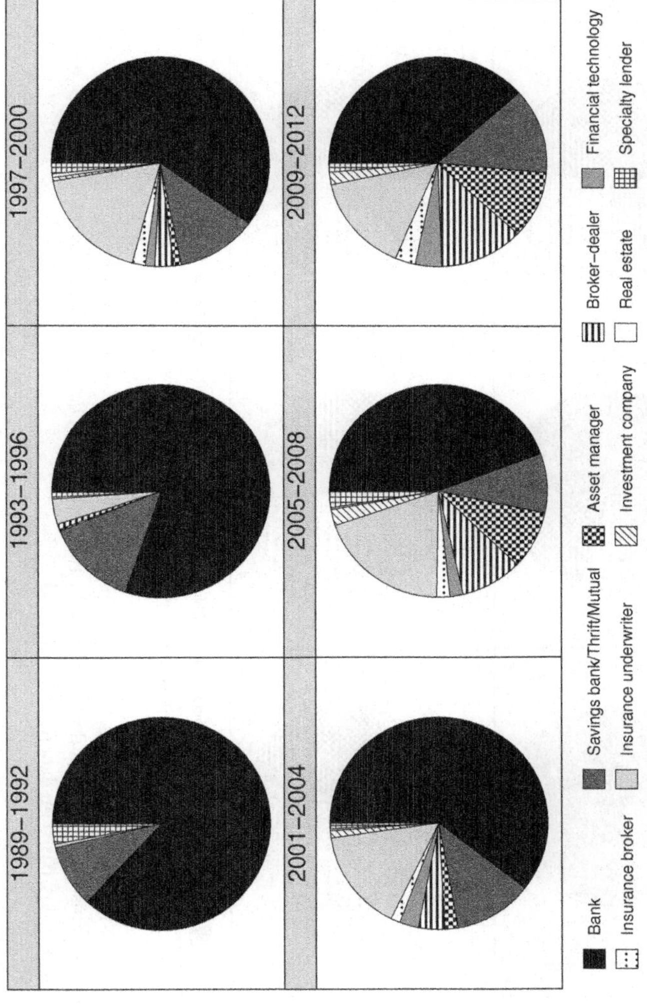

Fig. 7. Buyers in cross-industry acquisitions, by number.
Note: Cross-industry acquisitions represent deals in which the buyer and target have different types (off-diagonal).
Source: Authors' calculations, based on data from SNL financial.

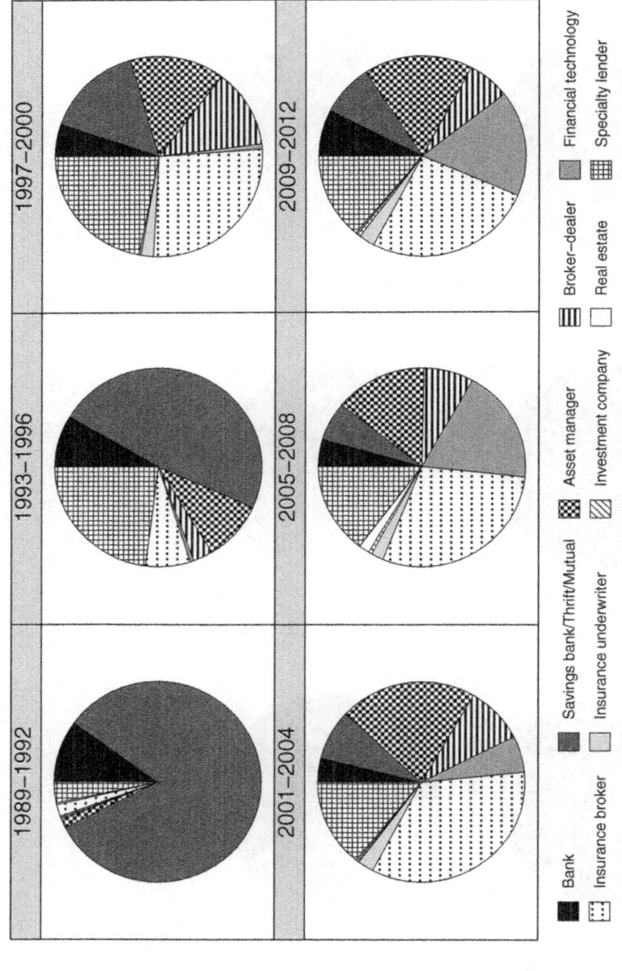

Fig. 8. Targets in cross-industry acquisitions, by number.
Note: Cross-industry acquisitions represent deals in which the buyer and target have different types (off-diagonal).
Source: Authors' calculations, based on data from SNL financial.

in itself, for our purposes, we want to maintain focus on organizations expanding to other industries within the financial sector. To this end, it is useful to report the breakdown of acquisition activity (for buyers and targets) separating on-diagonal and off-diagonal counts. Figure 6 shows that within-industry consolidation takes place quite diffusively across the various industries. Although banks dominated the activity during the geographic deregulation of the mid-1990s, there is considerable consolidation across the other industries as well, continuing into the present.

Figures 7 and 8 confirm and reinforce the message of the previous ones, which is that during our sample period the financial sector as a whole was reorganizing over time. Banks were buying non-banks, but not to the exclusion of substantial cross-industry acquisitions of other entity types. Moreover, targets were not concentrated in any particular industry, suggesting that the development was not driven by any particular industry-specific factors. Rather, it indicates a diffused transformation of the intermediation industry, with a progressive expansion of the organizational boundaries of intermediation firms.

Bank-specific dynamics

We shift our focus to banks themselves and follow their evolution. We start with a specific examination using the same deal data as above. Later in the paper, we present details of bank evolution from a family perspective, aggregating entities up at the family (BHC) level.

The next chart (Fig. 9) goes into the specifics of the off-diagonal evolution in bank organizational structure. Besides the substantial acquisition of thrifts in the early part of the period, the data denotes how banks expanded their footprint gradually. Banks proceeded first with the acquisition of entities that are arguably closer to their traditional mode of operations — specialty lenders and asset managers, both specialized intermediaries that increased their roles once securitization-based intermediation became more prevalent. The expansion progressed naturally with the incorporation of brokers and dealers later in the sample period. These entities rose in importance with the trading of a progressively increasing stockpile of securities created through asset securitization (Cetorelli and Peristiani, 2012). Moreover, the process continued by incorporating firms in insurance and financial technology, mostly firms offering payment-related services.

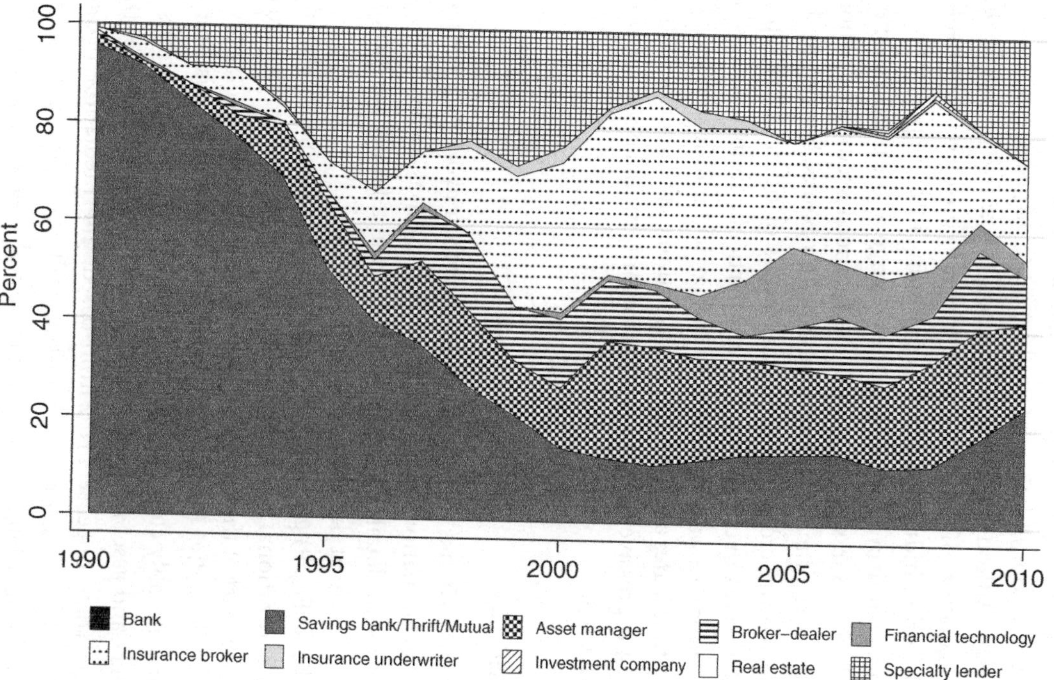

Fig. 9. Non-bank targets of bank buyers (share).
Note: Vertical cross-sections illustrate the average share of target by type in a given quarter.
Source: Authors' calculations, based on data from SNL financial.

Figure 10 instead displays the actual counts, rather than shares, of acquisition types through time. It shows that the process of expansion remained active throughout the period, perhaps slowing down only in the post-crisis years.

Evolution in bank families, or organizational changes in BHCs

The entity-level analysis in the previous subsection already gives a good indication of the evolution in complexity of US banking firms. However, maintaining the focus on individual entities actually understates the extent to which bank organizational boundaries really expand. Entity-level analysis misses the process of merging, changes in names, and branching into multiple levels of affiliation. As a result, entity, rather than family, analysis leaves us blind to the actual size and composition of entity families. For example, in Table 4, Bank of America and NationsBank are the first and second highest ranked entities by acquisition value. However, these entities are truly the same; most of NationsBank's history will fold into Bank of America upon creation. Within this new entity are many entities acquired along the way, perhaps representing a diversified portfolio, perhaps a hyper-focused industry giant. To track complexity accurately through time, we require a picture of the same entity's organization before and after the deal.

As explained in the fourth section, our methodology allows us to combine and track overall complexity, as captured by the amount and type of performed acquisitions (and sales). This build-up takes place within the walls of a banking family, defined by aggregating the information of individual entities under a common highest holder identifier.

What does the typical BHC family look like? How does its structure evolve over time? Figure 10 attacks these questions by depicting the evolution of organizational profiles in our sample. The typical BHC changed significantly over time. A BHC family was identified by having mostly commercial banks and thrifts subsidiaries in the early 1990s. However, the organizational boundaries expanded significantly starting in the mid-1990s, as BHCs began adding an increasing number of non-bank subsidiaries (Fig. 11).

We display the aggregate of this process in the cross-section. Table 5 shows snapshots of family complexity taken in a given year, capturing

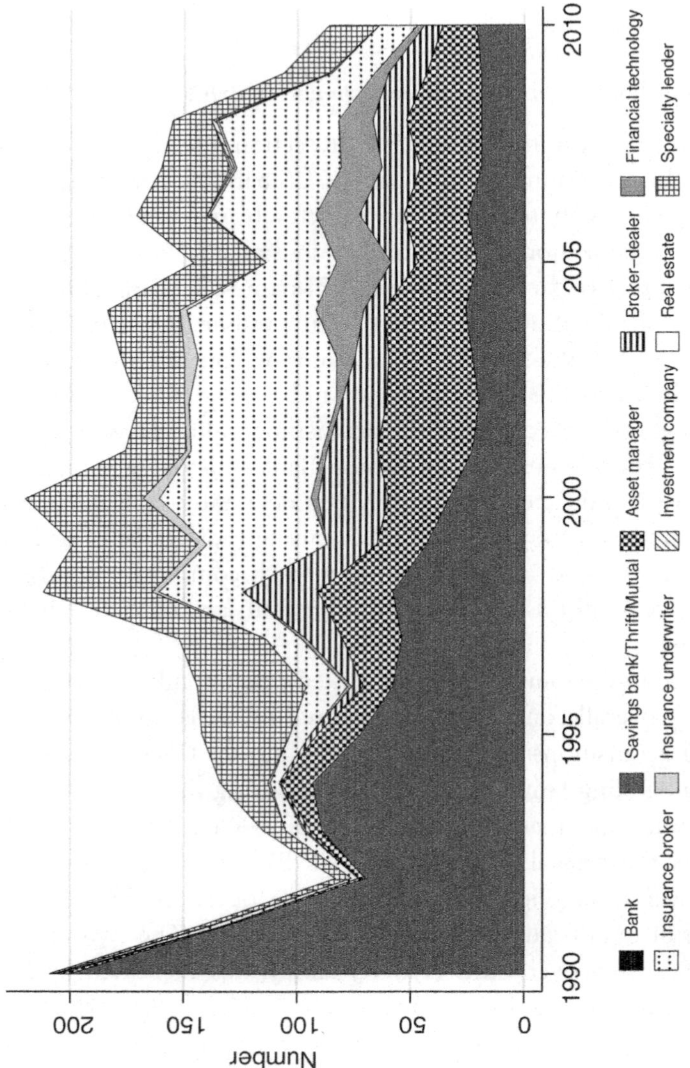

Fig. 10. Non-bank targets of bank buyers (number).
Note: Vertical cross-sections illustrate the average number of targets by type in a given quarter.
Source: Authors' calculations, based on data from SNL financial.

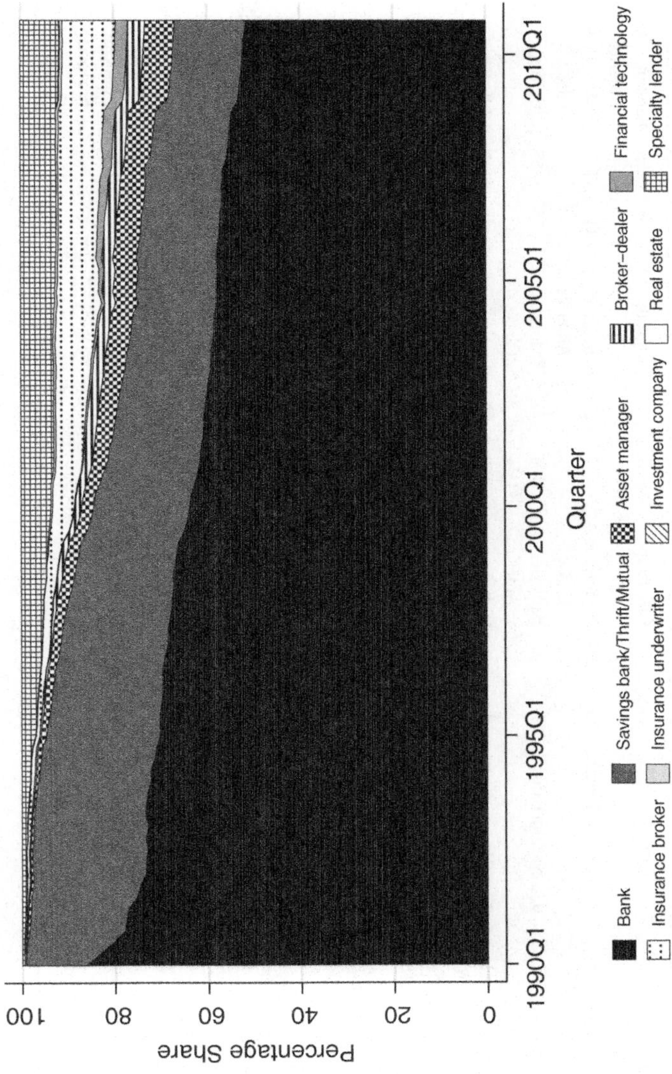

Fig. 11. Organizational evolution.
Note: Vertical cross-sections illustrate the average share of types within a bank family in a given quarter.
Source: Authors' calculations, based on data from SNL financial.

Table 5. Top fifty families by size and time.

	1990			1995			2000			2005			2010		
Rank	Name	Banks	Non-banks	Name	Banks	Non-banks	Name	Banks	Non-banks	Name	Banks	Non-banks	Name	Banks	Non-banks
1	Citi	6	1	Citi	5	2	Citigroup	1	37	Citigroup	6	59	Bank of America	117	166
2	BankAmerica	3	10	BankAmerica	16	28	JPMorgan Chase	17	25	Bank of America	114	113	JPMorgan Chase	81	97
3	Chase Manhattan	1	0	NationsBank	17	3	Bank of America	104	77	JPMorgan Chase	75	65	Citigroup	5	108
4	JPMorgan	1	0	JPMorgan	1	1	Wells Fargo	194	80	Wachovia	138	117	Wells Fargo	305	244
5	Security Pacific Corp	10	7	Chemical Banking	18	7	Bank One	74	20	Wells Fargo	211	119	Goldman Sachs	0	89
6	Chemical Banking	18	2	First Chicago NBD	1	0	First Union	73	77	MetLife	1	9	Morgan Stanley	0	25
7	NCNB	5	0	Bankers Trust New York	1	0	FleetBoston Financial	45	47	U.S. Bancorp	116	83	MetLife	1	22
8	Bankers Trust New York	1	0	First Union	22	25	SunTrust Banks	11	23	SunTrust Banks	12	34	US Bancorp	126	96
9	Manufacturers Hanover	1	0	Banc One	60	13	US Bancorp	77	53	Countrywide Financial Corporation	1	4	PNC Financial Services Group	69	117
10	C&S/Sovran	1	0	Fleet Financial Group	25	21	Key	26	20	National City	31	54	Bank of NY Mellon	6	98
11	First Interstate Bancorp	7	0	PNC Bancorp	14	10	Firstar	0	1	BB&T	105	161	Capital One Financial Corporation	54	41

(*Continued*)

Table 5. (*Continued*)

	1990			1995			2000			2005			2010		
Rank	Name	Banks	Non-banks	Name	Banks	Non-banks	Name	Banks	Non-banks	Name	Banks	Non-banks	Name	Banks	Non-banks
12	First Chicago	3	0	Norwest	65	18	Bank of New York Company	5	32	Fifth Third Bancorp	47	53	SunTrust Banks	25	41
13	PNC Financial	4	0	Key	26	12	PNC Financial Services Group	14	16	Bank of New York Company	5	59	State Street	2	26
14	Bank of New York Company	3	0	First Interstate Bancorp	23	4	State Street	1	8	State Street	1	15	BB&T	112	190
15	Banc One	16	5	Bank of New York Company	5	1	BB&T	55	89	Key	28	27	American Express Co	0	12
16	First Union	15	1	National City	12	6	Mellon Financial	20	19	PNC Financial Services Group	21	26	Regions Financial Corporation	191	163
17	SunTrust Banks	1	0	Bank of Boston	11	9	Fifth Third Bancorp	27	39	Capital One Financial Corporation	45	22	Fifth Third Bancorp	55	69
18	Bank of Boston	2	1	SunTrust Banks	6	2	SouthTrust	47	12	Regions Financial Corporation	158	70	Key	30	31
19	Fleet/Norstar Financial	4	1	Barnett Banks	7	9	Regions Financial Corporation	83	28	MBNA	0	6	Northern Trust	6	11
20	Barnett Banks	4	5	Mellon Bancorp	5	8	Comerica	25	9	North Fork Bancorp	8	17	M&T Bank	27	34

(*Continued*)

Table 5. (*Continued*)

Rank	1990 Name	1990 Banks	1990 Non-banks	1995 Name	1995 Banks	1995 Non-banks	2000 Name	2000 Banks	2000 Non-banks	2005 Name	2005 Banks	2005 Non-banks	2010 Name	2010 Banks	2010 Non-banks
21	Norwest	10	2	Comerica	24	10	Summit Bancorp	6	7	Comerica	23	10	Discover Financial	0	3
22	First Fidelity Bancorp	2	1	First Bank System	27	10	AmSouth Bancorp	33	17	Northern Trust	6	9	Comerica	23	10
23	Mellon Bancorp	2	0	Boatmen's Bancshares	29	7	MBNA	0	3	AmSouth Bancorp	30	75	Huntington Bancshares	51	34
24	Continental Bank	3	0	CoreStates Financial	6	5	Charles Schwab	3	14	Popular	15	9	CIT Group	0	21
25	NBD Bancorp	1	0	State Street Boston	1	2	Northern Trust	6	6	Charles Schwab	3	19	Zions Bancorp	55	17
26	Society	2	0	First of America Bank Corp	7	11	Union Planters Corporation	78	33	Zions Bancorp	50	17	Marshall & Ilsley	32	34
27	National City	2	1	SouthTrust	28	6	Charter One Financial	4	15	Mellon Financial	23	36	New York Community	5	12
28	Shawmut National	3	3	Southern National	6	31	M&T Bank	14	18	Commerce Bancorp	4	14	Popular	18	10
29	CoreStates Financial	2	0	Huntington Bancshares	20	8	Huntington Bancshares	33	11	First Horizon National	9	28	Synovus Financial Corp	29	15
30	Midlantic	4	0	Northern Trust	4	3	Popular	14	5	Huntington Bancshares	34	13	First Horizon National	9	29
31	Bank of New England	1	0	Firstar	1	1	Old Kent Financial Corporation	14	12	Compass Bancshares	45	14	BOK Financial Corporation	20	2

(*Continued*)

Table 5. (*Continued*)

Rank	1990 Name	1990 Banks	1990 Non-banks	1995 Name	1995 Banks	1995 Non-banks	2000 Name	2000 Banks	2000 Non-banks	2005 Name	2005 Banks	2005 Non-banks	2010 Name	2010 Banks	2010 Non-banks
32	Key	8	1	Crestar Financial Corporation	4	16	Zions Bancorp	35	9	Synovus Financial Corp	27	14	Associated Banc-Corp	25	7
33	First Bank System	8	3	AmSouth Bancorp	10	8	Compass Bancshares	45	4	New York Community	2	7	First Niagara Financial	8	34
34	Boatmen's Bancshares	2	1	Fifth Third Bancorp	9	7	First Tennessee National	10	15	Associated Banc-Corp	24	7	First Citizens Bancshares	14	16
35	First of America Bank Corp	5	3	Mercantile Banc	16	9	Banknorth Group	25	16	Colonial BancGroup	31	13	East West Bancorp	10	3
36	Comerica	13	4	UJB Financial	3	4	Hibernia	44	12	First Bancorp	7	6	TCF Financial Corporation	2	11
37	UJB Financial	2	0	BanPonce	4	2	National Commerce	18	25	Webster Financial	24	30	Webster Financial	21	32
38	Manufacturers National	5	1	Meridian Bancorp	9	4	GreenPoint Financial Corp	0	6	Doral Financial	1	1	Cullen/Frost Bankers	19	12
39	Meridian Bancorp	2	1	GreenPoint Financial Corp	0	3	Provident Financial	4	12	Mercantile Bancshares	16	10	SVB Financial Group	2	4
40	Crestar Financial Corporation	2	2	Integra Financial	2	3	North Fork Bancorp	5	15	BOK Financial Corporation	18	2	Fulton Financial	26	13

(*Continued*)

Table 5. (*Continued*)

	1990			1995			2000			2005			2010		
Rank	Name	Banks	Non-banks	Name	Banks	Non-banks	Name	Banks	Non-banks	Name	Banks	Non-banks	Name	Banks	Non-banks
41	Huntington Bancshares	4	1	Regions Financial Corporation	11	8	Pacific Century Financial Corporation	8	2	W Holding Company	2	1	First Bancorp	9	8
42	Northern Trust	1	1	MBNA	0	1	Associated Banc-Corp	14	1	Sky Financial Group	12	17	Valley National Bancorp	16	14
43	State Street Boston	1	0	Bancorp Hawaii	3	2	Colonial BancGroup	26	11	First Citizens	9	16	FirstMerit	4	11
44	Signet Banking	1	0	First Security	14	4	People's Mutual Holdings	2	5	South Financial Group	25	15	Wintrust Financial Corporation	10	10
45	Ameritrust	1	1	First Tennessee National	12	10	Centura Banks	18	17	Commerce Bancshares	28	6	Susquehanna Bancshares	16	27
46	Michigan National	4	1	BayBanks	5	2	TCF Financial Corporation	2	8	TCF Financial Corporation	2	10	BankSouth	29	18
47	Bancorp Hawaii	3	1	Old Kent Financial Corporation	4	3	Commerce Bancshares	28	5	Valley NBC	9	12	Bank of Hawaii	8	2
48	Valley National	1	0	First Empire State	3	4	First Citizens Bancshares	6	15	Fulton Financial	22	11	PrivateBancorp	5	2
49	Dominion Bancshares	1	0	Union Planters Corporation	33	7	FirstMerit	3	9	Investors Financial	1	3	UMB Financial Corporation	19	14
50	BayBanks	2	0	Signet Banking	3	2	BOK Financial Corporation	13	2	Cullen/Frost Bankers	15	8	Franklin Resources	0	13

Source: Authors' calculations, based on data from SNL Financial; Federal Reserve System, Form FR Y-9C, Schedule HC.

the number of both bank and non-bank entities amassed through the acquisition channel by the top 50 BHC families (ranked by total assets) up to that year. BHCs in the early 1990s were relatively simple in terms of organizational structure. Among the top 10 in 1990, only BankAmerica Corporation, back then a holding company headquartered in San Francisco, CA, had performed 10 non-bank acquisitions, and Security Pacific Corporation had performed 7. Among the remaining in the top 50, Bank One and Barnett had performed 5 non-bank acquisitions each. Five years later already, the picture was quite different. The number of acquisitions is much higher, both within and across industries. Some families from 1990 disappear from the subsequent list as they got absorbed by surviving ones (Security Pacific for instance, was acquired by BankAmerica Corp.).

The BHC organizational profiles only increase in complexity as time goes by, with very large numbers of entities that are wrapped under common ownership and control. Moreover, the lists indicate that the process takes place across institutions, and it is not a phenomenon that is confined to just the largest entities.

Another way to capture the sector-wide transformation is to look at time series metrics of BHC structures. Figure 12, for instance, displays

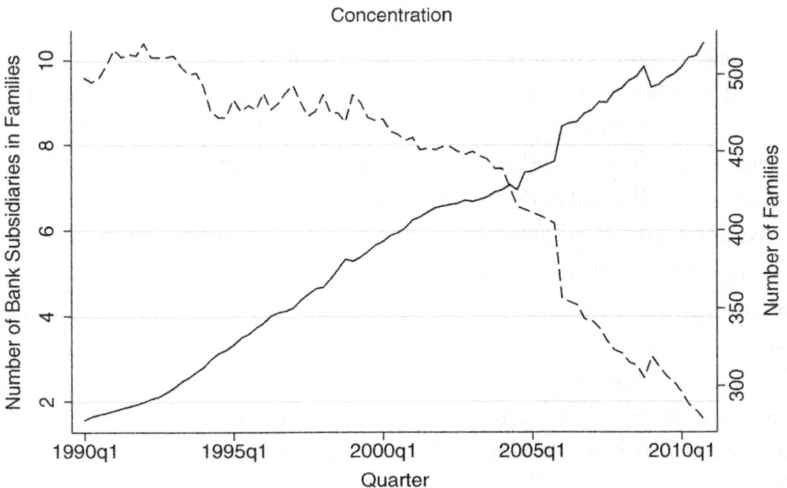

Fig. 12.
Notes: The solid line the average number of banks acquired and kept within a family. The dashed line illustrates the total number of families in a given quarter.
Source: Authors' calculations, based on data from SNL financial.

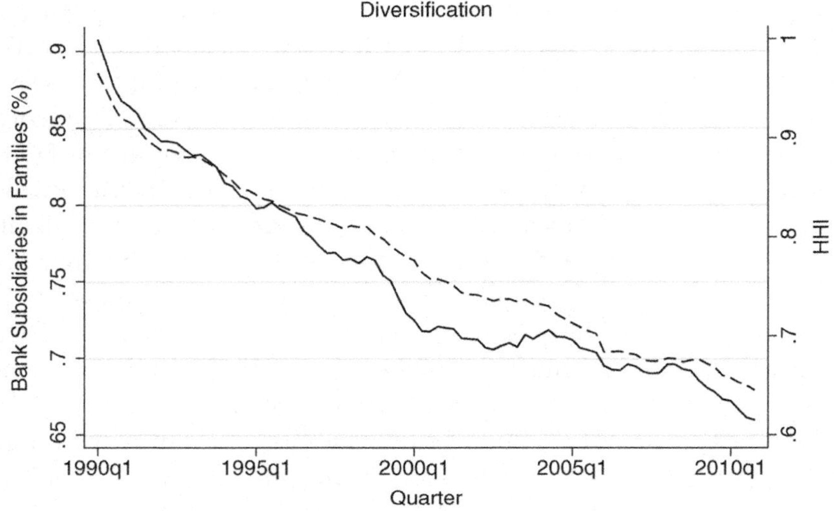

Fig. 13.
Notes: The solid line illustrates the share (by count) of banks in family organizational profiles. The dashed line represents the average Herfindahl–Hirschman Index calculated across the 10 types of bank families.
Source: Authors' calculations, based on data from SNL financial.

the average number of commercial banks that were acquired and that are kept within a family in a given year. This number, not surprisingly, steadily increases, again reflecting the process of geographic deregulation and consequent consolidation (also reflected in the steady decrease in the total number of families, also depicted in the figure). Figure 13, however, shows the average number of acquired commercial bank subsidiaries divided by the total number of acquired subsidiaries. This ratio is steadily declining over time, going from almost 1 at the beginning of the period to about 0.65 toward the end. The count of non-bank acquisitions could still not show true expansion across industries. For instance, BHCs could have performed many acquisitions that were concentrated in just one non-bank industry. In order to capture the extent of broad horizontal expansion, we calculate a Herfindahl index of industrial concentration. This index is 1 if the BHC only has commercial banks and smaller than 1 if the BHC acquires non-bank subsidiaries. Further, it progressively decreases the more "diverse" the acquisition profile among the 10 industries. In the same figure, we report the average HHI of BHC families over time. The steady downward trend does indicate a push toward broad expansion in organizational boundaries.

Conclusions

The evolution in the structure of financial firms can be summarized by four key observations. First, BHCs have become less bank-centric by expanding the types of their subsidiaries. Second, this phenomenon was very widespread. Third, financial firms other than BHCs also expanded their scope. Finally, BHCs expanded by adding additional banks to their firm in the early and mid-1990s. As we discussed earlier, there are several hypotheses that might be consistent with those observations. First, it appears that the geographic deregulation of banking in the US led to significant changes in the structure of banking markets (not covered in our paper, but this has been studied extensively) and BHCs, as they expanded their bank franchise across previously impenetrable geographic borders. Second, the GLB act may have also allowed BHCs to expand into activities from which they previously had been excluded, such as brokering and dealing.

While regulatory changes may have allowed firms to evolve in the ways we describe, it is unlikely that deregulation fully explains the changes. Instead, some other changes in the underlying technology of, or in the demand for, financial intermediation seem to be required to explain such widespread and thoroughgoing changes in the industry. Here again, there may be several possible candidates. For instance, it may be that the more geographically expansive nature of business enterprises gave rise to an increased demand for cross-border banking, both within the US and overseas. That could have provided an impetus to the bank acquisition wave we observe early in our sample. An alternative hypothesis is that specialized firms, whose contributions to finance are to add value along a chain of financial engineering that operates externally to any particular firm, are now more efficient than generalist firms, who build an integrated value chain internally. This hypothesis could be supplemented with one that accounts for the conglomerated form of the acquisitions of specialist firms by increasingly large BHCs. For example, information and credit frictions may be more difficult to overcome for isolated specialist firms, but more manageable with assistance from internal capital markets in larger firms. Our results are consistent with this move toward a model of finance oriented toward securitization. The hypothesis itself may be dependent on the long-term and ongoing revolutions in information technology and communications that have allowed more quantification of financial information and have improved the ability to communicate and manage that information. In that sense, Occam's razor may not apply: Complexity is a necessary adaptation by banking firms to remain viable organizations in a changing industry.

Is this evolution good or bad? Is posing a question in these terms even the right thing to do? The financial crisis of 2007–2009 raises concerns about the very existence of super-sized institutions. Why does society need incredibly large and complex banking institutions when they are a potential cause of systemic disruption? Possible "subsidies" from explicit or perceived government guarantees may distort incentives in failure resolution. Size and complexity may also lead to complicated and ineffective monitoring, such as duplication of rules or regulation that is too strict (or too weak!). Likewise, policy measures designed by hatchet or scalpel may add undesirable market distortions.

Regardless of the causes, the changes documented in this paper are clearly important across a number of dimensions. First, they highlight the expanded scope and complexity of individual firms. Second, they suggest that the industrial organization of finance is changing profoundly. Market interactions among more numerous and more specialized firms have displaced the prior organization of generalized firms engaged in most stages of finance using internal resources. Third, the increasingly less bank-centric the BHCs are, the more important the consolidated supervision of the BHCs and the cooperation among the larger set of functional regulators becomes.

References

Cetorelli, N. (2012). A Principle for Forward-Looking Monitoring of Financial Intermediation: Follow the Banks! Federal Reserve Bank of New York. *Liberty Street Economics Blog.*

Cetorelli, N. and S. Peristiani (2012). The Role of Banks in Asset Securitization. Federal Reserve Bank of New York. *Economic Policy Review*, Vol. 18, No. 2 (July), pp. 47–63.

Cetorelli, N., B.H. Mandel and L. Mollineaux (2012). The Evolution of Banks and Financial Intermediation: Framing the Analysis. Federal Reserve Bank of New York. *Economic Policy Review*, Vol. 18, No. 2 (July), pp. 1–12.

Financial Stability Board (2013). Global Shadow Banking Monitoring Report. Available at http://www.financialstabilityboard.org/publications/r_131114.htm [accessed on January 8, 2014].

Pozsar, Z., T. Adrian, A. Ashcraft and H. Boesky (2010). Shadow Banking. Federal Reserve Bank of New York. Staff Reports, No. 458, July.

IV
Implications for Financial Stability

Financial Stability Policies for Shadow Banking

Tobias Adrian*

Federal Reserve Bank of New York

This paper explores financial stability policies for the shadow banking system. I tie policy options to economic mechanisms for shadow banking that have been documented in the literature. I then illustrate the role of shadow bank policies using three examples: agency mortgage real estate investment trusts (REITs), leveraged lending, and captive reinsurance affiliates. For each example, the economic mechanisms are explained, the potential risks emanating from the activities are described, and policy options to mitigate such risks are listed. The overarching theme of the analysis is that any policy prescription for the shadow banking system is highly specific relative to the particular activity.

Introduction

The Financial Stability Board (2011) defines shadow banking as the system of credit intermediation that involves entities and activities outside the regular banking system. Shadow credit intermediation thus takes place in an environment where prudential regulatory standards and supervisory oversight are either not applied or are applied to a materially lesser or

*Adrian: Federal Reserve Bank of New York, 33 Liberty Street, New York, NY 10045 (E-mail: tobias.adrian@ny.frb.org). This paper was prepared for the Federal Reserve Bank of Chicago's *Sixteenth Annual International Banking Conference: Shadow Banking Within and Across National Borders*. The author would like to thank Adam Ashcraft, Nicola Cetorelli, Michael Holscher, Morgan Lewis, Antoine Martin, and Robert Patallano for feedback. The views expressed in this paper are those of the authors and do not necessarily reflect the position of the Federal Reserve Bank of New York or the Federal Reserve System.

different degree than is the case for regular banks engaged in similar activities. While the vast majority of shadow credit intermediation is regulated in some way, it is typically not subject to prudential supervision, which is the main objective to the regulation of the traditional banking system.

The majority of shadow banking activities are conducted outside of the commercial banking system. However, some activities take place under the umbrella of bank holding companies (BHCs) or insurance companies, and banks themselves feature prominently in the shadow banking system. For example, banks extend backup lines of credit that allow independent or off balance sheet entities to issue short-term liabilities. Furthermore, BHCs house money market funds, the tri-party repo market, and many different types of activities related to securitization. The connection between bank and non-bank credit intermediation activities thus has to be one focus of shadow bank policies.

More generally, shadow banking can be defined as maturity transformation, liquidity transformation and credit risk transfer outside of institutions with direct access to government backstops such as depository institutions, i.e., traditional commercial banks. This definition encompasses a large section of the financial system, as is illustrated by Fig. 1, which plots shadow bank liabilities and commercial bank liabilities as a fraction of the nominal gross domestic product since the 1960s. The figure illustrates that traditional bank liabilities have been roughly constant at around 70% of GDP over the past 50 years. Shadow credit intermediation, on the other hand, has grown from less than 1% of GDP in 1960 to over 70% today, with a peak close to 80% in mid-2007, just before the onset of the global financial crisis. In 2007, shadow bank liabilities were in fact larger than traditional commercial bank liabilities. Also plotted in Fig. 1 are liabilities of BHCs and broker-dealers. While large commercial banks in the US are part of BHCs, they are separate legal entities with distinct regulations. Importantly, only commercial bank subsidiaries have access to the discount window and deposit insurance, not the BHC, or other subsidiaries such as broker dealer subsidiaries. BHC and broker dealer liabilities have also grown in recent decades, though their size is relatively small.

The remainder of the chapter is organized as follows. I explain seven economic mechanisms of shadow bank intermediation in some detail in the next section. The third section provides an overview of financial stability policies aimed at risks emanating from the shadow banking sector,

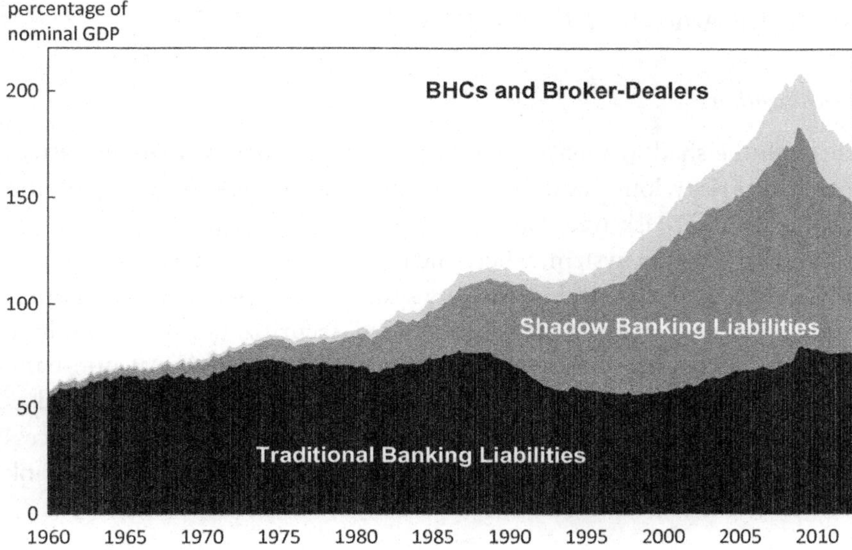

Fig. 1. Shadow banking and traditional banking.

Note: The figure shows the evolution of total liabilities by shadow banks, traditional banks, and BHCs and broker-dealers, based on data from the US Flow of Funds by the Board of Governors of the Federal Reserve, and the US National Accounts by the Bureau of Economic Analysis. The figure illustrates the stability of the size of traditional bank liabilities relative to GDP around 70% since the 1960s, and the rapidly increasing size of the shadow banking system over the past 50 years. The collapse of shadow banking after the financial crisis of 2007–2009 is also clearly visible. The plot is from Adrian, Covitz, and Liang (2012).

following the seven economic mechanisms from the next section. Sections after that provide three case studies of shadow banking activities. The fourth section explains agency mortgage REITs, the fifth section analyzes leveraged lending, and the sixth section dives into the shadow insurance sector. Each of the three case studies presents the economics of the respective activity, the risks emanating from the activity, and finally policy options. The final section concludes this chapter.

The Economics Shadow Banking

The literature has identified seven distinct economic mechanisms that motivate shadow bank activities. I discuss each of these mechanisms in more detail, drawing on previous work by Adrian and Ashcraft (2012b) and Adrian, Ashcraft, and Cetorelli (2013).

Specialization

Through the shadow intermediation process, the shadow banking system transforms risky, long-term loans (subprime mortgages, for example) into seemingly credit-risk-free, short-term, money-like instruments. Unlike the traditional banking system, where the entire process takes place within a single institution, the shadow banking system decomposes the credit intermediation into a chain of wholesale-funded, securitization-based lending. Shadow credit intermediation is performed through chains of non-bank financial intermediaries in a multistep process that can be interpreted as a "vertical slicing" of the traditional bank's credit intermediation process into seven steps. Pozsar *et al.* (2013) explain the seven steps of shadow bank credit intermediation in detail:

1. Loan origination (loans and leases, non-conforming mortgages, etc.) is performed by non-bank finance companies.
2. Loan warehousing is conducted by single- and multi-seller conduits and is funded through asset-backed commercial paper (ABCP).
3. The pooling and structuring of loans into term asset-backed securities (ABS) is conducted by broker-dealers' ABS syndicate desks.
4. ABS warehousing is facilitated through trading books and is funded through repos, total return swaps, or hybrid and repo conduits.
5. The pooling and structuring of ABS into CDOs is also conducted by broker-dealers' ABS.
6. ABS intermediation is performed by limited-purpose finance companies (LPFCs), structured investment vehicles (SIVs), securities arbitrage conduits, and credit hedge funds, which are funded in a variety of ways including, for example, repo, ABCP, MTNs, bonds, and capital notes.
7. The funding of all the above activities and entities is conducted in wholesale funding markets by money market intermediaries (money market funds, enhanced cash funds) and direct money market investors such as securities lenders.

This intermediation chain closely intertwined with commercial banks, BHCs, and security broker-dealers. The seven steps are furthermore complemented by risk repositories of insurance companies, which provide credit risk transfer at various stages of the intermediation chain.

Mispriced guarantees from government backstops

Since the creation of the Federal Reserve in 1914 and the Federal Deposit Insurance in 1935, the official sector has attempted to minimize the risk of runs in the banking system risk through the use of its own balance sheet by providing credit guarantees via deposit insurance and contingent liquidity via lending of the last resort. However, the risk-insensitive provision of credit guarantees and liquidity backstops creates well-known incentives for excessive risk-taking, leverage, and maturity transformation, motivating the need for supervision and prudential regulation. The traditional form of financial intermediation, with credit being intermediated through banks and insurance companies, but with the public sector standing close by to prevent destabilizing runs, dominated other forms of financial intermediation from the Great Depression well into the 1990s.

Pozsar *et al.* (2013) define shadow banking as credit intermediation without explicitly guaranteed liabilities. Credit intermediation outside of backstopped commercial banks grew significantly, as illustrated in Fig. 1. Outside of commercial banks, institutions have varying degrees of connectedness to government backstops. For example, uninsured liabilities outside of commercial banks are part of the shadow banking system since they do not benefit from access to official sector liquidity, thus making them vulnerable to concerns about credit as well as runs by investors. However, some shadow banking liabilities have indirect access to backstops via credit lines of commercial banks. The pricing of credit lines, which benefit from the government backstops, therefore influences the pricing of such uninsured liabilities. As the distortionary impact from official backstops is primarily contained via constraints on risk taking (e.g., via capital requirements), the pricing of the credit line to the shadow banking institution can benefit from the government backstop of the commercial bank. Examples of distorted pricing of shadow banking activities due to the closeness to government backstops are widespread and include the pricing of intraday credit in the tri-party repo market, the implicit guarantees of various shadow banking institutions under the umbrella of BHCs due to reputational reasons (for example SIVs and money market funds), or credit guarantees written by insurance companies that benefit from superior credit ratings due to state insurance funds.

Regulatory arbitrage

Among the motivations for shadow credit intermediation are regulatory and tax arbitrage. Regulation typically constrains institutions to behave in ways that they would privately not choose: pay taxes to the official sector, disclose additional information to investors, or hold more capital against financial exposures. The re-structuring of financial activity that aims at avoiding taxes, disclosure, and/or capital requirements, is referred to as regulatory arbitrage. While arbitrage generally refers to the simultaneous buying and selling of instruments for a riskless profit, regulatory arbitrage is generally a change in structure of activity which does not change the risk profile of that activity, but increases the net cash flows to the sponsor by reducing the costs of regulation.

An example of regulatory arbitrage is documented by Acharya, Schnabl, and Suarez (2013). The authors show that the rapid expansion of ABCP since 2004 was, at least in part, attributable to regulatory arbitrage triggered by a change in capital rules. In particular, Financial Accounting Standards Board issued a directive in January 2003 (FIN 46) and updated the directive in December 2003 (FIN 46A) suggesting that sponsoring banks should consolidate assets in ABCP conduits onto their balanced sheets.[1] However, US banking regulators clarified that assets consolidated onto balance sheets from conduits would not need to be included in the measurement of risk-based capital and instead used a 10% credit conversion factor for the amount covered by a liquidity guarantee. Acharya, Schnabl, and Suarez (2013) documented that the majority of guarantees were structured as liquidity-enhancing guarantees aimed at minimizing regulatory capital, instead of credit guarantees, and that the majority of conduits were supported by commercial banks subject to the most stringent capital requirements.

There is also a literature investigating the impact of taxes and tax avoidance activity on the recent financial boom and bust. Alworth and Arachi (2012) provide a broad discussion of the role of the tax advantages of home

[1] See http://www.fasb.org/summary/finsum46.shtml.

ownership, the use of debt in mergers and acquisitions by private equity, the use of hybrid debt instruments as capital by financial institutions, and the use of tax havens to structure securitization vehicles. Mooij, Keen, and Orihara (2013) document an empirical link between corporate tax rates and the probability of crises. Finally, Davis and Stone (2004) document that the severity of crises is larger when pre-crisis leverage is higher, suggesting that tax policy could have effects both on incidence and severity of financial stress.

Neglected risk

Another economic role of shadow banking activity is related to aggregate tail risk. Because shadow banks are tailored to take advantage of mispriced tail risk, they accumulate assets that are particularly sensitive to tail events. Academic literature argues that such tail risk might be mis-priced *ex-ante*, either due to irrational or due to rational reasons. This literature is broadly referred to as "neglected risk".

The behavioral literature on neglected risk is rooted in the psychological observation that market participants are fundamentally biased against the rational assessment of tail risk. Gennaioli, Shleifer, and Vishny (2012) develop a theory of individual decision making based on the behavioral evidence, positing that actors neglect risk. Gennaioli, Shleifer, and Vishny (2013) apply this theory to the economics of the shadow banking system. They model a world where investors systematically ignore the worst state of the world, generating overinvestment and overpricing during the boom and excessive collapse of real activity and the financial sector during the bust. An early paper warning of the financial system's exposure to such tail risk was presented by Rajan (2005) who asked whether financial innovation had made the world riskier. Coval, Jurek, and Stafford (2009) point out that the AAA tranches of private label asset backed securities behave like catastrophe bonds that load on a systemic risk state. Neglected risk also manifests itself through over-reliance on credit ratings by investors. For example, Ashcraft *et al.* (2011) document that subprime MBS prices are more sensitive to ratings than ex post performance, suggesting that funding is excessively sensitive to credit ratings relative to informational content.

Dang, Gorton, and Holmström (2009) present an alternative theory that generates neglected risk within a rational setting. Their theory is one of information opacity that can serve as a rationalization of excessive risk taking in the shadow banking system. According to this theory, debt contracts are optimal because they generate opacity. Opacity, in turn, minimizes adverse selection and provides the least possible incentives to collect information. This insight justifies the growth of relatively opaque securitized products in the run-up to the crisis. Mortgages and loans were packaged into MBS and ABS and funded by CDOs, SIVs, and MMMFs that had relatively little information about the underlying credit quality. However, Dang, Gorton, and Holmström show that systemic risk is exacerbated once a bad shock hits informationally opaque, debt-funded economies. The intuition is that a bad shock leads to an increase in private information collection, which exacerbates the incorporation of adverse information in market prices. As a result, adverse selection starts to accumulate as systemic crises deepen.

Agency problems

Ashcraft and Schuermann (2008) describe seven informational frictions in the securitization of subprime mortgage credit prior to the financial crisis, although these frictions can be generalized to all securitization transactions. They include asymmetric information problems between lenders and originators (predatory lending and borrowing), between lenders and investors, between servicers and investors, between servicers and borrowers, between beneficiaries of invested funds and asset managers, and between beneficiaries of invested funds and credit rating agencies. In addition, asymmetric information between investors and issuers results in risk-insensitive cost of funding. For example, Keys *et al.* (2010) document that mortgage borrowers with FICO scores just above a threshold of 620 perform significantly worse than borrowers with FICO scores just below 620. As it is more difficult to securitize loans below that threshold, the authors argue that this result is consistent with issuers exploiting asymmetric information, disrupting the otherwise monotone relationship between borrower credit scores and performance. Although securitization has a relatively short history, it is a troubled one. The first known securitization transactions in the United States occurred in the 1920s, when commercial real estate (CRE) bond houses sold loans to finance CRE to retail investors through a vehicle known as CRE bonds. Wiggers and Ashcraft (2012) document the performance of these bonds, which defaulted in large numbers following the onset of the Great Depression. Although the sharp deterioration in economic conditions played an important part in explaining their poor performance, so did aggressive underwriting and sales of the bonds in small denominations to unsophisticated retail investors. Over-reliance on credit ratings can create problems when the rating agencies face their own agency problems. For example, Mathis, McAndrews, and Rochet (2009) analyze a dynamic model of ratings where reputation is endogenous and the market environment may vary over time. The authors' model predicts that a rating agency is likely to issue less accurate ratings in boom times than it would during recessionary periods. Moreover, the authors demonstrate that competition among rating agencies yields similar qualitative results. Xia and Strobl (2012) document that the conflict of interest caused by the issuer-pays rating model leads to inflated corporate credit ratings. Cohen (2011) documents significant relationships between variables that should not affect a CRA's view of the credit risk of conduit/fusion CMBS transactions issued during 2001–2007, but that would affect issuers' and CRAs' incentives in an environment where rating shopping was present.

Private money creation

Gorton and Metrick (2011, 2012) argue that an important aspect of shadow credit intermediation is its role in money creation. The creation of money like shadow bank liabilities complement traditional forms of money creation. High powered money can only be created by central banks. Commercial banks create broader forms of money, such as checking accounts and savings accounts. Treasury bills also have money like features due to their liquidity and safety. Shadow bank money creation occurs primarily in the commercial paper market and the repo market, and is funded by money market funds and short-term investment funds. Money plays a crucial role in the economy, acting not only as a store of value, but also as a unit of account and means of exchange.

The role of shadow liabilities in the overall money supply is explored by Sunderam (2012), who analyzes the extent to which shadow banking liabilities constitute substitutes for high-powered money. He shows in a simple model that shadow bank liabilities should constitute substitutes for money in the private sector's asset allocation. Empirically, Sunderam shows that shadow banking liabilities respond to money demand, extrapolating that heightened money demand can explain about half of the growth of ABCP in the mid-2000s. He also confirms that regulatory changes to ABCP played a significant role in the growth of the shadow banking system. Moreira and Savov (2014) study the impact of shadow money creation on macroeconomic fluctuations. Intermediaries create liquidity in the shadow banking system by levering up the collateral value of their assets. However, the liquidity creation comes at the cost of financial fragility as fluctuations in uncertainty cause a flight to quality from shadow liabilities to safe assets. The collapse of shadow banking liquidity has real effects via the pricing of credit and generates prolonged slumps after adverse shocks.

Short-term funding and runs

The financial frictions that lead to excessive risk taking and exacerbated credit losses during downturns also interact with the fragility of funding. Per definition, funding sources for shadow banking activities are uninsured and thus runnable. In many ways, the fragility of shadow banks due to the run-ability of liabilities resembles the banking system of the 19th century, prior to the creation of the Federal Reserve and the FDIC. During that time, bank runs were common, and they often had severe consequences for the real economy.

The shadow banking system's vulnerability to runs bears resemblance to bank runs as modeled by Diamond and Dybvig (1983). Shadow banks are subject to runs because assets have longer maturities than liabilities and tend to be less liquid as well. While the fundamental reason for commercial bank runs is the sequential servicing constraint, for shadow banks the effective constraint is the presence of fire sale externalities. In a run, shadow banking entities have to sell assets at a discount, which depresses market pricing. This provides incentives to withdraw funding — before other shadow banking depositors arrive. However, the analogy between bank runs and shadow bank runs goes only so far. The reason is that shadow bank entities do not offer demand deposits, but instead obtain funding in wholesale money markets such as commercial paper or repo. Martin, Skeie, and von Thadden (2011) provide a model for a run in repo markets that takes the empirical facts of the Bear Stearns and Lehman crises as a starting point. In their model, repo borrowers face constraints due to the scarcity of collateral and the liquidity of collateral. Under sufficiently adverse conditions, self-fulfilling runs can occur. The model focuses in particular on the differences between the tri-party repo market and the bilateral repo market (see Adrian *et al.* (2013) for an overview of both markets). Arguably, runs occurred in both markets, but they were of very different natures. While the run in the bilateral market was characterized by a sharp increase in haircuts (as documented by Gorton and Metrick (2012)), the run in the tri-party repo market materialized as a simple withdrawal of funding with a rather limited impact on the level of haircuts (see Copeland, Martin, and Walker (2011)). Runs in the ABCP market were equally characterized by a withdrawal of funding (see Covitz, Liang, and Suarez (2012)). Gallin (2013) provides a comprehensive map of the amount of short-term funding from the shadow banking system to the real economy, based on the flow of funds statistics. Gallin's framework shows that much of the decline in credit supply in the crisis was due to the decline of short-term shadow bank funding. Gallin's work can be used to quantify fragility in shadow bank funding over time.

Shadow Bank Policies

The discussion of the economics of shadow banking in the previous section has demonstrated that some shadow banking activities are just market-based credit intermediation with specialized financial institutions, while others are regulatory arbitrage responses to particular regulations, and yet others are outcomes of market failures. Shadow banking activities are generally vulnerable due to the absence of government backstops, and such vulnerabilities can create externalities for other parts of the financial sector. The regulation of shadow banking activities aims to correct market failures, government failures, and other distortions. Of particular concern is the systemic nature of certain shadow banking activities, i.e., the potential of distress in the shadow banking system to cause distress in other parts of the financial system, and ultimately the real economy.

While the case studies in fourth, fifth and sixth sections present specific policy options in three shadow credit intermediation examples, the current section will discuss general principles that are motivated from the previous discussion on the economics of shadow banking. I discuss policy options for each of the seven economic mechanisms that were presented in the second section.

Specialization

Specialization has many economic benefits, and in well-functioning markets, specialized intermediaries are likely to increase economic efficiency. However, credit intermediation chains in specialized institutions can be subject to externalities along the chain. While credit intermediation within one and the same bank internalizes some of these externalities, credit intermediation along a chain of intermediaries can pass market failures on from one part of the chain to the next. Financial stability policies thus have to aim at internalizing such externalities, which depends on specific forms of the externality at each step of the chain. Externalities in shadow banking can be generated by network externalities, runs, and leverage cycles due to risk management constraints, among other. Policies to address such externalities are specific to each shadow banking activity. The case studies in fourth, fifth and sixth sections discuss specific examples.

Mispriced guarantees from government backstops

Government guarantees consist primarily of the liquidity backstop by the Federal Reserve, and the credit backstop by the Federal Deposit insurance. The backstops are created to ensure the stability of the traditional commercial banking system, particularly due to bank runs. The regulation of depository institutions by the Federal Reserve and the Federal Deposit Insurance Corporation is motivated by the moral hazard that is created by the backstops. Many shadow banking activities benefit indirectly from the backstops, via the pricing of tail risk for both liquidity and credit. To the extent that shadow banking institutions benefit indirectly from government backstops, without, however, being subject to the same prudential regulation as depository institutions, policies have to aim at either expanding the regulatory reach, or else at adjusting the pricing of government backstops.

In the aftermath of the financial crisis, both routes have been undertaken. The prudential regulatory reach has been expanded by the creation of the Financial Stability Oversight Council, as well as fundamental reforms to the regulation of banks, BHCs, and other credit intermediaries. In addition, the pricing of government guarantees has been adjusted. For example, the assessment fee of the Federal Deposit Insurance Corporation has been changed to better reflect the systemic footprint of member banks. Capital regulations have been tightened to reflect the size, interconnectedness, and complexity of financial institutions, leading to an increase in the pricing of government backstops that are passed to shadow banking activities.

Regulatory arbitrage

A number of shadow banking activities consist of regulatory arbitrage, primarily with the aim of minimizing capital requirements of core regulated institutions such as banks, dealers, or insurance companies. In the banking sector, capital requirements represent the primary regulatory tool, and much regulatory arbitrage activity aims at circumventing such requirements. The first order policy response to such regulatory arbitrage activity is, of course, to change capital requirements in such a way that the arbitrage will be prevented. Indeed, the Basel III capital regulation has closed many loopholes in capital regulation, preventing regulatory capital arbitrage. However, it is too early to tell to what extent new regulatory arbitrage activities will emerge in the future. In addition, new regulations such as liquidity rules might be arbitraged once fully implemented. The case study on shadow insurance in the sixth section provides a discussion of policy actions that can mitigate a particular form of capital arbitrage in the insurance sector.

Neglected risk

Neglected risks can arise due to behavioral reasons, or as an equilibrium phenomenon due to adverse selection. In general, the excessive buildup of risk due to neglected risk can be mitigated with reporting requirements and shadow bank risk monitoring systems. Indeed, after the financial crisis, much effort has been put into better reporting systems. For the banking system, stress tests have become the primary tool to assess forward looking risks. The tests include, at least to some extent, stresses due to balance sheet exposures to the shadow banking system. For the broader financial system, the Office of Financial Research has as goal to collect and analyze data in order to assess system wide risk, including in the shadow banking system. Furthermore, the Dodd–Frank Act provides regulatory agencies in the US with a broad mandate to regulate risk in the system as a whole, not just the risk of individual financial institutions. Internationally, the Financial Stability Board (2013a) is leading a global effort to analyze and collect data on shadow banking activity, and to propose regulations to mitigate risks emanating from such activities. Of course, risk reporting systems only go so far in being able to mitigate systemic shadow banking risks: risk negligence might be an equilibrium outcome, either due to behavioral biases or due to adverse selection. A first order question is to what extent regulators are subject to the same behavioral biases as market participants.

Adverse selection can be an equilibrium outcome in response to market frictions, generating informational insensitivity. Intuitively, funding liquidity in good times is only possible when funding arrangements are informationally insensitive. However, adverse shocks can lead to an unraveling of theses arrangement, leading to information sensitivity. Such unraveling can be excessive, justifying public liquidity injections. Hence, optimal policies relative to information insensitivity are *ex-post* backstops that mitigate market breakdowns due to adverse selection. Of course, the challenge of such policies are the information asymmetries that central bank faces. Gorton (2009) argues that the collapse of securitization activity was triggered by the emergence of synthetic products that allowed the shorting of the housing market. In particular, the ABX, a synthetic index of subprime mortgage-backed securities, was created shortly before the financial crisis. The ABX allowed market participants to take short positions in subprime mortgages, and lead to an unraveling of information opacity in securitized credit markets. One of the policy responses of the Federal Reserve to the collapse of securitization activity was the creation of the Term Asset-backed Securities Loan Facility (TALF) as described by Ashcraft, Malz, and Pozsar (2012). Under the program, the Federal Reserve extended term loans collateralized by securities to buyers of certain high-quality ABS and CMBS, with the intent of reopening the new-issue ABS market. Through the TALF program, the Federal Reserve was able to prevent the shutdown of lending to consumers and small businesses, while limiting the public sector's risk. While such backstops might be optimal *ex-post*, from an *ex-ante* perspective, tighter regulation is likely optimal (Farhi and Tirole, 2012).

Agency problems

Many reform efforts since the financial crisis have aimed at mitigating agency problems in the shadow banking system, particularly in the securitization process, and for credit rating agencies. The Dodd–Frank Act requires credit risk retention by securitizers (see Adrian, 2011). The risk retention is designed to reduce the moral hazard problem arising from the fact that mortgages and loans that are securitized are sold in the market place, and the underwriter thus generally does not have the right incentives to monitor underwriting standards. The risk retention provisions of the Dodd–Frank Act aims at investor protections and improvements to the regulation of securities. Securitizers are forced to retain not less than 5% of the credit risk of any asset that they sell through the issuance of an ABS, and prohibit securitizers from directly or indirectly hedging or otherwise transferring the retained credit risk. The issuer must disclose the amount and form of retention to investors, and must provide material assumptions which justify the aggregate face amount of liabilities. A menu approach to risk retention is offered where vertical, horizontal, or a mix of vertical and horizontal tranches can be retained. "Vertical" retention refers to holding a portion of all tranches, while under "horizontal" retention the securitizer retains a first-loss tranche restricted to receive only scheduled principal. The rule also includes a "premium capture mechanism" that disallows securitizers from structuring interest only securities which transfer the full cash value to the equity tranche holder at the time of issuance. The premium capture mechanism prevents the structuring of the equity tranche in such a way that the incentive alignment is removed as cash flows are no longer sensitive to the credit quality of the underlying securities. If the issuer of the security is a bank, the capital requirement applied to the retained risk is a key consideration for the economic rationale of securitization.

The reform of credit rating agencies has aimed at lowering conflicts of interest. The Securities and Exchange Commission, which gained oversight of the credit rating agencies in 2006, has started to implement rules that aim at removing conflicts of interest since 2009 (see Adrian and Ashcraft (2012a) for a discussion). For example, agencies are prohibited from structuring the same product that they rate, and analysts are not allowed to receive gifts exceeding $25 from companies that they rate. Furthermore, agencies are required to publish statistics about the performance of their ratings after 1, 3, and 10 years. Furthermore, the Dodd–Frank Act provided the Commission with greater authority over credit rating agencies with respect to disclosure, governance, and conflicts of interest. Credit rating agencies have to provide more granular information about their ratings methodology, and the assumptions underlying particular ratings. Material changes to ratings methodology need board approval. Furthermore, sales and analysis within credit rating agencies has been separated. Changes to the rating agency compensation model could furthermore have significant consequences. Investors are too small to have a meaningful influence over issuers to generate appropriately risk-sensitive funding, which suggests the need to either coordinate to have market power or have an agent negotiate with only their interests in mind. As coordination between investors might raise antitrust issue, hence making rating agencies effective representatives of investors is likely an important part of mitigating conflicts of interest. However, as long as agencies are chosen and paid by the issuer, it seems difficult to imagine them working exclusively as a fiduciary of investors. While a number of solutions are being discussed, the right conceptual model would appear to be rating agency risk retention. This might involve rating agencies being compensated for their services by the sponsor in the form of a vertical slice of securities rated. Alternatively, this might involve rating agencies having balance sheets, and only being permitted to disclose ratings to investors if they hold a vertical share of a security outstanding.

Private money creation

One role of the shadow banking system, emphasized by Gorton and Metrick (2012), is the creation of safe collateral that can be used in money markets. In particular, AAA tranches of securitized products were used as collateral in repo markets, and ABCP funded conduits of long term, risky mortgage pools prior to securitization. The first order policy response to a shortage of risk free collateral is the regulation of aggregate liquidity through the management of the maturity structure of government debt, and the management of aggregate liquidity in the banking system. Stein (2012) develops a conceptual framework to assess these issues in the context of an equilibrium model. Stein argues that the central bank can regulate aggregate financial stability risk via the amount of reserves in the banking system. Shortages of collateral are met by the creation of short-term wholesale shadow funding, which are subject to run risk, leading to inefficient fire sales. Demand pressures for short-term debt can be measured via the spread between the interest on excess reserves, and the federal funds rate. By supplying liquidity in the federal fund market, and setting the interest on excess reserves, the central bank can influence the availability of liquidity in the banking system and thus regulate incentives for shadow bank money creation. Greenwood,

Hanson, and Stein (2010) investigate the role of the maturity structure of government debt for incentives of the private sector to generate risk free collateral. They document that corporations tend to issue risk free debt at times when there is a shortage of Treasury collateral. Sunderam (2012) uncovers a similar mechanism for ABCP issuers, who respond to shortages in money markets. Krishnamurthy and Vissing-Jorgensen (2012) show an explicit link between the shortage of money like assets and financial crises. Financial stability considerations in the creation of risk free collateral by the Treasury and the central bank to regulate the extent to which the shadow banking system creates potentially vulnerable substitutes thus seems to be a goal for shadow bank policies.

Short-term funding and runs

Policy efforts with respect to runs in wholesale funding markets have been primarily concentrated on money market funds, and the tri-party repo market. While some progress has been achieved since the financial crisis, the risk of runs has not been eliminated. A 2010 reform of the money market fund sector by the Securities and Exchange Commission has tightened liquidity risk and credit risk constraints. Currently, three main reform proposals are under discussion. The first consists of the abolishment of the stable net asset value. Purchases and redemptions in money market fund shares are rounded to the nearest penny, and are not marked to market, except when asset values fall below $0.995, at which point the fund breaks the buck. Due to this stable net asset value rule, investors treat money market funds like demand deposits. However, once a fund breaks the buck, there is no public backstop, making the funds vulnerable to runs. While the abolishment of the net stable asset rule is likely to reduce run risk, it is important to note, however, that money market funds in countries with floating net asset values have also experienced runs. The second reform proposal is to institute capital requirements for money market funds, similar to the capital requirements imposed on banks (see McCabe, 2011). Capital requirements move the default barrier of the funds, allowing some losses in their portfolios without triggering bankruptcy. The equity tranche of the funds could be publicly traded at different prices than the safe money market shares. While a capital requirement can make default less likely, it certainly does not rule it out, and thus does not eliminate run risk entirely.

A third proposal consists of a liquidity requirement called "minimum balance at risk", which consists of a liquidity buffer that minimizes incentives for runs (see McCabe *et al.*, 2012).

The tri-party repo market reform addresses three shortcomings in the tri-party repo market: (1) the heavy reliance of market participants on intraday credit extension, (2) the weaknesses in credit and liquidity risk management practices by market participants, and (3) the lack of a mechanism to ensure that tri-party repo investors do not conduct disorderly fire sales immediately following a dealer default. The reliance of market participants on intraday credit is addressed via technological changes by the tri-party repo clearing banks, which is expected to lead to an elimination of this type of credit by late 2014. Risk management practices of dealers have improved due to heightened supervision of the largest dealers, leading to a decline in the fraction of overnight repo funding. The risk of fire sales in the event of a dealer failure remains an open issue, without any obvious solution.

Case Study 1: Agency Mortgage REITs

Economics of agency REITs

REITs are investment vehicles that primarily invest in real estate related assets. Agency mortgage REITs (agency REITs) are specialized REITs that invest in mortgage backed securities (MBS) issued by US government sponsored agencies (Fannie Mae, Freddie Mac, and Ginnie Mae). While there are hundreds of publicly listed REITs in the US, the publicly listed agency REIT market consists of only a handful of companies, the majority of which were created since the financial crisis (see Fig. 2). In 2013, there were 14 publicly traded agency REITs in the US, owning over $350 billion of agency MBS. While the latter only represents around 7% of the total outstanding agency MBS, the ownership share of agency REITs in that market has grown rapidly in recent years, as can be seen in Fig. 3.

US REITs are exempt from specific provisions of the Investment Company Act due to the large fraction of their assets invested in real estate related assets. In particular, the SEC requires REITs to invest at least 55% of their assets in mortgages or qualifying real estate interests, and at least 80% of assets in qualifying real estate interests and assets. Due to the exemption

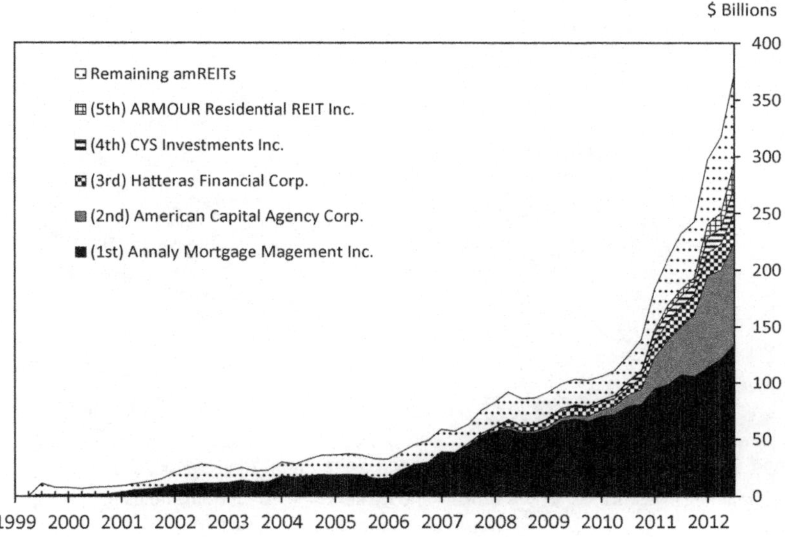

Fig. 2. Agency MBS holdings of agency mortgage REITs.

Note: The figure plots agency mortgage holdings by publicly listed agency mortgage REITs, based on 10K and 10Q filings with the Securities and Exchange Commission. The figure shows the rapid increase in the size of agency mortgage holdings by REITs, as well as the high degree of concentration in holdings by the top two firms.

from the Investment Company Act, REITs in general, and agency REITs in particular, are exempt from limits of leverage and other SEC regulations though, as publicly listed entities, they are subject to the SEC's investor protection rules and have to file reports such as 10Qs. However, agency REITs are not subject to prudential regulation.

REITs are also special with respect to their tax status. As long as REITs distribute at least 90% of their taxable net income annually, they avoid paying corporate taxes. To the extent that those distributions are done in the form of dividends, they are taxed at the shareholders' income tax rate, thus avoiding double taxation. The dividend yield of REITS in general, and agency REITs in particular, tend to be relatively high due to the high level of distributions required to avoid corporate taxation.

The business model of agency REITs relies on liquidity and leverage, but not credit transformation. Mortgage REITs obtain leverage in the bilateral repo market, from the broker-dealer sector. The repo contracts limit

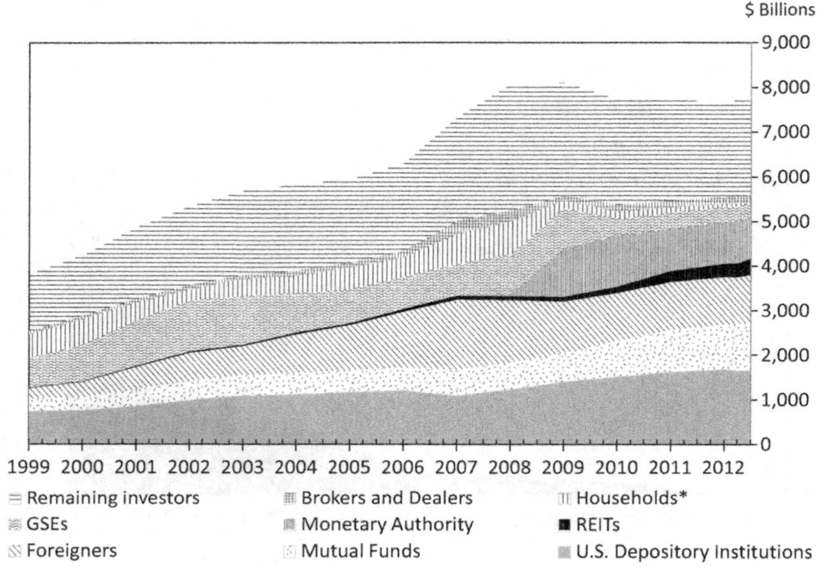

Fig. 3. Ownership of agency mortgages.

Notes: The figure plots ownership of agency mortgages by type of investors, based on data by the Board of Governors of the Federal Reserve. It illustrates that holdings by REITs have increased rapidly in recent years, but remain small in comparison to agency mortgage holdings by other investors.

the amount of leverage that REITs can obtain. Since the financial crisis, haircuts for agency MBS have increased. The current level of leverage is between 6 and 10, down from 10 to 16 pre-crisis, according to the 10K filings of the largest agency REITs. There is no credit transformation, as agency MBS only contain interest rate, prepayment, and liquidity risk, but no credit risk. The rapid growth of assets under management in the agency REIT sector since the financial crisis can be primarily attributed to the interest rate environment. As expansionary monetary policy has resulted in low yields across the maturity spectrum, investors have been reaching for yield by allocating funds to levered investments. As a result, agency REITs, bond mutual funds (and particularly high yield mutual funds) as well as collateralized loan obligations (CLOs) have grown rapidly. The high degree of leverage and the above mentioned requirement to pay out at least 90% of net income in order to achieve tax exemption results allows agency REITs to generate dividend yields that are among the highest among traded stocks. For example, in recent years, the largest agency REITs have achieved dividend yields around 20% in recent years, despite longer term interest rates that are only around 2–3%.

Risks of agency mortgage REITs

Agency REITs are exposed to two main sources of risk, duration risk and liquidity risk. Duration risk arises as their assets are longer term MBS, while liabilities are repos. Hence, when the slope of the yield curve steepens, agency REITs experience mark-to-market losses on their mortgage holdings. This can be seen from the historically tight relationship between return on assets and the slope of the yield curve (see Fig. 4). A steeper yield curve thus generates losses, translating into a fall of the REITs' equity value. In addition to slope risk, agency REITs hold convexity risk. Convexity risk

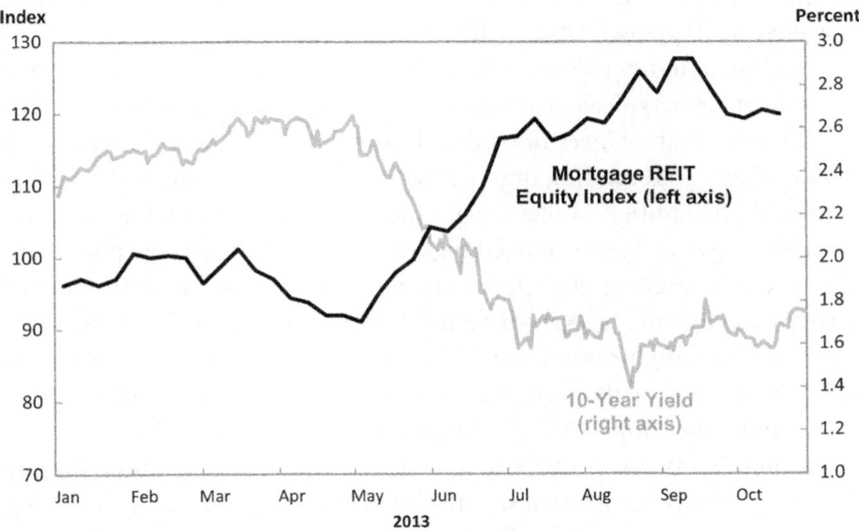

Fig. 4. REIT share price index versus 10-year yield.

Notes: The figure shows the level of the 10-year treasury yield, together with the share price of the agency mortgage REIT index based on data from the Board of Governors of the Federal Reserve and Bloomberg. The negative relationship between the yield and the REIT index reflects the mechanism through which agency REITs generate earnings: they borrow short (at low rates close to zero) and invest in longer term assets. When interest rates rise, REITs experience mark-to-market losses on their agency mortgage holdings, leading to lower earnings and a declining share price.

arises also in a rising yield environment. As agency mortgage pools consist of mortgages that can be prepaid, rising interest rates makes prepayment less likely, extending the duration of mortgages. The duration extension in a rising yield environment generates "negative convexity", meaning that the price of MBS is more and more sensitive to increasing rates, the higher rates are. Negative convexity has been linked to past bond market selloffs, particularly in 1994 and 2003.

Agency REITs are exposed to market liquidity and funding liquidity risks. Market liquidity risks arise in the agency MBS market during selloffs, as witnessed during the financial crisis in 2008 and the selloff in 2013. In selloffs, prices on agency MBS can be depressed due to fire sale externalities, leading to mark-to-market losses by agency REITs, and a corresponding decline in their book equity. The leveraged nature of agency REITs means that adverse price movements of agency MBS due to illiquidity have a magnified impact on their equity cushion: when leverage is 10, a 1% loss of agency MBS prices leads to a 10% loss of book equity.

Funding liquidity risk arises for agency REITs because their repo funding is short term, typically with either an overnight or a month long maturity. If money market investors suddenly withdraw funding to dealers, those can no longer pass funding onto agency REITs, exposing the REITs to liquidity risk. In addition, dealers might increase haircuts when liquidity and rate risk of agency MBS is judged higher, exposing REITs to the possibility of forced deleveraging. In fact, during the financial crisis, repo funding of agency MBS became severely distorted, leading the Federal Reserve to start a special financing program called "Term Securities Lending Facility". In addition, distress of the securities broker-dealer sector, as experienced in 2008, can further impact the funding liquidity of agency REITs.

Agency REITs can contribute to systemic risk during times of sharply increasing longer term interest rates by magnifying rates selloffs. Rising interest rates can force REITs to fire sale agency MBS, as agency REITs tend to manage their leverage ratio. Rising rates lead to market-to-market losses and hence a decline in their equity cushion, thus involuntarily increasing their leverage ratio. In order to restore target leverage, REITs have to sell MBS, thus contributing to market illiquidity and rising rates. The adverse rate and liquidity effects might spill over to other institutions, such as mutual funds, money market funds, insurance companies, and pension funds. Indeed, during the sharp rise in interest rates in the summer of 2013, agency REITs did sell significant amounts of agency MBS.

	2007	2008	2009	2010	2011	2012
REITs	88.9	89.6	105.1	143.3	239.1	368.2
Broker-Dealers	290.2	242.6	110.9	149.8	166.8	165.5
Ratio	0.3	0.4	0.9	1	1.4	2.2

Fig. 5. Agency mortgage holdings: Inventories of REITs and broker-dealers.

Notes: The table shows the agency mortgage holdings by REITs and by security broker-dealers, based on data form the US Flow of Funds of the Board of Governors of the Federal Reserve. The table documents that the fraction of agency bonds owned by REITs relative to broker dealers increased from one third to more than two between 2007 and 2013.

If the sector grows significantly larger in coming years, the high leverage and dependence on repo market funding might increase the systemic footprint of agency REITs. Endogenous adverse feedback loops in the agency MBS market might be exacerbated by the presence of leveraged investment vehicles that do not have access to lender of last resort facilities. The concern that risk management by REITs via selloffs in a rising rate environment is further magnified by the relative size of their agency holdings in comparison to the dealer-broker sector. Figure 5 illustrates that the size of agency MBS holdings by REITs has become very large relative to the agency MBS holdings of the securities broker-dealer sector.

Financial stability policies

Financial stability policies to address the systemic risks emanating from agency REITs can consist of policies aimed at improving the resilience of the repo market, enhanced disclosure requirements for REITs, and indirect regulation via supervised BHCs.

A recent study by the Financial Stability Board (2013b) has explored policy options to ensure the stability of shadow bank intermediation in relation to repo and securities lending markets. The recommendations of the FSB include the collection of more granular data on such activities, regulatory regimes for securities lenders and their agents, limits on the rehypothecation of client collateral, minimum standards for collateral valuation, and the review of the law governing bankruptcies that involve repo contracts. All of these recommendations aim at making repo and the (closely intertwined) securities lending market more resilient, which in turn helps to solidify funding liquidity of agency REITs, among other repo market borrowers. Of course, policies that enhance the resiliency of the broker-dealer sector, the tri-party repo market, and the money market fund sector will also enhance the funding liquidity of agency REITs. While such improvements of the repo market infrastructure benefit all repo market participants, agency REITs are likely beneficiaries due to their highly leveraged nature, and singular dependence on repo funding.

The second set of policies to mitigate systemic risks emanating from the agency REIT sector consists in data reporting and disclosure requirements. One of the cornerstones of regulations is the disclosure of data to investors, which allows market forces to constrain the behavior of financial institutions. The exemption of REITs from the Investment Company Act also implies exemption from more granular disclosure requirements that other investment vehicles are subjected to, such as disclosure of securities holdings and hedges. The Office of Financial Research, created by the Dodd–Frank Act, has an explicit mandate to collect data for institutions and activities that can potentially endanger the financial system, and whose data is not adequately collected by other agencies. The OFR has broad subpoena power that ensures its ability to collect data, even though it does not have any supervisory or regulatory authority.

A third avenue to address systemic risks emanating from the agency REIT sector is via the supervision of the counterparty credit risk management of the dealers that provide leverage via the bilateral repo market. As agency REITs rely on the dealers to obtain leverage, they are closely monitored by the counterparty risk management functions of dealers. This is putting constraints on the amount of interest rate risk, prepayment risk, and liquidity risk that the REITs can obtain. As most major dealers are now part of BHCs, Federal Reserve supervision has some indirect lever over the risk taking of the REIT sector. However, the constraint on this policy option is that there are major dealers that are not part of BHCs, as well as foreign dealers through which REITs can trade. Hence, the effectiveness of the indirect supervision channel is limited at best.

Case Study 2: Leveraged Lending

The economics of leveraged lending

Leveraged loans are loans extended to firms with credit ratings below investment grade. Leveraged loans are used to fund ongoing investments such as capital expenditures and working capital, and also to finance corporate events. The latter category includes leveraged buyouts of publicly listed firms. Leveraged loans are typically structured as floating rate balloon loans with limited amortization, making their performance highly dependent on refinancing conditions. The term of leveraged loans is usually between 5 and 7 years. Defaults on leveraged loans is sensitive to macroeconomic conditions, varying between 1 and 12% annually depending on the state of the credit cycle. Leveraged loans are typically collateralized and senior to other debt instruments, yielding high recovery rates of 70% on average, which is higher than recovery rages for corporate bonds.

The shadow credit intermediation chain of the leveraged loan market is represented in Fig. 6. Issuers consist of speculative grade corporations.

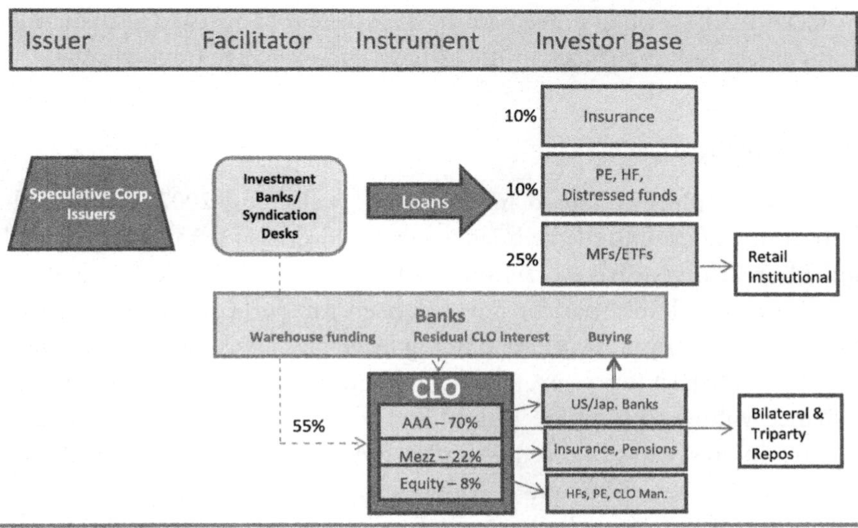

Fig. 6. Institutional leveraged loan markets.

Notes: The institutional leveraged loan market comprises bank syndicated loans distributed to institutional investors. CLOs represent the predominant investor in leveraged loans. Large US banks are at the heart of the originate-to-distribute model. They fund loan warehouses, take residual risk in CLOs, and buy AAA or AA tranches. The largest leverage risk is found in hedge funds and CLOs' equity tranches, exposing these investors to high losses. However, in both cases the maturity transformation is not high, as the liabilities are not of a short-term nature. The largest liquidity transformation is found in mutual funds and ETFs, which have grown significantly. As liquidity is normally robust, investors expect to be able to sell out of positions in market downturns, but may find liquidity is absent when they most need it. CLOs engage in risk arbitrage to secure equity returns. CLO AAA spreads are materially wider than corporate AAA bonds, but also experienced significant spread widening during the crisis.

Issuance is facilitated by the syndication desks of investment banks which also provide warehouse funding for loans that are securitized. Securitization of leveraged loans is via CLOs, which are portfolios of loans that are structured into different tranches according to their riskiness. The AAA tranche of a CLO makes up around 70% of total face value and is typically sold to banks. The mezzanine tranche makes up around 22% of the CLO and tends to be sold to insurance companies, pension funds, and asset managers. The equity tranche is around 8% of the CLO and tends to be sold to hedge funds, private equity firms, or independent CLO managers. CLOs are leveraged structures that perform some maturity transformation, and can be used for risk arbitrage. Around 55% of leveraged loans were securitized by CLOs in 2013, while the remaining 45% were sold outright to insurance companies, asset managers, mutual funds, and exchange traded funds.

Risks in leveraged lending

Leveraged lending collapsed in 2008 after peaking in 2007 of $680 billion. In the aftermath of the financial crisis, leveraged lending rebounded quickly, reaching nearly $1 trillion in 2013 (see Fig. 7). While issuance has been at record levels, part of that has been for purposes of refinancing. While the total amount of outstanding leveraged loans has been growing rapidly in the past two years, the change from year to year is less than total issuance volumes (compare Figs. 7 and 8). Refinancing activity reflects the low interest rates in recent years, as well as the rolling over of maturing loans. Leveraged buyouts are low by historical standards, and corporate events more generally have not been a primary source of leveraged lending activity. Credit metrics of leveraged buyouts have not deteriorated, with average Debt-to-EBITA and EBITA-to-Debt service within historical norms to date. However, there is some evidence of increasing leverage as Debt-to-EBITA for the high yield sector that requires further monitoring.

The fraction of covenant lite loans has increased significantly from 0 in 2010 to 60% in 2013, raising financial stability concerns. This deterioration in loan underwriting has come hand-in-hand with an increased presence of retail investors in the leveraged loan market primarily through mutual funds and exchange traded funds (see Fig. 9). Such investors are relatively less sophisticated than banks and hedge funds whose share in leveraged loan ownership is declining (though not necessarily their overall amount of

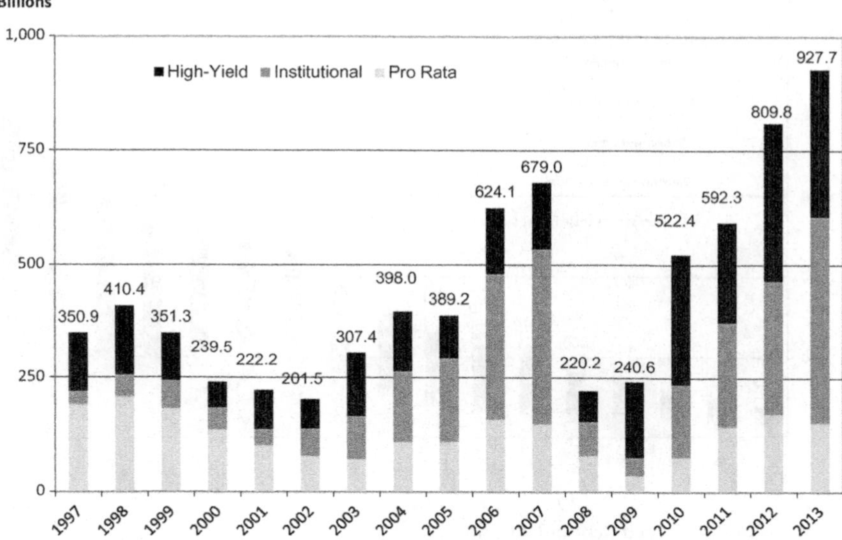

Fig. 7. Leveraged finance volume: Bank debt and bonds.

Notes: The figure plots the leveraged finance issuance volume for leveraged loans (gray), high yield bonds (black), and pro-rata (light gray), based on data from Standard & Poor's Capital IQ LCD. Issuance volume in 2012 and 2013 was at historical highs, exceeding volumes of 2006 and 2007, particularly in the high yield bond market.

holdings). The funding of leveraged loans by mutual and exchange traded funds represents a financial stability risk, as the loans have long maturities, are opaque and are inherently risky. Mutual and exchange traded fund shares, on the other hand, are demandable on a daily basis. These funds thus engage in maturity and credit transformation. The funding of leveraged loans on balance sheets that perform maturity and credit transformation makes the activity classifiable as shadow credit intermediation. While leveraged loan funds do use risk management techniques such as minimum liquidity holdings and backup lines of credit, such hedges are inherently expensive, and unlikely to withstand a major selloff of leveraged loans.

In the leverage lending intermediation chain presented in Fig. 6, the largest leverage risk is found in hedge funds and in CLOs' equity tranches, exposing these investors to high losses. However, in both cases the maturity transformation is not high, as the liabilities are not of a short-term

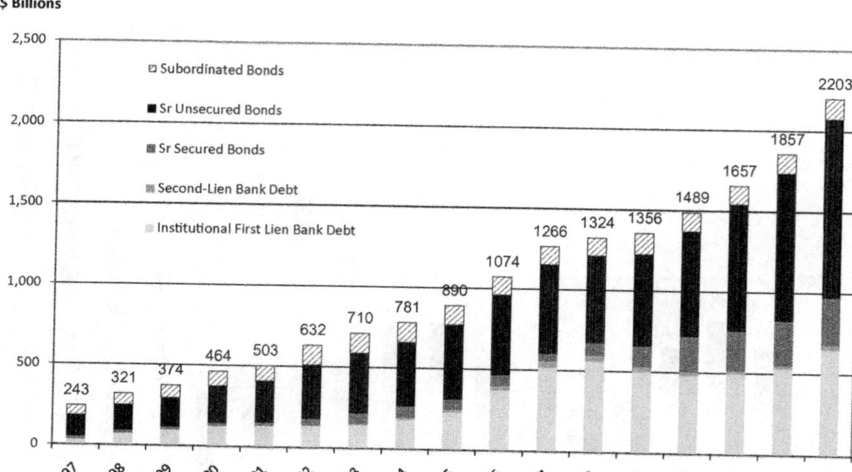

Fig. 8. Total leveraged debt outstandings.

Notes: The figure plots total leveraged debt outstandings, based on data from Bank of America/Merrill Lynch Global High-Yield Strategy and Standard & Poor's Capital IQ LCD. Total outstandings grew substantially in 2012 and 2013, reaching 2.2 trillion by the end of 2013.

nature, so forced unwinding is generally not a concern. The largest liquidity transformation is found in mutual funds and ETFs, which have grown significantly. As liquidity is normally robust, investors expect to be able to sell out of positions in market downturns, but may find liquidity is absent when they most need it. CLOs engage in risk arbitrage to secure equity returns. CLO AAA spreads are materially wider than corporate AAA bonds, but also experienced significant spread widening during the crisis.

Leveraged loan policies

Banking agencies have recently issued new regulatory guidance on leveraged lending (supervisory rule 13-03[2]). The rule is important as it takes a macroprudential approach to the supervision of underwriting standards for leveraged lending. While supervision is historically concerned with the safety and soundness of individual institutions, the Dodd–Frank Act of

[2]See http://www.federalreserve.gov/bankinforeg/srletters/sr1303.htm.

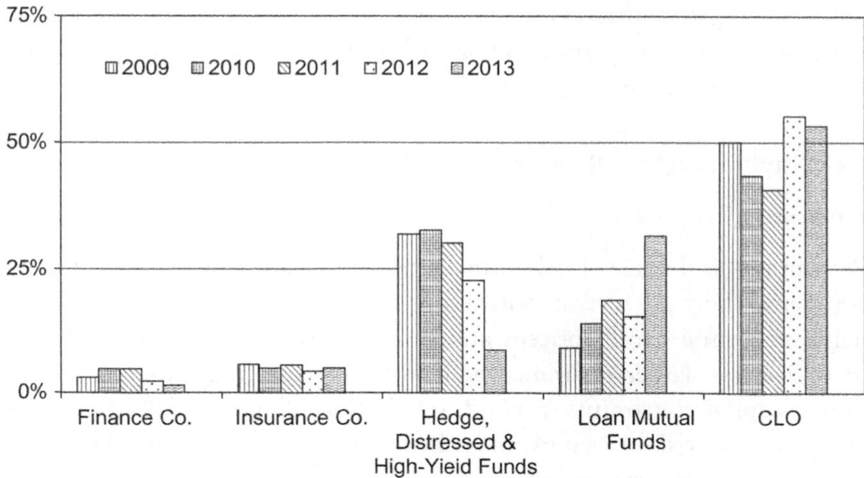

Fig. 9. Primary market for institutional loans by investor type excluding banks.

Notes: The figure plots the share of investments in the institutional loan market by investor type since 2009, based on data by Standard & Poor's Capital IQ LCD. It also shows the rapid growth of loan mutual funds among primary loan market investors. The growth of mutual fund investors is primarily offset by declining investments of hedge, distressed, and high yield funds.

2010 has given regulatory agencies an explicit mandate to ensure the safety and soundness of the financial system as a whole. The way in which SR 13-03 implements that mandate is by requiring examiners of banks that underwrite leveraged loans to enforce underwriting standards even if those loans are not intended to be held by the bank in question. This is in contrast to some of the supervisory rules prior to the financial crisis, when poor underwriting of loans (or mortgages, for that matter) was not prevented as long as the loans under question were resold in the market place.

The rule provides specific guidance to examiners when reviewing leveraged lending, including standards for underwriting of specific loans, as well as overall risk management. The underwriting guidelines will raise scrutiny in the face of excessive leverage, limited amortization, and over-reliance on refinancing. As explained above, these underwriting standards apply both to loans intended for distribution as well as for the bank's own portfolio. Guidance related to risk management requires institutions to have a clearly articulated risk appetite, limits for pipeline and commitments, as well as for the aggregate book and individual borrower concentration. Banks must stress test both the pipeline and retained portfolio, and hold adequate capital against all positions.

Case Study 3: Captive Reinsurance Affiliates

Economics of reinsurance

Reinsurance is the sale of risk from an insurance company to a reinsurance company. There are several motivations for reinsurance. First, reinsurance helps an insurer avoid concentrations in its own portfolio, permitting it to underwrite larger insurance policies by relaxing regulatory and economic capital constraints. Second, solicitation of third-party evaluation and pricing of risk can supplement the insurer's own evaluation and pricing, reducing uncertainty about the risk. Third, when markets are segmented, the insurer can earn arbitrage profits. Segmentation can be driven by reinsurers who have more expertise, are better able to diversify, or have different funding sources. The usage of reinsurance by insurance companies can thus enhance their efficiency and competitiveness. While the usage of reinsurance can be advantageous from the point of view of individual insurers, it might be costly from society's point of view. In particular, the usage of reinsurance can lead to laxer regulation, excessive risk taking, and a potentially higher burden for taxpayers in the case of insurance company distress.

One particular form of reinsurance is captive reinsurance, where an insurance company purchases reinsurance from an affiliate, reducing the cost of regulation of the insurer. Captives are subject to different accounting rules that facilitate lower reserves. In addition, captives do not face regulatory capital requirements, thus offering a regulatory arbitrage opportunity for insurers. While insurance company regulation imposes restrictions on liquidity and credit risk taking, captives are generally not subject to these rules. Captives also face weaker transparency requirements limiting market discipline. Unlike insurance companies, captives are able to back reinsurance with low cost letters of credit or parental guarantees instead of more expensive capital. In a typical captive insurance arrangement, risk is transferred from the insurance company to the parent, which reduces the insurance company's regulatory capital requirements. The arrangement permits the consolidated organization to lower capital requirements,

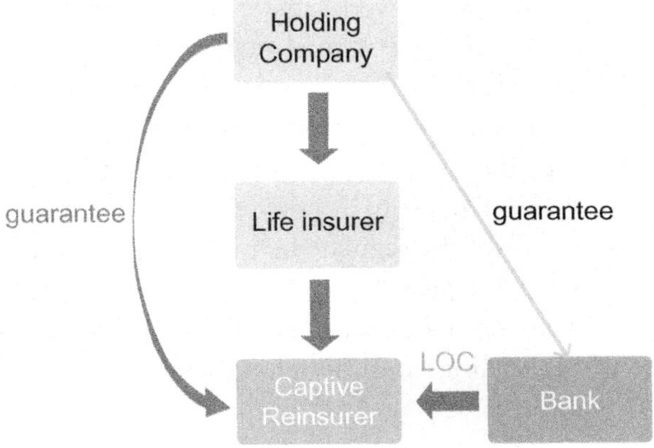

Fig. 10. Shadow insurance intermediation.

Notes: This figure shows the functioning of reinsurance captives for life insurance companies. Life insurance assets and liabilities are moved from the life insurance subsidiary to an affiliated captive reinsurer that typically resides in a different state with lower or no capital requirements. The holding company provides a guarantee either directly to the captive reinsurer, or to a bank that provides a LOC to the captive. Hence, risk is not transferred out of the insurance holding company, but total capital held by the holding company is lowered due to this capital arbitrage.

thus enhancing return on equity. Many captive reinsurance agreements are backed by letters of credit from the holding company to the captive reinsurer (see Fig. 10). Alternatively, the captive reinsurer can be guaranteed with a letter of credit (LOC) from a bank, which is in turn guaranteed by the holding company. The bottom line is that while risk is transferred out of insurance subsidiaries, it is still part of the holding company, i.e., it is not transferred out of the holding company. However, the required capital is lower for the captive.

Insurance company regulators have the authority to reject transactions with a captive. However, insurance companies are regulated at the state level, and not the holding company level. From the state's point of view, risk transfer to captives represents a reduction in the risk at the subsidiary, even though the risk at the holding company level might not experience a decline of risk, and typically experiences increased risk due to the lower capital requirement at the captive. Insurance companies argue that captive insurance is used to reduce the cost of excessively conservative regulation, which require them to hold reserves above the actuarial risk of their insurance policies. Moreover, captive reinsurance helps to protect the insurance company from the capital market volatility of variable-rate annuities. As the insurer provides a guaranty on the principal value of these investments, they are required to increase reserves when the market value of those investments declines in value, which reduces earnings and capital of the insurance company. The use of a captive insurance reduces volatility in regulatory capital ratios of the regulated entity. Furthermore, insurer provides guaranty on the principal value of these investments, they are required to increase reserves when the market value of those investments declines in value, which reduces earnings and capital of the insurance company.

Risks of captive reinsurance

Life insurers' reinsurance to captives has grown significantly in recent years, from $11 billion in 2002 to an estimated $364 billion in 2012 according to Koijen and Yogo (2013), see Fig. 11. Koijen and Yogo further document that

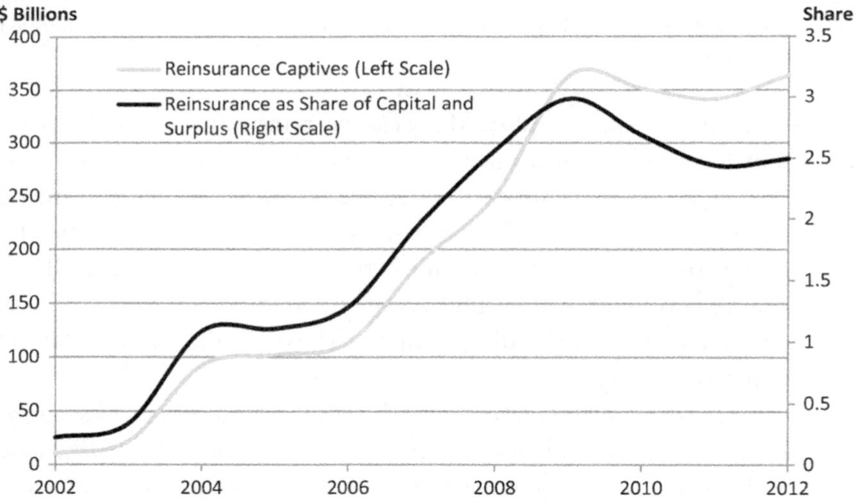

Fig. 11. Shadow insurance.

Notes: This figure reports life and annuity reinsurance ceded by US life insurers to shadow reinsurers, both in total dollars and as a share of the capital and surplus of the ceding companies, based on data from Koijen and Yogo (2013). Reinsurance ceded is the sum of reserve credit taken and modified coinsurance reserve ceded. Shadow reinsurers are affiliated and unauthorized reinsurers without an A.M. best rating.

captive reinsurance is primarily used by the largest insurance companies which are estimated to cede one quarter of all insured dollars to shadow reinsurers in 2012. Koijen and Yogo further estimate that risk based capital is reduced by 53 percentage points due to the usage of captives. They estimate that the total amount of this risk transfer corresponds to a three notch ratings downgrade. The authors argue that the cost of life insurance is significantly impacted by the usage of captives, as is the risk of the companies who are using them. The usage of shadow insurance is thus quantitatively large, and has a potentially significant impact on the risks in the insurance sector.

The growth of captive reinsurers has been attracting the attention of regulators. For example, the New York State Department of Financial Services recently issued a report highlighting findings from a study of reinsurance captives.[3] The New York state regulators refer to the activity as "shadow insurance", noting broader financial stability concerns, and calling for a moratorium on new activity. In the report, the regulators note significant volume of activity, significant reductions in regulatory capital ratios, inconsistent and incomplete disclosure to the market and regulators, and evidence of a regulatory race to the bottom.

A December 2013 study by the Federal Insurance Office of the US Treasury on the modernization and improvement of insurance regulation in the US pursuant to the Dodd–Frank Act argues that reinsurance captives for life insurance companies represent two risks.[4] Reinsurance captives allow an insurer to receive credit against its reserve and capital requirements by transferring risk to the captive even though the captive is not bound by consistent capital rules across the states. Reinsurance captives can be established with a small percentage of the capital required to establish a commercial insurance license in the same state. In particular, the standards that govern the quality of capital that reinsurance captives must hold are not sufficiently robust. For example, some state laws currently allow intra-company letters of credit, parental guaranties, or intra-company guaranties to constitute capital for captives. These instruments may not be sufficiently

[3] See http://www.dfs.ny.gov/reportpub/shadow_insurance_report_2013.pdf.

[4] See http://www.treasury.gov/initiatives/fio/reports-and-notices/Documents/How%20to%20Modernize%20and%20Improve%20the%20System%20of%20Insurance%20Regulation%20in%20the%20United%20States.pdf.

loss-absorbing if a significant adverse event were to occur. In many cases, a significant adverse event would cause a captive to fail and spread losses retained within the holding company or to another affiliate within the group, thereby accentuating group risk.

The Federal Insurance Office also points to the lack of transparency regarding the risk transfer to captives. The lack of transparency is not just *vis-à-vis* investors and the public, but also with regard to regulators. While financial statements of traditional insurers are made publicly available, the financial statements of captives are kept confidential between the captive manager and the domestic state. This is particularly troublesome in light of the limits on state regulatory authority, as state regulators must rely on information from another state in which a reinsurance captive is domiciled.

Financial stability policies for insurance captives

Insurance company regulators have the authority to reject transactions with a captive. However, the fragmented nature of insurance regulation in the US represents a high hurdle. Disclosure requirements limit regulators ability to assess the extent to which insurance companies transfer risks to captives in other states. Furthermore, as captives tend to make the insurance subsidiary in a given state less risky, they tend to be approved, even if the holding company risk has not declined.

The Federal Insurance Office recommends for states to develop a uniform and transparent solvency and oversight regime for the transfer of risk to reinsurance captives. The oversight of captives should not only cover the liabilities transferred to a reinsurance captive, but also of the nature of the assets that support a reinsurance captive's financial status. In addition, the Office recommends for states to develop and adopt a uniform capital requirement for reinsurance captives, including a prohibition on those types of transactions that do not constitute a legitimate transfer of risk.

The National Association of Insurance Commissioners has put out a white paper with recommendations regarding the treatment of captives and other special purpose vehicles that includes accounting, confidentiality and reinsurance regulatory matters. However, the paper notes that state insurance regulators disagree about the regulation of captives, with some arguing for a nationwide level playing field, while others prefer the current regime of incomplete opacity and differential capital treatment.

Among the state regulator, the New York State Department of Financial Services aggressively argues for a change in the regulation of life insurance captives by recommending disclosure requirements for captives of New York based insurers and their affiliates, by pressing the National Association of Insurance Commissioners to develop enhanced disclosure requirements for all jurisdictions. The New York regulator has also called for an immediate national moratorium on approvals of shadow insurance transactions until investigations are complete.

One avenue of regulation that is relevant for the captives of the largest, most systemically important insurance companies is the designation by the Financial Stability Oversight Council as systemically important financial institutions (non-bank SIFIs). Some of the largest insurance companies have recently been designated by the Financial Stability Oversight Council as systemically important, and will thus be subject to Federal Reserve supervision at the consolidated level. The designation of non-bank firms as systemically important is an important method of the Dodd–Frank Act to address the risk of so-called "too big to fail" financial institutions.

The Dodd–Frank Act explicitly mandates that designated systemically important financial institutions have to be subject to *enhanced prudential standards*, which include enhanced risk-based capital and leverage requirements, liquidity requirements, single-counterparty credit limits, stress testing, risk-management requirements, an early remediation regime, and resolution-planning requirements. Sections 165 and 166 of the Act also require that these prudential standards become more stringent as the systemic footprint of the firm increases. The Federal Reserve's proposed rules apply the same set of enhanced prudential standards to covered companies that are BHCs and covered companies that are non-bank financial companies designated by the Council.

In SR letter 12-23, issued on December 20, 2013, the Federal Reserve sets forth supplemental guidance regarding risk transfer considerations when assessing capital adequacy of large financial institutions. While the Federal Reserve generally recognizes that risk reducing transactions can represent sound risk management practices, the Fed points out that certain risk transfers to unconsolidated, sponsored affiliate entities give rise to supervisory concern as such transactions may result in a significant reduction of the capital requirements without a significant reduction of the firms' risk. To the extent that captive reinsurance affiliates lead to a reduction in regulatory capital for insurance holding companies, the Federal Reserve's treatment might become a binding constraint on the size of such affiliates.

Conclusion

Shadow banking activities evolve in response to changing regulations and market conditions. As a result of this evolution, policies towards financial stability for the shadow banking system need to adapt. While some of the risks that were relevant in the run-up to the financial crisis remain risks today, new shadow banking activities have emerged, requiring new policy approaches. For example, run and funding risks emanating from the tri-party repo market and the money market fund sector remain current, while risks from ABCP conduits, SIVs, and CDOs have receded, in part due to regulatory and accounting changes. The discussions and case studies in this article also underline that shadow bank policies are highly specific to the particular activity under consideration. Policies cover areas as diverse as capital regulation, wholesale money market funding, insurance company structure, disclosure policies, underwriting standards, among many others.

Policies aimed at mitigating risks from shadow credit intermediation have to start with an analysis of the economic mechanism that motivates the particular activity. We have listed seven motivations for shadow credit intermediation. A major challenge for financial stability policies for shadow banking is the fragmented nature of the regulatory system in the US. The creation of the Financial Stability Oversight Council by the Dodd–Frank Act provides some additional scope for regulators to address threats from shadow banking, primarily via designation of non-bank financial institutions as systemically important. Policies will need to react dynamically to the changing financial landscape to contain threats effectively. Importantly, shadow bank policies need to take a system wide, macroprudential view, due to the tight interconnections and potentially powerful spillovers among shadow banking entities, and between shadow banks and core regulated financial institutions.

References

Acharya, V., P. Schnabl and G. Suarez (2013). Securitization without Risk Transfer. *Journal of Financial Economics*, Vol. 107, No. 3, pp. 515–536.

Adrian, T. (2011). Dodd–Frank One Year On: Implications for Shadow Banking. *Published in the CEPR Conference Volume Pew Charitable Trust–New York University Conference "Dodd–Frank: One Year On".*

Adrian, T. and A.B. Ashcraft (2012a). Shadow Bank Regulation. *Annual Review of Financial Economics*, Vol. 4, pp. 99–140.

Adrian, T. and A.B. Ashcraft (2012b). Shadow Banking: A Review of the Literature. In *Palgrave Dictionary of Economics*, S.N. Durlauf and L.E. Blume (eds.). Palgrave: Macmillan.

Adrian, T., A.B. Ashcraft and N. Cetorelli (2013). Shadow bank monitoring. In *Oxford Handbook of Banking*. New York: OUP.

Adrian, T., B. Begalle, A. Copeland and A. Martin (2013). Repo and securities lending. In *Quantifying Systemic Risk Measurement: NBER Research Conference Report Series*, J.G. Haubrich and A.W. Lo (eds.). Chicago: University of Chicago Press.

Adrian, T., D. Covitz and J.N. Liang (2012). Financial stability monitoring. *Federal Reserve Bank of New York Staff Reports* 601.

Alworth, J. and G. Arachi (2012). *Taxation and the Financial Crisis*. Oxford: Oxford University Press.

Ashcraft, A.B. and T. Schuermann (2008). Understanding the Securitization of Subprime Mortgage Credit. *Foundations and Trends in Finance*, Vol. 2, No. 3, pp. 191–309.

Ashcraft, A.B., A. Malz and Z. Pozsar (2012). The Federal Reserve's Term Asset-Backed Securities Loan Facility. *Federal Reserve Bank of New York Economic Policy Review*, pp. 29–66.

Ashcraft, A.B., P. Goldsmith-Pinkham, P. Hull and J. Vickery (2011). Credit Ratings and Security Prices in the Subprime MBS Market. *American Economic Review*, Vol. 101, No. 3, pp. 115–119.

Cohen, A. (2011). Rating Shopping in the CMBS Market. Presented at Regulation of Systemic Risk, Washington, DC, September 15–16.

Copeland, A., A. Martin and M. Walker (2011). Repo Runs: Evidence from the Tri-Party Repo Market. *Federal Reserve Bank of New York Staff Report* 506.

Coval, J., J. Jurek and E. Stafford (2009). The Economics of Structured Finance. *Journal of Economic Perspectives*, Vol. 23, No. 1, pp. 3–25.

Covitz, D., N. Liang and G. Suarez (2012). The Evolution of a Financial Crisis: Panic in the Asset-backed Commercial Paper Market. *Journal of Finance*. Forthcoming.

Davis, E.P. and M. Stone (2004). Corporate Structure and Financial Stability. *IMF Working Paper* 04/124.

Dang, T.V., G. Gorton and B. Holmström (2009). Opacity and the Optimality of Debt for Liquidity Provision. *Yale/MIT Working Paper.*

Diamond, D. and P. Dybvig (1983). Bank Runs, Deposit Insurance, and Liquidity. *Journal of Political Economy*, Vol. 91, pp. 401–419.

Farhi, E. and J. Tirole (2012). Collective Moral Hazard, Maturity Mismatch, and Systemic Bailouts. *American Economic Review*, Vol. 102, No. 1, pp. 60–93.

Financial Stability Board (2011). Shadow Banking: Strengthening Oversight and Regulation.

Financial Stability Board (2013a). Policy Framework for Strengthening Oversight and Regulation of Shadow Banking Entities.

Financial Stability Board (2013b). Policy Framework for Addressing Shadow Banking Risks in Securities Lending and Repos.

Gallin, J. (2013). Shadow Banking and the Funding of the Nonfinancial Sector. *Federal Reserve Board Finance and Economics Discussion Series* 2013-50.

Gennaioli, N., A. Shleifer and R. Vishny (2012). Neglected Risks, Financial Innovation, and Financial Fragility. *Journal of Financial Economics*, Vol. 104, No. 3, pp. 452–468.

Gennaioli, N., A. Shleifer and R. Vishny (2013). A Model of Shadow Banking. *Journal of Finance*, Vol. 68, No. 4, pp. 1331–1363.

Gorton, G. (2009). The Subprime Panic. *European Financial Management*, Vol. 15, No. 1, pp. 10–46.

Gorton, G. and A. Metrick (2011). Regulating the Shadow Banking System. *Brookings Paper on Economic Activity*, pp. 261–312.

Gorton, G. and A. Metrick (2012). Securitized Banking and the Run on Repo. *Journal of Financial Economics*, Vol. 104, pp. 425–451.

Greenwood, R., S. Hanson and J. Stein (2010). A Gap-Filling Theory of Corporate Debt Maturity Choice. *Journal of Finance*, Vol. 65, No. 3, pp. 993–1028.

Keys, B., T. Mukherjee, A. Seru and V. Vig (2010). Did Securitization Lead to Lax Screening? Evidence from Subprime Loans. *Quarterly Journal of Financial Economics*, Vol. 125, No. 1, pp. 307–362.

Koijen, R. and M. Yogo (2013). Shadow Insurance. *NBER Working Paper* 19568.

Krishnamurthy, A. and A. Vissing-Jorgensen (2012). Short-Term Debt and Financial Crisis: What can We Learn from the U.S. Treasury Supply. *Northwestern University Working Paper.*

Martin, A., D. Skeie and E. von Thadden (2011). Repo Runs. *Federal Reserve Bank of New York Staff Report* 444.

Mathis, J., J. McAndrews and J.C. Rochet (2009). Rating the Raters: Are Reputation Concerns Powerful Enough to Discipline Rating Agencies? *Journal of Monetary Economics*, Vol. 57, No. 5, pp. 657–674.

McCabe, P. (2011). An A-/B-share Capital Buffer Proposal for Money Market Funds. *Working Paper.*

McCabe, P.E., M. Cipriani, M. Holscher and A. Martin (2012). The Minimum Balance at Risk: A Proposal to Mitigate the Systemic Risks Posed by Money Market Funds. *Federal Reserve Bank of New York Staff Report* 564.

Mooij, R., M. Keen and M. Orihara (2013). Taxation, Bank Leverage, and Financial Crises. *IMF Working Paper* 13/48.

Moreira, A. and A. Savov (2014). The Macroeconomics of Shadow Banking. *Yale University Working Paper.*

Pozsar, Z., T. Adrian, A.B. Ashcraft and H. Boesky (2013). Shadow Banking. *Federal Reserve Bank of New York Economic Policy Review*, Vol. 19, No. 2, pp. 1–16. Available at http://www.newyorkfed.org/research/epr/2013/0713adri.html.

Rajan, R. (2005). Has Financial Development Made the World Riskier? *Proceedings of the Federal Reserve Bank of Kansas City Economics Symposium*, pp. 313–369.

Stein, J. (2010). Securitization, Shadow Banking, and Financial Fragility. *Daedalus*, Vol. 139, No. 4, pp. 41–51.

Stein, J. (2012). Monetary Policy as Financial-Stability Regulation. *Quarterly Journal of Economics*, Vol. 127, No. 1, pp. 57–95.

Sunderam, A. (2012). Money Creation and the Shadow Banking System. *Harvard Business School Working Paper.*

Wiggers, T. and A.B. Ashcraft (2012). Defaults and Losses on Commercial Real Estate Bonds during the Great Depression Era. *Federal Reserve Bank of New York Staff Report* 544.

Xia, H. and G. Strobl (2012). The Issuer-Pays Rating Model and Ratings Inflation: Evidence from Corporate Credit Ratings.

Shadow Banking — What Are We Really Worried About?

Laura E. Kodres*

International Monetary Fund

This morning I would like to take a step back from some of the more detailed topics that have been on the agenda for this conference and provide you with a somewhat broader perspective. Let me apologize in advance to some of my colleagues in the room for perhaps a very basic treatment of some of the issues surrounding systemic risk and shadow banking. I hope my value added is to try to "connect the existing dots". The reason that I think it is important to do this is that, ultimately, the policy fixes are different depending on the diagnosis of the problem. Thus, understanding whether shadow banking contributes to systemic risk and how it does so will be important in determining the policy solutions.

Let me start by looking backward and examine the events during this last crisis that generated the interest in this topic. During the crisis we observed runs — not the usual retail runs but wholesale funding runs. We observed the drying up of repo funding for heavily dependent US investment banks; runs on money market mutual funds (MMMFs) that had provided funding to commercial and universal banks (both in the United States and in Europe); runs on asset-backed commercial paper (ABCP) funding where the assets were backed by mortgages or by structured credit products. Although initially the runs were of a wholesale nature, we also witnessed some retail deposit runs — for instance, commercial banks in the

*Assistant Director and Division Chief for the Asian Division in the Institute for Capacity Development at the International Monetary Fund. The content of this paper represents my own view and not those of the International Monetary Fund's executive board, its management, or its staff.

United States and United Kingdom. As well, we saw runs on MMMFs — such as the Reserve Fund — initially instigated from corporate cash pools, but where retail investors also got nervous.

We also observed a higher-than-normal degree of leverage in the system. We saw institutions that held insufficient backing for their activities — even if not termed "capital". We saw insufficient cash for redemptions in money market funds, insufficient means of taking losses in non-traditional insurance activities such as derivatives transactions or guarantees, and insufficient backing for off-balance sheet vehicles, such as SIVs and conduits. Even now, we observe leverage and maturity mismatches between assets and liabilities in some new vehicles. The wealth management products in China and the M-REITS in the United States are two examples.

Before I try to connect how shadow banking might be related to systemic risk, let me outline two ways of thinking about systemic risk.

First, consider a time series component. This mainly describes a build-up of leverage in a credit context or a differential mismatch between assets and liabilities. In the context of markets, this can also be viewed as the procyclicality of margin or collateral valuation, which as noted yesterday by Ana Fostel, adds a further component to a normal credit cycle.

Second, we can consider a cross-sectional or interconnectedness component. This would encompass the knock-on effects of a shock, potentially leading to runs on multiple types of securities or institutions simultaneously. The simultaneous interaction between funding and market liquidity, that is, the fact that funding difficulties can lead to fire sales and or a "flight to quality" which differentiates risks across asset types, is part of this conceptualization of systemic risk.

Now let me return to the connection between shadow banking and systemic risk: What we are generally concerned about is the uncontrolled, or hidden, amount of leverage in non-banks that may be harmful to the financial system, and ultimately affect the real economy. In particular, as noted by Governor Stein yesterday, we are concerned about the "innocent bystanders" that get hurt when unwinding or fire sales take place — when there are externalities involving those who cannot protect themselves.

We are concerned about non-linear, or amplified, responses to relatively small shocks and how this magnification can affect the real economy. We are especially concerned about shadow banks that affect the banking sector. The work of Ana Fostel and John Geanokoplos, and many others, is focused on explaining exactly how various amplification mechanisms operate in modern financial markets.

We are also concerned about "runs" — that is, when investors abruptly want their money to be money-like. This can include bank-like activities that are executed by non-banks but marketed or viewed as if they taking place under the purview of supervisors or contain some type of public sector backstop (as banks typically have). This can be types of investments where customers believe they can withdraw their money at par value, even if not technically guaranteed. Examples include items like MMMFs in the United States, the wealth management products in China, and even, one might argue, the M-REITs that are getting so much attention in the United States. Two features regarding runs that are relatively new are that they can be perpetrated by so-called "sophisticated" investors (like a non-financial corporate treasurer) and can move money across borders relatively quickly.

However, we should be careful to avoid viewing all non-bank activity as somehow "shadowy". It is worth noting that the FSB's monitoring exercise that quantifies "shadow banks" from various jurisdictions from the national flow of funds data is actually capturing just the assets of "other financial institutions" without a judgment about the leverage, maturity structure, or other characteristics of the activities. For instance, in part, the category of "asset managers" is likely largely unlevered investments in public equities. Hedge funds in the FSB sample cover anything from unlevered long-short equity strategies to levered credit transfer products. In generally, we are not really concerned if savers are using capital market-based financing instruments to enhance their welfare. Nor are we concerned about the movement of funds through normal, well-constructed payment systems. The use of e-payments systems to reach previously unbanked parts of a countries' population would be an example.

Having identified, conceptually, what we are worried about, the next step to figure out *when* we should be worried. Clearly, this is a much harder task and requires some amount of measuring the "size" of the problem. Again, conceptually, we will need to make a judgment on the elements that feed into systemic risks.

These elements include: the degree of leverage, the degree of maturity mismatch, the cash holdings that might be available for redemptions, the protections against operational risk such as legal documentation, the robustness of clearing and settlement (such as the timing of flows through the tri-party repo system) and so on.

Even in cases where we know what we need to know, it may be difficult to find it. For instance, the "assets under management" are not necessarily a good measure of risk exposure. Moreover, we do not even have AUM for all non-banks. For instance, for some non-bank financial intermediaries in some jurisdictions, such as those in India, the government is not permitted to collect information unless that entity is regulated, but without the information the authorities cannot determine whether the entity *should* be regulated. Hence, there can be a "chicken and egg" problem in which one cannot discover whether an institution or activity poses a systemic risk unless one can collect basic information about it.

Even if we were able to collect the information, we would then need to discover whether it poses a systemic risk — for instance, how much leverage in a typical finance company is too much? As we noted yesterday, even this answer may depend on the other conditions of the financial system. Leverage could be quite high and not be problem in a so-called "stable" or "benign" environment, but would be in a fragile or volatile environment. Runs may be less likely until one or more institution experiences a run, then the risk of more runs increases.

Recall, we are mostly concerned with the "innocent bystanders" or those who unwittingly end up in the cross-fire. How do we tell whether investors really understand the risks they are assuming? How large does the typeface need to be on disclosure statements? Which types of investors are sophisticated, or which ones have deep enough pockets that we think they can realistically absorb their own mistakes?

How much information about interconnectedness do we need to see if the networks are basically stable, or whether they are exceeding some threshold that makes them fragile? If we collected enough information about cross-exposures to determine systemic risks, how widely should we distribute such information? When?

Figure 1, in the pre-crisis period, represents statistically significant connections among banks, insurance companies and sovereigns.

Figure 2 represents the same exercise in the post-crisis period. The question then arises, should we have been concerned before, after, or not at all? My point is that we have not yet figured out how to interpret even the information that we are able to collect and transform.

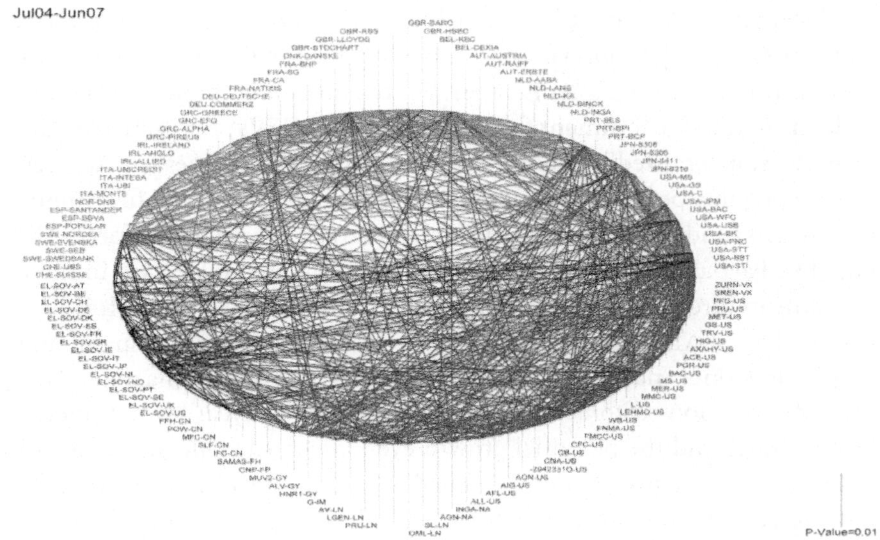

Fig. 1. Sovereign, bank, and insurance company connections: Pre-crisis period.
Source: Billio *et al.* (forthcoming).

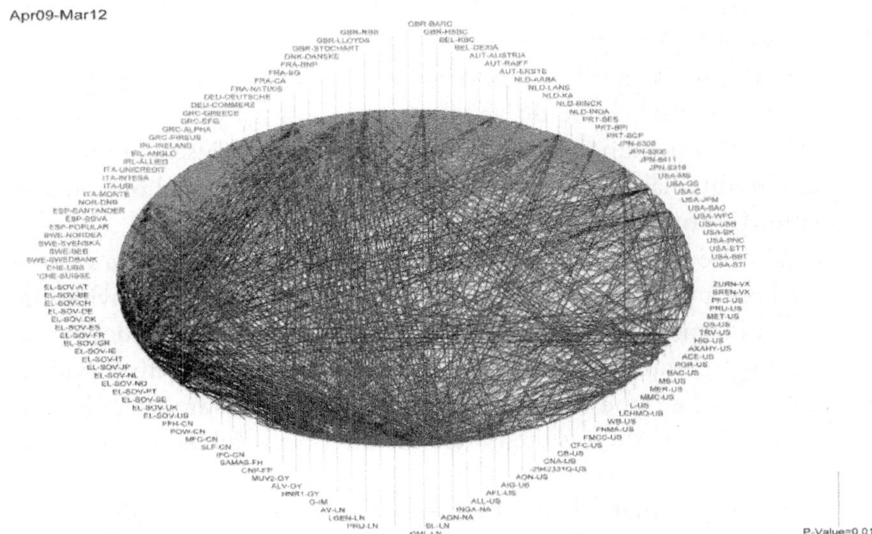

Fig. 2. Sovereign, bank, and insurance company connections: Post-crisis period.
Source: Billio *et al.* (forthcoming).

Yesterday, we talked a bit about China's wealth management products, which may well be a concern. Many investors believe they can obtain their money from these investments at par; but the investments are now likely to be loans to local government financial vehicles (LGFVs) for infrastructure projects, collateralized by public land that could well be overvalued. Even more worrying, perhaps, is the launch of Yu'E Bao. This is the first online investment fund. It is connected to the 3rd largest payment platform, Alipay (like Paypal in the United States). The service uses spare cash in these accounts to directly invest in a private fund (TIANHONG), which is now China's largest MMF. Apparently, the investments are in government and corporate money markets. The growth numbers are pretty amazing with a total of 13 million customers as of end-September this year from its inception in June. And the potential growth even larger, since those connected to the payment platform number some 800 million customers. Please note, however, that I have not been able to verify these statistics with any formal source. The reason for both the Wealth Management Products and this new online MMF is clear, though. With deposit interest rates at 35 basis points and returns in this vehicle of close to 5% — with again the ability to redeem immediately at, presumably, par value — the investment is very attractive. Should we worry? Hard to know. Do investors realize the risks? Is the payments platform safe?

Assuming we deem some type of activity or institution as posing a risk to the system what do we do about it? Here is a list of possibilities — ranging from extending the regulatory perimeter for closer monitoring, or more traditional micro-prudential regulation (like capital or liquidity regulation), or outlawing the activity or closing the institutions.

In the case of private-label securitization, a number of "fixes" have already been put in place. While we cannot be sure what is driving the decline in issuance, whether it is lack of demand for the product or the high cost of attempting to execute the business (especially with two giant GSEs in the background), we can observe that the volumes are basically dead (Figure 3). The question is then, were the multiple regulations warranted or not.

Let me suggest that when we believe we have found some shadow banking activity that poses a systemic risk, we think deeply about what the root cause is. Yesterday, we discussed financial repression. This really points to

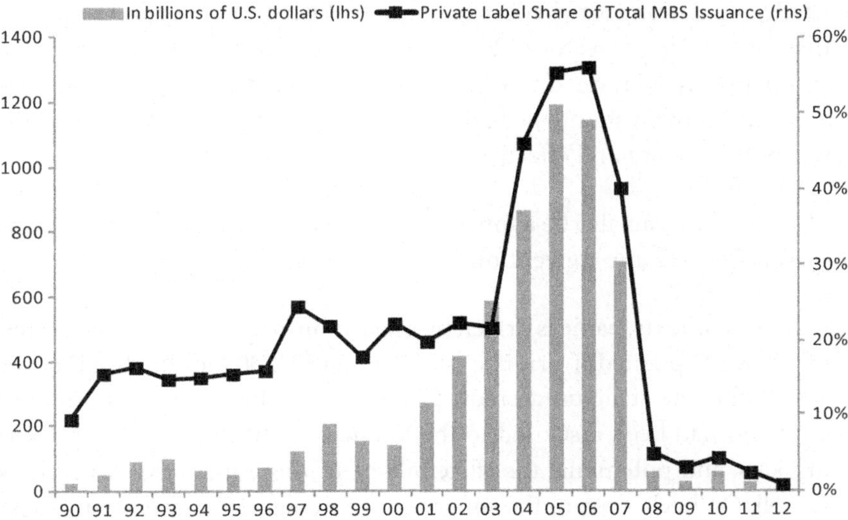

Fig. 3. US private label mortgage-backed security issuance.
Source: Inside Mortgage Finance and IMF Staff Estimates.

considering incentives — and not just the incentives of the private sector. Let me suggest three items.

- First, better link private sector compensation schemes to long-run risks, not just short-run returns. There is a tendency to put short-run profits in front of all else. Witness the credit growth when mortgage originators were rewarded for the quantity, not the quality, of the loans they originated. Also, consider the incentives of the five types of investors Zoltan Posnar identified yesterday that are active this arena. Why should those requesting safe assets be rewarded by receiving them at no cost?
- Incentives also need to improve for supervisors and regulators. For instance, supervisors and regulators need to have the incentive to report the buildup of risks and aberrant behavior of their regulatees to their superiors without the fear that they (perhaps anticipating the response of lobbyists and politicians) will be ignored, or worse, fired. What has been the influence, for instance, of non-financial corporate treasurers on the members of the regulatory community regarding the use of a fixed net asset value for the MMF complex in the United States?

- Lastly, regulations for shadow banking will need to factor in the incentives of the private sector to follow them. We used to call this "incentive compatible regulation" and it seems to have been dropped from the lexicon, but I think it should be revived as it is likely the only way regulations will both efficient and effective.

Information can also be a touchstone for removing systemic risk. Allow me to challenge some conventional wisdom here.

- In many contexts, panic is driven by a lack of information. Consider what may have happened if prior to the summer of 2007 all the holdings of ABCP and the structured credit products and the mortgages underlying them had been disclosed to the financial institutions active in these markets, and potentially the stakeholders of those financial institutions as well. Or, heck, even to the supervisors and regulators overseeing these institutions.
- I contend that at least part of the solution to preventing systemic events, and runs in particular, from repeating themselves it to provide much more basic information to those involved in funding various financial activities. The cross-exposures of institutions, if released constantly (not during the high-point of a systemic crisis), would allow providers of funds to extract enough return to compensate them for the risks they bear. While the technical requirements of looking through the first level of exposures to additional counterparties are not easy, it can be done.
- The key will be to remove some types of confidentiality agreements, and to collect and provide the raw data to regulators and supervisors and, importantly, devise some method of providing it to the public in a way that does not overly compromise competition. There are difficult issues here, no doubt, but the protection of the financial system from runs may need to be explicitly preferred to the protection of confidentiality for the benefit of competition.
- I agree that there are benefits of many types of capital market activities that fall into the category of shadow banking, but if they were more transparent and investors were cognizant of what was happening and why, then systemic risks arising from asymmetric or incomplete information could be mitigated — and this would certainly help remove some of the activity from the shadows and put it into the daylight.

Reference

Billio, M., M. Germansky, D. Gray, A. Lo, R. Merton and L. Pelizzon (forthcoming). Sovereign, Bank, and Insurance Credit Spreads: Connectedness and Systemic Networks. *Sloan School of Management Working Paper*, Massachusetts Institute of Technology, Cambridge, Massachusetts.

Derivatives and Bankruptcy*

Steven L. Schwarcz[†] and Ori Sharon[‡]

Duke University School of Law

Bankruptcy law in the United States, which serves as an important precedent for the treatment of derivatives under insolvency law worldwide, gives creditors in derivatives transactions special rights and immunities in the bankruptcy process, including virtually unlimited enforcement rights against a bankrupt counterparty (hereinafter, the "safe harbor"). The concern is that these special rights and immunities grew incrementally, primarily due to industry lobbying and without a systematic and rigorous vetting of their consequences.

Thus, creditors can exercise their contractual enforcement remedies against a bankrupt counterparty or its property — including closing out, netting, and setting off their derivatives positions and liquidating collateral in their possession — notwithstanding the automatic stay of enforcement actions. Creditors are also exempt from the so-called "trustee-avoiding powers", such as preference rules and constructively fraudulent transfers, regarding any payments and collateral received prior to the bankruptcy. The US bankruptcy law also allows creditors to enforce bankruptcy-termination ("*ipso facto*") clauses, and to net all existing derivatives contracts with the

---

*This chapter is based on the authors' forthcoming article, *The Bankruptcy-Law Safe Harbor for Derivatives: A Path-Dependence Analysis*, 71 Washington and Lee L. Rev. issue no. 3 (forthcoming 2014); Available at http://ssrn.com/abstract=2351025.

[†]Stanley A. Star Professor of Law & Business, Duke University School of Law, and Founding Director, Duke Global Capital Markets Center; schwarcz@law.duke.edu. The authors thank participants in the Federal Reserve Bank of Chicago-International Monetary Fund conference on "Shadow Banking Within and Across National Borders" for their valuable comments.

[‡]S.J.D. candidate, Duke University School of Law.

bankrupt counterparty. This effectively exempts derivatives contracts from a debtor's ability to terminate unfavorable contracts.

Many scholars believe there is a serious question whether the benefits of the safe harbor exceed its costs, and some argue that the safe harbor may even have unintended harmful consequences.

Path Dependence

This type of legislative accretion process is a form of path dependence — a process in which the outcome is shaped by its historical path. To understand path dependence, consider Professor Mark Roe's example of an 18th century fur trader who cuts a winding path through the woods to avoid dangers.[1] Later travelers follow this path, and in time it becomes a paved road and houses and industry are erected alongside. Although the dangers that affected the fur trader are long gone, few question the road's inefficiently winding route.

Legal path dependence occurs when an initial path effectively blinds lawmakers to alternative paths. Informational and political burdens can cause the blindness.[2] Informational burdens arise when the choice of one legislative path makes it harder to assess other paths. Political burdens are created when groups wield their influence to maintain and perhaps magnify an initial path.

Evolution of the Bankruptcy-Law Safe Harbor for Derivatives

The derivatives safe harbor exemplifies legal path dependence. It is an outcome of decades of sustained industry pressure on Congress to exempt the derivatives market from the reach of bankruptcy law, with each exemption serving as an historical justification for subsequent broader exemptions.

The initial exemptions — which were included in 1977 in the bill that became the Bankruptcy Code — were promoted by a derivatives-industry representative who suggested that Congress grant commodities brokers authority to "close out" an insolvent customer's account, in order to prevent "a potential domino effect". He argued such an effect could occur

[1] Roe (1995–1996).

[2] Ruhl and Ruhl, Jr. (1996–1997).

because the commodities futures market is fragile.[3] But as sole evidence of market fragility, he merely cited a court case.[4] And he did not explain why the inability of a commodities broker to freely close out an insolvent customer's account could cause a domino effect. Nonetheless, Congress followed his suggestion and included several narrow exemptions in the Bankruptcy Code.

These exemptions were later used as precedent to justify broader exemptions, which in turn themselves served as precedent for increasingly broader exemptions. For example, a 1982 amendment to the Bankruptcy Code that further expanded the safe harbor exemptions beyond commodities futures markets was viewed by Congress as merely continuing the goal of preventing systemic risk, with the "*potential* domino effect" now being termed a "*threat of market collapse*".[5] Similarly, in 1990, the International Swaps and Derivatives Association ("ISDA"), a leading industry group, urged Congress to further amend the Bankruptcy Code to exempt its application to swap transactions. ISDA noted that "Congress has for many years recognized the need for certainty and speed in the treatment of securities and other similar financial transactions in bankruptcy", and that former amendments to the Bankruptcy Code with regard to securities, commodities, and repurchase agreements "worked well in practice and have provided needed certainty".[6] ISDA argued that the requested new protections "closely paralleled" those provided by earlier amendments.

Perhaps the only expansion of the safe harbor that was not clearly due to path dependence was a 2005 amendment to the Bankruptcy Code, which allowed creditors to terminate and net amounts owing under most financial market contracts. This expansion was based on a recommendation in a report by the President's Working Group on Financial Markets (the "PWG Report"), which studied the near failure of the Long-Term Capital

---

[3]Testimony of Stuart D. Root. Bankruptcy Reform Act of 1978: Hearings before the Subcommittee on Improvements in Judicial Machinery of the Committee on the Judiciary, United States Senate, Ninety-fifth Congress, first session, on S. 2266 and H.R. 8200, November 28, 29 and December 1, 1977, pp. 521–524. Available at http://www.archive.org/stream/bankruptcyreform1978unit/bankruptcyreform1978unit_djvu.txt.

[4]Geldermann & Co. v. Lane Processing, Inc., 527 F.2d 571 (8th Cir. 1975).

[5]H.R. Rep. No. 420, H.R. REP. 97-420, 1, 1982 U.S.C.C.A.N. 583, 583.

[6]Statement of International Swap Dealers Association in Support of S.2279, June 10, 1988, at 674.

Management hedge fund ("LTCM"). The PWG Report argued that if LTCM had defaulted, the ability of creditors to terminate and net amounts owing under derivatives contracts, free of bankruptcy law's automatic stay of enforcement actions, would have mitigated their losses and reduced the likelihood of instability in the financial markets. Congress did not appear to take into account opposing views, however, such as those of the National Bankruptcy Conference, which advised that there is "no indication that the absence of" these expanded rights "has led to widespread difficulties or systemic disruptions in the financial markets".[7] Congress also ignored the Conference's warning that certain aspects of the "netting could deprive a [bankrupt counterparty] of much-needed cash collateral, which in some instances may lead to conversion and liquidation to the detriment of other creditors".[8]

Is the Derivatives Safe Harbor Path Dependent?

The derivatives safe harbor is, at least, largely path-dependent. Congress usually assumed that an expanding safe harbor would help protect against systemic risk. With each passing amendment, that assumption became more entrenched as a truth. This reflects an informational blindness, discouraging alternative views. The informational blindness was almost certainly exacerbated by both the complexity of derivatives and uncertainty over how systemic risk is created and transmitted. Being concerned about systemic risk, members of Congress tended to see what they expected to see, the expectation in this case being driven by powerful derivatives-industry lobbying pressure. From a public choice standpoint, no powerful interest groups presented Congress with opposing views (although the National Bankruptcy Conference presented opposing views, it was not a powerful interest group and its views were ignored[9]).

[7] Bankruptcy Reform Act of 1999 (Part III), Hearing on H.R. 833 Before the Subcomm. on Commercial and Administrative Law of the House Comm. on the Judiciary, 106th Cong., 1st Sess. 369 (statement of Randal Picker, on behalf of the National Bankruptcy Conference), available at http://commdocs.house.gov/committees/judiciary/hju63847.000/hju63847_0.HTM.

[8] *Id.*

[9] *See supra* notes 10–11 and accompanying text.

To the extent the 2005 expansion of the safe harbor was recommended by the PWG Report, it might not appear to represent legal path dependence. Nonetheless, that Report does not address opposing viewpoints. Furthermore, ISDA played a "significant role in the drafting of the relevant provisions of [the 2005 expansion and] worked in close collaboration" with the President's Working Group on Financial Markets. ISDA "prepared a position paper . . . setting forth the need for [the expansion] and proposing [its statutory] language". ISDA also "participated in many of the hearings that led up to the eventual adoption of the" expansion.[10]

ISDA's significant influence reflects the fact that as the derivatives industry skyrocketed in size, lobbyists such as ISDA became much more powerful, creating a political burden that discouraged alternative views. Ironically, the increase in the size of the derivatives industry was itself partly fostered by the safe harbor, which encouraged firms to deviate away from traditional financing into exotic derivatives, to avoid application of bankruptcy law. And that, in turn, has made the financial system even more complex, further reinforcing the informational blindness.

Reassessing the Derivatives Safe Harbor. Path-dependent legislation is not necessarily bad. Nonetheless, if the legislation is not fully vetted, its significance and utility should not be taken for granted. Although we have not made an independent analysis of the merits of the derivatives safe harbor, our review indicates that some scholars seriously question whether its benefits exceed its costs. Consider this in the context of the substantive issues surrounding derivatives and systemic risk.

The characteristics of the derivatives market have contributed to the belief that a collapse of a derivatives counterparty might precipitate a systemic meltdown. Because the trade in derivatives is concentrated among relatively few major firms, it is feared that the collapse of a single firm, especially a highly connected one, might systemically disrupt the derivatives market, which could then impact the financial system more broadly.[11] But this systemic risk story is far from proved. There is "little actual evidence

---

[10] pp. 1–2 and note 1 of ISDA's Amicus Curiae brief in *In re* Nat'l Gas Distributors, LLC, 556 F.3d 247 (4th Cir. 2009).

[11] United States General Accounting Office, "Financial Derivatives: Actions Needed to Protect the Financial System", Report to Congressional Requestors, GAO/GGD-94-133, 7 (May 1994).

to support" the story.[12] On the other hand, economists have estimated that the net exposure of the major derivatives dealers to their five largest dealer counterparties is relatively small.[13]

Ironically, the safe harbor itself may be exacerbating the movement toward market concentration of the derivatives industry. The safe harbor enables creditors to ignore counterparty risk because a creditor can terminate derivatives contracts, net amounts owing thereunder, and foreclose on collateral notwithstanding the counterparty's bankruptcy. That reduces a creditor's incentive to diversify its counterparties. The safe harbor's unrestricted netting provisions can also contribute to increased market concentration. Unrestricted netting permits derivatives positions to be adjusted by executing an offsetting position with the same party without incurring additional costs. That induces market participants to concentrate their positions with relatively few dealers.[14]

The safe harbor may not even be focused on the right parties. Some scholars argue that the fear of derivatives-induced systemic risk is warranted only in the case of an insolvency of a major financial market participant holding a massive derivatives portfolio. The safe harbor's exemptions, however, operate independently of the size of the counterparty or its portfolio. They also apply to non-financial, as well as to financial, firms. Thus a bank that makes a secured loan cannot enforce its collateral against a bankrupt borrower, whereas an ordinary business firm can enforce its collateral against a bankrupt derivatives counterparty.

Another concern is that the safe harbor, which is now so broad that virtually any ordinary financial transaction can be documented to fall within it, may well have unintended harmful consequences. Because derivatives transactions are exempted from bankruptcy law, parties are tempted to try to document ordinary financial transactions as derivatives transactions in order to benefit from the exemption. Some textbooks are openly encouraging parties to design financing contracts as derivatives transactions, in order to circumvent the Bankruptcy Code's restrictions.

Another possible unintended consequence is that unrestricted netting can trigger the equivalent of bank runs. Using LTCM as an example,

[12] Lubben (2010).

[13] Bliss and Kaufman (2006).

[14] *Id.* at 61–62.

Professors Edwards and Morrison argue that unrestricted netting would have motivated LTCM's creditors to rush to net and close out their positions. That, in turn, could have caused or exacerbated "liquidity shortages, resulting in systemic illiquidity with the potential to cause widespread contagion."[15] In contrast, absent unrestricted netting, Edwards and Morrison believe that "LTCM's major creditors almost certainly would have opted to . . . put[] in more capital. . .".[16]

ISDA's Head of Research has responded to this criticism, but only in generalities, including observing that there is an international legal harmonization towards allowing unrestricted netting.[17] The fact that something is occurring does not necessarily mean, however, that it should be occurring — especially when lobbying is a cause of what is occurring.

Conclusions

Because the derivatives safe harbor has important consequences for systemic risk, a more fully informed discussion of its merits — under US bankruptcy law, and under foreign insolvency laws to the extent such laws incorporate similar derivatives exemptions — may well be timely. Our analysis also suggests that heightened informational burdens due to complexity and uncertainty can increase the influence of interest-group politics. That, in turn, can make legislation more vulnerable to legal path-dependency, especially when, as in the case of the derivatives safe harbor, no powerful interest groups present opposing views. In the face of increasing financial complexity, further research into the causes and consequences of legal path-dependency may be warranted.

---

[15] Edwards and Morrison (2005).

[16] *Ibid.*

[17] Beyond maintaining that "inability to terminate or net contracts with an insolvent firm would leave surviving firms vulnerable to losses caused by sudden market changes" — an argument that takes into account *ex-post* but not *ex-ante* implications, disregarding how increased exposure would motivate derivatives counterparties to diversify and monitor — ISDA's Head of Research observes that, "more generally, changing the treatment of derivatives and other financial contracts would represent a major departure by the United States from the trend toward cross-border convergence of the treatment of derivatives in insolvency and from the widespread acknowledgement by policymakers of the contribution of netting to financial stability"). David Mengle, ISDA Research Notes, *The Importance of Close-Out Netting* 5 (November 1, 2010).

References

Acharya, V.V. *et al.* (2011). Market Failures and Regulatory Failures: Lessons from Past and Present Financial Crises. In *Financial Market Regulation and Reforms in Emerging Markets*. M. Kawai and E. Prasad (eds.). Washington DC: Brookings Institution Press, p. 64.

Acharya, V.V., R.F. Cooley, R. Matthew and W. Ingo (2011). *Regulating Wall Street: The Dodd–Frank Act and the New Architecture of Global Finance*, pp. 27–28. John New York: Wiley & Sons, Inc.

2012 Annual Report of the Financial Stability Oversight Council, at 133. Available at http://www.treasury.gov/initiatives/fsoc/Pages/annual-report.aspx.

Baird, D.G. (1998). Bankruptcy's Uncontested Axioms. *Yale Law Journal*, Vol. 108, pp. 573–583.

Bebchuk, L.B. and M.J. Roe (1999). A Theory of Path Dependence in Corporate Ownership and Governance. *Stanford Law Review*, Vol. 52, pp. 131–156.

Bergman, W.J., R.R. Bliss, C.A. Johnson and G.G. Kaufman (2004). Netting, Financial Contracts, and Banks: The Economic Implications. *Federal Reserve Bank of Chicago Working Paper* No. 2004–02.

Bliss, R.R. and G.G. Kaufman (2006). Derivatives and Systemic Risk: Netting, Collateral, and Closeout. *Journal of Financial Stability*, Vol. 2, pp. 57–68.

Campbell, R.G. (2005). Financial Markets Contracts and BAPCA. *American Bankruptcy Law Journal*, Vol. 79, pp. 699–712.

Edwards, F.R. and E.R. Morrison (2005). Derivatives and the Bankruptcy Code: Why the Special Treatment? *Yale Journal on Regulation*, Vol. 22, pp. 95–121.

Faubus, B.G. (2010). Narrowing the Bankruptcy Safe Harbor for Derivatives to Combat Systemic Risk. *Duke Law Journal*, Vol. 59, pp. 828–829.

Final Report of the National Commission on the Causes of the Financial and Economic Crisis in the United States, 50 (January 2011).

Franklin, R.E. and E.R. Morrison (2005). Derivatives and the Bankruptcy Code: Why the Special Treatment? *Yale Journal on Regulation*, Vol. 22, p. 101.

Gerard, A. (2001). Institutions, Path Dependence, and Democratic Consolidation. *Journal of Theoretical Politics*, Vol. 13, p. 254.

Greenspan, A. (1999). Financial Derivatives. Remarks Before the Futures Industry Association, Boca Raton, Florida March 19, 1999.

Hansen, B.A. and H.M. Eschelbach (2007). The Role of Path Dependence in the Development of US Bankruptcy Law, 1880–1938. *Journal of Institutional Economics*, Vol. 3, p. 206.

Hathaway, O.A. (2001). Path Dependence in the Law: The Course and Pattern of Legal Change in a Common Law System. *Iowa Law Review*, Vol. 86, pp. 603–604.

Hedge Funds, Leverage, and the Lessons of Long-Term Capital Management, Report of the President's Working Group on Financial Markets (1999).

Judge, K. (2012). Fragmentation Nodes: A Study in Financial Innovation, Complexity, and Systemic Risk. *Stanford Law Review*, Vol. 64, p. 696.

Keath, H.J. (2008). Derivatives in Bankruptcy: Lifesaving Knowledge for the Small Firm. *Washington and Lee Law Review*, Vol. 65, pp. 739–761.

Lubben, S.J. (2009). Derivatives and Bankruptcy: The Flawed Case for Special Treatment. *University of Pennsylvania Journal of Business Law*, Vol. 12, pp. 63–75.

Lubben, S.J. (2010). Repeal the Safe Harbor. *American Bankruptcy Institute Law Review*, Vol. 18, pp. 328–331.

Mahoney, J. (2000). Path Dependence in Historical Sociology. *Theory and Society*, Vol. 29, p. 513.

Mark, J.R. (1996). Chaos and Evolution in Law and Economics. *Harvrad Law Review*, Vol. 109, pp. 643–644.

Mengle, D. (2010). The Importance of Close-Out Netting. *ISDA Research Notes*, pp. 4–6.

Morrison, E.R. and J. Riegel (2005). Financial Contracts and the New Bankruptcy Code: Insulating Markets from Bankrupt Debtors and Bankruptcy Judges. *American Bankruptcy Institute Law Review*, Vol. 13, pp. 641–663.

Partnoy, F. and D.A. Skeel Jr. (2007). The Promise and Perils of Credit Derivatives. *University of Cincinnati Law Review*, Vol. 75, p. 1050.

Perotti, E. (2014). The Roots of Shadow Banking. In *Shadow Banking Within and Across National Borders*, S. Claessens, D.D. Evanoff, G.G. Kaufman and L. Laeven (eds.). New Jersey: World Scientific Publishing Co. Pte. Ltd.

Redd, C.J. (2005). Treatment of Securities and Derivatives Transactions in Bankruptcy, Part I. *American Bankruptcy Law Journal*, Vol. 24–26, p. 37.

Robert, R.B. and G.G. Kaufman (2006). Derivatives and Systemic Risk: Netting, Collateral, and Closeout. *Journal of Financial Stability*, Vol. 2, p. 67.

Roe, M.J. (1996). Chaos and Evolution in Law and Economics. *Harvard Law Review*, Vol. 109, pp. 643–662.

Roe, M.J. (2011). The Derivatives Market's Payment Priorities as Financial Crisis Accelerator. *Stanford Law Review*, Vol. 63, pp. 554–562.

Ruhl, J.B. and H.J. Ruhl Jr. (1997). The Arrow of the Law in Modern Administrative States: Using Complexity Theory to Reveal the Diminishing Returns and Increasing Risks the Burgeoning of Law Poses to Society. *U.C. Davis Law Review*, Vol. 30, p. 415.

Ruhl, J.B. and J. Salzman (2003). Mozart and the Red Queen: The Problems of Regulatory Accretion in the Administrative State. *Georgetown Law Journal*, Vol. 91, pp. 785–788.

Schwarcz, S.L. and L. Chang (2012). The Custom-to-Failure Cycle. *Duke Law Journal*, Vol. 62, p. 768.

Schwarcz, S.L. and O. Sharon (2014). The Bankruptcy-Law Safe Harbor for Derivatives: A Path-Dependence Analysis. *Washington and Lee Law Review*, Vol. 71, No. 3 (forthcoming 2014).

Skeel, D. (2011). *The New Financial Deal: Understanding the Dodd–Frank Act and its (Unintended) Consequences*, pp. 135, 161–162. New York: John Wiley & Sons, Inc.

Stephen, J.L. (2010). Repeal the Safe Harbor. *American Bankruptcy Institute Law Review*, Vol. 18, p. 331.

Stulz, R.M. (2009). Financial Derivatives: Lessons from the Subprime Crisis. *The Milken Institute Review*, p. 61.

United States General Accounting Office (1994). Financial Derivatives: Actions Needed to Protect the Financial System. Report to Congressional Requestors, GAO/GGD-94-133.

Vasser, S. (2005). Derivatives in Bankruptcy. *The Business Lawyer*, Vol. 60, pp. 1509–1542.

Waldman, A.R. (1994). OTC Derivatives and Systemic Risk: Innovative Finance or the Dance into the Abyss? *American University Law Review*, Vol. 43, pp. 1031–1063.

The Roots of Shadow Banking

Enrico Perotti*

University of Amsterdam, ECB and CEPR

We propose a precise definition of shadow banking based on the type of transactions (as opposed to entities) that replicate a fragile bank-like funding structure, and are thus relevant for macroprudential policy. We claim that secured financial credit is the pivot for replicating banking in an un(der)regulated framework. This contractual arrangement enables financial intermediaries to promise liquidity on demand to investors just as insured deposits, thanks to major financial innovation fed by recent changes in bankruptcy law. We review the advantages of the underlying legal construction, the so-called safe harbor status. While safe pledgeability promotes credit growth and liquidity in good times, it reduces liquidity in times of stress, specifically by accelerating fire sales, and thus reinforces rapid deleveraging. We summarize the history of the legal development underlying safe harbor and its impact on lending composition in the credit boom. Finally, we join the policy debate among academics about possible remedies. An important conclusion is that shadow banking's reliance on a special legal construction enables shadow banking to expand rapidly outside the regulated area, leading to a loss of control over its scale, with an adverse impact on contingent liquidity risk incurred by authorities.

Introduction

The shadow banking sector is an ill-defined financial segment that expands and contracts credit outside the regulatory perimeter. It was critical in the

*I would like to thank Stijn Claessens, Darrel Duffie, Viral Acharya, Markus Brunnermeier, Jeremy Stein, David Skeel, and the editors for excellent feedback.

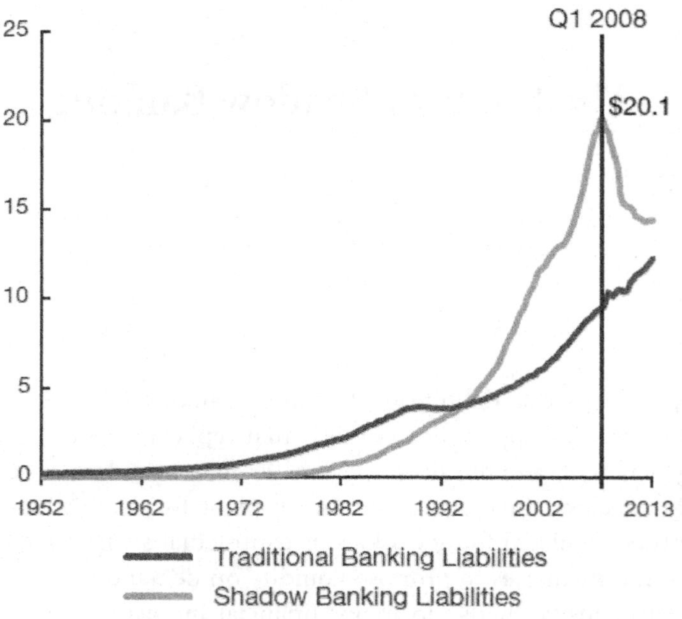

Fig. 1. Evolution of regulated and shadow banking credit volumes.

Note: Traditional banking liabilities refer to total liabilities of US chartered depository institutions, foreign banking offices in the United States, banks in US affiliated areas, credit unions, and holding companies, less corporate bonds they have issued and other long-term liabilities. Shadow banking liabilities (netted from overlaps with the Federal Reserve Flow of Funds Table L.110) refer to the sum of total outstanding open market paper, total repo liabilities, net securities loaned, total GSE liabilities and pooled securities (prior to Q4 2008), total liabilities of asset-backed securities issuers, and total shares outstanding of money market funds.

Source: Office of Financial Resources, 2013.

buildup and demise of the credit boom. While much reduced since 2008, in the US, its size still exceeded bank assets in 2011. Figures 1 and 2 shows how rapidly the sector can expand as well as contract.[1]

The opinions stated here are mine and do not necessarily reflect those of the ECB. What have we learned since the crisis on shadow banking? As Paul Tucker has observed (Tucker, 2012), not all intermediaries

[1]Note that the decrease in shadow banking credit is in part due to incorporation of SIVs, acquisitions, and transformation of shadow banks into banks.

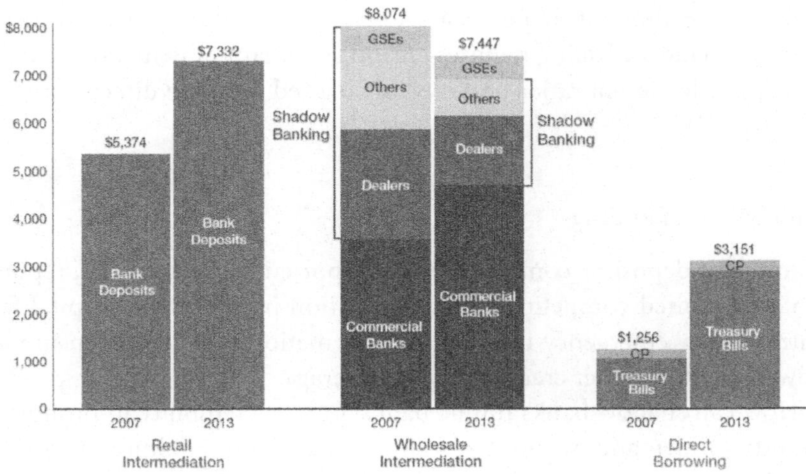

Fig. 2. Changes in regulated and shadow banking system since 2007.
Source: Federal Reserve, US Treasury, Haver Analytics, Securities Industry and Financial Markets Association, OFR analysis.

deemed shadow banks do banking.[2] I will propose a transaction-based definition, which implies that even banks are active in some shadow banking activities.

The essential structure of banking is about funding risky assets with demandable debt. Banks perform various key risk transformations through their balance sheet (diversification, maturity, and liquidity transformation). Banks are special as they can support long-term investment at a low funding cost, thanks to their (perceived) ability to promise liquidity on demand. This promise is made credible by deposit insurance and access to central bank refinancing, and enables very high bank leverage. Confidence on immediacy ensures that demandable debt is routinely rolled over, thus supporting long-term lending.

As most savers prefer risk-free liquid claims, more intermediation (and risk absorption) by banks results in more credit for the economy, but it also increases their vulnerability when confidence is shaken. To ensure stability, bank credit volume is constrained by regulatory capital ratios. So financial

[2]For instance, money market funds are simply pools of uninsured depositors and neither do proper lending nor monitoring.

markets have thought of new ways to carry risky assets on inexpensive funding. Shadow banking requires creating a variant of demandable debt, not subject to capital ratios and credibly backed by some direct claim on liquidity.

Shadow Bank Funding

Historically, depositor confidence was supported by high capital, reputation, and limited competition. As competition increased and capital fell, central banks' emergency liquidity transformation and deposit insurance allowed steadily higher credit and bank leverage.

How can shadow banks mimic banks' unique credibility in promising liquidity on demand, without access to central bank liquidity or insured deposits? Shadow banks may simply rely on bank credit lines for emergency liquidity. A large part of securitization was placed in Special Investment Vehicles (SIVs), funded with very short-term paper backed by credit lines by the sponsoring banks. These were allowed to be off balance sheet, though the sponsor banks bore all the contingent liquidity risk. While this specific regulatory arbitrage has now been closed, the ability to conduct unregulated shadow banking transactions has largely survived.

I argue that shadow banks' distinctive liquidity guarantees arise from their issuing of collateralized financial credit, such as repurchase agreements (repos). These are often combined with collateral swaps to maximize liquidity transformation. This is the source of shadow banking's very short-term, inexpensive funding source, as well as of the risk externality it creates. But how can these liabilities deliver investors credible liquidity upon demand?

How to Jump a Running Queue? Superior Bankruptcy Rights

Security pledging grants access to easy and cheap funding thanks to the steady expansion in the EU and US of "safe harbor status", the so-called bankruptcy remote privileges for lenders secured on financial collateral (also called qualified financial contracts, QFCs). Their claims are now uniquely excluded from mandatory stay under the EU and the US bankruptcy law. Critically, creditors using such contracts can immediately repossess and resell pledged collateral. They also escape most other bankruptcy restrictions such as cross default, netting, eve-of-bankruptcy, and preference rules. These privileges ensure immediacy for their holders. Unfortunately, they do so by undermining orderly liquidation, the foundation of bankruptcy law.

The consequences became visible upon Lehmann's default, when its massive portfolio of repos and derivative collateral was taken out of the bankruptcy estate and resold within hours. This produced a shock wave of fire sales of Asset-Backed Securities (ABS) holdings by other safe harbor lenders. While these lenders broke even, their rapid sales led to lower price and spread losses to all others, eventually forcing public interventions. It thus became clear that safe harbor not only undermines the value of unsecured claims of a specific entity (even deposit insurance or tax claims),[3] but also may create external effects on markets. Because safe harbor offers superior claims to for some lenders over others, it inevitably reduces for everyone else their security. Most of the time, the privilege appears innocuous; after all, default of financial intermediaries is a rare event. But the extreme safety in tail events produces a formidable risk externality.

Next to accelerating fire sales, safe harbor provisions have also a significant ex ante effect on the quality of credit risk, as the time series of risk taking during the credit boom suggests. The privileges were massively expanded in a coordinated legislative push in the US and EU (Devos, 2006; Perotti, 2011).[4] This immediately led to an acceleration of shadow banking funding for mortgage risk taking. The guaranteed ease of escape for repo lenders led to the final burst in the pace of mortgage lending and repackaging during 2004–2007, where credit standards fell through the floor. Lehmann was simply the most exposed of all shadow banks, with an average debt maturity of less than three days, carrying a huge exposure in mortgage credit.

---

[3] Unsecured creditors had to wait five years to get around 20 cents on the dollar.

[4] Limited safe harbor status was granted as exceptions in the 1978 US Bankruptcy code, limited to Treasury repos and margins on futures exchanges for qualifying intermediaries. They were broadened progressively to include margins on OTC swaps. The massive changes took place in 2004, when any financial collateral pledged under repo or derivative contracts, whether OTC or listed, by any financial counterparty, came to enjoy the bankruptcy privileges (Perotti, 2011).

Liquidity Transformation Along the Credit Chain

Shadow banks expanded massively with securitization, where the "most liquid" part of mortgage loans were pledged under safe harbor. However, shadow banks can also expand by relying on the liquidity of assets they do not own, via collateral swaps. A major source of pledgeable financial collateral is "mined" by borrowing liquid assets from long-term asset managers, such as insurers, pension and mutual funds, custodians, and collateral reinvestment programs (Poszar and Singh, 2011). In exchange, beneficial owners receive fees, booked as yield enhancement. The borrowed securities are then pledged to repo lenders or posted as margins on derivative transactions. Experienced asset managers protect themselves via collateral swaps, where the security borrower pledges collateral of lower liquidity as a guarantee. The liquidity risk transformation chain may have more links.

Security pledging can be a force for good if incentives are appropriate. It activates the liquidity value of assets from long-term holders who do not need it. Such extraction of unused collateral service value may be seen as enhancing "financial productivity", and it certainly increase asset liquidity. Its expansion clearly boosted securitization. It enables overstretched borrowers to further increase leverage (certainly if other lenders fail to fully appreciate its effects). Yet this can be an illusory gain, flattering market depth in normal times, at the cost of greater illiquidity at times of distress.

Shadow Banking Runs

A jump in market haircuts, and ultimately a refusal to roll over security loans or repos, is the shadow banking system equivalence to a classic bank run. As a security borrower cannot raise as much funding from its own illiquid assets, it is forced to deleverage fast or it goes bust. In both cases this triggers fire sales. Once repo lenders seize collateral, they have all reasons to wish to sell fast for a number of reasons. First, they are not natural holders. Second, they do not suffer from a lower price as long as the price drop is less than their haircut. Third, they are aware that others are repossessing similar collateral at the same time, so they have an incentive to front sell. In addition, real money investors which lost their original holdings are likely to sell the repossessed, less liquid collateral, as they wish to re-establish their portfolio profile. More critically, they legally need to sell within days to be able to claim any shortfall in bankruptcy court. Thus resale incentives associated with repossessed collateral lead to an acceleration of sales even for assets originally invested for a long holding period.

Finally, although central banks are not in charge of shadow banks, they come under pressure to extend credit or purchase assets to stop fire sales. This completes the banking analogy.

The Safe Harbor Debate

It is now evident that shadow banks (or rather, shadow banking activities, wherever performed) need the safe harbor privileges to replicate banking. No financial innovation to secure escape from distress can match the proprietary rights granted by the safe harbor status, which ensure immediate access to sellable assets.

Safe harbor has long been an obscure detail even for senior policymakers and academics. A reason is that few repossessions took place, as only one major shadow bank was allowed to go bust (though its effect on MF Global clients has been notable). Traditional unsecured lenders have taken notice, and now request more collateral, squeezing bank funding capacity, and limiting future flexibility.

Many attentive observers find such an unconditional assignment of superpriority to repo and derivative claimants excessive, and encouraging excess risk taking (Bolton and Oehmke, 2014). Duffie and Skeel (2012) discuss in an excellent summary the merit of safe harbor. In their words, "*safe harbors could potentially raise social costs through five channels*: (1) *lowering the incentives of counterparties to monitor the firm*; (2) *increasing the ability of, or incentive for, the firm to become too-big-to-fail*; (3) *inefficient substitution away from more traditional forms of financing*; (4) *increasing the market impact of collateral fire sales; and* (5) *lowering the incentives of a distressed firm to file for bankruptcy in a timely manner*".

While these arguments are well understood, we wish to reinforce the *ex-ante* effect of safe harbor. Repo lenders and derivative counterparties are extremely safe. Not only do they enjoy immediacy in default, they also reset margins daily. By construction, just as insured depositors, these claimants can afford to neglect credit risk. Thus this source of funding cannot be entrusted to perform any monitoring role. Supportive evidence comes from the critical role played by repo financing in funding the last wave of securitization, where lending standards fell continuously. Another critical ingredient of that last fatal phase of the credit boom were the credit enhancements provided by derivatives. Between 2004 and 2007 the CDS market grew from 5 to 60 trillion dollar. Thus the expansion of safe harbor privileges appears to have contributed significantly to the creation of excess risk in the credit boom.

Duffie and Skeel cite as a benefit: "*a reduction of the incentives of repo and derivatives counterparties to "run" as soon as the debtor's financial condition is suspect*". This is true, but it simply reflects the fact that margins can be adjusted daily. A rapid increase in repo haircuts is equivalent to a shadow bank run. More importantly, a larger amount of superpriority claims makes other lenders run earlier and faster, as they come to realize how their claims have been diluted. The recent major shift from traditional unsecured creditors toward secured debt, which is undermining traditional bank funding patterns, reflects this new awareness.

Duffie and Skeel also cite the enhanced reliability of derivative transactions. Indeed, safe harbor does facilitate hedging transactions, but also speculative ones. But surely it is questionable whether the highest level of protection should be granted to collateralized lenders, and to shadow bank funding, over all other investors. For all these reasons, regulators and public society needs to make an informed decision, which does not seem to have happened (see Schwarcz and Sharon, in this volume, for the legislative history of the safe harbor provision in the US).[5]

The ultimate financial stability concern is that shadow banking funding can be scaled up easily by securitization or collateral mining (as long as real money investors agree). The implicit capital ratio is as low as security lenders choose to tolerate it, and thus becomes highly procyclical. Whenever liquidity is abundant, the channel can expand very rapidly. Both micro- and macro-prudential oversight authorities have limited tools to control the associated contingent liquidity risk (including for the part of shadow banking which is pursued within banks). Collateral lending, by splitting up liquidity transformation, lengthens credit chains and expands the number

[5]Creation of new proprietary rights is an exceedingly rare legal innovation. Limited liability and the bankruptcy stay were the last main instances in the area of financial contracting.

of connections among intermediaries, further contributing to systemic risk (Gai, Haldane, and Kapadia, 2011).

The main argument used by the industry in the US Congress debate on bankruptcy reforms was that safe harbor ensures immediate freeing up of pledged securities upon an individual large-scale failure. It was meant to prevent distress in cases such as LTCM (although emergency Fed lending had promptly resolved the problem). Such an episode was termed naively "systemic risk". With hindsight, it was equivalent to declare any financial institution as systemic and thus deserving of absolute priority. Most clearly, none understood the real systemic risk externality it would create (Schwarcz and Sharon, in this volume).

A First Step: A Public Registry

Any prudential policy aimed at containing the risk externality associated with safe harbor requires proper measurement. Perotti (2011) suggests that claims be publicly registered (just as secured real credit generally is) as a precondition for safe harbor status. This will ensure proper disclosure, essential to macro prudential regulators, and avoids unauthorized or misunderstood (re)hypothecation. The need of a central repository seems by now well accepted among senior policymakers, especially once all securities will be securely identified by an unique identifier code (as in the case of the newly introduced Legal Entity Identifier, or LEI).

Changing bankruptcy law against well established lobbies will not be simple, however sensible (Schwarcz and Sharon, in this volume).[6] With this in mind, central banks may take a lead by establishing a standard. In their position as the main supplier of liquidity and secured refinancing, they can demand that securities pledge under safe harbor be regularly registered in order to be eligible for refinancing. Concretely, such assets may be considered eligible provided their safe harbor status had been registered earlier in time, such as in the previous month. This would avoid having securities registered only when the chance of default becomes significant.

[6]Remarkably, safe harbor status is being further extended since the crisis, without much scrutiny. A EU directive amendment (Directive 2009/44/EC) grants eligibility to all credit claims "in the form of a loan". More legislation has been prepared for central securities depositories, amending Directive 98/26/EC.

Limiting eligibility to safe harbour status to secured credit beyond a minimum maturity would also be beneficial to this purpose.

Broader Reform Proposals

The main proposals to reform the safe harbor status aim at firmly restricting eligibility. Tuckman (2010) suggested that only cleared derivatives should enjoy the status. Duffie and Skeel argue that it may be limited to appropriately liquid collateral (thus not ABS!) and only transparent uses (e.g., derivatives listed on proper clearing exchanges). Implementing these proposals would defuse the Damocles' sword of dangling fire sales, since the eligible collateral would be precisely the type of assets in demand in a liquidity crisis. This would achieve the goal of putting back in the bottle the most explosive feeder of shadow banking, containing the scope of quasi money to currency and bank deposits. It would essentially limit it to a form of "narrow" shadow banking.

While limiting eligibility to safe collateral is probably the best solution, it is meeting intense resistance from the industry, which has become quite addicted to this legal construction. It is important to recall that intermediaries have become used to pledge borrowed or even clients' assets as collateral to their repo funding and even their derivative positions.[7] Indeed it amounts to a major (socially welcome) change in its business model, and would constrain significantly the scale of funding for entities and transactions not subject to capital requirements.

Another solution would be to bring this form of funding under the regulated periphery, by mandatory haircuts for collateralized secured credit. This would satisfy the basic principle — to avoid regulatory arbitrage, equivalent transactions leading to systemic liquidity risk must be subject to similar rules for both banks and shadow banks. This would essentially extend Basel III rules to shadow banking. Yet, international negotiations at the FSB to establish minimum haircuts have failed so far to achieve any

[7] In some cases the re-use of the collateral is not well understood or appreciated even by the beneficial owners. MF Global pledged assets held in custody for clients to fund their own activity. Owners recognized the exposure only once their assets were repossessed by third parties. But because the safe harbor status grants a proprietary right to the repo lenders, the original owners had in fact been legally expropriated.

results, leaving at present no global policy in place. For a proposal to link capital adequacy requirements to the use of collateralized secured credit, see Tarullo, 2013, and Stein, in this volume.

A Repo Resolution Authority has been proposed as a solution to maintain the pledgeability of less liquid collateral under safe harbor (Acharya and Oncu, 2012). The idea is to prevent the immediate release of all collateral, while avoiding the effect of a complete mandatory stay. In this approach, the authority would take over the exposure under safe harbor, transferring repo and derivative counterparties immediately a large fraction (over 90%) of their claim. The collateral would be disposed in an orderly resolution, with the lenders remaining fully liable for any residual loss. This would resolve the urgent issue of avoiding propagation via fire sales, and the residual risk bearing would surely contain the risk externality.

At the macro-prudential level, once collateral held under safe harbor were registered, policymakers would be able to track its evolution, finally enabling to map contingent liquidity risk. If the stock appears to grow too fast, various steps may be undertaken.

Perotti (2011) proposes that safe harbor claimants should be paying for the privilege, thus internalizing the risk externality created. In normal times, a low charge should be levied on registered claims. Such charges should be adjusted countercyclically, lowered in difficult times, and raised when aggregate liquidity risk builds up, to slow down an otherwise uncontrollable expansion.

A more drastic solution involves limiting the stock of safe harbor claims directly (Stein, 2012). This approach may be achieved by a cap-and-trade model, which a registry receiving fees could support. Yet past experiences in controlling externalities within a cap-and-trade system have failed, thanks to predictable over issuance. The cap may be adjusted with some frequency, but this takes away its main advantage as well as undermines its credibility. It seems much easier to adjust a systemic charge on the privilege.

Conclusions

Due to the safe harbor rules, a shadow bank can hold risky illiquid assets and earn risk and term premia with funding at the overnight repo rate. In what is essentially a synthetic bank, repo and collateral swap haircuts act as market-defined capital ratios, and stretching the degree of maturity transformation. Both features result in potentially large excess volatility following asset liquidity shocks.

Safe harbor was created by investors seeking extreme safety, a form of quasi money. Yet investors who claim superpriority in distress seek a scarce resource. As such, contracts may be created at will, they may be overexploited, leading to a novel "tragedy of the common".

Safe harbor volume at present reflects private contracting choices. As its use grants an ability to create quasi money, it enables unregulated banking, with capital ratios set by cyclical market margins, and subject to shadow bank runs.

This liquidity transformation across states and entities has procyclical effects, enhancing credit and asset liquidity in normal or boom times, at the cost of accelerating fire sales in distress (when arguably it really matters).

Any reform to the shadow banking funding model should take into account its favorable effects on asset liquidity and credit in normal times. Yet the scale of the contingent liquidity risk in the shadow banking sector is not at present controllable (nor is it well measured!). There is an academic consensus that a balance has to be struck (Acharya *et al.*, 2011; Brunnermeier *et al.*, 2011; Gorton and Metrick, 2010; Shin, 2010). Appropriate tools are also necessary to align capital and risk incentives in banks and shadow banks (Haldane, 2010). Security lending may also undermine Basel III liquidity (LCR) rules.[8]

Since the crisis, many shadow banks have either been absorbed by banks, gained a state guarantee, defaulted or massively deflated. Though measurement of security lending against illiquid collateral is still very imprecise, it seems to have abated. Yet the powerful liquidity promise allowed by safe harbor status creates a permanent channel for a buildup in systemic liquidity Risk.[9]

---

[8]A simple rolling 30-day collateral swap enables banks to (temporarily) transform illiquid assets into LCR-compliant holdings. As a result, resilience to runs is ensured only for a month, but completely vanishes afterwards (since in distress, the swap counterpart will close out). LCR implementation rules need to contain such window dressing, which is hard to detect without any registration of encumbrances.

[9]So-called real estate investment trusts (REITs) have emerged as a novel category of shadow banks. These are funds invested in mortgage-backed securities (MBS), and rely on repo financing to leverage returns. Although at present much better capitalized than SIV, they are subject to sudden liquidity needs, especially when rates rise (see Fig. 3).

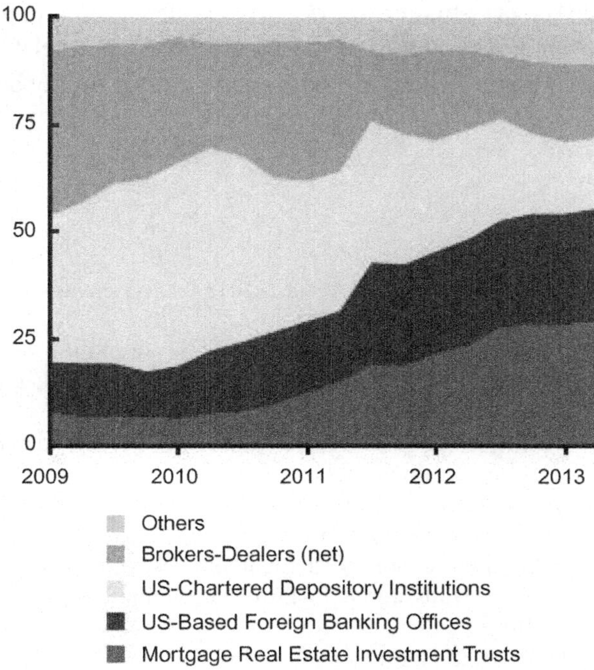

Fig. 3. Evolution of Fed funds and repo liabilities by entity types (%).
Source: Federal Reserve, Haver Analytics, OFR analysis.

The privileges enjoyed by secured credit are now fully appreciated by market participants. Traditional long-term unsecured lenders to banks are now demanding considerable financial collateral, with pernicious consequences on access to stable funding for many intermediaries undermining the traditional interbank and long-term funding market. But this awareness only reinforces the desire for superpriority. It does not solve the simple problem that not everyone can be first in line, nor the simple fact that not all bank funding may be secured. In particular, insured deposits will end up having no asset left to cover the claim, shifting the entire problem to the tax payer.

At a time when all lenders seek security, questioning the logic of safe harbor provision may seem unwise. Yet at the system level, it is simply impossible to promise security and liquidity to all. Uncertainty on the stock of pledged assets may create a self-reinforcing effect, feeding a frenzy among lenders to all seek ever-higher priority. This is already taking place, and is ultimately unsustainable at the individual and aggregate level. Control over either the volume of potential fire sales or the money supply becomes lost to private choices.

References

Acharya, V., A. Krishnamurthy and E. Perotti (2011). A consensus view on liquidity risk. VoxEU.org, 14 September.

Acharya, V. and S. Öncü (2012). A Proposal for the Resolution of Systemically Important Assets and Liabilities: The Case of the Repo Market. *CEPR Working Paper* 8927.

Bolton, P. and M. Oehmke (2014). Should Derivatives Be Privileged in Bankruptcy? *Journal of Finance* (forthcoming).

Brunnermeier, M., G. Gorton and A. Krishnamurthy (2011). Risk Topography. *NBER Macroeconomics Annual 2011.*

Devos, D. (2006). Legal Protection of Payment and Securities Settlement Systems and of Collateral Transactions in European Union Legislation. *BIS Legal Department Paper.*

Duffie, D. and D. Skeel (2012). A Dialogue on the Costs and Benefits of Automatic Stays for Derivatives and Repurchase Agreements. *Rock Center for Corporate Governance Working Paper* No. 108, Stanford University, March.

Gai, P., A. Haldane and S. Kapadia (2011). Complexity, Concentration and Contagion. *Bank or England Discussion Paper.*

Gorton, G. and A. Metrick (2010). Regulating the Shadow Banking System. *Brookings Papers on Economic Activity*, Vol. 2, pp. 261–297.

Haldane, A. (2010). The $100 Billion Question. Bank of England, March.

Perotti, E. (2011). Targeting the Systemic Effect of Bankruptcy Exceptions. *CEPR Policy Insight* No. 52, 2010 published in *Journal of International Banking and Financial Law* (2011).

Schwarcz, S. and O. Sharon. The Bankruptcy-Law Safe Harbor for Derivatives: A Path-Dependence Analysis. In this volume.

Shin, H.S. (2010). Macroprudential Policies Beyond Basel III. *Policy memo.*

Stein, J. (2012). Monetary Policy as Financial-Stability Regulation. *Quarterly Journal of Economics*, Vol. 127, No. 1, pp. 57–95.

Stein J. (n.d.) The Fire-Sales Problem and Securities Financing Transactions, in this volume, also www.federalreserve.gov/newsevents/speech/stein20131107a.htm

Tarullo, D. (2013). Shadow Banking and Systemic Risk Regulation. Speech at the Americans for Financial Reform and Economic Policy Institute Conference, 22 November, Washington, DC.

Tucker, P. (2012). Shadow Banking: Thoughts for a Reform Agenda. Speech at the European Commission High Level Conference, 27 April, Brussels.

Tuckman, B. (2010). Amending Safe Harbors to Reduce Systemic Risk in OTC Derivatives Markets. Centre for Financial Stability, New York.

Ex-ante Securitization versus *Ex-post* Fire-Sales under Various Policy Interventions*

Alexandros P. Vardoulakis†

Federal Reserve Board of Governors

This paper examines how existing policy options to deal with fire-sales risk interact with the desire of traditional financial institutions to securitize part of their loans and engage in repurchase agreements with shadow banks. We use the model developed by Goodhart *et al.* (2012) to compute the effect of capital requirements, conventional and unconventional monetary policy on the level of securitization and haircuts charged on repos. These policies can reduce fire-sale risk, but distort the incentives to securitize and do not sufficiently account for fire-sales externalities stemming from repurchase agreements. We argue that margin requirements are useful tools to mitigate fire-sales risk and that they can be used as complements to the aforementioned policy interventions.

Introduction

A vast literature analyzing the financial crisis of 2007–2008 points to fire sales through capital markets as another source of financial and economic instability. Financially distressed institutions liquidate their assets to meet their debt obligations, and, by doing so, they reduce the value of their own

*The views expressed in this paper are solely the responsibility of the authors and should not be interpreted as reflecting the views of the Board of Governors of the Federal Reserve System or of anyone else associated with the Federal Reserve System.

†Federal Reserve Board of Governors; Constitution Ave NW, Washington DC, USA; E-mail: alexandros.vardoulakis@frb.gov.

and other institutions' portfolio, which reinforces the fire sale and deteriorates further their debt position. Fire sales give rise to a pecuniary externality if they impede financial stability by tightening borrowing constraints of other institutions holding the same assets or by increasing the possibility of default of distressed institutions and the loss suffered by debt-holders.[1]

Policy interventions can mitigate the adverse effects of fire-sales. Intuitively, the level and severity of fire-sales depends on the maturity mismatch of financial institutions, the availability and the relative cost of alternative sources of liquidity, and the total amount of resources used to purchase distressed assets. Conventional monetary policy can reduce the cost of obtaining liquidity for commercial banks, while unconventional monetary policy intervenes directly in the market for distressed assets and enhances demand to increase their price. On the other hand, banking regulation, such as capital requirements, can be made stricter to reduce the level of maturity mismatch and hence the need of institutions to sell assets at distressed prices.

Apart from the three aforementioned frictions, securities financing transactions, such as repurchase (repo) agreements, play a significant role in the build-up of leverage which gives rise to potential fire-sales.[2] This paper uses the model developed by Goodhart *et al.* (2012-GKTV henceforth) to examine how the three policy interventions described above interact with the activity in the shadow banking system and the desire of traditional banking institutions to fund their credit extension through securitization and the use of repo contracts.

GKTV study an economy that is at risk from an occasional asset price collapse. Their primary contribution is the introduction of a model that includes both a banking and a "shadow banking system" that each help households finance their expenditure and smooth their consumption intertemporally. But if asset prices collapse, the consumers default and the financial system acts as an amplifier of the primitive shocks.

In their model default can interfere with the supply of credit. Households sometimes choose to default on their loans, and when they do, this

---

[1]See Korinek (2011) and Stein (2012) for a discussion of the market failure induced by fire sales.

[2]See Gorton and Metrick (2012) and Stein (2013) for a discussion of how the repo market interacts with fire-sales externalities.

triggers forced selling by the shadow banks. The banking sector, which faces a maturity mismatch, can choose to liquidate part of its assets to gain liquidity and in the process of doing so it contributes to a fire sale. The latter magnifies the effects of the resulting credit crunch on economic performance. Although the presence of both the banking and the "shadow" banking sector facilitates consumption smoothing, the interaction between default and fire sales results in a market failure due to marginal spirals and a deeper credit crunch.

The following sections describe the building blocks of our model, analyze in more detail the knock-on effects of default and fire-sales externalities on the supply of credit, and present quantitative results on the effect of capital requirements, and conventional and unconventional monetary policy on the level of securitization.

Model Structure

An important feature of the GKTV model is its general equilibrium character with fully endogenous prices and interest rates charged on loans. Financial regulation will not only affect the supply of credit, but also the price of loans. Some aspects of default involve choices. This means that default is endogenous. It is true that the easiest way to incorporate financial frictions into a macro model is to add an exogenous credit-risk premium into the expenditure function, a la Curdia and Woodford (2010). But the exogeneity of that credit-risk premium means that such an approach offers no guidance about factors that cause financial crises. The difference between endogenous and exogenous default risk matters greatly for regulatory policies. GKTV framework allows the examination of important regulatory tradeoffs. For example, regulations that mitigate the risk of default and fire-sales may also raise the costs of financial intermediation, thus resulting in higher borrowing rates, and potentially lower welfare. This approach allows for the consideration of potential risk and efficiency trade-offs.

Financial regulation is dynamic in nature and a regulatory tool can have different *ex-ante* and *ex-post* effects. GKTV consider a two-period economy with uncertainty being realized in the second period. Households trade in each period to correct for the differences in their endowments and smooth their consumption over time. One household type (R) is very well endowed with "housing", which is a durable good. A second household type is less well endowed with "potatoes", a non-durable. Some of these agents are old households (P) who live and consume in both periods, and others are young households (F) who enter the economy in the second period as first-time buyers and serve the role of supporting the demand for housing.

The two types of households' trade with each other using money as the stipulated means of exchange. The role of the financial system is to intermediate funds between borrowers and lenders. Most importantly, it supplies credit to support purchases and facilitate the inter-temporal smoothing of consumption.

The desire to study the shadow banking system and the potential effects of regulatory arbitrage requires the inclusion of two types of financial institutions, a commercial bank and a shadow bank. Household R, being the natural lender, deposits some of the revenues from housing sales to the commercial bank, which extends credit to household P in order to accommodate its housing purchases in the initial period. Deposits are unsecured and can be withdrawn at any point in time, while credit to household P takes the form of a mortgage contract with the houses bought that are pledged as collateral in the event of default. Mortgages mature at the end of the second period while deposits are optimally withdrawn in the beginning of that period, thus creating a maturity mismatch and a need for liquidity by the commercial bank.

Apart from collecting deposits and extending mortgages, the commercial bank offers short-term loans to all households to facilitate their transactions in every period. Short-term loans are repaid at the end of the respective period and are free of credit risk. The bank faces a portfolio problem and can choose to securitize some of the mortgages it extended and package them in mortgage-backed securities (MBS). The shadow bank having a higher appetite for risk is the natural buyer of these securities. Securitization allows the commercial bank to extend more credit without compromising its liquidity position. In addition, the introduction of a new asset (MBS) enhances the hedging opportunities of the commercial bank. The shadow bank finances its MBS purchases with its own capital and a repo loan from the commercial bank. The purchased MBS are pledged as collateral in the event of default. Finally, the bank funds its operations with its equity capital, deposits and with short-term borrowing from the "central bank", which stands in for the rest of the world. The borrowing from the central bank is always limited to what can be completely repaid.

The decision to default is endogenous and depends on the relative value of collateral to the value of the loan obligation. Accounting for additional costs of default, such as reputational penalties, it is individually optimal for household P to default on its mortgage and have its house foreclosed when the market value of collateral is low enough. Similarly, the shadow bank will choose to surrender the MBS it holds when mortgages, which are the underlying asset, are in default. As discussed below, the fall in housing prices and the subsequent defaults on mortgages creates a number of knock-on effects: fire-sales, marginal spirals, and a credit-crunch. Financial regulation tries to mitigate the adverse effects of default due to a fall in asset/house prices. Regulation can be imposed either on the contributors to risk, i.e., household P and the shadow bank, or instead on the commercial bank, which is exposed to housing price risk and can amplify this risk when defaults on its depositors.

Figure 1 presents the structure of the model, the financial relationships and the flow of goods and houses in the real economy.

Default, Fire-Sales and Amplification

When the endowment of potatoes is low (which can be loosely thought of as an adverse productivity shock) house prices will collapse. This collapse is unavoidable and default on mortgages is optimal from an individual's point

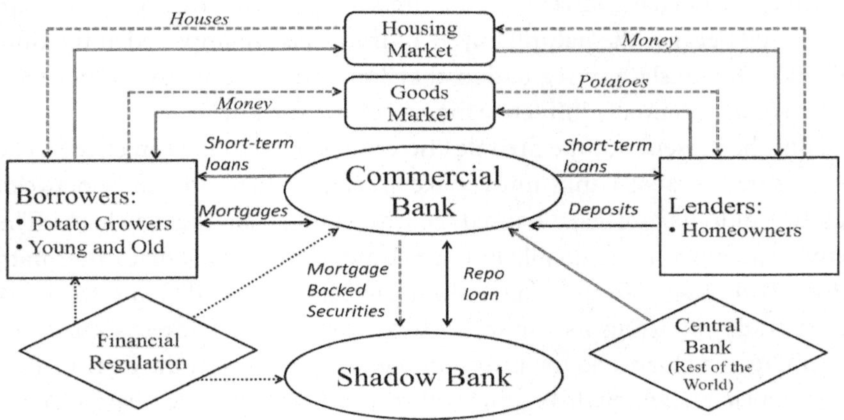

Fig. 1. Structure of the economy.

of view. However, there are several channels through which the financial system may amplify the initial impulse that will lead to other inefficiencies. Regulations may be useful if they can limit this amplification. One important property of the model is that there are no magic bullets. In particular, any regulations that dampen the effects of defaults create other distortions.

The effective return on mortgages depends on the market value of houses, which the bank forecloses and puts up for sale, and it is lower than the promised mortgage rate. Consequently, the value of the MBS that the shadow bank holds in its portfolio goes down as well. When the fall in housing prices is big enough, this induces a second round of default on the repo loans and the commercial bank takes the MBS pledged as collateral back on its balance sheet. The commercial bank sees its assets fall in value and faces the decision to default on its deposit obligations. Given that deposits are withdrawn in the beginning of the period, the bank sells some of the MBS returned by the shadow bank in order to attain liquidity to repay its depositors. By doing so it contributes to a fire-sale.

This is the first channel of financial amplification which stems from the assumed cash-in-the-market pricing that governs sales of MBS. The shadow bank, which is the natural buyer of MBS, finds its capital depleted in the state of the world where housing prices collapse. Thus, the more MBS that the commercial bank returns to the market, the lower is the price of MBS. This simple formulation is intended to capture the Shleifer and Vishny (2011) characterization of a fire sale whereby prices for assets are depressed because the natural buyers of the assets are impaired at the time of sale. Obviously any regulation that limits the size of the initial repo default can potentially influence the size of the fire sale.

But the presence of the fire sale also creates three follow-on effects. The first comes because banks must make an active portfolio choice between holding onto its mortgage-backed securities and extending new loans. The bank is assumed to be unable to issue equity (in the immediate aftermath of the bad shock), so its balance sheet capacity is limited. Thus, the bank must trade off using its capital to hold a mortgage-backed security or to initiate new loans. So the losses on the MBS sales from the cash-in-the-market pricing tighten this capital constraint and potentially create a "credit crunch" for new borrowers (in that the bank's capital problem reduces the supply of loans that are available).

The second potential inefficiency comes because the repo default also raises the incentive for the bank to default on its deposit contracts. The losses to the depositor (R) reduce his wealth, causing him to sell additional housing to finance his purchases of goods. The additional housing sales will lead to lower housing prices.

Finally, there is a third channel that arises from the interaction of the cash-in-the-market fire sale and the other two follow-on effects. The bank always considers the arbitrage relation between MBS prices and the price of houses. When the bank receives the MBS that are issued against defaulted mortgages (from the shadow bank), either it can hold the MBS to maturity or it can sell the MBS right away, which depresses further not only MBS but also house prices. Therefore, the model also embodies the kind of downward spiral described in Brunnermeier and Pedersen (2009).

A fire-sale does not always impose an externality from the financial system to the real sector of the economy. In good times when there is no default on mortgages and financial institutions are solvent, fire-sales are a redistribution of profits from the commercial bank to the shadow bank, which has the cash to facilitate the funding needs of the former. However, fire-sales during times of distress reduce the ability of the commercial bank to repay its depositors and drive it further into insolvency. This results in the additional effects described above, which further depress housing prices and results in a marginal spiral.

Policies to Mitigate Fire-Sales

There are three modeling elements necessary for a fire-sale. First, the financial institution selling assets at distressed prices (commercial bank in the model) should face a maturity mismatch between its liabilities and its assets. Thus, there is a need for interim funding liquidity. Second, the commercial bank should face a cost for attaining the interim liquidity needed to bridge the maturity gap between its liability and assets as in the GKTV model. Alternatively, one could consider limits for the funding that the commercial bank can get from the central bank either in the form of collateral constraints or an inability to access the discount window. Finally, the natural buyers of liquidated assets (the shadow bank in the model) should have a limited amount of funds, which results in cash-in-the-market pricing.

These three frictions provide useful intuition for the design of policies to mitigate the resulting fire-sales risk: A regulator could impose higher capital requirements to narrow the maturity mismatch between assets and liability, and the central bank could engage in accommodative monetary policy to prevent extensive fire-sales *ex-post*. Conventional monetary policy reduces the cost of liquidity and thus increases the opportunity cost of liquidating assets by affecting the supply side, i.e., the commercial bank's incentive to sell at distressed prices. Unconventional monetary policy boosts the demand for liquidated assets and relaxes cash-in-the-market pricing.

All three policies are successful in reducing fire-sales risk *ex-post*, but they distort *ex-ante* incentives to securitize if regulatory arbitrage is possible or if they are anticipated in the case of monetary interventions. The magnitude of fire-sales depends on the extent of initial securitization, which allows for higher mortgage extension, more leverage, and subsequently higher losses when a bad shock realizes and mortgages default.

Higher capital requirement reduces the leverage of commercial banks, but is vulnerable to regulatory arbitrage. The commercial bank can choose to securitize a higher percentage of the mortgages it extends to relax its regulatory constraints, and can provide more repo loans to the shadow bank to fund these purchases. The total amount of mortgages originated would not substantially decrease if the risk-weights for repo loans are not adjusted upwards to reflect the underlying risk of higher securitization. Finally, margins on repo loans would decrease to facilitate higher securitization and circumvent capital regulation. Figure 2 presents the effect of stricter capital regulation on the level of securitization and the margins charged on repo loans.

Alternatively, one could consider *ex-post* interventions as efficient backstops to fire-sales. Conventional and unconventional monetary policies operate through different channels. Reducing the interest rate for discount borrowing enables the bank to obtain more funding liquidity to gap its maturity mismatch rather than selling MBS. Equivalently, the commercial bank is willing to sell MBS only at higher prices and fire-sales risk is contained. If a reduction in interest rates is anticipated, the ability of the commercial bank to obtain cheaper funding *ex-post* increases the incentives to take more risk *ex-ante*. Figure 3 shows the effect of anticipated conventional monetary policy on the level of securitization and the margins charged on repo loans.

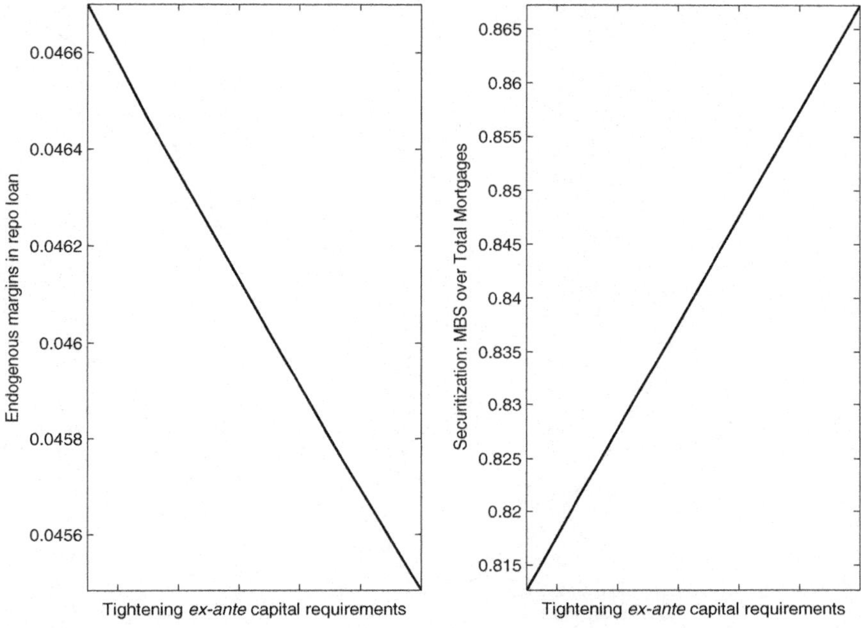

Fig. 2. Capital regulation and fire-sales.

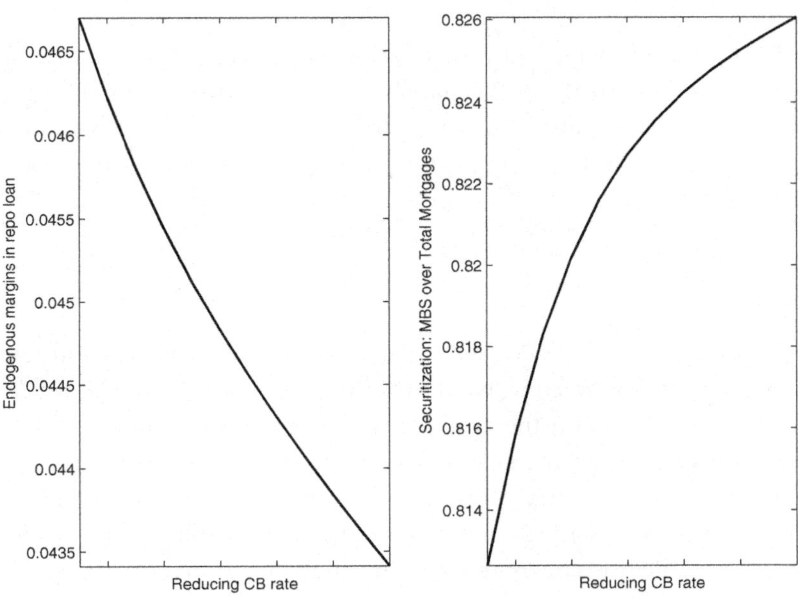

Fig. 3. Conventional monetary policy and fire-sales.

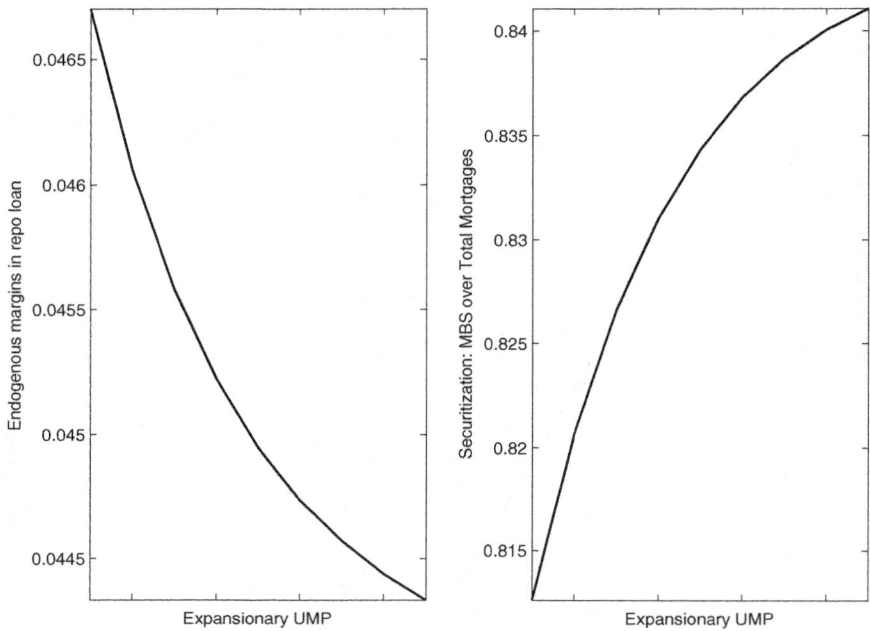

Fig. 4. Unconventional monetary policy and fire-sales.

Finally, the monetary authority can use unconventional measure and intervene directly in the MBS market to buy securities. This relaxes the cash-in-the market constraint, but distorts *ex-ante* incentives to securitize and take more risk by charging lower margins on repo loan as shown in Fig. 4.

Conclusions

An institution can sell assets at distressed price to obtain liquidity and bridge the maturity gap between its liabilities and assets. The possibility and level of fire-sales depends on the availability of alternative sources of funding for the institution, on the cost it has to pay for it, and on the resources that the natural buyers have to purchase the assets sold at distressed prices. However, distressed selling is a transfer of the intermediation surplus from one financial institution to another and they do not necessarily warrant policy intervention. Fire-sales lead to an externality when they interact with financial stability and default on third parties. Financial regulation and monetary interventions aim at mitigating this risk, but they operate through different channels.

Capital regulation aims at reducing the maturity mismatch between liabilities and asset, and increase the loss absorbency of the commercial bank when its assets default. The presence of a shadow banking system allows the commercial bank to circumvent stricter capital requirement and fund mortgage extensions through securitization. Regulatory arbitrage is possible as long as the risk-weights for repo loans are not adjusted upwards to reflect this.

Monetary policy can also alleviate fire-sales risk *ex-post* by providing more liquidity to distressed institutions or directly intervening in the asset market to boost asset prices. If such interventions are anticipated, they can distort *ex-ante* incentives to take-on more risk, increase credit extension through securitization, and results in lower margins on repo loans, since the *ex-post* risk for commercial bank is perceived to be lower.

The analysis in this paper argues that the aforementioned policies are not sufficient to address an important element affecting fire-sales risk: Excessive securitization in the presence of a shadow banking system allowing for higher leverage and effective maturity mismatch within the traditional financial system. Although they can reduce the size of the fire-sale, they lead to higher securitization. The analysis shows that this is accompanied by lower margins on repo loans suggesting that margin requirements can be used as a complement to the aforementioned policies to control fire-sales externalities. Indeed, Goodhart *et al.* (2013) argue that margin requirements are an essential element of the regulatory toolbox and that they can be used in combination with capital requirements to achieve financial stability and higher welfare.

References

Brunnermeier, M. and L.H. Pedersen (2009). Market Liquidity and Funding Liquidity. *Review of Financial Studies*, Vol. 22, No. 6, pp. 2201–2238.

Curdia, V. and M. Woodford (2010). Credit Spreads and Monetary Policy. *Journal of Money, Credit and Banking*, Vol. 42, No. 1, pp. 3–35.

Goodhart, C.A.E., A.K. Kashyap, D.P. Tsomocos and A.P. Vardoulakis (2012). Financial Regulation in General Equilibrium. *NBER Working Paper* 17909.

Goodhart, C.A.E., A.K. Kashyap, D.P. Tsomocos and A.P. Vardoulakis (2013). An Integrated Framework for Analyzing Multiple Financial Regulations. *International Journal of Central Banking*, Vol. 9, No. 1, pp. 109–143.

Gorton, G. and A. Metrick (2012). Securitized Borrowing and the Run on Repo. *Journal of Financial Economics*, Vol. 104, No. 3, pp. 425–451.

Korinek, A. (2011). Systemic Risk-Taking: Amplification Effects, Externalities, and Regulatory Responses. *ECB Working Paper*.

Shleifer, A. and R. Vishny (2011). Fire Sales in Finance and Macroeconomics. *Journal of Economic Perspectives*, Vol. 25, No. 1, pp. 29–48.

Stein, J. (2012). Monetary Policy as Financial-Stability Regulation. *Quarterly Journal of Economics*, Vol. 127, No. 1, pp. 57–95.

Stein, J. (2013). The Fire-Sales Problem and Securities Financing Transactions. Speech at Federal Reserve Bank of Chicago and International Monetary Fund Conference, Shadow Banking Within and Across National Borders, Chicago, November 7, in this volume.

V

Challenges for Supervision and Regulation

Financial Market Infrastructure: A Challenge to the Supervision and Regulation of the Financial System

Darrell Duffie*
Stanford University

A key goal of financial system regulation and supervision is to reduce to a manageable level the damage to the economy caused by any financial firm's failure. Aside from the direct cost of failure, a common view that the failure of a particular firm could be extremely damaging incites the moral hazard of allowing that firm to believe that its failure would be dangerous to the financial system and that it would therefore likely receive significant government assistance when its solvency is suddenly threatened.

While orderly failure resolution is a desirable principle, I do not believe that it currently applies to all financial firms. In this chapter, I argue that failure resolution could not yet be safely applied to certain firms that operate key financial market infrastructures (FMIs) used for clearing over-the-counter derivatives or tri-party repurchase agreements (repos). The failure of key FMIs could indeed be dangerous to the financial system, even with the best available approaches to failure resolution.

---

*Distinguished Professor of Finance, Graduate School of Business, Stanford University, and National Bureau of Economic Research. I am grateful for comments from many. All errors and opinions are my own, exclusively. This paper is intended for publication in *Shadow Banking Within and Across National Borders*, and is based substantially, and with permission, on "Financial Market Infrastructure: Too Important to Fail", in *The US Financial System — Five Years After the Crisis*, edited by Martin Bailey and John Taylor, forthcoming, Hoover Press Stanford University, 2014. For potential conflicts of interest, please see darrellduffie.com/outside.cfm. Please email remarks to duffie@stanford.edu.

By implication, a financial institution should not operate key FMI backed by the same capital that supports much more discretionary forms of risk-taking, such as speculative trading or general lending. Not only would such a combination of activities expose a key FMI to losses caused elsewhere in the same financial institution, it would raise the firm's moral hazard based on the importance to the economy of the survival of the FMI and, thus, the entire firm.

Later in this chapter I will focus special attention on tri-party repo (TPR) clearing, because this key FMI is currently operated in the United States by two large, complex banks that have significant latitude for risk-taking in their other lines of business. The failure of these banks could sharply reduce access by the largest US broker-dealers to TPR financing for their securities inventories. This would be dangerous to the financial system, possibly through the impact of fire sales of large quantities of securities. Every day, each of the larger US broker-dealers receives $100 billion or more in overnight financing that depends from an operational perspective on one of these two TPR clearing banks.

Central Clearing Parties

Central clearing parties (CCPs) for derivatives are FMIs that guarantee derivatives payments to surviving clearing members of a CCP in the event of the failure of other clearing members. The potential loss exposures of some CCPs are extremely large in practice. These losses are intended to be covered by a "waterfall" of default management resources, including the initial margins and default guarantee funds of clearing members and the capital of the CCP.[1]

The failure of a CCP cannot be safely and effectively treated by currently available forms of bankruptcy or by the Dodd–Frank Act's Title II administrative failure resolution.

For treating the failure of a systemically important bank holding company (BHC), the Federal Deposit Insurance Corporation (FDIC, 2013) has suggested that it would exercise its authority under Title II of the Dodd–Frank Act by using a "single point of entry" approach by which the BHC

[1] For details, see the Appendix of Duffie (2010), ISDA (2013), and Elliott (2013).

can in principle be quickly recapitalized through a conversion of some of its debt to equity. This single-point-of-entry approach may not apply to a CCP, which has almost no debt relative to the largest plausible losses that could arise through the failure of its clearing members. Once the capital of a CCP is wiped out, the tail risk is held by clearing members, who are generally themselves systemically important firms. It is not even clear at this point whether Title II failure resolution authority applies to CCPs, as discussed by DeCarlo and Steigerwald (2013). If Title II does apply, it is also uncertain whether the FDIC is prepared to use this authority for resolving a failing CCP.[2] No other available form of administrative failure resolution authority is evident. The US bankruptcy code is not currently adapted to safely resolve a failing CCP. Even a proposed new Chapter 14 of the code that is designed to treat a range of systemically important non-bank financial companies, as outlined by Jackson (2012), would be poorly adapted to the special case of CCPs.

Altogether, this absence of systemically effective failure resolution methods for US CCPs is an unsatisfactory situation and is contrary to recommendations by the Committee on Payment and Settlement Systems, Technical Committee of the International Organization of Securities Commissions (CPSS-IOSCO, 2013), as well as official-sector guidance from the European Commission (2012) and the Financial Stability Board (2013).

A mitigating factor here is the restricted scope of risk-taking actions by a CCP, which cannot make general loans and has limited discretion over the manner in which it invests collateral. Lower discretion in risk-taking implies lower scope for moral hazard. Given the systemic importance and relatively limited scope for risk-taking of large CCPs, it is reasonable to treat them as "too important to fail". That said, CCPs do fail from time to time. For example, in October 1987 the clearing house of the Hong Kong Stock and Futures Exchange had a disorderly failure described by the Hong Kong Securities Review Committee (1988). Careful regulation, supervision, and failure planning should be used to reduce to the greatest

[2]To my knowledge, the FDIC has not declared its intent in this area, for example in any response to a letter of November 10, 2010 from the general counsel of the CME Group Inc., Kathleen Cronin, to Ronald Feldman, executive secretary of the FDIC, requesting clarification regarding whether the CME is subject to the FDIC's Orderly Liquidation Authority under Title II of the Dodd–Frank Act.

possible extent the adverse impact of CCPs' failures. There is room for significant improvement in this area. For now, CCPs are too important to fail, as key regulators have acknowledged.[3]

Tri-Party Repo Clearing

A repurchase agreement, or repo, is the sale of a portfolio of securities combined with an agreement to repurchase that portfolio on a specific future date at a pre-arranged price. Abstracting from some legal distinctions concerning their bankruptcy treatment, repos are essentially collateralized loans. The cash provided at the purchase leg of a repo is effectively the proceeds of the loan; the repurchase price is the effective loan repayment amount; and the underlying securities are the loan collateral. Repos are normally over-collateralized in order to protect the cash provider from exposure to loss associated with a decline in the value of the collateral before the repo matures.

Broker-dealers finance substantial amounts of their securities inventories with TPRs. The three parties involved in a TPR are the borrowing dealer; the cash lender; and an agent that assists with trade confirmations, settlements of the cash and securities transfers, the allocation of each dealer's collateral to its various lenders, and other forms of operational assistance. Copeland *et al.* (2012) provide details on the operation and systemic importance of the TPR market. In the United States, two large banks, JPMorgan Chase and The Bank of New York Mellon, act as the agents for the vast majority of TPRs. Currently, a total of roughly $1.5 trillion of TPRs is handled by these two banks every day.

---

[3]In testimony provided in October 2013 to the Treasury Select Committee of the UK Parliament, Bank of England Deputy Governor Paul Tucker stated that "central counterparties have almost been mandated by the G20 leaders to be too important to fail. We need to make sure these institutions are sound and well-regulated and could recover in distress". See http://www.telegraph.co.uk/finance/newsbysector/banksandfinance/10363688/Clearing-houses-are-the-biggest-risk-says-Tucker.html. In Dudley (2012), the president of the Federal Reserve Bank of New York, William C. Dudley, stated that "for the system to be safer it is not sufficient to ensure that trades are standardized and that they are mandated to be cleared through CCPs, but also it is necessary that CCPs be 'bullet proof'. They have to have the ability to perform and meet their obligations regardless of the degree of stress in the financial system and even if one or more of their participants were to fail in a disorderly manner". See http://www.newyorkfed.org/newsevents/speeches/2012/dud120322.html.

There is nothing in principle that requires a TPR agent bank to be exposed to losses on the repurchase agreements that it handles for borrowers and lenders, nor to expose repo counterparties to its own failure. In US practice, however, both directions of loss exposure exist and represent systemic risk.

The two large clearing banks offer intraday credit to a securities dealer between the times at which its previously arranged repos mature and the times at which new repos are funded by new cash investors. Until recently, this intraday credit provided by the two TPR agent banks was extensive, covering essentially all repos for a substantial part of each day. The Federal Reserve Bank of New York (2010) has encouraged a financial industry task force to dramatically reduce the extent of this intraday credit. Significant progress has been made toward this goal. But for now the TPR agent banks could nevertheless suffer significant losses in the most extreme plausible scenarios.

The other direction of exposure, of the repo borrower and lender to a potential failure of the TPR agent bank, is the main focus of my remarks here. If one of the two large TPR agent banks were to become illiquid or insolvent due to losses in some other line of business such as trading or general lending, a systemic crisis could be triggered by the potential discontinuation of its TPR clearing function.

First, the dealers who rely on the TPR agent bank for handling their repos could find themselves without the means to quickly obtain financing from other sources. They may not have operationally feasible backups, given their dependence on the specific infrastructure of their TPR agent banks. A fire sale of a large quantity of securities could follow. This could depress the prices of the securities, causing other levered investors to add to the aggregate magnitude of the fire sale, further reducing the securities prices, and possibly creating a general financial crisis. Begalle *et al.* (2013) have examined the potential size of the fire sales relative to typical daily trade volumes, pointing to some large asset classes that could be heavily affected.

Second, in US practice, cash borrowers and lenders settle their TPR cash transfers in the form of deposits in the TPR agent banks. This exposes repo counterparties to a potential failure of their TPR agent bank, for example, through losses to the TPR agent bank that stem from its unrelated lines of business. Even a perceived threat to the liquidity or solvency of an agent bank could provide a sufficient incentive for cash investors to fail to renew TPRs with dealers using that agent bank. This in turn could cause extreme stress to those dealers and possibly the earlier mentioned risk of fire sales.

The settlement of FMI transactions in commercial bank deposits is contrary to clear and well-justified principles set down by CPSS-IOSCO (2012), whose Principle 9 for FMI states:

> *An FMI should conduct its money settlements in central bank money where practical and available. If central bank money is not used, an FMI should minimize and strictly control the credit and liquidity risk arising from the use of commercial bank money.*

CPSS-IOSCO (2012) continues by stating, "One way an FMI could minimize these risks is to limit its activities and operations to clearing and settlement and closely related processes". Applying the CPSS-IOSCO principles to US TPR clearing practice, either a TPR agent bank should have no other significant lines of business or the agent bank should arrange for cash settlement in central bank deposits or in a separate "narrow bank" that is not exposed to losses from unrelated lines of business. While the current US practice of settling TPRs in the agents' commercial bank deposits may offer operational efficiencies, this benefit is trumped by the imperative to insulate system-critical FMIs and systemically important FMI users from unnecessary exposures.

When a large multi-line financial institution operates a systemically important FMI, as is current practice in the US TPR market, its government and central bank are under pressure to forestall the failure of the financial institution in order to assure continuity of services provided by the FMI. In some cases, a government official should not stand rigidly on the principle that no such financial institution should receive extra assistance to avoid failure. By this point, it would be too late to prevent the too-important-to-fail moral hazard with a better design of the TPR market architecture. The exigencies of preventing a significant financial crisis would take priority.

References

Begalle, B., A. Martin, J. McAndrews and S. McLaughlin (2013). The Risk of Fire Sales in the Tri-Party Repo Market. *Federal Reserve Bank of New York Staff Report* 616. Available at http://www.newyorkfed.org/research/staff_reports/sr616.html.

Copeland, A., D. Duffie, A. Martin and S. McLaughlin (2012). Key Mechanics of the U.S. Tri-Party Repo Market. *Economic Policy Review*, Federal Reserve Bank of New York. Available at http://www.newyorkfed.org/research/epr/2012/1210cope.html.

CPSS-IOSCO (Committee on Payment and Settlement Systems, Technical Committee of the International Organization of Securities Commissions) (2012). *Principles for Financial Market Infrastructures*. Madrid: IOSCO. Available at http://www.bis.org/publ/cpss101a.pdf.

CPSS-IOSCO (2013). Recovery of Financial Market Infrastructures. Consultative report. Madrid: IOSCO. Available at http://www.bis.org/publ/cpss109.pdf. Comments: http://www.bis.org/publ/cpss103/comments.htm.

DeCarlo, D. and R. Steigerwald (2013). Orderly Liquidation under Title II of Dodd–Frank. Part I: Do Financial Market Utilities Qualify as 'Financial Companies'? Draft *Working Paper*, Federal Reserve Bank of Chicago.

Directorate General Internal Market and Services. Brussels: DG Internal Market and Services. Available at http://ec.europa.eu/internal_market/consultations/2012/nonbanks/consultation-document_en.pdf.

Dudley, W. (2012). Reforming the OTC Derivatives Market. Remarks at the Harvard Law School's Symposium on Building the Financial System of the 21st Century, Armonk, New York, March. Available at http://www.newyorkfed.org/newsevents/speeches/2012/dud120322.html.

Duffie, D. (2010). *How Big Banks Fail and What to Do About It*. Princeton, NJ: Princeton University Press.

Elliott, D. (2013). Central Counterparty Loss-allocation Rules. *Financial Stability Paper No.* 20, Bank of England.

European Commission (2012). Consultation on a Possible Recovery and Resolution Framework for Financial Institutions Other than Banks.

FDIC (2013). *The Resolution of Systemically Important Financial Institutions: The Single Point of Entry Strategy*. Washington, DC: FDIC. Available at http://www.fdic.gov/news/board/2013/2013-12-10_notice_dis-b_fr.pdf.

Federal Reserve Bank of New York (2010). *Tri-Party Repo Infrastructure Reform*. New York: Federal Reserve Bank of New York. Available at http://www.newyorkfed.org/banking/tpr_infr_reform.html.

Financial Stability Board (2013). Application of the Key Attributes of Effective Resolution Regimes to Non-Bank Financial Institutions. Consultative document. Basel, Switzerland: FSB.

Hong Kong Securities Review Committee (1988). *The Operation and Regulation of the Hong Kong Securities Industry*. Hong Kong: Securities Review Committee.

ISDA (International Swaps and Derivatives Association) (2013). *CCP Loss Allocation at the end of the Waterfall*. New York: ISDA.

Jackson, T. (2012). Bankruptcy Code Chapter 14: A Proposal. In *Bankruptcy Not Bailout, A Special Chapter 14*, K. Scott and J. Taylor (eds.). pp. 25–72. Stanford CA: Hoover Institution Press.

Dividing (and Conquering?) Shadows: FSB and US Approaches to Shadow Banking Entities and Activities

Edward F. Greene and Elizabeth L. Broomfield*

Cleary Gottlieb Steen & Hamilton LLP

Introduction

In the wake of the 2008 crisis, it soon became apparent that the fault lines of the global financial system extended far beyond the regulated banking sector. When national and international efforts to address non-bank risk commenced, efforts were primarily organized on the basis of identifying "entities" and "activities" that were engaged in credit intermediation. These entities and activities comprised what was referred to as the "shadow banking" sector, and there was a presumption that both should be subject to bank-like regulation. At the Financial Stability Board ("FSB"), this distinction between "entities" and "activities" was evidenced by the creation of five shadow banking workstreams, two of which focused on activities (securities lending and repurchase agreements, and securitization), while three

*Edward F. Greene is Senior Counsel in the New York office of Cleary Gottlieb Steen & Hamilton LLP. Mr. Greene served as General Counsel of the Securities and Exchange Commission from 1981 to 1982 and Director of the Division of Corporation Finance from 1979 to 1981. From 2004 to 2008, Mr. Greene served as General Counsel of Citigroup's Institutional Clients Group. Elizabeth L. Broomfield is an investment banker in the Financial Institutions Group at Morgan Stanley in New York. Previously, she was an associate in the New York office of Cleary Gottlieb Steen & Hamilton LLP. Ms. Broomfield graduated from Yale University in 2008, where she double majored in Electrical Engineering and Ethics, Politics, and Economics. She completed a JD degree in 2011 from Columbia Law School, where she was a James Kent Scholar, recipient of the Parker School Certificate in Foreign and Comparative Law, and law clerk at the Securities and Exchange Commission. She simultaneously completed an LLM in International Business Law with Distinction from the London School of Economics as part of Columbia Law School's JD/LLM program.

were entity-centric (such as the workstream on money market funds). In the United States, the Dodd–Frank Act ("Dodd–Frank") empowered the Financial Stability Oversight Council ("FSOC") to designate systemically significant non-bank financial institutions for additional oversight and regulation under Section 113 by the Federal Reserve Board ("FRB") and to identify, and prescribe regulatory responses for, systemically significant activities under Section 120.

This article will address how this bipartite approach to "shadow banking" has evolved and the consequences of this strategy.[1] We note that the concept of "shadow banking activities" has, at both the global and national level, focused to an increasing extent on the risks associated with short-term financing. Both the FSB and the US are looking closely at securities lending and repurchase agreements ("repos"), and securitization. However, the regulatory approach with respect to shadow banking entities has diverged at the global and national level; the FSB approach to "shadow banking entities" is organized by sector, whereas the US entities based approach, reflected in Dodd–Frank, focuses primarily on size. As a result, vastly different non-bank entities are grouped into one category — SIFIs — and then subject to bank-like prudential regulation by the FRB, a key bank regulator in the US.

We conclude that activities-based reforms are a more promising means of addressing shadow banking risks at both the national and international level. Where entity-specific reforms are necessary, the US would benefit from the FSB's sector-based approach, which targets specific sectors and entities within those sectors, rather than the blunderbuss approach of targeting just large systemically important institutions whose failure from a regulatory perspective would materially affect financial markets, and broadly treating them all the same. The FSOC would also benefit from the FSB's policy of relying on existing regulatory bodies with relevant sector-expertise in the formation of legal and policy recommendations. We conclude by observing that, while shadow banking reform efforts have been divided into "entities" and "activities", regulators must consider the implications of how entity-based and activity-based reforms interact.

[1] In its "Green Paper" on shadow banking released in March 2012, the EU explicitly stated that the shadow banking system was based on "two intertwined pillars" of entities and activities. However, the EU approach to shadow banking is beyond the scope of this article.

Financial Stability Board

The G-20 called on the FSB to develop recommendations to strengthen the regulation and oversight of the "shadow banking system" in November 2010. In response, the FSB created its five "shadow banking workstreams": three based on entities, and two based on activities. The "activities" workstreams were focused on (i) securitization and (ii) securities lending and repos, and the entities workstreams addressed regulation of (i) banks' interactions with shadow banking entities; (ii) money market funds ("MMFs"); and (iii) "other shadow banking entities".

The FSB's workstream on securitization was, in turn, delegated to the International Organization of Securities Commissions ("IOSCO"), which released a report with final recommendations in November 2012. These recommendations included better aligning incentives through risk retention requirements, improving asset-level disclosure through standardized templates, standardizing products to encourage secondary market trading, and reforming underwriting and accounting practices. IOSCO is currently in the process of conducting a peer review of national approaches to align incentives associated with securitization (specifically risk retention requirements) and plans to report its results in 2014. While harmonization is a key objective, the significant difference already in the US and the EU with respect to risk retention indicate that such a goal will not be achieved.

To address securities lending and repos, an FSB Taskforce ("WS5") released a November 2012 consultation with a description of recommended policies. In addition to relatively uncontroversial proposals for enhanced transparency and improved disclosure, the consultation also called for minimum standards for the methodologies that firms use to calculate collateral haircuts. In November 2013, the FSB released consultative proposals for these minimum standards and the FSB is currently soliciting feedback on these proposals.

The other three "entity-based" workstreams are proceeding at a similar pace. The workstream targeting bank interaction with shadow banking has been delegated to the Basel Committee on Banking Supervision ("BCBS"), which has focused on consolidation rules for prudential purposes, limits on the size and nature of a bank's exposures to shadow banking entities, risk-based capital requirements for banks' exposures to shadow banking entities, and treatment of reputational risk and implicit support. On December 13, 2013, the BCBS published a final standard that revises the capital treatment of banks' investments in the equity of funds held on the banks' balance sheet, including, but not limited to, hedge funds, managed funds, and investment funds. This revised standard is intended to more accurately reflect the risk of exposure to a fund's underlying investments and the fund's leverage. Within the next year, the BCBS is expected to finalize its proposed supervisory framework for banks' large exposures as well.

The FSB delegated the task of proposing reforms for MMFs to IOSCO. IOSCO's final recommendations in its October 2012 report included limiting the use of constant net asset value, imposing capital buffers, requiring redemption restrictions, liquidity and maturity portfolio requirements, and stress testing. A peer review process to assess implementation of the recommendations at a national level will be launched by IOSCO in 2014.

To address "other shadow banking entities", the FSB created an internal FSB taskforce ("WS3"), which released its proposed "Policy Framework for Strengthening Oversight and Regulation of [Other] Shadow Banking Entities" in November 2012. This framework to address "other shadow banking entities" was noteworthy in its clear rejection of an entity-specific focus, despite the mandate of the workstream to focus on "other shadow banking entities". The FSB observed that concentrating on entities was unhelpful due to the "high degree of heterogeneity and diversity in business models and risk profiles not only across the various sectors in the non-bank financial space, but also within the same sector (or entity-type)". Cross-border differences in existing regulatory frameworks and legal names and forms exacerbated the challenge of prescribing reforms.

Instead, the FSB WS3 proposed assessing risk posed by "an economic function-based (i.e., activities-based) perspective for assessing shadow banking activity in non-bank entities". The five economic functions addressed in the report include: management of client cash pools with features that make them susceptible to runs; loan provision that is dependent on short-term funding; intermediation of market activities dependent on short-term funding; facilitation of credit creation; and securitization and funding of financial entities. As discussed in greater detail in the report, each economic function is meant to address concerns related to short-term financing and other forms of credit considered volatile and/or susceptible to runs.

Therefore, the FSB shadow banking workstreams are now primarily focused on activities that facilitate short-term financing. Only the MMF workstream focuses explicitly on shadow banking entities; the other "entity" workstream is dedicated to improving the regulation and oversight of banks' interaction with the "shadow banking" sector. The three remaining workstreams are focused on risks associated with short-term financing activities.

In addition to its shadow banking workstreams, the FSB has pursued a parallel initiative to designate systemically significant entities ("G-SIFIs"), which includes institutions considered to be "shadow banks". G-SIFIs are defined by the FSB as "institutions of such size, market importance, and global interconnectedness that their distress or failure would cause significant dislocation in the global financial system and adverse economic consequences across a range of countries". All such G-SIFIs will be required to craft resolution plans and to develop institution-specific cross-border cooperation agreements so that home and host authorities have a framework for coordination when responding to a crisis in the future.

To designate G-SIFIs, the FSB took a sector-specific approach, designating systemically important banks ("G-SIBs"), insurance companies ("G-SIIs"), and non-bank non-insurance financial institutions ("NBNI G-SIFIs"). The FSB initially designated 29 global systemically important banks ("G-SIBs") in November 2011. To do so, it relied on an "indicator-based measurement approach" methodology developed by the BCBS comprising both quantitative and qualitative metrics. The selected indicators reflect the size of banks, their interconnectedness, substitutability in the market, complexity, and cross-border activity. The FSB and BCBS are committed to updating the list and identification methodology annually.

On July 18, 2013, the International Association of Insurance Supervisors ("IAIS"), in response to a mandate from the FSB, published a methodology for identifying G-SIIs, as well as a set of policy measures that will apply to such entities. The FSB then endorsed the IAIS methodology and relied on it to designate an initial list of nine G-SIIs. The FSB also endorsed the IAIS policy measures, which include enhanced group-wide supervision and higher loss absorbency requirements for non-traditional and non-insurance ("NTNI") activities, including credit-default swaps, variable annuities and life insurance contracts with various guarantees. By the end of 2015, the IAIS will develop implementation details for these higher loss absorbency requirements, which will apply starting from January 2019. Most recently, on December 16, 2013, the IAIS released, for public consultation, proposed options for the development of global Basic Capital Requirements ("BCR") for G-SIIs as a first step in the development of group-wide global capital standards for insurance companies. Comments on the proposal are due in February 2014. In July 2014, the FSB, in consultation with the IAIS and national authorities, will make a decision on the G-SII status of, and appropriate risk mitigating measures for, major reinsurers.

The FSB, in consultation with IOSCO, will finalize a proposed assessment methodology for identifying systemically important non-bank non-insurance financial institutions ("NBNI G-SIFIs"). While the proposal has not yet been released, the FSB has stated that the methodologies will capture the "systemic impact posed by the failure of financial entities in each type or sector, while maintaining consistency across the spectrum of non-bank financial entities".

There are several noteworthy points about the FSB's approach that will be discussed more fully below. First, the FSB has addressed non-bank entities by sector, such as MMFs, insurance, and reinsurance. When developing regulatory reform policies targeting each sector, the FSB delegated the work to authorities with relevant expertise in that field (i.e., there would be a change in rules governing capital, and perhaps structure, but not necessarily a change in existing regulator(s)). This approach produced recommendations that focused on the "bank-like" risky activities conducted by non-bank entities. This strategy stands in sharp relief with the strategy adopted by the US in Dodd–Frank, discussed below.

United States

The US addressed shadow banking in Dodd–Frank in July 2010, before the FSB received its mandate from the G-20. Although Dodd–Frank did not explicitly use the phrase "shadow banking", it set forth procedures for identifying non-bank entities and activities that pose systemic risk. Under Section 113, an entity may be designated systemically significant if the FSOC determines that the "material financial distress at the US non-bank financial company, or the nature, scope, size, scale, concentration, interconnectedness, or mix of the activities of the US non-bank financial company, could pose a threat to the financial stability of the United States". An activity may be designated systemic under Section 120 if, as determined by the FSOC, the "conduct, scope, nature, size, scale, concentration, or interconnectedness of such activity or practice could create or increase the risk of significant liquidity, credit, or other problems spreading among bank holding companies and non-bank financial companies, financial markets of the United States, or low-income, minority, or underserved communities".

On April 3, 2012, the FSOC approved a final rule setting forth the criteria and three-stage process for determining that a non-bank financial company is systemically important to US financial stability under Section 113, and therefore should be designated a "non-bank SIFI". Among other factors, the FSOC will look to a company's size (including off-balance sheet assets and exposures), interconnectedness to other significant financial companies, substitutability (the extent to which the group could be replaced in a timely manner in the market), leverage, short- and long-term liquidity risk, resolvability, opacity of operations, complexity, and existing regulatory scrutiny. The FSOC has repeatedly emphasized that no single factor is determinative in this analysis.

Once designated, these non-bank SIFIs will be subject to enhanced prudential and remediation requirements under Sections 165 and 166 of Dodd–Frank and subject to oversight by the Federal Reserve Board. The complex bank regulatory regime overseen by the FRB is layered on top of the existing regulatory structure and legal requirements already applicable to the non-bank SIFI. Thus, the December 2011 proposed rule implementing Dodd–Frank Sections 165 and 166 subjects non-bank SIFIs to the enhanced capital requirements, liquidity requirements, short-term debt limits and public disclosure rules that are also applied to large bank holding companies. While the FRB may tailor the application of these onerous standards to non-bank SIFIs, it is unclear how such tailoring will be carried out in practice; these entities were therefore designated before the regulatory consequences were determined.

In a June 3, 2013 closed-door meeting, the FSOC voted to designate three financial services companies as the first non-bank SIFIs under Section 113 — AIG, GE Capital, and Prudential. Though Prudential challenged the designation, the FSOC reaffirmed its designation in a 7-to-2 vote in September 2013. MetLife Inc., the largest US life insurer, has reported that it has been moved to the third and final stage of review to be designated systemically important by the FSOC.

The decision to label Prudential as a SIFI sheds light on how the FSOC has applied, and will likely continue to apply, the designation criteria set forth above. Prudential had argued, among other objections, that it does not pose systemic risk because exposures to Prudential are small relative to the capital of its individual counterparties. In response, the FSOC found that, while true, "aggregate exposures are significant enough that they could amplify the risk of contagion" among other financial institutions if Prudential were to experience material financial distress.

In their dissents, both Edward DeMarco (acting director of the Federal Housing Finance Agency) and Roy Woodall (FSOC's independent member with insurance expertise) criticized the designation, arguing that the FSOC did not accurately assess the characteristics of Prudential and misunderstood key characteristics of the insurance industry. For example, the FSOC's assumptions, as set forth in the decision justifying Prudential's designation, were dependent upon "an assumed run by millions of life insurance policyholders, who would collectively surrender or withdraw a significant portion of life insurance cash values". DeMarco and Woodall argued that such assumptions were unrealistic and not supported by any historical, quantitative or qualitative evidence. Furthermore, DeMarco and Woodall stated that the FSOC failed to understand key distinctions between insurance products and bank products due to existing mitigants to delay and/or limit run risk present in insurance products. Due to these features, even during the height of the financial crisis, traditional insurance products did not experience runs.

These dissents are illuminating in several respects. First, they reflect a clear concern that the FSOC designation was a mistake resulting from the FSOC's lack of understanding of insurance companies, products, and the sector as a whole. Moreover, DeMarco, Woodall, and the FSOC agreed that no large financial institution has more than a de minimus amount of its equity capital exposed to Prudential. However, the FSOC's decision to look at "aggregate exposures" indicates that size and fear of contagion are the overwhelmingly predominant factors in the FSOC's non-bank SIFI designations. As a result, the non-bank SIFI designations focus on financial entities that are large, regardless of their sector or other factors purportedly considered by the FSOC in its analysis.

Recent developments indicate that large asset management companies may be the next target for designation by FSOC under Section 113. In September 2013, the Office of Financial Research ("OFR") delivered a report on "Asset Management and Financial Stability", in response to the FSOC's request for a study to better inform the FSOC's analysis and potential designation of asset management firms under Section 113. To that end, the OFR report covered ways that activities in the asset management industry might create, amplify, or transmit stress through the financial system. Specifically, the report examined potential sources of risk for asset management firms, specifically: "reaching for yield" and herding behaviors; redemption risk in collective investment vehicles; and leverage. The report also examined how the failure of an asset management firm could pose a threat to financial stability.

The report was severely criticized by the asset management industry. Several members of the asset management profession, such as BlackRock, argued that the report mixed the risks that are associated with an investment product or investment practice versus the risks associated with an asset management firm. Other comment letters, such as a submission by the Investment Company Institute, argued that the OFR study did not reflect an accurate understanding of the asset management sector and failed to recognize that the structure, operation, and regulation of registered funds and their managers actually protects investors and serves to mitigate risk to the financial system. The report also failed to consider the many requirements already applied to asset managers, such as daily valuation, standards for liquidity, limits on leverage, and strict custody arrangements. In addition, several commentators argued that SIFI designation was not an effective means of addressing the risks hypothesized by the OFR in its report. As stated by the ICI, the bank regulations imposed on non-bank SIFIs under Dodd–Frank "are designed to moderate bank-like risks and are ill-suited or unnecessary for registered funds and their advisers, which ... do not present the types or scale of risks that would warrant application of such requirements".

Section 113 is not only a blunt tool with respect to large firms, but it also fails to address systemic risk posed by smaller financial companies. Due to Section 113's focus on size, the FSOC could not rely on this provision to capture small, connected entities that are "systemic as a herd", such as MMFs. However, as noted above, Dodd–Frank Section 120 empowers the

FSOC to designate an activity as systemically significant. In November 2012, the FSOC relied on Section 120 to issue proposals to address systemic risk posed by money market funds. FSOC's need to rely on Section 120, rather than Section 113, underscores the limited utility of Section 113 and provides further support for the contention (addressed below) that the FSOC should rely more heavily on Section 120 in the future.

As part of a separate initiative, the Federal Reserve recently stated that it has been considering new regulations related to short-term funding, specifically securities financing transactions ("SFTs") that include "repo and reverse repo, securities lending and borrowing, and securities margin lending". In a speech in November 2013, Federal Reserve Board Governor Tarullo discussed several possible options for targeting these SFT transactions to incentivize the use of more stable funding by institutions.

In his remarks, Governor Tarullo suggested that new margin requirements might be a useful tool for addressing the risks of short-term financing transactions. Citing the recent consultative paper by the FSB under its securities lending and repo shadow banking workstream, Governor Tarullo stated that the concept of a universal minimum margining requirement applicable directly to SFTs should be considered in the US. He also stated that such requirements would be applied based on the activity, and not depend on prudential regulation of the entity engaged in the short-term financing. This scope would present less risk of regulatory arbitrage, as SFT activities would be captured by new regulations even if conducted by non-bank entities typically subject to less prudential restrictions.

Governor Tarullo did not completely eschew regulation at the entity-level. He observed that the "most work" is needed in addressing the risks arising from the use of short-term wholesale funding by systemically important firms — both banks and non-banks. Such institutions could be subject to Basel capital and liquidity requirements, such as the net stable funding ratio ("NSFR") and liquidity coverage ratio ("LCR"). The Federal Reserve is also considering capital surcharges for large firms, both banks and non-banks, that substantially rely on short-term wholesale funding.

Analysis

Both the US and the FSB began addressing shadow banking by dividing the "shadow banking universe" into entities and activities. That initial framework has now evolved to address short-term financing activities, on the one hand, and non-bank systemic entities, on the other. Given the extraterritorial scope of both the US and other national and international regulatory regimes, international coordination and harmonization is essential.

It is therefore promising that the FSB and the US broadly agree that short-term funding activities must be addressed, including: securities lending, repos, and securitization. The consensus at this high-level to focus on these short-term funding activities is a promising first step towards international cooperation. Also, as noted by Governor Tarullo, a focus on short-term financing activities targets the source of risk while preventing arbitrage; entity-specific restrictions on such activities could just encourage, in his words, moving "more securities financing activity completely into the shadows".

When targeting shadow banking, regulators should therefore concentrate principally on short-term financing transactions that allow non-bank entities to achieve the maturity and liquidity transformation that defines shadow banking and increases the risk of runs in the non-bank sector. This targeting of bank-like activities, rather than entities, was contemplated by the IAIS and its recommendation that certain NTNI activities be subject to capital surcharges. If the bank-like activities themselves cannot be targeted, regulators should then consider how the industry, including the large systemic entities, can be regulated in a way that contemplates the risk profile of the financial institutions and their role in the financial markets more broadly. For example, AIG's difficulties during the financial crisis were caused by these bank-like activities conducted by specific units. Ideally, nuanced regulations would target those systemic activities, rather than more traditional, secure insurance products and practices. Blunt regulations at the entity-level should be imposed only when a more nuanced activity-based approach is not sufficient.

We are therefore skeptical about the effectiveness of entity-specific reforms. Restricting the behavior of particular entities will likely migrate risky activities to entities and sectors subject to less oversight. In addition, as noted by the FSB in its WS3 workstream, international consistency in entity-specific rules is difficult to achieve due to the diversity in business models and risk profiles both across and within non-bank financial sectors.

To the extent that entity-specific reforms are deemed necessary, the US would benefit from adopting the FSB sector-based approach, rather than applying bank prudential regulation to a category of non-bank entities defined by their size. Grouping large, but vastly different, companies together is likely to be a fruitless endeavor that risks being a distraction from more productive pursuits. In addition, imposing rules just on the few large actors in an industry could result in distorting the market and forcing risky activities into smaller competitors.

Systemically significant companies must be understood in the context of their particular industry. This lens would also encourage regulators to carefully consider the level and nature of pre-existing regulation applied to that sector. Then, instead of simply extending banking law to cover the largest entities in these sectors, the US regulators could have modified existing laws. For example, instead of imposing bank prudential rules on insurance companies such as AIG and Prudential, US lawmakers could have modified or supplemented the existing insurance regime with respect to its regulation of financial activities not linked to traditional insurance products. Such an approach would be better tailored to the structure and market position of the insurance industry and far less complex than subjecting large insurance companies to bank regulation.

In addition, the FSOC designation subjects non-bank SIFIs to oversight by the Federal Reserve, whose experience supervising and regulating non-bank institutions is limited. The FSOC should learn from the FSB approach, and place greater reliance on the expertise and tools of regulators with a history of oversight of the sector or industry in question. For example, the FSB delegated the MMF workstream to IOSCO, an organization comprising securities commissions and/or the main financial regulator from each country. The IOSCO was therefore deemed to have the relevant expertise in oversight of MMFs. Similarly, the FSB tasked the BCBS with crafting rules for banking institutions and the IAIS with insurance sector reform; the new basic capital requirements ("BCR") proposed by the IAIS were proposed specifically for insurance companies, and the FSB did not simply endorse applying the Basel bank capital rules to insurers. While the US comment solicitation process and mixed representation on FSOC in theory provide for input from actors with industry knowledge, it is troubling that the two dissenting members of FSOC in the Prudential designation were those with insurance experience and expertise. While insurance regulation is primarily conducted at the state level, new rules could have been crafted by the Federal Insurance Office ("FIO") which released a report on December 12, 2013, with suggestions on how to modernize and improve the system of insurance regulation in the United States. The FIO, in concert with state regulators, are resources that should be utilized in the formation of insurance sector reforms.

We therefore suggest that the FSOC reconsider its application of Section 113 and 120 to adopt a more sector-specific approach. Rather than designate entities pursuant to Section 113, the FSOC could increase its reliance on Section 120, which was used to propose MMF reforms. In addressing insurance companies, the FSOC could, as was suggested by DeMarco in his Prudential designation dissent, regulate insurance products through Section 120. This approach would still target risky activities of systemic entities, but would also be less likely to force the migration of such activities to smaller entities in the same sector. Section 120 could also be used to improve existing laws governing all insurance companies, which is preferable to grafting banking laws onto the insurance regulatory regime. When applying Section 120, the FSOC should continuously solicit participation and input from industry actors and regulators and the tools they already have at their disposal to mitigate the risks being targeted.

Conclusion

The financial crisis demonstrated the need for structural change of entities and activities outside the banking sector. Moreover, the vulnerabilities of specific sectors and institutions, including insurance companies, money market funds, and asset managers, cannot and should not be left unaddressed. However, large companies in those sectors should not be subject to bank-like regulation solely because they are large and operate in the shadow banking sector. Dodd–Frank's blunt targeting of large entities fails to target the true source of risk (short-term funding volatility) and simultaneously has the potential to distort markets and encourage arbitrage as bank-like activities migrate to smaller, and possibly more vulnerable, entities.

Targeting activities, as discussed above, is a more promising and nuanced means of addressing shadow banking risk. It is therefore promising that the US and the FSB are broadly considering similar strategies for mitigating the risks of short-term financing transactions, such as "skin in the game" rules for securitization and minimum haircut requirements for securities lending and repo transactions. However, such agreement is necessary, but not sufficient. If the details of these requirements and implementation are inconsistent in different jurisdictions, the benefits of cooperation at a high level may be lost through failure to coordinate on the details.

While shadow banking has been divided into entity-specific and activity-specific reforms, these changes must be viewed as a coherent whole. In particular, entity-specific proposals must consider how activity-centric reforms may affect "shadow banking" entities. For example, capital surcharges on specific "activities" may obviate the need to force an entity to comply with Basel capital and liquidity rules. The FSOC and FSB were created in response to the need for bodies with a mandate to take a macro-level view of the economy. Therefore, as both entity-based and activity-based reforms are proposed, the FSB and FSOC must remain cognizant of how these new rules interact. This macro-level oversight will be essential to avoid inefficiencies and unintended consequences that, rather than improve the resilience of the international financial system, only impede the functioning of global players in global markets.

Money Market Funds: Reconsidering the Mutual Fund Model

Patrick E. McCabe*

Board of Governors of the Federal Reserve System

Over half a decade since the run on money market funds (MMFs, or "money funds") in September 2008 intensified and deepened the financial crisis, money funds remain vulnerable to runs that can threaten financial stability. Policymakers and academics have made repeated calls for reforms, and new rules have tightened portfolio restrictions and added disclosure requirements. Still, the fundamental fragility remains: In a crisis, investors have strong incentives to redeem MMF shares before other investors do. Indeed, episodes since the crisis have provided reminders that the structural vulnerabilities of MMFs continue to pose risks to the financial system.

This paper focuses on one complication in reforming MMFs that has perhaps received less attention than others: These funds have diverged from the classic mutual fund model, in which the risks and rewards associated with a portfolio are *dispersed* to a broad group of mutual fund investors — that is, the funds' shareholders.[1] In contrast, money fund risks generally have not been borne broadly by all investors. Instead, risks usually have been absorbed by investors who do not redeem quickly, by MMF sponsors, and — in 2008 — by the government itself. This allocation of risks, together with other features of money funds, gives them a hybrid nature that straddles the roles and functions of mutual funds and banks.

---

*Senior economist at the Board of Governors of the Federal Reserve System. I would like to thank Matthew Eichner and Josh Gallin for helpful comments and Alexander Prairie for help with data and charts. The views expressed here are mine and do not necessarily reflect those of the Board of Governors of the Federal Reserve System or its staff.

[1] I use both "shareholder" and "investor" to refer to the individuals and institutions that own MMF shares.

The hybrid nature of MMFs suggests two directions for possible reforms: MMFs could become more like banks or more like mutual funds. This paper suggests that the mutual fund model continues to offer much promise for both the design and assessment of options for reform. Several approaches could be effective in mitigating the vulnerability of MMFs to runs, in part because they would disperse risks broadly to MMF shareholders, including those who redeem quickly in a crisis.

The next section outlines the vulnerability of MMFs to runs, provides a brief review of the run in 2008 and its consequences, and examines developments since the crisis that underscore that MMFs continue to pose risks. The second section describes how MMFs have deviated from the mutual fund model, including by taking on bank-like characteristics — but without bank-like protections. The third section reviews and examines the degree to which some recent proposals for MMF reform might reduce systemic risks by returning MMFs to the mutual fund model in which risks are dispersed to shareholders. Conclusions are offered in the final section.

MMFs are Vulnerable to Runs that Threaten Financial Stability

MMFs are mutual funds that are regulated by the US Securities and Exchange Commission (SEC) under the Investment Company Act of 1940. Unlike other mutual funds, MMFs typically offer shareholders a stable, $1 share price (net asset value, or NAV). An innovation of the 1970s, MMFs were mostly purchased by retail investors until the 1990s, when institutional MMFs grew rapidly. By November 2013, money assets fund stood at $2.7 trillion, with institutional funds accounting for 66% of the total.[2]

What makes MMFs vulnerable to runs?

Some of the features that make MMFs popular with investors also make the funds vulnerable to runs.[3] To pay their investors attractive yields, MMFs

---

[2]These figures, which are based on data from the Investment Company Institute and iMoneyNet, are for MMFs that are sold to the public. Based on SEC filings, aggregate assets of *all* MMFs, including those that are not registered for sale to the public, were $3.0 trillion at the end of November 2013.

[3]For more complete discussions of the vulnerability of MMFs to runs and the consequences of those runs, see President's Working Group on Financial Markets (PWG, 2010); Financial Stability Oversight Council (FSOC, 2012b); and McCabe *et al.* (2013).

hold assets with credit, interest-rate, and other risks. For example, "prime" MMFs hold commercial paper (CP), certificates of deposit (CDs), and other short-term debt instruments. Nonetheless, MMFs have no formal buffer or insurance to maintain the $1 NAV if a problem occurs, so shareholders do not shoulder the costs of such protection *ex ante*. Instead, the funds rely on rules that allow them to round their share prices to the nearest cent to cushion small declines in value, and, when that fails, voluntary, ad hoc support from MMF sponsors, which are asset management firms and their affiliates and parents.[4] In addition to the stable NAV, MMFs offer shares that may be redeemed on demand, despite the funds' limited same-day liquidity. Rounded share prices, the relative illiquidity of some portfolio holdings, and uncertainty about sponsor support create strong incentives to exit when a fund's NAV appears to be at risk, and the ability to redeem shares on demand facilitates quick exits that can deplete a fund's liquidity and concentrate risks and potential losses on remaining investors. Furthermore, the funds' stable NAVs and unrestricted redemptions have attracted a highly risk-averse investor base that is — as noted above — now dominated by institutional investors who have proven to be particularly reactive. Thus, the characteristics of MMFs and their investor base interact in a manner that heightens the chance of runs when risks become apparent.

Runs on MMFs can threaten financial stability because MMFs are large and highly interconnected with one another and with the financial and payments systems. MMFs are key providers of short-term finance in capital markets. These funds hold large shares of outstanding CP in the US (about 40% in mid-2007 and even more in 2013), and they provide much of the funding in other short-term markets, such as the repo and negotiable CDs markets.[5] Most of this lending goes to large financial firms; in November 2013, 83% of all funding that MMFs extended to private entities was in

---

[4]The role of sponsor support for MMFs is discussed in more detail in the second section. See also McCabe (2010); Brady, Anadu, and Cooper (2010); and Moody's Investor Service (2010).

[5]*Sources*: For 2007 MMF share of aggregate CP outstanding, Federal Reserve Board and Investment Company Institute; for 2013 share, Federal Reserve Board and MMF filings of form N-MFP with the SEC. The figures for 2007 and 2013 are not directly comparable, since the data for 2007 do not include the CP holdings of MMFs that were not registered for sale to the public.

the form of financial sector obligations, including CDs, financial CP, asset-backed CP, repo, and other MMF shares.[6] Just 50 private issuers accounted for 86% of non-governmental investments of prime MMFs as of September 2013, and all but four of these issuers were financial institutions.[7] So, an initial shock to one issuer may affect multiple MMFs, and if a run develops, it can quickly affect the availability of short-term financing for the financial sector, even for firms that were not affected by the initial shock (Chernenko and Sunderam, 2013).

In addition, MMFs are used as cash-management vehicles by individuals, businesses, other institutions, and governments, and MMF shares outstanding are large relative to money stock measures.[8] Hence, a widespread run on MMFs could lead quickly to severe strains in short-term funding markets, liquidity problems for millions of investors, and, if large volumes of assets are tied up in lengthy MMF liquidations, severe consequences for the payments system.

The run on MMFs in 2008 and its consequences

Although the structural vulnerability of MMFs to runs was present before the financial crisis, these funds were largely seen as safe, by academics as well as by investors (McCabe, 2010). When dozens of MMFs suffered significant portfolio losses in late 2007 because of exposures to structured investment vehicles (SIVs) and other souring asset-backed CP, sponsors absorbed those losses and apparently enhanced the funds' reputation for safety. Indeed, institutional MMF assets grew 56% from June 2007 to August 2008, as institutions shifted money from other financial products (such as private liquidity funds) that seemed less safe than MMFs.

This belief in the safety of MMFs vanished abruptly in September 2008. As shown by the bars in Fig. 1, the bankruptcy of Lehman Brothers Holdings, Inc. ("Lehman") on September 15, 2008 triggered heavy outflows from

[6] *Source*: MMF filings of SEC form N-MFP.

[7] *Source*: MMF filings of SEC form N-MFP and author's calculations. See also Scharfstein (2012) and Hanson, Scharfstein, and Sunderam (2012).

[8] As of October 31, 2013, assets in MMFs registered for sale to the public were 24% of the size of the Federal Reserve's M2 money stock measure (M2 includes the value of retail MMF shares, except IRA and Keogh balances at MMFs, but M2 does not include institutional MMF shares).

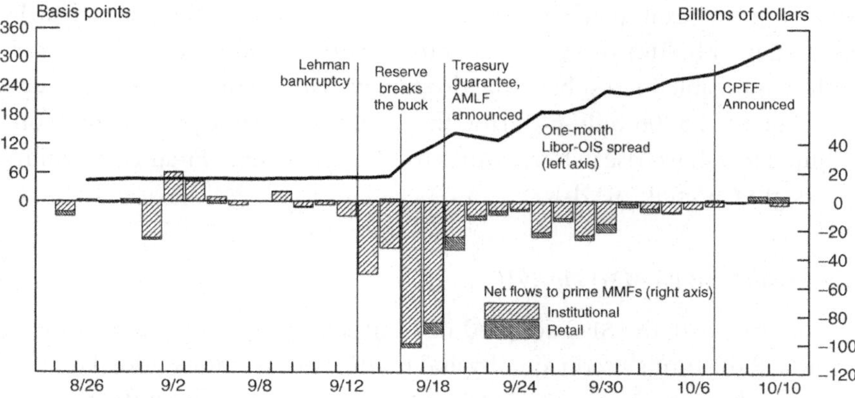

Fig. 1. Daily net flows to prime money market funds and Libor-OIS spread, August–October 2008.

Source: For MMF flows — Investment Company Institute, iMoneyNet, and author's calculations. For Libor-OIS spread — Bloomberg, FRBNY.

MMFs. The following day, the Reserve Primary Fund, a $62 billion MMF, announced that it had "broken the buck" — its per-share value had fallen far enough below $1 that rounding was no longer permissible under SEC rules — because of losses on Lehman debt that had represented 1.2% of the fund's portfolio. Reserve's announcement triggered a widespread run on MMFs, and redemptions from other prime MMFs exceeded $100 billion on the next day, September 17. As the line on Fig. 1 shows, the spread between one-month LIBOR and the overnight index swap (OIS) rate, which already had been elevated, began to rise steeply after Reserve's announcement, as short-term funding markets began to seize up (see Federal Open Market Committee, 2008; Board of Governors of the Federal Reserve System, 2009; SEC, 2009; PWG, 2010). The run's damaging consequences were so severe that, on September 19, the US Department of the Treasury ("US Treasury") announced an unprecedented guarantee program for virtually all MMF shares and the Federal Reserve Board announced a program to finance purchases of asset-backed CP (which was highly illiquid at the time) from MMFs.

The run on MMFs in September 2008 led to a rapid decline in the availability of money market lending for private firms and worsened stress in financial markets as these firms struggled to roll over their short-term financing. For example, between September 9 and 30, 2008, prime MMFs reduced their holdings of CP by $202 billion (29%).[9] This pullback was partially responsible for a substantial drop in availability of financing through CP, which fell $206 billion during the same three-week period, and contributed to a sharp rise in borrowing costs for CP issuers (Financial Stability Oversight Council, 2012b).

New regulations for MMFs in 2010

In January 2010, the SEC adopted new rules for MMFs that, for example, tightened the funds' credit-quality and maturity restrictions, added reporting and disclosure requirements, introduced specific liquidity requirements, and gave MMFs the option to halt redemptions and liquidate if they are in danger of breaking the buck. MMFs are now required to hold at least 10% of their assets in "daily liquid assets" and 30% in "weekly liquid assets". The SEC also reduced the maximum allowable weighted average maturity for MMF portfolios from 90 days to 60 days, tightened limits on holdings of "tier two" securities, and strengthened diversification requirements for some repo holdings.

However, MMFs remain vulnerable to runs. Their portfolios still have credit and other risks, they lack any buffer to absorb losses, they maintain stable NAVs by rounding their share prices to the nearest cent, their shares are still redeemable on demand, and their investor base remains highly risk-averse. Hence, investors continue to have clear incentives to redeem quickly — before others do — when risks become apparent.

Concerns about these risks have prompted the FSOC to recommend MMF reform in every one of its annual reports (FSOC, 2011, 2012a, 2013). Moreover, the FSOC in November 2012 proposed to use its authority under Section 120 of the Dodd–Frank Wall Street Reform and Consumer Protection Act to "recommend that the SEC proceed with much-needed structural reforms of MMFs" (FSOC, 2012b). In June 2013, the SEC responded to the FSOC action by proposing two alternatives for reform "to address money market funds' susceptibility to heavy redemptions, improve their ability to manage and mitigate potential contagion from such redemptions,

[9] *Source*: iMoneyNet. These figures exclude reported reductions in CP held by the Reserve Primary Fund, which provided inaccurate information to iMoneyNet.

and increase the transparency of their risks, while preserving, as much as possible, the benefits of money market funds" (SEC, 2013). The SEC has indicated that it intends to finalize rules.[10]

Reminders of MMF vulnerabilities after 2010

Events since the financial crisis — and after the 2010 reforms were in place — have provided further evidence of the continuing vulnerability of MMFs to runs. For example, as illustrated on Fig. 2, over an eight-week period in the summer of 2011, institutional investors withdrew $180 billion from prime MMFs amid growing concerns about the funds' exposures to European banks and sovereigns, as well as stalled negotiations over the US federal government debt ceiling. These heavy redemptions occurred even though no MMF suffered any material loss during this period. In contrast, in 2007, when many MMFs did suffer losses related to holdings of asset-backed CP, sponsors bailed out their funds and institutional investors generally did *not* redeem shares, even from funds that experienced the losses (McCabe, 2010). Hence, a comparison of these two episodes suggests that institutional investors may have become *more* sensitive to MMF risks and

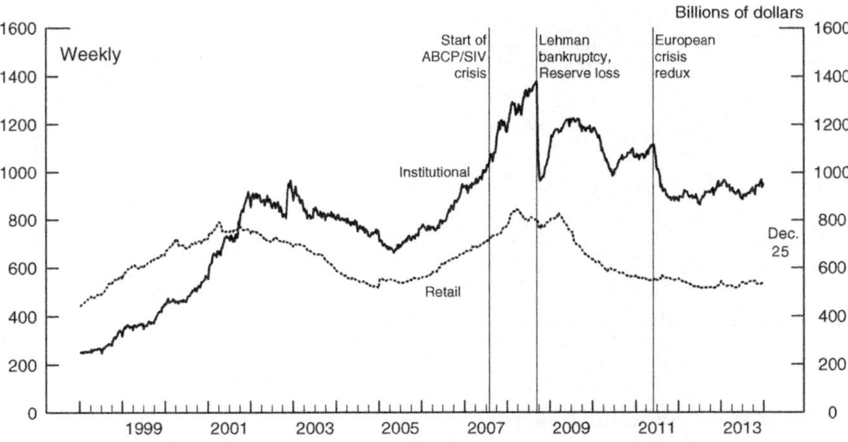

Fig. 2. Assets under management in US prime money market funds by investor type. *Source*: Investment Company Institute.

[10] See www.reginfo.gov/public/do/eAgendaViewRule?pubId=201310&RIN=3235-AK61.

the possibility of losses, and hence more prone to run, since the 2008 crisis (FSOC, 2012b).

The 2013 debt-ceiling standoff provided another reminder of MMF vulnerabilities. In late September, Secretary of the Treasury Lew wrote that "the extraordinary measures we are employing to preserve borrowing capacity . . . will be exhausted no later than October 17".[11] As of the end of September 2013, MMFs held large amounts of "at risk" Treasury securities — that is, those maturing from October 17 to November 15 — and such securities represented more than 50% of assets for some Treasury MMFs.[12] As Fig. 3 shows, money fund investors redeemed shares in the two weeks before October 17; in that period, Treasury-only MMF assets declined by 4%. Portfolio managers also reacted by reducing MMFs' aggregate holdings of Treasury securities 10% in the same two weeks. More surprisingly, they also cut the funds' CP holdings by 10% over the same period, even though the assets of prime MMFs (the only funds that hold significant amounts of CP) declined only 1%.[13]

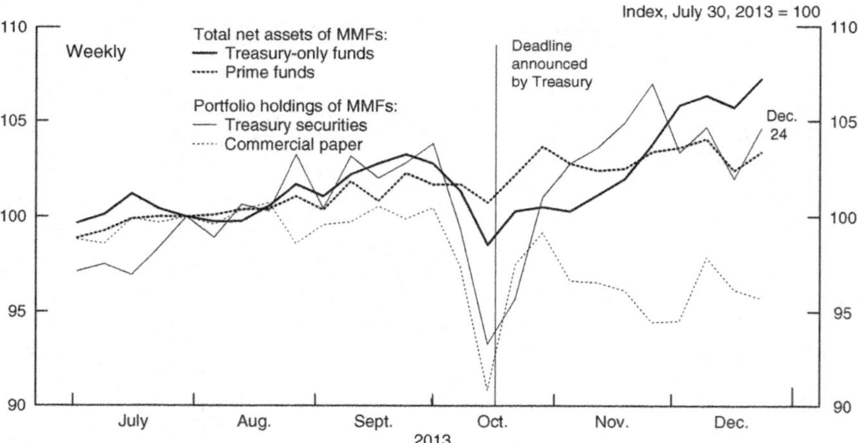

Fig. 3. MMF total assets and selected portfolio holdings during debt-ceiling standoff.
Source: iMoneyNet.

[11] See www.treasury.gov/Documents/Debt%20Limit%2020130925%20Boehner.pdf.
[12] *Source*: MMF filings of SEC form N-MFP.
[13] *Source*: iMoneyNet.

The drop in MMFs' CP holdings in this episode is, in some respects, reassuring evidence that portfolio managers were actively managing risk by boosting their funds' liquidity ahead of possible outflows. But it also serves as a reminder that MMFs are vulnerable to liquidity shocks, and that these shocks have the potential to cause strains in one sector (such as Treasury securities) to spill over to others (such as the CP market) through MMFs.

Mutual Funds or Banks?

The range of MMF features described in the first section makes money funds vulnerable to runs. But a more basic problem contributes to the systemic risk posed by MMFs and complicates strategies for reforming them: MMFs have diverged from the classic mutual fund model, in which the risks and rewards associated with a fund's portfolio are *dispersed* to a broad group of shareholders. The mutual fund model mitigates systemic risk in part because when losses do occur, they are absorbed by mutual fund shareholders in proportion to their holdings. That is, the mutual fund model disperses risks, rather than concentrating them.

In contrast, MMF risks historically have not been borne proportionally by all shareholders, but instead have been concentrated upon those who redeem slowly, upon MMF sponsors, and — at least in 2008 — upon the federal government. Notably, the overwhelming share of MMF losses over time has been borne by MMF sponsors, which include large, potentially systemically important institutions. Hence, the *de facto* allocation of risks in the MMF industry contributes to systemic risk, even as it appears to shield investors from losses and fosters a perception that MMF shares are similar to deposits. These deviations from the mutual fund model make today's MMFs hybrid financial entities that function like mutual funds most of the time but are tied to and supported by institutions at the core of the financial system during periods of stress.

Legally, MMFs *are* mutual funds. MMF investors own equity claims on the fund's portfolio, earn a pro rata share of its portfolio income, and legally bear a pro rata share of its risk. And MMF prospectuses and advertisements must warn that "it is possible to lose money by investing in the Fund" (SEC, 1998; 2003).

However, money fund risks and losses historically have almost never been passed on to investors, particularly those who redeem quickly in a crisis. Instead, those risks and losses have been shouldered by others, for three reasons. First, MMFs round their share prices to the nearest cent, so investors who redeem after an MMF has suffered small loss (less than 0.5% of assets) still receive $1 per share but shift potential losses to investors who do not redeem. Second, when losses are too large to be rounded away, MMF sponsors routinely absorb them. Third, amid the run in 2008, the federal government insured virtually all MMF shares.

The historical record of who absorbs MMF losses is particularly lopsided. Money fund sponsors have absorbed MMFs losses *more than 200 times* in the 30 years since the SEC first adopted Rule 2a-7 in 1983 to govern money funds.[14] In contrast, MMF investors have absorbed losses *just twice*: once in 1994 and then again when the Reserve Primary Fund announced its loss on September 16, 2008. Moreover, data from the SEC and US Treasury analyzed in McCabe, Cipriani, Holscher, and Martin (2013) show that at least 29 different MMFs had losses in September and October 2008 that exceeded 0.5% of assets and were thus large enough to cause them to break the buck without sponsor support. As Fig. 4 illustrates, some of these losses were quite substantial; for example, five funds had losses exceeding 3% of their assets. What made the Reserve Primary Fund unique in the crisis was not its losses but the inability of its sponsor to absorb them.

This long record of sponsor support — together with the US Treasury's guarantee of MMF shares in 2008 when confidence in sponsors' capacity to provide support was undermined by the Reserve Primary Fund's loss — has, not surprisingly, influenced investors' expectations for their MMFs. The Association for Financial Professionals (AFP) reported that 37% of the institutional investor respondents to its 2013 Liquidity Survey expected that the "fund sponsor would provide additional capital to ensure the orderly, ongoing operation and liquidity of its MMF" if the NAV of the fund falls below $1 (AFP, 2013). Moreover, another 14% believed that "the US Government would provide *adequate capital* to ensure the orderly, ongoing

[14]Moody's Investors Service (2010) reported 144 cases from 1989 to 2003 in which US MMFs received such support, and Brady, Anadu, and Cooper (2012) report 123 instances of support for 78 different money funds between 2007 and 2011. MMF sponsors reportedly intervened as recently as November 2011 to support their MMFs (Henriques, 2012).

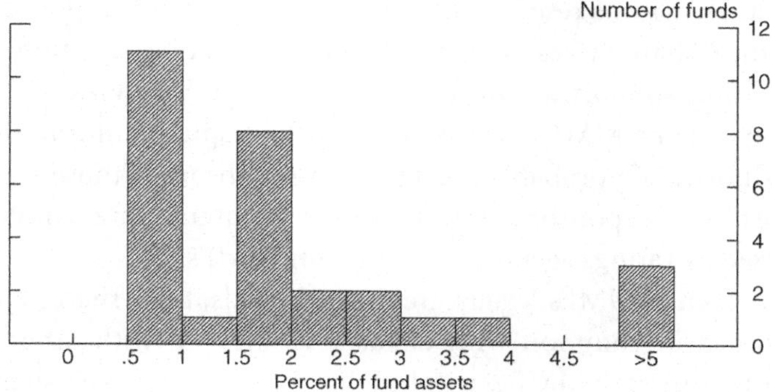

Fig. 4. MMF's reported losses in excess of 0.5%, September 5 to October 17, 2008.
Source: US Treasury and Securities and Exchange Commission.

operation and liquidity of the MMF" (emphasis mine).[15] For comparison, only 34% conceded that an MMF investor "would lose some amount of its principal investment".[16]

The principal stability provided by share-price rounding and enhanced by expectations of sponsor (and perhaps government) support has helped MMFs become a key component of the cash-management strategy for many large institutional investors. According to the AFP's 2013 Liquidity Survey, "over three-quarters of organizations consider money funds as a destination for corporate cash, including more than four in five large organizations with annual revenues of at least $1 billion". Prime MMFs, on average, were institutional investors' second-largest short-term investment — after bank deposits and ahead of Treasury bills. The importance of the rounded share price is evident in the answers to the same survey's question about an SEC proposal that this feature of MMFs be eliminated for institutional prime

[15]The implications of past government support for MMFs in 2008 are probably not limited to their effects on investors' expectations for future support; government support may have helped preserve the MMF industry. Other types of money market vehicles that encountered serious strains in 2007 and 2008, such as SIVs and auction-rate securities (ARS), did not receive government support and essentially disappeared.

[16]This view of sponsor support as an important component of MMF safety predates the 2007–2008 financial crisis. *Stigum's Money Market,* a classic reference guide to money markets, notes that "... a money fund run by an entity with deep pockets, while it may not have federal insurance, certainly has something akin to private insurance ... [and] that insurance is likely to prove adequate to cover any losses sustained by the fund" (Stigum and Crescenzi, 2007, p. 1117).

MMFs: Nearly half of respondents said that they would stop investing in MMF if their share prices floated.[17] As noted in the first section, the key role of sponsor support was evident after the SIV crisis in late 2007, when institutional prime MMF assets grew robustly despite significant losses in the funds' portfolios, probably because sponsors absorbed those losses. And the importance of sponsor support remains apparent, for example, in the criteria used by ratings agencies in evaluating MMFs.[18]

Hence, even if MMFs legally are mutual funds, their shares appear to have as much in common with deposits as they do with other mutual fund shares. Although MMF portfolios fluctuate in value, their share prices almost never do, so money fund investors, like depositors, largely do not bear the risks associated with the assets that back their claims. Indeed, the "cliff effect" when an MMF's portfolio value falls below $0.995 per share — so that it can no longer round its NAV up to $1 — has little in common with the regular fluctuations in NAVs of other mutual funds. As noted above, MMFs, like deposits, are heavily used for cash management by institutional investors. Adding to the similarity is the fact that most retail MMFs offer check-writing privileges to their shareholders.[19,20]

Of course, MMFs also deviate from the bank model. Depository institutions have a legal obligation to pay depositors in full, while MMF sponsors' support for money fund shares is expressly voluntary. No supervisory regime monitors the ability of MMF sponsors to provide support, nor must sponsors hold capital against the contingent liability associated with MMFs. As such, sponsor support for MMFs is always uncertain and is likely to be

[17]Notwithstanding institutional investors' apparent dislike for MMFs with floating NAVs, the SEC, recognizing the significance of MMF usage for cash management, offered reassurance in its proposed rules that MMFs with floating NAVs could continue to be classified as cash equivalents (SEC, 2013, pp. 121–122).

[18]Fitch's "Global Money Market Fund Rating Criteria", for instance, states, "Fitch's rating analysis also considers the fund sponsor and investment advisor", in part because a sponsor acts "as a potential source of stability to the fund during periods of stress". Thus, "[a]t the 'AAAmmf' rating level, a fund sponsor typically would be rated (or deemed to be rated) investment grade and demonstrate an appropriate level of financial resources" (Fitch Ratings, 2013).

[19]Based on data from iMoneyNet, as of the end of November 2013, retail funds that offered check-writing services accounted for 69% of retail MMF assets.

[20]Another link between MMFs and banks is the fact that sponsors affiliated with banks and thrifts operated 52% of MMF assets as of September 2013 (based on MMF filings of SEC form N-MFP and author's calculations).

more so during financial crises. In fact, uncertainty about weaker sponsors' ability to provide support contributed to outflows from MMFs during the run in 2008 (McCabe, 2010). Thus, the hybrid MMF model concentrates risk on the balance sheets of MMF sponsors, some of which are themselves large, systemically important financial institutions, without any regulatory or supervisory regime to ensure that sponsors have adequate resources to provide support.

The hybrid role of MMFs thus contributes to systemic risk by creating channels for transmission of stress between sponsors and their nominally off-balance-sheet MMFs. Losses in a money fund's portfolio can raise questions about the financial condition of sponsors that are widely expected to provide discretionary support. During the run in 2008, MMF bailouts cost sponsors scarce capital at a time when liquidity was in short supply and worsened some sponsors' financial condition (Standard & Poor's, 2008). On the other hand, a sponsor's inability to provide support that investors expect can be disastrous for MMFs and for short-term funding markets, as the Reserve Primary Fund example illustrates.

The hybrid role of MMFs also complicates reform efforts, in part because MMF shareholders may appear to have had the best of both worlds: The safety associated with deposits and the low costs associated with mutual funds. Hence, reforms that move MMFs back toward the mutual fund model by dispersing — that is, reallocating — risks to investors may cause many of them to shift assets away from money funds, potentially toward less regulated products. And reforms that would push MMFs closer to the banking model, for example, by requiring sponsors to hold capital, would impose costs on shareholders that would reduce yields. Hence, industry-sponsored surveys typically find that large fractions of MMF investors oppose virtually every option for reform.

Two possible directions for reform

MMFs' hybrid role suggests two possible strategies for reform. Policymakers could pursue remedies that add protections to MMFs that make them more like banks, or reforms could be designed to make MMFs more like other mutual funds.

Academicians have described the benefits of applying MMF-like asset restrictions for some portion of the banking sector at least since the early 1990s (Kobayakawa and Nakamura, 2000). For example, "narrow banks" that hold only money market instruments were seen as a means of ameliorating the asymmetric information and moral hazard associated with lending, deposit taking, and deposit insurance. After the run on MMFs in 2008, as the need for money fund reform became apparent, some suggested that a version of a narrow (or "special-purpose") bank might hold promise for addressing the vulnerability of MMFs to runs (see, for example, Group of Thirty, 2009; BlackRock, 2010; President's Working Group on Financial Markets (PWG), 2010). One impediment to such a reform strategy is that it probably would require legislation, as it would expand the financial safety net. In addition, because narrow banks would have concentrated positions in systemic risk, these entities would be a challenge for traditional bank regulation.

A second possible direction for money fund reform would be to make MMFs more like other mutual funds. The next section examines that alternative.

Returning to the Mutual Fund Model?

Although MMFs have deviated significantly from the mutual fund model, that model continues to hold promise for the design of MMF reforms. This section reviews several MMF reform options that have been discussed elsewhere. My aim is not to provide a complete analysis of the advantages and disadvantages of each option, but rather to discuss how some options might help disperse risks broadly to all MMF shareholders — not just to those who are slow to redeem in a crisis — and hence help mitigate the financial stability risks posed by MMFs.

Require MMFs to have floating NAVs

A straightforward way to return MMFs to the mutual fund model would be to require them to have floating NAVs, so that they "would value their portfolios like all other mutual funds" (FSOC, 2012b).[21] A floating NAV

[21]Opponents of a floating NAV have noted that MMF portfolio values do not fluctuate *much* (see, for example, Investment Company Institute, 2013). Of course, the same can be said for the values of the money market instruments that MMFs hold, but variations in the prices of those instruments are nonetheless economically significant. Both the FSOC (2012) and SEC (2013) floating NAV options would require that MMFs' share prices be computed to the nearest basis point.

would help disperse portfolio risks to *all* investors; those who redeem would receive a pro rata share of the value of the portfolio at the time of their redemption, not $1 per share when share prices have been rounded up to the nearest cent. A floating NAV also could hamper sponsor intervention to maintain stable $1 share prices, since the repeated interventions needed to provide stability could put sponsors at risk of having to consolidate their money funds on their own balance sheets. In addition, the floating NAV would enhance the transparency of MMF risks and facilitate better alignment of investor expectations and actual portfolio risks.[22]

To be sure, even with a floating NAV, investors still would have reason to redeem quickly from troubled MMFs (FSOC, 2012b; Hanson, Scharfstein, and Sunderam, 2012; Gordon and Gandia, 2013). For example, because MMFs typically meet net redemptions by disposing of their more liquid assets, remaining investors are left with claims on a less liquid portfolio. And empirical evidence for the effectiveness of a floating NAV in stemming runs is mixed (Witmer, 2012; Gordon and Gandia, 2013).

An additional concern about the floating NAV — particularly if it were to be implemented as the only reform option for money funds — is that it may be *too effective* in dispersing risks to shareholders. As noted above, the key deviations of MMFs from the mutual fund model — share-price rounding, sponsor support, and government intervention — have enhanced the apparent safety of MMFs. The stable $1 NAV has been called the "hallmark" of MMFs, and it is probably responsible for their disproportionate size relative to their closest floating-NAV cousins, ultrashort bond mutual funds (Investment Company Institute, 2009). Notably, more than two-thirds of the respondents to the AFP's liquidity survey cited safety of principal as their most important objective for short-term investing (AFP, 2013). Hence, elimination of MMFs' stable NAVs may prompt institutional investors with cash balances that far exceed caps on deposit insurance to seek other systemically risky vehicles that offer stable values, such as private liquidity funds and offshore MMFs. Alternatively, such investors might increase their holdings of uninsured deposits, which could add volatility and risk to the banking system.

[22]For a more complete discussion, see PWG (2010); FSOC (2012b); SEC (2013).

These concerns indicate that the vulnerabilities of MMFs and the systemic risks they pose cannot be eliminated solely through a simple return to the mutual fund model. Still, the floating NAV could have an important place in a broader strategy for MMF reform. If new rules gave investors a choice between floating-NAV and stable-NAV MMFs with additional protections, such as substantial capital buffers, the most risk-averse investors who primarily seek principal stability likely would move to the protected stable-NAV funds. This presumably would leave floating-NAV funds with a more risk-tolerant investor base that is less likely to run. Moreover, if protected stable-NAV funds are still allowed to invest in private debt securities, some investors who withdraw from floating NAV funds in a crisis might switch to the safer stable-NAV funds and hence not exacerbate aggregate liquidity pressures in the private money markets (PWG, 2010).

Capital buffers for MMFs

A second reform option would require MMFs to maintain pre-funded capital buffers. One attraction of capital is that it could bolster money funds' stable NAVs, eliminate the rationale for share-price rounding, and diminish the role of voluntary sponsor support in shielding investors from MMF risks. Disadvantages of capital include its cost and that it may be ineffective in stopping runs if investors fear that an MMF's losses could exceed the size of its buffer.

A capital-buffer mandate would appear to move MMFs closer to the banking model. But capital could be introduced in a manner consistent with the mutual fund model in a manner that disperses risk; the key question is who funds and owns the buffer. Giving MMF sponsors that role would make MMF shares even more like deposits. This approach could heighten systemic risks by further concentrating the tail risks associated with the $2.7 trillion MMF industry onto the balance sheets of a few asset-management firms, some of which already are affiliated with large, potentially systemically important institutions.[23]

[23]Data from MMF filings of SEC form N-MFP show that, as of September 2013, just 20 MMF sponsors operated funds accounting for 90% of the industry's assets. As noted above, affiliates of banks and thrifts sponsored MMFs with over half of the industry's assets.

However, capital buffers also could be funded in a way that utilizes the mutual fund model and disperses risks across a broad group of shareholders. For example, MMFs might issue two types of securities: stable-value shares and buffer shares (see Hanson, Scharfstein, and Sunderam, 2012, for a discussion of such a scheme). The latter would absorb variations in the portfolio's value so that the value of the stable-value shares could remain constant. Hence, the buffer shares, which would be levered claims on the MMF's portfolio that would *not* be redeemable on demand, would be riskier and presumably would offer higher yields than the stable-value shares.[24] If buffer shares were sold in capital markets, the buffer could be funded by a diverse group of mutual fund shareholders who presumably would be more tolerant of risks than stable-value shareholders. The funding costs of such a buffer presumably would come from the fund's gross income and would reflect the market price of an MMF's risk, so greater portfolio risks would diminish income available for stable-value shares and give portfolio managers incentives for prudent risk management. In summary, a capital buffer requirement for MMFs could be introduced in a way that would maintain the advantages of the mutual fund model.

Restrictions or fees for redemptions

A third set of options for MMF reform would create restrictions or fees for redemptions, with the aim of slowing potential runs or dampening investors' incentives to redeem in a crisis. A shortcoming of redemption constraints is that they would be less effective than capital buffers in displacing or reducing the likelihood of sponsor support. Still, these options can be assessed for how they address the current uneven allocation of risks among MMF shareholders.

Redemption restrictions may be imposed conditionally — in emergencies only — or at all times. An example of conditional restrictions is included in the SEC's proposed MMF reforms (SEC, 2013). Under that proposal, MMFs would have a system of "standby" fees and gates that would be triggered if a fund's "weekly liquid assets" fall below 15% of assets. In that

[24]Hanson, Scharfstein, and Sunderam (2012) suggest that the buffer shares could be "perpetual closed-end first-loss shares", but other types of securities, such as laddered-maturity debt securities, might also be feasible.

event, the fund could impose a 2% redemption fee or the fund's board could decide to impose a lower fee, halt all redemptions temporarily, permanently close, or do nothing.

A drawback for conditional restrictions is that they create incentives for investors to redeem *before* any conditions are met and effectively shift forward the "deadline" for exiting a troubled fund. For example, in the version proposed by the SEC, investors who redeem before a fund's liquid assets drop below 15% would exit without restrictions or fees. Conditional restrictions thus may heighten run risks (FSOC, 2012b; Rosengren *et al.*, 2013).

Furthermore, rather than dispersing MMF risks to all shareholders, conditional restrictions may exacerbate the uneven allocation of risks among money fund investors. If the threshold for imposing restrictions is based on a fund's liquid assets, for example, investors who redeem from a fund that is near the threshold are likely to reduce the fund's stockpile of liquid assets, push it closer to the threshold, and worsen other investors' expected outcomes. Moreover, conditional restrictions may put additional pressure on sponsors to provide liquidity (voluntarily) to prevent money funds from crossing a threshold.

Alternatively, redemption restrictions may be imposed at *all* times. An example of this approach is the minimum balance at risk (MBR) proposed by McCabe *et al.* (2013). The MBR would be a small fraction — perhaps 3 to 5% — of an investor's balance that could only be redeemed with a delay. Although this restriction would always be in place, it would not affect an investor's transactions as long as her balance remains larger than her MBR. The MBR would even out the allocation of risks among investors by ensuring that those who redeem quickly in a crisis do not shift all risks to others. Moreover, the MBR can create a *disincentive* to redeem by subordinating redeeming investors' MBRs, which would give a greater portion of risks to investors who redeem early. Although this would not be the pro rata allocation of risks called for by the mutual fund model, it may be desirable, given the liquidity advantages enjoyed by investors who redeem rapidly and the considerable negative externalities associated with runs on MMFs.

To be sure, MMF sponsors probably would continue to face pressures to provide voluntary support for money funds with MBRs. McCabe *et al.* (2013) suggest that pairing an MBR with a capital buffer might displace sponsor support and provide greater protections for MMFs and for the financial system than either capital or an MBR alone.

Conclusions

Five years after the damaging run on MMFs in 2008, these funds remain vulnerable to runs that threaten financial stability. The SEC's 2010 reforms strengthened regulatory constraints on the funds' portfolios, but events since 2010 have served as reminders that the risk persists.

One complication in designing reforms for MMFs is that the funds have deviated from the basic mutual fund model in which the risks and rewards arising from a fund's portfolio are allocated among its investors in proportion to their shareholdings. MMF investors who redeem quickly from a troubled fund can shift risks and losses to other investors, in part because MMFs maintain a stable share price by rounding their NAVs. In addition, sponsors have, as a rule, acted to protect even those investors who do not redeem quickly, so that in practice money fund investors, like depositors, usually do not bear the risks associated with the assets that back their claims. Hence, except in crises, MMF investors seem to enjoy the best of both worlds — the apparent safety of banks without the costs of capital or insurance.

The hybrid nature of today's MMFs suggests two possible strategies for reform: MMFs could become more like mutual funds or more like banks. This paper argues that the mutual fund model still offers considerable promise for the design and assessment of MMF reform options. Moreover, several options — including a floating NAV (particularly if it is paired with an option that preserves stable-NAV funds with new protections), a capital buffer funded in capital markets, and an MBR — could reduce the vulnerability of MMFs to runs, in part by clarifying that MMF investors bear the risks of their funds, even if those investors redeem shares quickly during the next crisis.

References

Association for Financial Professionals (AFP) (2013). AFP Liquidity Survey: Report of Survey Results. June. Available at www.citizensbank.com/pdf/commercial/2013_AFP_Liquidity_Survey.pdf [accessed on June 20, 2014].

BlackRock (2010). ViewPoint: Money Market Funds, A Proposal for a Capitalized Special Purpose Entity. February 7. Available at www2.blackrock.com/webcore/litService/search/getDocument.seam?venue=PUB_IND&source=GLOBAL&contentId=1111124986 [accessed on June 20, 2014].

Board of Governors of the Federal Reserve System (2009). Monetary Policy Report to the Congress. February 24. Available at www.federalreserve.gov/monetarypolicy/mpr_20090224_part2.htm [accessed on June 20, 2014].

Brady, S.A., K.E. Anadu and N.R. Cooper (2012). The Stability of Prime Money Market Mutual Funds: Sponsor Support from 2007 to 2011. Risk and Policy Analysis Unit *Working Paper No.* 12-3, Federal Reserve Bank of Boston, August 13. Available at www.bos.frb.org/bankinfo/qau/wp/2012/qau1203.pdf [accessed on June 20, 2014].

Chernenko, S. and A. Sunderam (2013). Frictions in Shadow Banking: Evidence from the Lending Behavior of Money Market Mutual Funds. Mimeo, December 24. Available at www.people.hbs.edu/asunderam/mmmf_2013-12-24_with_names.pdf [accessed on June 20, 2014].

Federal Open Market Committee (2008). Minutes of the Federal Open Market Committee. October 28–29. Available at www.federalreserve.gov/monetarypolicy/files/fomcminutes20081029.pdf [accessed on June 20, 2014].

Financial Stability Oversight Council (FSOC) (2011). Annual Report. July. Available at www.treasury.gov/initiatives/fsoc/documents/FSOCAR2011.pdf [accessed on June 20, 2014].

Financial Stability Oversight Council (FSOC) (2012a). Annual Report. July. Available at www.treasury.gov/initiatives/fsoc/Documents/2012%20Annual%20Report.pdf [accessed on June 20, 2014].

Financial Stability Oversight Council (FSOC) (2012b). Proposed Recommendations Regarding Money Market Mutual Fund Reform. *Federal Register*, Vol. 77, No. 223, November 19, pp. 69455–69483. Available at www.gpo.gov/fdsys/pkg/FR-2012-11-19/pdf/2012-28041.pdf [accessed on June 20, 2014].

Financial Stability Oversight Council (FSOC) (2013). Annual Report. April. Available at www.treasury.gov/initiatives/fsoc/Documents/FSOC%202013%20Annual%20Report.pdf [accessed on June 20, 2014].

Fitch Ratings (2013). Global Money Market Fund Rating Criteria. March 26.

Gordon, J.N. and C.M. Gandia (2013). Money Market Fund Risk: Will Floating Net Asset Value Fix the Problem? Columbia University School of Law Center for Law and Economic Studies *Working Paper No.* 426, March.

Group of Thirty (2009). Financial Reform: A Framework for Financial Stability. January 15. Available at www.group30.org/images/PDF/Financial_Reform-A_Framework_for_Financial_Stability.pdf [accessed on June 20, 2014].

Hanson, S.G., D.S. Scharfstein and A. Sunderam (2012). An Evaluation of Money Market Fund Reform Proposals. Comment letter regarding Financial Stability Oversight Council, "Proposed Recommendations Regarding Money Market Mutual Fund Reform" December 20. Available at www.regulations.

gov/#!documentDetail;D=FSOC-2012-0003-0032 [accessed on June 20, 2014].

Henriques, D.B. (2012). Money Funds Could Face More Changes. *New York Times*, Business Day, January 8, p. 11. Available at www.nytimes.com/2012/01/08/ busines/mutfund/money-market-funds-may-soon-face-more-changes.html? pagewanted=all&_r=1&.

Investment Company Institute (2009). Report of the Money Market Working Group. March 17. Available at www.ici.org/pdf/ppr_09_mmwg.pdf [accessed on June 20, 2014].

Investment Company Institute (2013). Comment Letter of the Investment Company Institute to the Securities and Exchange Commission: Money Market Fund Reform; Amendments to Form PF. September 17. Available at www.sec.gov/comments/s7-03-13/s70313-200.pdf [accessed on June 20, 2014].

Kobayakawa, S. and H. Nakamura (2000). A Theoretical Analysis of Narrow Banking Proposals. *Monetary and Economic Studies*, Vol. 18, No. 1, May, pp. 105–118. Available at http://www.imes.boj.or.jp/research/papers/english/me18-1-4.pdf [accessed on June 20, 2014].

McCabe, P.E. (2010). The Cross Section of Money Market Fund Risks and Financial Crises. *Federal Reserve Board Finance and Economics Discussion Series Working Paper* No. 2010-51, September 12. Available at www.federalreserve.gov/pubs/feds/2010/201051/201051pap.pdf [accessed on June 20, 2014].

McCabe, P.E., M. Cipriani, M. Holscher and A. Martin (2013). The Minimum Balance at Risk: A Proposal to Mitigate the Systemic Risks Posed by Money Market Funds. *Brookings Papers on Economic Activity*, Spring, pp. 211–256. Available at www.brookings.edu/~/media/Projects/BPEA/Spring%202013/ 2013a_mccabe.pdf [accessed on June 20, 2014].

Moody's Investors Service (2010). Sponsor Support Key to Money Market Funds. August 8.

President's Working Group on Financial Markets (PWG) (2010). Report of the President's Working Group on Financial Markets: Money Market Fund Reform Options. October. Available at www.treasury.gov/press-center/press-releases/Documents/10.21%20PWG%20Report%20Final.pdf [accessed on June 20, 2014].

Rosengren, E.S. *et al.* (2013). Comment Letter Regarding Securities and Exchange Commission's Money Market Fund Reform; Amendments to Form PF, September 12. Available at http://www.sec.gov/comments/s7-03-13/s70313-111.pdf [accessed on June 20, 2014].

Scharfstein, D.S. (2012). Testimony on 'Perspectives on Money Market Mutual Fund Reforms' before U.S. Senate Committee on Banking, Housing, and Urban Affairs. Washington. June 21. Available at www.banking.senate.gov/public/index.cfm?FuseAction=Files.View&FileStore_id=ca1f8420-b2de-46dd-aee1-9a22d47b198c [accessed on June 20, 2014].

Standard & Poor's (2008). Money-Market Fund Support Weighs on Fund Managers and Bank Sponsors. December 4.

Stigum, M. and A. Crescenzi (2007). *Stigum's Money Market*, 4th edn. New York: McGraw-Hill.

US Securities and Exchange Commission (SEC) (1998). Final Rule: Registration Form Used by Open-End Management Investment Companies. File No. S7-10-97, March 18. Available at www.sec.gov/rules/final/33-7512r.htm [accessed on June 20, 2014].

US Securities and Exchange Commission (SEC) (2003). Final Rule: Amendments to Investment Company Advertising Rules. File No. S7-17-02, October 1. Available at www.sec.gov/rules/final/33-8294.htm [accessed on June 20, 2014].

US Securities and Exchange Commission (SEC) (2009). Money Market Fund Reform: Proposed Rule. Release No. IC-2880730, June 30. Available at www.sec.gov/rules/proposed/2009/ic-28807.pdf [accessed on June 20, 2014].

US Securities and Exchange Commission (SEC) (2010). Money Market Fund Reform: Final Rule. Release No. IC-29132, February 23. Available at www.sec.gov/rules/final/2010/ic-29132.pdf [accessed on June 20, 2014].

US Securities and Exchange Commission (SEC) (2013). Money Market Fund Reform; Amendments to Form PF. Release No. 33-9408, June 5. Available at www.sec.gov/rules/proposed/2013/33-9408.pdf [accessed on June 20, 2014].

Witmer, J. (2012). Does the Buck Stop Here? A Comparison of Withdrawals from Money Market Mutual Funds with Floating and Constant Share Prices. *Bank of Canada Working Paper No.* 2012-25, August. Available at www.bankofcanada.ca/wp-content/uploads/2012/08/wp2012-25.pdf [accessed on June 20, 2014].

VI

Shadow Banking around the World and Cross-Border Issues

Shadow Banking and the Global Financial Eco-System

Zoltan Pozsar*

US Treasury, Office of Financial Research

Understanding the global financial eco-system that dealer banks operate in is imperative, as it can influence the types of lending activities they engage in and the types of liabilities they issue. This can be done at two levels: first, by profiling the range of institutional investors that dealers interact with on both their asset and liability sides and their needs (questions of "who" and "what"), and second, by identifying the global macro drivers behind the rise of these institutional investors and their needs (questions of "why").

Risk Intermediation

Our analytical framework to understand what dealer banks do is muddled by trying to draw parallels with what commercial banks do. Commercial banks engage in credit intermediation by issuing loans and insured deposits, linking ultimate borrowers with ultimate savers.

Dealer banks do something different. They finance institutional bond portfolios with un-insured money market claims, and rather than linking

*Zoltan Pozsar is a Senior Adviser at the Office of Financial Research. The views and opinions expressed are those of the author and do not necessarily represent official OFR or Treasury positions or policy.

ultimate borrowers with ultimate savers, they link cash portfolio managers and risk portfolio managers (PMs) who in turn manage ultimate savers' savings. In linking cash PMs and risk PMs through collateralized repurchase agreements (repos), dealers effectively function as money dealers (see Mehrling *et al.*, 2013).

Cash PMs invest in the money market and are characteristically risk-averse. Think for example of a corporate treasurer who wants only minimal credit, duration, and liquidity risk in a portfolio.

Risk PMs invest farther out on the duration and credit curve and search for yield using leverage. Think of hedge funds that aim to beat a benchmark by taking extra credit, duration, and liquidity risks.[1]

Cash and risk PMs are natural complements to each other. Cash PMs are "cash rich" but "safety poor" since they are too large to be eligible for deposit insurance. This drives them toward insured deposit alternatives such as repos (see for example, Pozsar, 2011).

On the other hand, risk PMs are "securities rich" but "return poor" in the sense that they are mandated to beat their benchmarks. To that end, they employ the techniques of funding, shorting, and derivatives.[2]

Risk PMs are often secured cash borrowers in the repo market, using their securities as collateral — they repo securities out and cash in. On the flipside, cash PMs are secured cash lenders — they repo securities in and cash out. Through the repo market, cash PMs have their safety thanks to the securities posted by risk PMs as collateral, and risk PMs have their enhanced return thanks to the leverage provided by cash PMs' cash loans in exchange for collateral.

Dealer banks are intermediaries between risk PMs and cash PMs. Risk PMs interface with dealers on the asset side of dealers' balance sheets and cash PMs interface with dealers on the liability side of dealers' balance sheets. In this process, dealers intermediate risks (credit, duration, and

[1]What sets risk PMs apart from long-only investment managers is risk PMs' ability to use leverage. Risk PMs may be hedge funds or any investment fund, separate account, or allocation with a mandate that allows the use of leverage.

[2]Excess returns can come in two basic forms: pure alpha (through smart portfolio selection, market timing, and hedges) and alpha masquerading as levered beta (through the use of funding, securities lending, and derivatives).

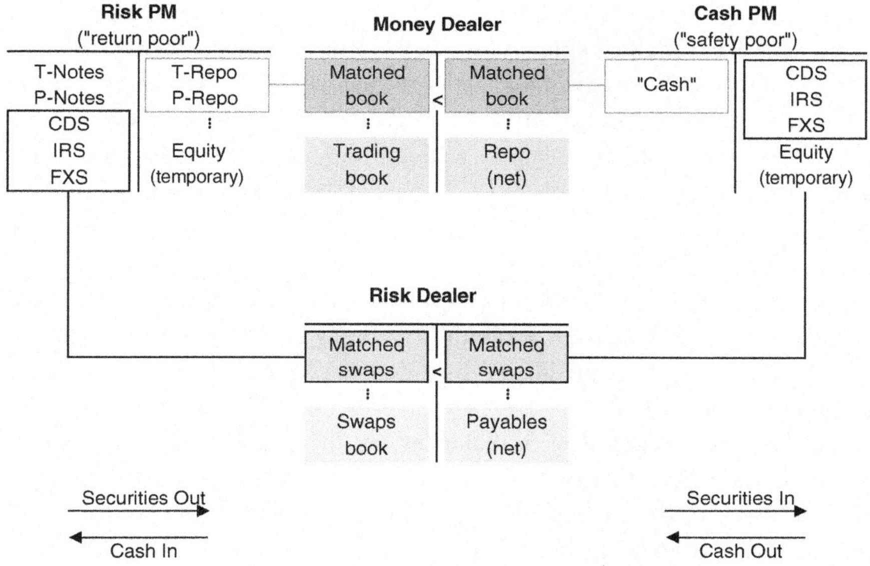

Fig. 1. Risk intermediation.

Source: Zoltan Pozsar expanding on "**Bagehot Was a Shadow Banker**" (Mehrling *et al.*, 2013).

liquidity risks) away from cash PMs and toward risk PMs using repos and derivatives.[3] This is risk intermediation (see Fig. 1 and Checki, 2009; Pozsar and Singh, 2012; Mehrling, 2010).

Dealers and the Global Financial Eco-System

Turning to questions of "why", the secular rise of cash PMs seeking safety and risk PMs reaching for yield has been driven by macro imbalances — both global and local, and present and future.

First, the secular rise of cash PMs (or institutional cash pools, see Pozsar, 2011) can be attributed to three factors.

[3]Derivatives may be used by risk PMs as hedges or as means to take leveraged bets. Risk PMs offload or take on risks using derivatives by trading with dealers, and dealers pass on the bulk of these positions (through matched swap books) to other investors looking to take the other side of the trade.

On the global level, managed exchange-rate arrangements *vis-à-vis* the US dollar are a major explanation for the rise of cash pools held by foreign exchange (FX) reserve managers (in the form of FX reserve's so-called *liquidity tranches* estimated at $1.3 trillion).[4] The secular increase in capital's share of income versus labor's share of income is one important driver behind the rise of cash pools at the largest global corporations (estimated at $1.6 trillion).[5]

On the local level, the rise of cash pools within the asset management complex (estimated at $3.1 trillion) is explained by consolidation among asset managers, the centralized liquidity management of fund complexes, and the growth in securities lending and derivative overlay investment strategies.

These examples reflect imbalances in the distribution of present incomes — between countries with structural current account surpluses and deficits, and between capital and labor — and that ever more savers' portfolios are managed by ever fewer asset managers.[6]

---

[4]The shares of countries under a freely floating FX arrangement *vis-à-vis* the US dollar has declined from just over 45% of world GDP and world exports in 2000 to just over 35% in 2007 (see Eichengreen *et al.*, 2011).

[5]Numbers are as of the second quarter of 2013 (see OFR, 2013a). On FX reserve accumulation contributing to the rise of short-term dollar assets, see Pozsar (2011) and McCauley and Rigaudy (2011). Corporate cash pools are a stock measure of accumulated profit flows over time. The increase in corporate cash pools has been driven to a great extent by the fact that corporate profit margins as a share of GDP (capital's share of national income) have increased to historical highs at the expense of wages as a share of GDP (labor's share of national income) — see for example Labour pains, *The Economist*, November 2, 2013. That said, high profit margins do not explain why corporations chose to hold on to more of the cash they generated. Debate about this is unsettled, but one oft-cited argument is the rapid declines of the cost of capital goods, especially those associated with information technology (see for example Summers, 2013). For the purposes of this article, the question of why corporations ended up holding more cash over the past two decades is irrelevant. What is relevant to highlight is greater pace of cash accumulation, the secular rise of corporate cash pools within the system, and what this means for the mix of instruments banks use for funding.

[6]See for example Asset management hits record level, FT, July 9, 2013 which notes that the asset management "industry is also taking on winner-takes-all characteristics. For example, the top 10 US managers took almost two-thirds of all net new fund assets among managers with positive net flows in 2012 compared with 54% in 2011". Also see the OFR study on asset managers which notes: "Economies of scale in portfolio management and administration, combined with index-based strategies, have increased industry concentration in recent years" (OFR, 2013b).

Secondly, the secular rise of risk PMs (or levered investment strategies) reflects imbalances between the present value of future pension promises, which exceeds the expected present value of unlevered, long-only investment incomes.[7] This underfundedness is the principal driver of the trend that pension funds and endowments allocate an increasing share of their portfolios to hedge funds and separate accounts at asset managers (see for example Caballero, 2013).[8]

In a low-yield environment, risk PMs may have an extra incentive to increase their use of funding, shorting, securities lending, and derivatives, with an aim to enhance returns and avoid major portfolio drawdowns. They are all aiming to provide equity-like returns with bond-like volatility.[9]

FX reserve managers'[10] needs are somewhat similar to those of pension funds, for whom the maintenance of FX pegs is a negative carry proposition: the bonds issued to sterilize the exchange of foreign currency to domestic currency yield more than the foreign currency bonds reserves are held in, which is a fiscal cost. To minimize these costs, reserve managers also employ the techniques of securities lending and derivatives to enhance their returns (see Fig. 2).[11]

---

[7]On the degree of corporate pension funds' structural under-funded status (see Towers Watson, 2013) and on the degree of state and local pension funds' structural under-funded status (see Novy-Marx and Rauh, 2014). On the secular rise of risk PMs see the rise in hedge fund's assets under management from less than \$50 billion in 1990 to \$500 billion in 2000 and \$2.25 trillion in 2012 (see Farrell *et al.*, 2007). Finally, on the rise of pension funds' and endowments' increased allocation to hedge funds, see the increase in hedge funds' capital under management from pension funds and endowments rise from about 15% in the mid-1990s to 30% in the mid-2000s and nearly 35% as of March, 2012 (see Farrell *et al.*, 2007; FSA, 2012) as well as US pension funds' allocations to alternatives doubling from 10% in 2002 to 20% in 2012 (see Towers Watson, 2013, p. 31)

[8]See p. 19 in Caballero (2013) presentation at the Bank of England by Ricardo Caballero. The chart shows a strong positive correlation between pension funds degree of underfundedness and their tendency to increase their allocation to riskier assets and asset management strategies.

[9]Since risk PMs are mandated to beat their benchmark, they always search for yield. However, there may be added pressures to search for yield if ultimate investors' yield expectations do not adjust to an ever-lower-yield environment.

[10]Unlike FX reserves' liquidity tranches, this section refers to FX reserves' long-duration segments where search for yield is more prevalent.

[11]See for example, The SNB's bond buying: now with more context, FTAlphaville, October 8, 2012.

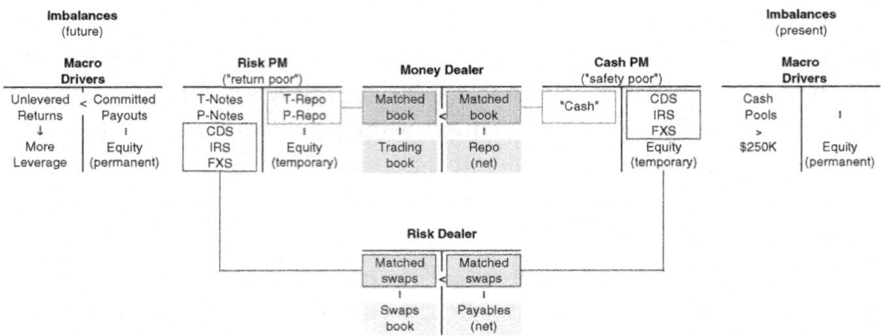

Fig. 2. Dealers and the global financial ecosystem.
Source: Zoltan Pozsar.

Four Goals Shaping Dealers' Balance Sheets

Thus, from a bird's eye perspective, the modern financial eco-system has five groups of players, each with a well-defined goal.

CIOs at pension funds, foreign central banks, and sovereign wealth funds — the first group — are tasked with reducing their underfundedness. They do this by allocating more of their portfolios to hedge funds and separate accounts — the second group — whose managers (risk PMs) employ leverage, shorting, and derivatives in order to beat their benchmarks (or in other words, reach for yield).

Treasurers (or cash PMs) — the third group — are tasked with not losing any money on the cash pools they manage. They shun credit, duration, and liquidity risks and invest cash on a collateralized basis. These cash pools are the by-products of the decisions of sovereign and corporate CEOs — the fourth group — who are tasked with generating growth in the real economy and profits respectively.

The goals of these market participants — asset-liability matching for CIOs, beating benchmarks for hedge funds (risk PMs), liquidity at par for treasurers (cash PMs), and growth for CEOs — represent nominal rigidities in the system that drive what dealers — the fifth group — do.

Dealers' role is to make markets and intermediate risks away from cash PMs to risk PMs, enabling them to preserve their wealth in the present and to help meet their promises in the future.

Dealers for the most part engage in risk intermediation through their matched book positions and only engage in risk transformation through

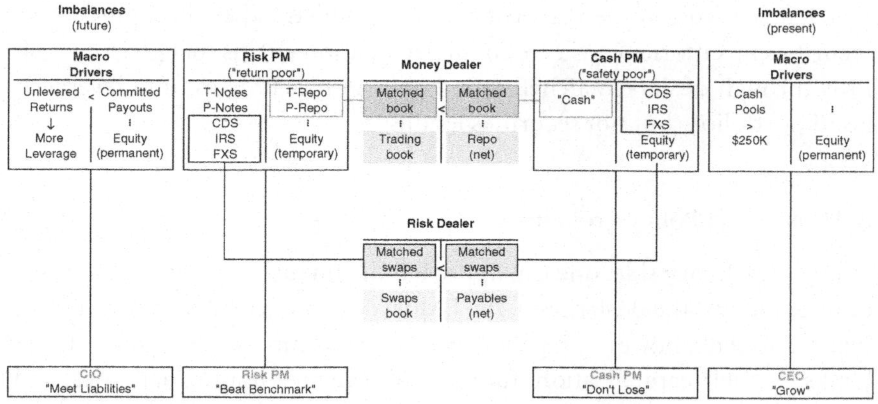

Fig. 3. Four goals shaping dealers' balance sheets.
Source: Zoltan Pozsar.

their inventory positions (either in the form of a portfolio of securities or derivatives), which — as more than "just" brokers — they accumulate through market making activities (see Fig. 3).[12]

This is the broadest perspective in which we can understand the rise of the shadow banking system and why it is misleading to think about credit, duration, and liquidity transformation and more appropriate to think about the intermediation of credit, duration, and liquidity risks between cash and risk PMs across the financial eco-system and, by inference, the real economy more broadly.[13]

---

[12] It follows that risk intermediation corresponds to matched book activities and risk transformation corresponds to net long or short positions. If a risk PM sheds risks to a dealer using derivatives and a cash PM assumes the same risks from the dealer using derivatives through a matched book transaction, then risks have been intermediated. However, if a risk PM sheds risks but the dealer is unable to offload it to anyone, then, from the PM's perspective, the dealer transformed these risks through its equity, much like banks would transform the credit, maturity and liquidity risk of loans from depositors' perspective via deposits.

[13] Shadow banking is defined many different ways. For example the FSB defines it as "the system of credit intermediation that involves entities and activities outside the regular banking system", the OFR defines it as "credit intermediation by unregulated financial institutions in combination with the creation of money-like liabilities, involving leverage and maturity transformation, in opaque markets" and the Shadow Banking Colloquium at INET defines it as "money market funding of capital market lending" (see Mehrling *et al.*, 2013). The context provided in this article is broader than these definitions as it highlights

That is, credit to the real economy is extended either through dealers' securities inventories or via credit intermediation chains that go from cash PMs through dealers' matched repo books to risk PMs to fund leveraged bond portfolios (but not securities lending).[14]

A Three-Level Policy Problem

On the regulatory side, one can approach the financial eco-system at three different levels: the dealer level, the PM level or the global macro level (see Fig. 4). To date, however, regulatory reform has mostly focused on dealer banks — their capitalization, funding, proprietary trading activities, and separation from retail banking.

However, focusing on dealers only, while leaving the needs of risk and cash PMs and that of their CIO and CEO "masters" unaddressed will only

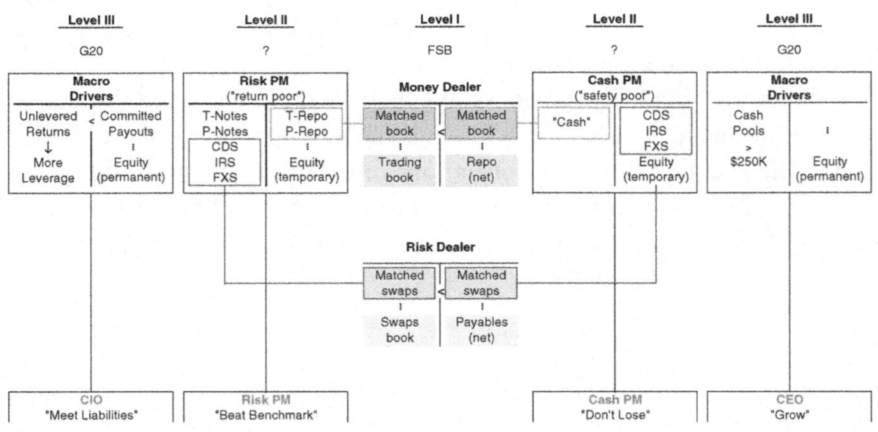

Fig. 4. A three level policy problem.
Source: Zoltan Pozsar.

the importance of repos and derivatives to enhance portfolio returns, which have less to do with credit intermediation and more with the generation of excess returns by risk PMs.

[14]Exactly what share of repos funds credit extension to the real economy is not clear from the existing literature on repo and shadow banking. While — as our discussion suggests — some repo funding is directly related to credit extension, the precise quantification of this should be a research priority.

shift problems around but not solve them. Ultimately, the policy extremes are (1) aiming to reduce the imbalances in present and future incomes,[15] or (2) accommodating the system as it is by giving the dealers at its core access to official liquidity (dealer of last resort, see Mehrling (2010) and the BoE's recently updated SMF (2013)).

In either case, the fundamental problem we are dealing with is a financial eco-system that has outgrown the safety-net that has been put around it many years ago. Today we have new types of savers (cash PMs versus retail depositors), new types of borrowers (risk PMs to fund pensions versus ultimate borrowers to finance investments and consumption) and also new types of banks (dealer banks that do securities financing versus traditional banks that finance the real economy more directly via loans) to whom discount window access and deposit insurance do not apply.

These twin pillars of the official safety net were erected around traditional, deposit-funded banks to address retail runs. In contrast, the crisis of 2007–2009 was a crisis of institutional runs where cash PMs ran on dealers and dealers ran on risk PMs. But importantly, as our examples demonstrate, beyond the institutional façade of the eco-system, it is ultimately retail wealth and promises that are at stake.

Therefore if neither of the above policy options (that is, shrinking imbalances or broadening the safety net) are palatable, the third option is to offer partial solutions[16] and to recognize that the eco-system's existing needs will be met by new structures that need to be understood and monitored to avoid new systemic excesses.

But we cannot monitor what we do not measure. The Flow of Funds accounts do not measure the eco-system described above.

[15]This may happen either through rewriting corporate tax regimes or providing incentives for capital expenditures, with the former affecting the pace of cash accumulation and the latter the pace of cash decumulation (see G20 back fundamental reform of corporate taxation, Reuters, July 19, 2013, and Japan can put people before profits, FT, February 5, 2013).

[16]These include increased Treasury bill issuance or access to the Fed's full allotment reverse repo facility to absorb cash PMs' money demand. However, these policy measures only address cash PMs' but not risk PM's needs.

We Cannot Monitor What We Do Not Measure

The Flow of Funds have been designed to show who borrows, who lends and through what types of instruments.[17] It does not provide information on the asset-liability mismatches at pension funds and FX reserve managers; it does not cover hedge funds and separate accounts which make up a rising share of institutional investors' portfolios; it does not provide a breakdown of dealers' matched repo books to gauge the volume of funding passed on to hedge funds and asset managers, or the purpose of that funding: whether it was to fund a bond position or a short position, or to raise liquidity for margin.

Moreover, the Flow of Funds accounts end where derivatives begin: derivatives effectively separate the flow of risks (credit, duration and FX risks) from the flow of funds and hence looking at exposures to bonds without looking at accompanying derivatives makes the Flow of Funds accounts' usefulness somewhat limited. Without these measures, our ability to understand asset prices dynamics is also limited.

To improve on this, one recommendation would be for the Flow of Funds accounts to be augmented over time to incorporate measures of structural asset-liability mismatches and supplemented with a set of Flow of Risks satellite accounts and a set of Flow of Collateral satellite accounts in order to tabulate the types of collateral that back the flow of funds and risks across the eco-system.

Conclusions

Compared with earlier decades, risk PMs' bond portfolios have become more and more leveraged and bonds have become more and more valuable as collateral for cash PMs.[18]

Leveraged bond portfolios (through the techniques of funding, shorting, securities lending and derivatives) help risk PMs beat their benchmarks

[17]The US Flow of Funds were recently renamed as the US Financial Accounts.

[18]One can infer this from the increased matched book volumes of dealers on recent decades (see for example, TBAC and King, 2013, slide 16). This involves willing securities lenders (risk PMs) who lend securities for cash and willing repo investors (cash PMs) who lend cash against collateral.

to help CIOs achieve asset-liability matching in an ever-lower-yield environment, and collateral gives cash PMs a sense of safety in a financial eco-system with an increasingly outdated safety net.

In this system, credit intermediation is just a by-product. Risk PMs go to work every day not to lend to the real economy but to beat their benchmark or to generate absolute returns. In this sense, shadow banking is primarily about the financing of pre-existing securities, rather than credit extension to the real economy, which is just a second derivative.

Credit, maturity and liquidity transformation is only the tip of the iceberg in understanding shadow banking and the contribution of Pozsar *et al.* (2010) should be viewed in that light. Importantly, we must also ask why these activities are being undertaken, and the answer here is: to manage future and present imbalances.

Dealing with the shadow banking system — the system that grew up to intermediate these imbalances — will have to involve either moderating these imbalances via entitlement, currency and tax reforms or giving it some form of an official backstop. Like in 1913 and 1933, it is retail assets that are at stake, but this time around they are harder to see due to the veil of institutional investors managing them.

References

Bank of England (2013). Liquidity Insurance at the Bank of England: Developments in the Sterling Monetary Framework. October.

Caballero, R., 2013, The Shortage of Safe Assets: Macroeconomic Policy Implications, presented at the Bank of England, Chief Economist's Workshop, May. Available at http://www.bankofengland.co.uk/research/Documents/ccbs/cew2013/presentation_caballero.pdf

Checki, T.J. (2009). Beyond the Crisis: Reflections on the Challenges. Remarks at the Foreign Policy Association Corporate Dinner, New York City, December 2.

Eichengreen, B., M. El-Erian, A. Fraga, T. Ito, J. Pisani-Ferry, E. Prasad, R. Rajan, M. Ramos, C. Reinhart, H. Rey, D. Rodrik, K. Rogoff, J.S. Shin, A. Velasco, B. Weder di Mauro and Y. Yuarry (2011). Rethinking Central Banking, Report of the Committee on International Economic and Policy Reform, Brookings Institution. Available at http://www.brookings.edu/~/media/events/2011/9/14%20central%20banking/rethinking%20central%20banking.pdf.

Farrell, D., S. Lund, E. Gerlemann and P. Seeburger (2007). The New Power Brokers, McKinsey Global Institute, October. Available at http://www.mckinsey.

com/~/media/McKinsey/dotcom/Insights%20and%20pubs/MGI/Research/Financial%20Markets/The%20new%20power%20brokers%20-%20shaping%20global%20capital%20markets/MGI_Power_brokers_shaping_global_markets_full_report.ashx.

Financial Services Authority (FSA) (2012). Assessing the Possible Sources of Systemic Risk from Hedge Funds, August: London. Available at http://www.fsa.gov.uk/static/pubs/other/hedge-fund-report-aug2012.pdf.

McCauley, R.N. and J.F. Rigaudy (2011). Managing Foreign Exchange Reserves after the Crisis. *BIS Working Paper* # 58. Available at http://www.bis.org/publ/bppdf/bispap58b.pdf.

Mehrling, P. (2010). *The New Lombard Street: How the Fed Became the Dealer of Last Resort.* Princeton: Princeton University Press.

Mehrling, P., P. Zoltan, J. Sweeney and D.H. Neilson (2013). Bagehot was a Shadow Banker: Shadow Banking, Central Banking, and the Future of Global Finance. *INET Working Paper.*

Novy-Marx, R. and J. Rauh (2014). The Revenue Demands of Public Employee Pension Promises. *American Economic Journal: Economic Policy*, Vol. 6, No. 1, pp. 193–229.

Office of Financial Research (OFR) (2013a). 2013 Annual Report, Washington, DC: U.S. Government Printing Office: Washington. Available at http://www.treasury.gov/initiatives/ofr/about/Documents/OFR_AnnualReport2013_FINAL_12-17-2013_Accessible.pdf.

Office of Financial Research (OFR) (2013b). Asset Management and Financial Stability, U.S. Department of the Treasury. Available at http://www.treasury.gov/initiatives/ofr/research/Documents/OFR_AMFS_FINAL.pdf.

Pozsar, Z. (2011). Institutional Cash Pools and the Triffin Dilemma of the US Banking System. *IMF Working Paper* No. 11/190.

Pozsar, Z. (2012). A Macro View of Shadow Banking: Do T-Bill Shortages Pose a New Triffin Dilemma?, in *Is US Government Debt Different?* F. Allen, A. Gelpern, C. Mooney and D. Skeel (eds.), pp. 35–44. Philadelphia, USA: FIC Press.

Pozsar, Z., T. Adrian, A. Ashcraft and H. Boesky (2010). Shadow Banking. *Federal Reserve Bank of New York Staff Report* 458.

Summers, L.S. (2013). Why Stagnation Might Prove to be the New Normal, *Financial Times*, December 15. Available at http://www.ft.com/intl/cms/s/2/87cb15ea-5d1a-11e3-a558-00144feabdc0.html#axzz351TyJXWb.

Towers Watson (2013). Global Pensions Asset Study, Thinking Ahead Group within Towers Watson. January.

Cross-Border Challenges in Addressing Shadow-Banking Risks

Yasushi Shiina and Eva H. G. Hüpkes*

Financial Stability Board

Introduction

The 2007 global financial crisis demonstrated that the fault lines of the global financial system extended far beyond the regulated banking sector. Growing amounts of leverage, maturity and liquidity transformation (or shadow banking risks) were built-up through non-bank financial entities, such as structured investment vehicles (SIVs) and conduits that are often less prudentially regulated than banks. They are nonetheless interconnected with other parts of the financial system, most notably, overseas banking systems. Thus, when these risks finally materialized, they not only caused a dramatic drop in the non-bank credit intermediation but also spread both into the regular banking system and beyond national borders culminating in a global crisis.

At the November 2010 Seoul Summit, the G20 Leaders called on the Financial Stability Board (FSB), in collaboration with other international standard setting bodies, to develop recommendations to strengthen the oversight and regulation of the "shadow banking system" noting that "[w]ith the completion of the new standards for banks, there is a potential that regulatory gaps may emerge in the shadow banking system".[1]

A "global" approach in addressing shadow banking risks is crucial not only for preventing such risks from spreading beyond borders (through

*The views expressed are those of the authors and do not necessarily reflect the views of the FSB or its members.

[1]The Group of 20, 2010.

interconnections within the financial system) but also to discourage incentives to arbitrage regulation (through using non-bank financial entities residing in other jurisdictions). This is why the FSB, which brings together national authorities responsible for financial stability in 24 jurisdictions, has been working to develop policy recommendations to strengthen the oversight and regulation of the shadow banking system.

This paper provides an overview of FSB's multipronged policy approach to addressing shadow banking risks or bank-like systemic risks in the non-bank financial space, with specific focus on how it is trying to overcome cross-border challenges associated with such risks.

What is Shadow Banking?

Shadow banking can be broadly defined as "credit intermediation involving entities and activities (fully or partially) outside the regular banking system", also known as non-bank credit intermediation.[2] Such intermediation takes a wide range of forms and continues to evolve in response to changing market and regulatory conditions. It provides a valuable alternative to bank funding, supporting real economic activity and introducing competition to traditional intermediation of credit by banks, thereby reducing borrowing costs for businesses and households. Since non-bank financial entities tend to have focused business models and/or specific financial expertise, they may also lead to a more efficient credit allocation in the economy, or create innovations in the ways credit is extended.

Although there are huge benefits from non-bank credit intermediation, the 2007 financial crisis demonstrated that it poses serious risks to financial stability if it combines maturity and liquidity transformation, and leverage on a substantial scale like banks (e.g., longer-term credit extension based on short-term funding and leverage). Such risk creation may take place at the level of an individual entity, but it can also form part of a complex chain of transactions among multiple entities, in which leverage and maturity transformation occur in stages. Often banks are involved at various points, thus creating multiple forms of feedback channels into the regular banking system. If some entities in these chains of transactions reside in different

[2]For details, please see http://www.financialstabilityboard.org/publications/r_110412a.pdf and http://www.financialstabilityboard.org/publications/r_121118.pdf.

jurisdictions, underlying risks can remain undetected and turn local risks into cross-border or global risks.

Like banks, leverage and maturity-transformation within the shadow banking system can create the risk of depositor-like "runs" that can generate contagion risk, and amplifying risk in the financial system. Such activity can also exacerbate procyclicality by boosting credit supply and asset price increases during surges in confidence. At the same time, this dynamic can also lead to greater risk of precipitate falls in asset prices and credit by creating credit channels that are vulnerable to shocks and sudden loss of confidence. These effects were in evidence in 2007–2009 in the dislocation of asset-backed commercial paper (ABCP) markets, the failure of an originate-to-distribute model employing SIVs and other securitization conduits, "runs" on money market funds (MMFs) and a sudden reappraisal of the terms on which securities lending and repos were conducted. The policy focus of FSB is on non-bank credit intermediation that poses bank-like risks to financial stability and is typically subject to no or less stringent prudential oversight arrangements as banks.

The FSB Policy Framework[3]

The objective of the FSB's work on shadow banking is to ensure that the shadow banking system is subject to appropriate oversight and regulation to address bank-like risks to financial stability while not inhibiting sustainable non-bank financing models. In other words, it aims to limit the excessive build-up of leverage and maturity transformation in the shadow banking system so that businesses and households would be able to obtain stable non-bank financing that contributes to sustainable economic growth.

In accomplishing this goal, the policy framework needs to be designed to be proportionate to financial stability risks and focused on those activities that are material to the system, using as a starting point those that were a source of problems during the crisis. It also needs to establish a process for monitoring the shadow banking system, so that rapidly growing new activities that pose bank-like risks can be identified at an early stage and addressed accordingly. At the same time, given the interconnectedness of

[3]For detailed discussions on the overview of FSB's policy framework to address shadow banking risks, see http://www.financialstabilityboard.org/publications/r_130829a.pdf.

markets, its cross-border nature, and the strong adaptive capacity of the shadow banking system, the policies in this area necessarily have to be comprehensive and global in scope.

The FSB has followed a two-pronged strategy in building such policy framework in addressing shadow banking risks: First, it has created a monitoring framework that would enhance authorities' capabilities to track developments in the shadow banking system and identify the build-up of systemic risks, so as to enable them to take corrective actions where necessary.

Second, the FSB has coordinated the development of policies in the five areas where oversight and regulation needs to be strengthened to reduce systemic risks:

(i) mitigating risks in banks' interactions with shadow banking entities;
(ii) reducing the susceptibility of MMFs to "runs";
(iii) improving transparency and aligning incentives in securitization;
(iv) dampening pro-cyclicality and other financial stability risks in securities financing transactions such as repos and securities lending; and
(v) assessing and mitigating financial stability risks posed by other shadow banking entities and activities.

The first area is led by the Basel Committee on Banking Supervision (BCBS), which tries to ensure that all banks' activities, including interconnections with the shadow banking system and their offshore funding vehicles, are adequately captured in prudential regimes and any significant spill-overs of risks are addressed appropriately. Work on the second, third and fourth areas are led by the International Organization of Securities Commissions (IOSCO) and the FSB respectively, and focus on excessive build-up of leverage and maturity transformation in non-bank financial entities and activities that materialized during the 2007 financial crisis. Finally, the fifth area led by the FSB sets out a forward-looking high-level policy framework for identifying and addressing sources of financial stability risks from shadow banking, which would allow authorities to capture innovations that occur outside the bounds of bank regulation and which would take actions on identified sources of shadow banking risks as necessary.

Most of these policy measures are now finalized and will be adopted by FSB member authorities in an internationally coordinated manner. Some measures, such as proposed minimum haircut standards for securities financing transactions under the fourth area above, will be further elaborated in light of public consultation results and assessments of their potential impact on the financial system.

Overcoming Cross-Border Challenges

Cross-border challenges associated with shadow banking

As noted earlier, the shadow banking system often spans national borders. Entities involved in shadow banking take a variety of legal forms, business models and risk profiles depending on the jurisdictions where they are established, and continuously evolve so as to adapt to changing market and regulatory conditions.

This feature of the shadow banking system creates significant cross-border challenges in designing and implementing the FSB's policy framework to address shadow-banking risks. First, it is difficult for national authorities to detect the full extent of risks in the shadow banking system. The establishment of a system-wide monitoring framework able to identify "global" risks in the shadow banking system is essential.

Second, the wide range of legal forms and business models of shadow banking entities creates huge difficulties in developing and implementing regulatory policies that can be applied consistently across jurisdictions. The continuous evolving nature of these entities makes the development of internationally consistent policies and their implementation across jurisdictions still more challenging. It is therefore crucial to develop and apply a policy framework that is sufficiently flexible to take into account national differences, but that is effective in addressing shadow banking risks in an internationally consistent manner so as to not create incentives for regulatory arbitrage.

Establishing a system-wide monitoring framework

One of the most poignant lessons from the crisis is the need for authorities to establish better system-wide monitoring arrangements, capable of assessing sources of systemic risks outside that part of financial system traditionally subject to prudential regulation. Such monitoring arrangements also need to be able to capture non-bank financial vehicles in other jurisdictions that constitute part of the credit intermediation chain and any cross-border activities associated with the shadow banking system.

Hence, the FSB began conducting annual monitoring exercise to assess global trends and risks of the shadow banking system in 2011.[4] These exercises have prompted an increasing number of national and regional authorities to assess regularly the risks of shadow banking, so that the monitoring now covers 25 jurisdictions, capturing jurisdictions representing about 80% of global GDP and 90% of global financial system assets.

The annual global shadow banking monitoring exercise adopts a stylized monitoring process (Exhibit 1) that first assesses the broad scale and trends in non-bank financial intermediation in the financial system ("macro-mapping"). It draws on information such as flow of funds and sector balance sheet data, and complemented with other relevant information such as supervisory data. Authorities then narrow down their focus to credit intermediation activities that have the potential to pose bank-like systemic risks, concentrating in particular on activities involving the key shadow banking risk factors, i.e., maturity/liquidity transformation, imperfect credit risk transfer and/or leverage.

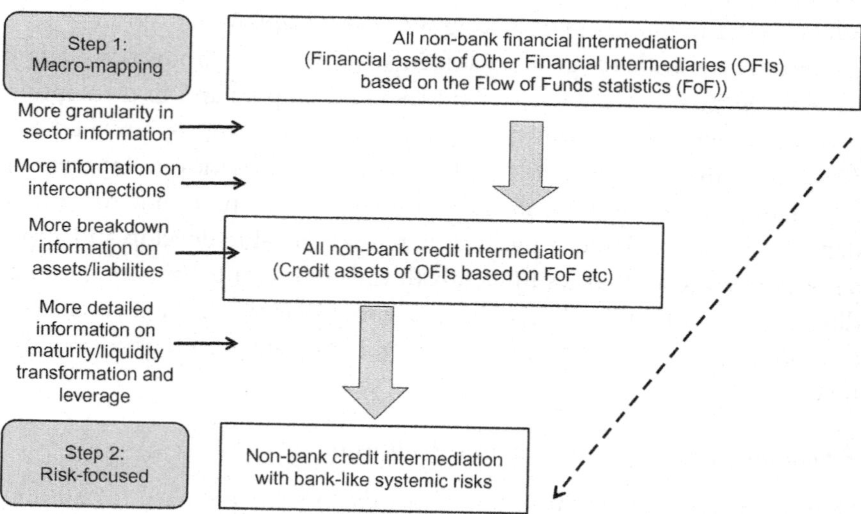

Exhibit 1. A stylized shadow banking monitoring process.

Source: http://www.financialstabilityboard.org/publications/r_121118c.pdf.

[4]The most recent results of the FSB annual global shadow banking monitoring exercise was published on November 14, 2013. Please see http://www.financialstabilityboard.org/publications/r_131114.htm.

The first step allows authorities to map the scale and trends of all non-bank financial intermediation based on generally high-quality, consistent data that are available in many jurisdictions. Although not all non-bank financial intermediation poses shadow banking risks, their mapping allows authorities to cover all areas where shadow-banking-related risks might potentially arise. This would alert the authorities to areas where developments could pose risks for the system. Also, the use of internationally consistent data allows comparisons of national trends and aggregation at the global level. However, further enhancement in data collection is needed to be able to also assess linkages between sectors.

The second step meanwhile would allow authorities to identify the subset of non-bank credit intermediation activities that could pose risks to the financial system. However, data for such risk-based monitoring is often lacking and the FSB is currently working to improve risk-related data collection by national authorities. It is also working to introduce activity-based monitoring to complement the stylized monitoring process. Implementation of policy recommendations on strengthening oversight and regulation in the identified five areas will help in this regard as they include enhanced data reporting and disclosure requirements.

Adopting a function-based policy framework

Designing a suitable policy response that effectively addresses shadow banking risks is challenging due to the high degree of heterogeneity and diversity in business models and risk profiles not only across the various sectors in the non-bank financial space, but also within the same sector (or entity-type). This diversity in function and form is exacerbated by different legal and regulatory regimes that govern shadow-banking entities and activities across jurisdictions as well as the dynamic nature and constant innovation in the non-bank financial sectors. Together, these factors tend to obscure the activities and functions performed by different entities and hence complicate the determination of the appropriate regulation that should apply to them. For example, "finance companies" in one jurisdiction may have very different business models and risk profiles from "finance companies" in other jurisdictions.

Because shadow banking entities take a variety of forms and are evolving over time, the FSB has adopted a functional approach that is designed to enable authorities to assess the extent of non-bank financial entities' involvement in shadow banking by looking through the legal form to the underlying economic functions that may be performed by a single entity or through a chain of transactions among multiple entities. The high-level policy framework developed by the FSB should enable authorities to capture innovations that occur outside the bounds of bank regulation and adopt suitable policy measures where these pose a threat to financial stability.

The policy framework consists of the following three steps (Exhibit 2)[5]:

(i) *Assessment based on economic functions*: Authorities will identify the potential sources of shadow banking risks in non-bank financial entities in their jurisdictions from a financial stability perspective by categorizing these with reference to five economic functions,

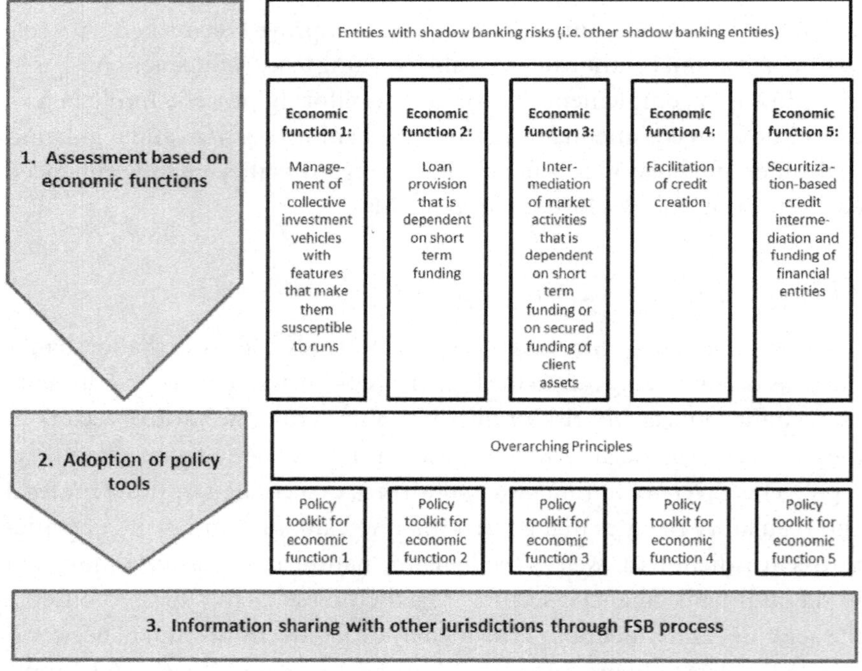

Exhibit 2. Function-based high-level policy framework for oversight and regulation of shadow banking entities.

Source: http://www.financialstabilityboard.org/publications/r_130829c.pdf.

[5]For details of the policy framework, see http://www.financialstabilityboard.org/publications/r_130829c.pdf.

independent of legal form the entities take. They are: (1) management of collective investment vehicles with features that make them susceptible to runs; (2) loan provision that is dependent on short-term funding; (3) intermediation of market activities that is dependent on short-term funding or on secured funding of client assets; (4) facilitation of credit creation (e.g., through credit insurance); and (5) securitization-based credit intermediation and funding of financial entities. The FSB may revise the economic functions and add new ones if deemed appropriate.

(ii) *Adoption of policy tools*: Authorities will refer to agreed overarching principles for oversight of non-bank financial entities that are identified as posing a threat to financial stability. In addition, where necessary to mitigate financial stability risks, authorities will apply appropriate policy tools from a menu of optional policies for each economic function as they think best fits the non-bank financial entities concerned, the structure of the markets in which they operate, and the degree of financial stability risks posed by such entities in their jurisdictions. Such policy tools may include existing regulatory measures as well as newly introduced ones.

(iii) *Information-sharing process*: Authorities will share information on (i) non-bank financial entities (or entity types) that are identified as being involved in economic functions and the rationale for their decisions based on the shadow banking risk factors; as well as (ii) the policy tool(s) the relevant authority adopted and how, it is seeking to address shadow banking risks.

By focusing on the underlying economic functions (or activities) rather than legal forms or names, this framework allows authorities to assess the extent of non-bank financial entities' involvement in shadow banking in a consistent manner across jurisdictions. Furthermore, this approach is forward-looking in that it will be able to capture new types of entities that perform these economic functions generating shadow banking risks.

In addition, it is expected that the framework will provide a structured process to further enhance the FSB's annual monitoring exercise as well as for authorities to assess the need for extending the regulatory perimeter. The FSB will develop detailed procedures for information-sharing by March 2014 so that the FSB would be in a position to start a peer review process of national implementation of the framework by 2015.

Conclusion

The shadow banking system can have important benefits and can contribute to the financing of the real economy. However, it can also become a source of systemic risk, especially when shadow banking entities perform bank-like functions (e.g., maturity transformation and leverage) and when they are closely interconnected with other parts of the financial system, most notably the banking system. The 2007 crisis demonstrated that such systemic risks within the shadow banking system can easily spread beyond national borders culminating in a global crisis through involvement of foreign non-bank financial entities and strong interconnections with overseas banking system. Thus, any policy actions to mitigate such risks in the shadow banking system have to be fundamentally "global". The FSB has so far adopted such global approach in addressing shadow banking risks through: (i) establishing a system-wide monitoring framework (by conducting annual monitoring exercises with global scope on an agreed process and generally high-quality, consistent data that are available in many jurisdictions); and (ii) introducing a forward-looking function-based policy framework that allows authorities to identify and address shadow banking risks in the non-bank financial space by focusing on underlying economic functions rather than legal forms.

The launch of information-sharing based on the function-based policy framework from May 2014 onwards should help authorities deepen their understanding of the shadow banking system and refine their policy responses. To promote the consistent implementation of the FSB's policies, the FSB plans to undertake a peer review on the status of national implementation in 2015.[6]

Reference

Caballero, R. (2013). The Shortage of Safe Assets: Macroeconomic Policy Implications. Presented at the Bank of England, Chief Economist's Workshop, May. Available at http://www.bankofengland.co.uk/research/Documents/ccbs/cew2013/presentation_caballero.pdf.

[6]In this regard, IOSCO will conduct in 2014 a peer review on the implementation of its recommendations on MMFs and securitization, the results of which will be reported to the FSB.

Shadow Banking: A European Perspective

Stan Maes*

European Commission

To date, the economic and financial statistics collected for the EU (and euro area) are neither detailed enough nor have sufficient coverage to allow for a full understanding of shadow banking-related policy concerns, such as the leverage and maturity transformation achieved by the shadow banking sector and the possible channels for systemic contagion towards the regulated banking sector. Relevant time series statistics are of particular importance when evaluating possible regulatory measures at the European level. Work is currently being undertaken by the European Central Bank (ECB), European Systemic Risk Board (ESRB), and European Supervisory Authorities (EBA, EIOPA, and ESMA) to fill EU shadow banking data gaps.

It is of particular importance to produce consistent data, indicators, and risk metrics on shadow banking and the role played therein by large European banks. First, because recent US evidence suggests that modern financial intermediation is "less shadowy than we thought" (Cetorelli and Peristiani, 2012). Regulated banks have kept a considerable footprint

*Stan Maes is an Economist at the European Commission (Directorate-General for the Internal Market and Services) and is also affiliated as guest professor with the Center of Economic Studies (CES) at the University of Leuven. I have benefited from discussions with several colleagues at the European Commission and the European Securities and Markets Authority and would like to thank them and others for their very useful comments. The views expressed in this paper are those of the author and do not represent those of the European Commission.

in modern financial intermediation. The business model of the banking system has over time shifted from a deposit-funded, credit-risk intensive, spread-based, originate-to-hold model towards a wholesale funded, less credit-risk-intensive but more market-risk-intensive, fee-based, originate-to-distribute business model in which shadow banking entities and activities have surged (Boot and Ratnovski, 2013; Adrian and Shin, 2010b; Ratnovski, 2013). Many shadow banking activities are shown to be operated from *within* systemically important banks (Pozsar and Singh, 2011; Singh, 2012; Fein, 2013). Second, the mapping and understanding of the shadow banking role played by systemically important EU banks should be even more important for European regulators than for US regulators, given that the EU financial system is significantly more bank-intermediated than the US financial system. A consistent and ambitious financial-system-wide regulatory approach will be required given that shadow banking is a phenomenon that defies institutional and national boundaries.

To further motivate the ongoing data collection workstreams, this paper reviews and highlights the significant role played by European banks in influencing overall US credit conditions, notably through shadow banking entities and activities. EU banks are shown to be important players in US credit intermediation through relying on US money market funds (MMF), sponsoring USD ABCP vehicles, engaging in USD collateral repo transactions, and investing in US MBS and ABS (Shin, 2012; Bouveret, 2011). As a result, the EU and US financial systems are intimately linked and connected, albeit asymmetrically. Several shadow banking activities and links have collapsed following the recent financial crisis, but there is a persistent and significant transatlantic asymmetry in the EU–US banking system, which has a bearing on financial stability.

Measuring Shadow Banking in the Euro Area

The Financial Stability Board (FSB) defines shadow banking broadly as "credit intermediation that involves entities and activities fully or partially outside the regular banking system" or non-bank credit intermediation in short. The literature has formulated a number of weaknesses about the retained FSB definition. First, the focus on entities and activities outside the regular banking system underestimates the role of large banking groups (Pozsar and Singh, 2011; Cetorelli and Peristiani, 2012). Second, the definition may cover entities that are not commonly thought as being part of the shadow banking sector, such as leasing and finance companies, credit-oriented hedge funds, corporate tax vehicles, etc. Third, the definition does not allow to pro-actively detect new shadow banking activities (Claessens and Ratnovski, 2013).

Shadow banks are an alternative channel, next to regulated banks, to transform risky illiquid long-term loans into seemingly credit-risk-free, short-term, and money-like instruments. In practice, shadow banks cover entities which raise funding with deposit-like characteristics, perform maturity and/or liquidity transformation, are exposed to borrower default, or use borrowed money, directly or indirectly, to buy assets (European Commission, 2013a). Measuring the relative size of shadow banks and shadow banking is challenging in general due to the heterogeneity of entities and activities, due to the fact that shadow banking is not always easy to distinguish from traditional banking, and due to its scalability and quickly evolving nature.

Whereas there is a sizeable and growing analytical and empirical literature on shadow banking in the US (Adrian and Ashcraft, 2012a; 2012b; Adrian *et al.*, 2013; Claessens *et al.*, 2012; Pozsar *et al.*, 2013), relatively few comparable papers to date are available for the European shadow banking sector. This is unfortunate given the fact that (i) the size of the shadow banking sector in the euro area and the UK combined is reported to be greater than that in the US and (ii) the sharp decline in US shadow banking since the financial crisis is more than compensated by increasing volumes in the UK, euro area, and other jurisdictions (FSB, 2012; 2013a).

First attempts to "fill the gap" are made by ESMA (2013) and Bouveret (2011) for Europe at large and by Bakk-Simon *et al.* (2012) for the euro area, but there is no flow of funds report for Europe or the euro area, unlike the case in the US. Some countries may not even be able to execute meaningful monitoring, as some authorities are not permitted to ask for data from unregulated entities to assess a need for regulation. Current efforts necessarily compile and combine several databases that have not been designed for these purposes and which are managed by central banks, industry associations, and commercial data providers.

Table 1 presents a rough proxy for the relative size of shadow banking entities in the form of "Other Intermediaries" in the euro area financial

Table 1. Relative size of financial institutions in the euro area.

	2011Q2	
	EUR trillion	% total
Regulated banks	**28.0**	**51.5**
Other intermediaries	**10.8**	**19.9**
Money Market Funds (MMFs)	1.1	2.0
Financial vehicle corporations	2.2	4.1
Other miscellaneous intermediaries	7.6	13.9
Insurance corporations and pension funds	**6.8**	**12.6**
Regulated investment funds other than MMFs	**5.6**	**10.3**
Eurosystem	**3.1**	**5.8**
Total assets of euro area financial institutions	**54.4**	**100.0**
Memo: Repo market outstanding value in the EU (lending and borrowing)	**6.1**	

Source: Bakk-Simon *et al.* (2012).

system as of mid-2011.[1] "Other Intermediaries" is the residual mixed bag of financial entities after excluding regulated banks, insurance companies, pension funds, regulated investment funds, and the Eurosystem balance sheet itself from the euro area financial system. Total assets of regulated banks made up roughly 50% of the total assets of the entire euro area financial system. The other half is made up as follows: 13% by insurance companies and pension funds, 10% by investment funds other than MMFs, 6% by the Eurosystem balance sheet, and 20% by "Other Intermediaries". "Other intermediaries" include amongst others MMFs, financial vehicle corporations (financial vehicles engaged in securitization), and other miscellaneous intermediaries (such as securities dealers, venture capital companies, leasing and factoring companies, and financial holding companies).

Bakk-Simon *et al.* (2012) subsequently analyze in more detail and to the extent possible the following shadow banking activities and entities in

[1] This proxy is not fully comparable with the measures provided in the US literature (Adrian and Ashcraft, 2012a; 2012b; Adrian *et al.*, 2013; Claessens *et al.*, 2012; Pozsar *et al.*, 2013), due to data limitations. The information from the US Flow of Funds allow for a more granular breakdown of the liabilities of the different sectors. Lacking this type of data granularity, the "other intermediaries" proxy covers most of the institutions engaged in shadow banking activities, but not only and not all.

the euro area: (i) securitization activities, (ii) money market funds, (iii) the repo market,[2] and (iv) hedge funds.[3]

They also document the connections of shadow banking with the regulated banking system, the difference in the importance of shadow banking in different countries, and the maturity transformation and leverage behavior of the euro area shadow banking sector. Following the crisis, it seems that the euro area shadow banking sector faces a decline in maturity mismatch (similar to what is being reported in the US), suggesting a decline in bank-like activities due to the financial crisis. It is found that a significant share of bank funding comes from parts of the financial sector that are not regulated as banks and/or are entirely unregulated. Moreover, the connections between the regulated banks and "other financial intermediaries" has increased considerably over the last decade, effectively increasing the risk of contagion through transmission of shocks across institutions.[4] Bank credit to ultimate borrowers is funded by either the equity of the banking system or by the funding that non-banks provide (i.e., households, pension funds, insurers, non-financial corporates, non-bank firms). Rapid increases in the aggregate volume of credit supplied through the banking system must come through increased leverage, interbank exposures, and interconnectedness with the shadow banking institutions (Adrian and Shin, 2010a; Hahm *et al.*, 2012; Singh, 2013). Finally, Bakk-Simon *et al.* (2012) also illustrate that the shadow banking sector has been catching up with regulated banks in terms of leverage and that the driver of the overall increase in leverage in

[2]The EU rules on capital requirements require supervisory reporting of aggregate data on repo transactions of credit institutions, but existing requirements are not detailed and frequent enough for the purposes of monitoring of financial stability.

[3]Total assets of hedge funds are not included in the non-banking aggregate "other intermediaries" but are reported to amount to 0.1 trillion EUR. This number is underestimating the relative importance of the European hedge fund industry, as many hedge funds engaging in business with euro area residents are actually located outside the euro area and are therefore not covered by the available EAA and monetary statistics.

[4]Caution is required, however, as European aggregates are shown to hide important differences across countries. Data for a given country may also include financial vehicles that are used to channel financial instruments issued by financial institutions with headquarters in other euro area countries, and beyond. The interconnection is likely underestimated by the available data, which does not sufficiently take into account financial institutions that are for legal and statistical purposes outside of the EU, but are carrying out financial activities in the EU.

the euro area financial system comes from the euro area shadow banking sector.

Securities lending and repurchase agreements, also called securities financing transactions (SFTs), and rehypothecation are techniques used by almost all actors in the financial system, be they banks, securities dealers, insurance companies, pension funds, or investment funds. SFTs use assets belonging to an entity to obtain funding from or to lend them out to another entity. The main purpose of SFTs is therefore to obtain additional cash or to achieve additional flexibility in carrying out a particular investment strategy (Dive *et al.*, 2011). Securities lending is an important shadow banking activity, but there is no publicly available data on securities lending transactions in the EU.[5] FSB (2013b) provides a summary of the data available to regulators on securities lending and repo, showing the lack of frequent and granular data on EU securities financing markets. Similarly, ESRB (2013) concludes that the information available to EU regulatory authorities is not sufficient for the purpose of monitoring the systemic risks that may arise from SFTs. Existing industry data or data collected in other publicly available surveys displays weaknesses in relation to the level of granularity, coverage of instruments and of institutions and their geographic coverage across Member States. This makes it particularly difficult to compare and use the data from different surveys for prudential purposes.

In sum, European empirical results are yet limited, incomplete, and tentative. The few empirical studies on European shadow banking acknowledge that data sources have been used that have not been designed for these purposes and that no official data are available for certain shadow banking activities and entities. Almost 70% of the assets of the "Other Intermediaries" aggregate in the euro area are held by miscellaneous financial institutions for which regular statistical information is not available (Bakk-Simon *et al.*, 2012). Also, maturity transformation is difficult to assess and map given the existing databases, as available breakdowns often refer to maturity at inception, rather than residual maturity, or lack even initial maturity data. Similarly, scarce and non-standardized information is available on repo market activity.

[5] Several private data vendors, however, conduct private market surveys on securities lending. According to International Securities Lending Association, global securities lending stands at €1.4 trillion.

One cannot but conclude that an important part of the European financial sector remains relatively unexplored by official statistics. An in-depth assessment of the activities of the shadow banking sector in Europe requires an improvement in the availability of data and other related qualitative information. Several database initiatives have been and are taken by the ECB, ESRB, and ESAs to improve the intelligence on shadow banking activities, in particular with a view to add granularity in (i) the breakdown within non-bank financial institutions so as to better identify leverage and maturity transformation concerns, (ii) the counterpart information to monitor relationships between regulated banks and shadow banks, and (iii) the residual maturity breakdowns of exposures (current statistics often focus on original maturity only).

Why Did Shadow Banking Arise and Grow as much as It Did?

The academic literature explores this question at length (Adrian and Ashcraft, 2012a, 2012b; Adrian *et al.*, 2013; Claessens *et al.*, 2012). The four main drivers for the growth of shadow banking are briefly discussed below:

- Genuine efficiencies;
- Accommodating the increased investor demand for safe assets (demand side);
- Regulatory and tax arbitrage (supply side); and
- Institutional factors.

Each of these four drivers is briefly discussed below.

Genuine efficiencies

Regulated banks transform risky, long-term and illiquid assets (such as loans) into seemingly credit-risk-free, short-term, money-like instruments (i.e., insured deposits). The shadow banking sector does something similar by decomposing the above transformation into a long chain of distinct wholesale funded securitization-based lending steps, making use of securitization, securities finance transactions, etc.[6]

[6]The two shadow banking activities that are most important in the financial system and raise most concerns in terms of financial stability are securitization and collateral intermediation. Whereas the former is about pooling, tranching, liquidity puts, and other support, the latter deals with repo, securities lending, and collateral rehypothecation. See Keller (2012) for a review of the economics of shadow banking.

In the pre-crisis conventional wisdom, key shadow banking activities such as securitization and securities finance transactions were believed to deliver important and unambiguous benefits to society, in particular (i) additional credit creation, market liquidity, and economic growth, (ii) improved price discovery and enhanced market efficiency, and (iii) increased financial stability.

For example, it was believed that securitization enables price discovery because it allows the pricing of credit risk through the capital markets ("liquefying what was previously illiquid"). As such, it would allow for third-party discipline and market pricing of assets that would be opaque otherwise. Credit risk was believed to be dispersed towards those that are best suited to bear the risks. Long intermediation chains were believed to promote more efficient maturity transformation which would be able to more precisely meet the preferences of investors. Securitization would allow banks to limit their concentration to certain borrowers, loan types and geographies. It would also allow them to raise long-term maturity-matched funding to manage their asset–liability mismatches. It would permit lenders to realize economies of scale from their loan origination platforms, branches, and call centers. It would allow market forces to help in better allocating scarce capital.

However, the subsequent and ongoing financial crisis has casted serious doubts on these alleged benefits (at least when stated in an unconditional and unqualified manner) and highlighted the systemic risk resulting from sharply increased intra-financial-sector connectedness. In the past 15 years, the financial system has proven to be highly unstable and excessively procyclical (Turner, 2012a, 2012b; Adrian and Shin, 2010a, 2010b; Acharya *et al.*, 2010b). Securitization has not achieved risk transfer, but has effectively concentrated risks in the leveraged financial sector (Greenlaw *et al.*, 2008). The biggest growth in short-term debt was between financial intermediaries. "Complex" securitization has not proven to be crisis-resilient and did not lead to price discovery. Allegedly safe assets (e.g., senior CDO tranches) became risky assets and safe entities (e.g., MMFs) became risky entities. Negative feedback loops and strong procyclicality arose (loss price loss spirals, haircut deleveraging, etc.). Regulatory gaps and regulatory arbitrage possibilities were exploited. Maturity and liquidity mismatches increased sharply outside the regulatory perimeter (through

SIVs, broker-dealers, etc.). Excessive leverage arose in the financial system and when wholesale funding dried up throughout the system, an unprecedented systemic crisis had been triggered which to date requires significant and exceptional government and central bank intervention. Private obligations became public obligations and private assets became public assets (Boudghene and Maes, 2012). The recent financial crisis has shown how critical funding liquidity risks can be in shaping the fate of individual institutions and in transmitting contagion across the financial markets. The procyclicality of funding liquidity created by private financial players, especially shadow banking entities, can be disruptive. The rehypothecation of collateral to support multiple deals, in particular securities lending and repurchase agreements, helped to fuel the financial bubble and allowed for increased liquidity as well as the build-up of hidden leverage and interconnectedness in the system. When confidence in the value of assets, safety of counterparties and investor protection collapsed, it created wholesale market runs leading to a sudden deleveraging and/or public safety nets (central bank facilities, etc.). EU banks have been estimated to have had a shortfall of stable funding of €2.89 trillion in 2010. Adrian and Shin (2010a) find that shadow banking reinforces the natural procyclicality of banking, as secured finance plus mark-to-market accounting creates strong procyclicality. Brunnermeier and Pedersen (2009) emphasize that "funding liquidity", "market liquidity" and asset values are linked in self-reinforcing procyclical cycles.

Accommodating the increased investor demand for safe assets (demand side)

Shadow banking developments are driven by increased corporate and institutional demand for safe liquid assets (Pozsar and Singh, 2011 and Turner 2012a). Over the past decade, the strong surge in institutional cash pools has exceeded the available pool of insured deposits and government bonds. Shadow banking has allowed to accommodate the significant increase of investor demand for safe assets, as shadow banking liabilities have been perceived to be good substitutes for money. Shadow banking creates safe, short-term, and liquid instruments, or money, from risky, long-term, and illiquid assets. This process requires "risk stripping", i.e., the elimination of credit, maturity, and liquidity risk through a chain of interconnected shadow banking intermediaries. Re-hypothecation of collateral increases the credit and quasi-money creation potential for shadow banking. Pozsar (2011) explains why institutional investors chose to fund modern banks through wholesale funding markets and instruments rather than through deposits. Stein (2010) suggests that the amount of private money creation may be excessive because private agents do not internalize the costs of crises.

Regulatory and tax arbitrage (supply side)

A clear motivation for private actors to avoid intermediation through the traditional banking system is to evade regulation and taxes. The academic literature documents that this driver explains part of the growth of shadow banking in the US and Europe (Acharya *et al.*, 2010a; Acharya and Schnabl, 2009). Regulatory arbitrage has exploited loopholes and has led to a sharp build-up of risk and leverage along the way (Haldane and Madouros, 2012).

Institutional factors

Bouveret (2011) documents differences in shadow banking trends between the US and the EU throughout the crisis. The role of institutions and the different nature of financial system intermediation is emphasized in explaining the discrepancy between the early crisis stages collapse of the US ABCP and US ABS market on the one hand (despite unprecedented policy action) and the significant peaking of EUR ABS 2008 issuance in the euro area on the other hand.

Specifically, unlike the Fed and Bank of England, the ECB monetary policy framework allowed for a wide range of collateral to be used for repo transaction purposes. As a result, almost all of the EUR ABS issuance in 2008 was retained by the issuer and used as collateral for ECB refinancing operations. This was one of the ways in which the ECB provided liquidity backstops to the euro area banks (as ABS issuers), similar to the alphabet soup of public safety nets put in place by the Fed and US Treasury to stop the runs (Commercial Paper funding facility (CPFF), ABCP MMF liquidity facility (AMLF), US Treasury MMF guarantee, Primary Dealer Credit Facility (PDCF), Term Security Lending Facility (TSLF), etc. (Baba *et al.*, 2009; Adrian and Ashcraft, 2012a)).

Why Regulate Shadow Banking

Important policy concerns and market failures arise in the area of shadow banking, as mentioned above and discussed in Adrian and Ashcraft (2012b). On the assets side, the main concern is inadequate asset quality. On the liability side, the main concern is the fragility of wholesale funding.

Inadequate asset quality

Shadow banking institutions have produced and accumulated assets that are particularly sensitive to tail events (Acharya *et al.*, 2010b).[7] Why is tail risk not adequately priced and curtailed? Gennaioli *et al.* (2011) posit that actors neglect risk for behavioral reasons, thereby giving rise to overinvesting and underpricing in the boom and excessive collapse of real activity and negative externalities in the financial sector in the bust. The underestimation of correlation enabled financial institutions to hold insufficient amounts of liquidity and capital and to sell cheap insurance against negative shocks. Neglected risks are one way of interpreting the widely perceived risk-free nature of highly rated structured credit products, such as the AAA tranches of ABS. As investors tend to overestimate the value of private credit and liquidity enhancement purchased through these cheap puts, the result has been an excess supply of cheap credit.

Another theory developed by Dang *et al.* (2009) emphasizes the rational optimality of debt contracts and instruments because they generate opacity, which in turn minimizes adverse selection and provides the least possible incentives to collect information. This reasoning is able to explain the growth of relatively opaque securitized products in the run-up to the crisis and the exacerbation of systemic risk once a negative shock hits information-opaque, debt-funded economies. The severity and negative externalities of a financial crisis is again being neglected, but this time based on rational grounds rather than on behavioral grounds.

Other related market and regulatory failures need to be mentioned, in particular the misaligned incentives and numerous conflicts of interest faced by credit-rating agencies (CRAs). First, CRAs are paid by the issuers

[7] Implicit subsidies enjoyed by large TBTF banking groups also lead to an underpricing of tail risk and the excessive build-up of systemic risk.

or sellers of the financial instruments, rather than by the buyers who face the lack of information and knowledge. Consequently, the issuer may threaten to shop elsewhere for a better rating if the CRA does not accommodate to the issuer's expectations. Second, CRAs sell multiple and often interdependent products and services. The issuer may hence put additional pressure on the CRA by conditionally promising more business. Moreover, advice sold by CRAs to achieve a better rating should arguably be backed up by a higher rating. Third, due to their omnipresence, CRA rating changes amplify procyclicality and cause systemic disruptions. Fourth, model risk is much more important for structured finance products, given their complexity and absence of prior crisis experience. The decades-long experience in deep and liquid corporate and sovereign debt markets has proven to be of limited value for rating complex, untested, OTC financial instruments. CRA ratings have been too narrowly focused on default risk and expected loss (first moment of loss distribution). Market and tail risk was not reflected (second and higher moments of the loss distribution), leading to the situation that AAA senior CDO tranches were able to pay out higher returns than equally rated AAA corporate bonds.

Fragility of wholesale funding

Shadow banking has revealed that regulated banks are prone to modern runs by wholesale market institutional actors: shadow banking funding sources are uninsured and thus runnable. Gorton and Metrick (2011; 2012) emphasize that the crisis of 2008 can best be understood as a run on repo. The fundamental cause of a run is the presence of fire sale externalities (Stein, 2013) and not the Diamond and Dybvig (1983) sequential servicing constraint. Wholesale funding may give rise to additional procyclicality, possibly stronger than already is the case in the traditional banking sector (Adrian and Shin, 2010a). Regulatory arbitrage exploits loopholes and has proven to lead to further build-up of risk and leverage.

Moral hazard from public safety nets

Given their *de facto* similarity to regulated banks, numerous shadow banking activities and entities have enjoyed the *ex post* coverage of public safety nets (Singh, 2012). Safety nets serve useful purposes *ex post*, but create incentives for excessive risk-taking and significant competition and other distortions *ex ante*. As is the case in the bank structural reform debate (European Commission, 2013b), the question that arises is why and to what extent shadow banking activities necessarily need to enjoy taxpayer support. It may need to be ensured that public safety nets only cover (i) activities essential to the economy and (ii) liquidity risk (not solvency risk), so as to curtail moral hazard and aggressive and inappropriate growth of the activities under consideration. If performed by entities more alienated from safety-net-enjoying commercial banks, shadow banking activities may not create systemic risks to the same extent. We may need to adequately distinguish (shadow) banking activities that are essential to the real economy, resolve a genuine market failure, and hence deserve to be government-backed, from those that are useful but need not be promoted through implicit or explicit subsidies.

Large European Banks' Reliance on the US Shadow Banking Sector

As visualized in Fig. 1, regulated banking groups are potentially intertwined with shadow banking entities and activities through their asset and liability side, both on-balance and off-balance sheet. Regulated banking groups pool and securitize loans through their broker-dealer arms, provide credit insurance through their insurance arms, invest in securitized assets, provide credit and liquidity lines to SPVs, conduits, MMFs, and receive short-term wholesale market funding (from MMFs or repo markets).

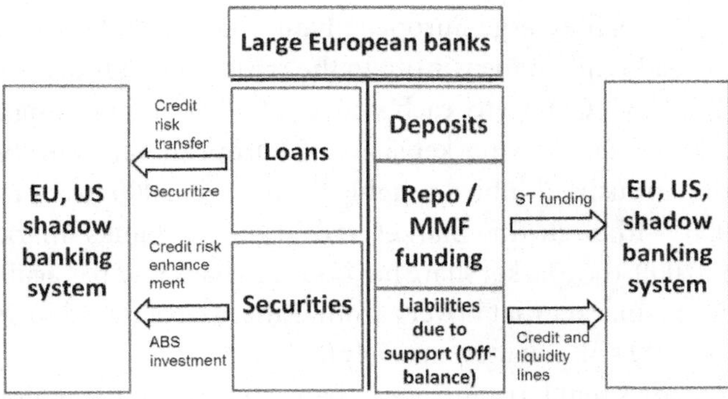

Fig. 1. Stylized illustration of how large European banks are potentially linked to shadow banking entities and activities.

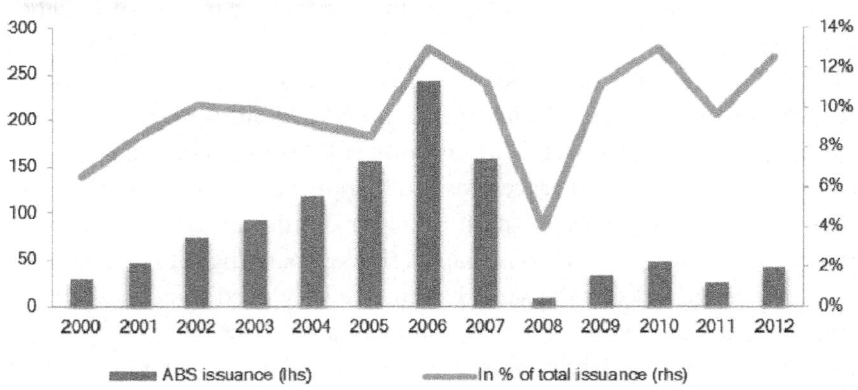

Fig. 2. Issuance of US ABS by European institutions in the period 2000–2012.
Note: Issuance of ABS, in USD bn.
Source: Dealogic ESMA.

It turns out that the *cross-border* intertwining is particularly important and striking between EU regulated banks and US shadow banks. Large European banks have aggressively expanded their intermediation activity in the US in the run-up to the crisis, notably through relying on the USD wholesale funding markets and through investments and sponsorship activity in the US shadow banking sector. Figures 2 and 3 and Table 2 are all empirical illustrations of the significant and sharply increasing exposures of large European banks to the US shadow banking system.

Figure 2 shows that large European banks have been key issuers of US ABS in the broad sense in the run-up to the crisis, issuing more than 100 bn USD of ABS, MBS, CDO, etc. each year as of 2003 and peaking at almost 250 bn USD in 2006. The market share of European banks in the surging securitization industry doubled roughly from 6% in 2000 to approximately 12% in 2006. Although this market and European banks' market shares collapsed in 2008, the market share has bounced back and has again reached 12%, albeit in a market that hovers around the size achieved in 2000/2001 (below 50 bn USD of issuance annually).

Table 2 reports that large European banks have been the main sponsors of USD ABCP vehicles in the run-up to the financial crisis. German, UK, and Dutch banks sponsored almost 140 bn, 93 bn, and 57 bn USD of USD

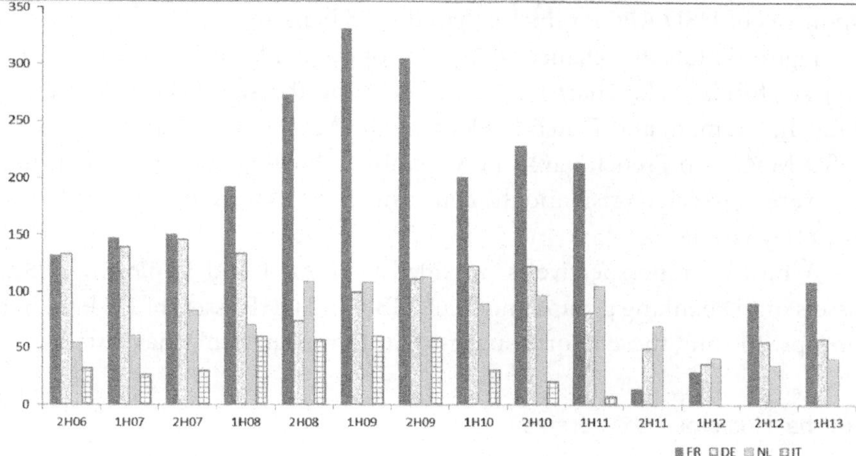

Fig. 3. Amounts owed to US prime money market funds by European banks for selected EU countries in the period 2006q2–2013q2.

Note: [a]All prime MMFs (extrapolated by Commission Services). In billion USD.
Source: Fitch.

Table 2. ABCP sponsor location and funding currency (January 2007).

	Funding currency			
Country of ABCP sponsor location	USD	EUR	Other	Total
US	302.1	0.0	2.9	305.0
DE	139.1	62.8	2.6	204.5
UK	92.8	62.3	3.2	158.3
NL	56.8	65.8	3.21	125.8
FR	51.2	23.6	0.9	75.7
BE	30.5	4.7	0.0	35.2
JP	18.1	0.0	22.7	40.8
SW	13.1	0.0	0.0	13.1
DK	1.8	0.0	0.0	1.8
SE	1.7	0.0	0.0	1.7
IT	1.4	0.0	0.0	1.4
Europe	388.4	219.2	9.9	617.5
US	302.1	0.0	2.9	305.0
Other	23.6	0.0	22.7	40.8
Total	714.0	219.2	35.6	963.3

Source: Acharya and Schnabl (2009) based on Moody's rating reports.

ABCP conduits in 2007. Taken as a whole, European banks have been bigger sponsors of USD ABCP vehicles than the US banking sector.

Figure 3 plots the reliance of large European banks on US prime money market funds.[8] The chart serves to underline the significant reliance of French, German, and Dutch banks on USD MMFs. The dramatic run by USD MMFs on French banks in May 2011 following concerns about the euro area sovereign crisis and the concerns about its resolution and fall-out is clearly visible.

A bird's eye perspective is provided by Figs. 4 and 5, plotting USD assets of EU banking groups and EUR, GBP, and CHF assets of US banking groups. In sum, these figures suggest that European banks have made use

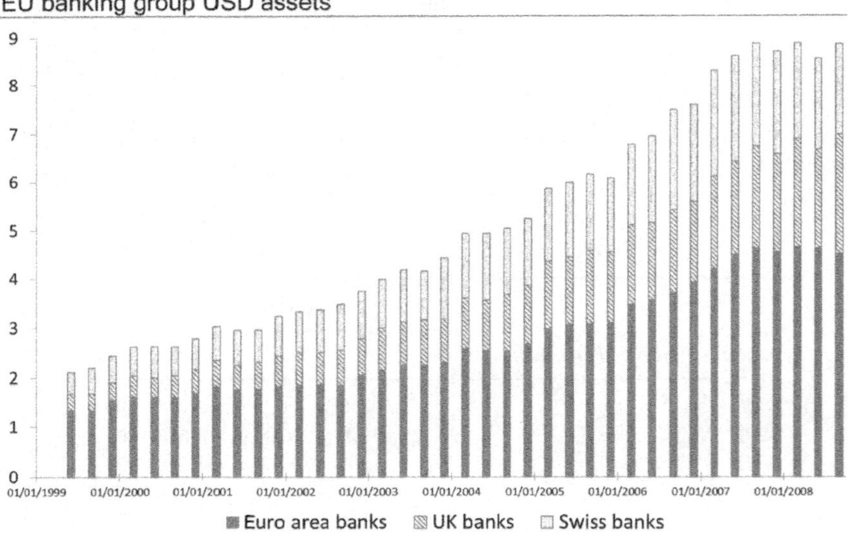

Fig. 4. USD assets held by European banking groups in the period 1999q2–2008q3.
Note: USD trillion.
Sources: BIS; Baba *et al.* (2009).

[8] Fitch data for the 10 largest prime money market funds are being extrapolated toward all prime MMFs for illustration purposes only. The 10 largest MMFs held 47% of total assets under management of the entire MMF sector in August 2013. The extrapolation may imply a bias, to the extent that smaller MMFs have investment profiles toward European banks, which significantly deviate from the average profile of a top 10 prime MMF.

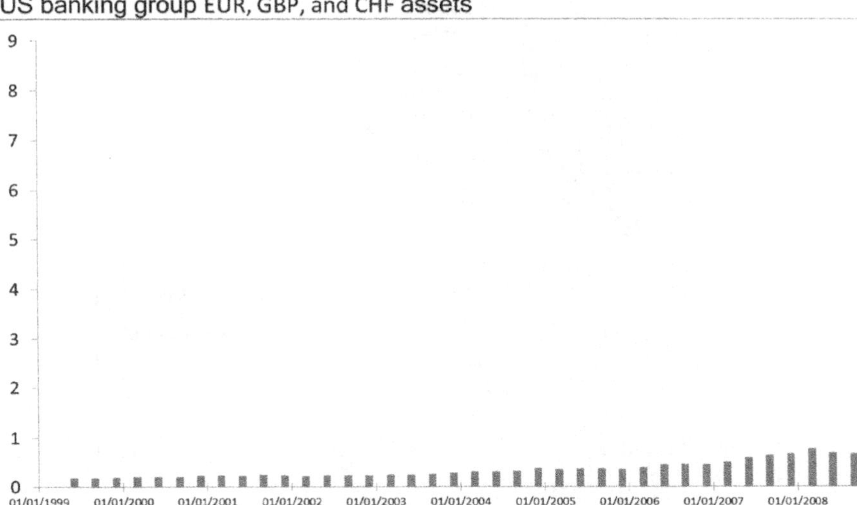

Fig. 5. EUR, GBP, and CHF assets held by US banking groups in the period 1999q2–2008q3.

Note: USD trillion.
Sources: BIS; Baba *et al.* (2009).

of US shadow banking entities and activities to build up claims exceeding 5 trillion USD against US borrowers at the peak of the credit boom. Large European banks have expanded aggressively in US credit intermediation, up to the point that EU banks seem to have played an equally important role at the peak of the credit boom than US commercial banks (Shin, 2012). However, US banks did not build up equally large assets in EUR, GBP, and SWF over the same time period, giving rise to an asymmetry in the EU–US banking system (Baba *et al.* 2009).

European banks have hence influenced credit conditions in the US market, as visualized in a stylized manner in Fig. 6. It is not obvious why large European banks would have a comparative advantage over US commercial banks in intermediating US savings to US borrowers. Why did European banks expand in US credit intermediation so rapidly? What has been driving the strongly increasing asymmetry in the EU–US banking system? These are research questions that have not yet been answered in a satisfactory way. Obviously, as the primary reserve currency, the dollar attracts much

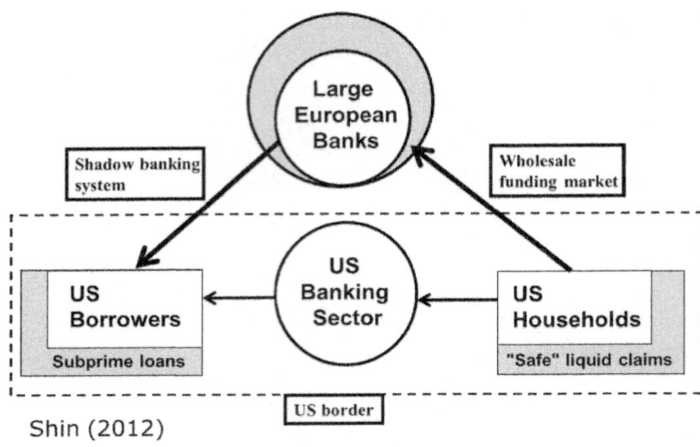

Fig. 6. Stylized illustration of the role of European banking groups in US credit intermediation.

demand for safe assets. Also, project and trade finance are mainly executed in USD. Many US, as well as non-US, firms manage their cash balances largely in USD, because international transactions are often financed and settled in dollars. European investors and asset managers, such as pension and hedge fund managers, also choose the USD for their needs. However, the rapid growth of large European banks in USD assets seems to outpace any reasonable growth of the above-mentioned real economy activities. Another potential explanation is the forward guidance of the Fed to keep rates low for a considerable period, which has put upward pressure on the prices of USD assets. Shin (2012) also refers to the regulatory environment as potential explanation for the observed dynamics, namely the fact that European banks have more quickly circumvented the spirit of Basel I and implemented the internal-ratings-based philosophy of Basel II earlier than their US peers, in a buoyant environment that allowed rapid bank balance sheet growth (given the advent of the euro).

As a result of the asymmetry in the EU–US banking system, US banks did not face a complementary need for European currencies, when both US and European banks faced an outflow of funding sources in September 2008. As a result, the FX swap market became vulnerable to shocks and disruption. Figure 7 is a stylized visualization of the fact that the large European banks faced a dollar run when USD MMFs switched their investments away from European banks into US T-Bills in September 2008. The run on European

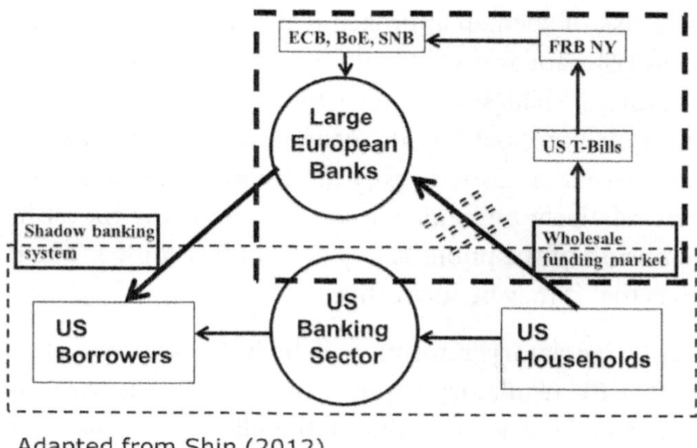

Fig. 7. Stylized illustration of USD run on European banking groups engaged in US credit intermediation.

banks in USD could only be met thanks to the introduction of swap lines between the ECB and BoE on the one hand, and the Fed on the other hand.[9]

Regulation of Shadow Banking in Europe

In general, financial system regulation should be designed to mitigate well-articulated problems, be efficient, be fair and seen to be fair, not stifle valuable innovation, and avoid being circumvented easily. The crisis has been a painful reminder that the financial sector is of paramount importance and that the costs are potentially huge when regulators and supervisors get it wrong.

Claessens *et al.* (2012) present the different polar approaches towards shadow banking regulation:

- One polar approach is to broaden the regulatory perimeter to hitherto less or unregulated shadow banking entities and to require that shadow banks become regulated like traditional banks or be merged into traditional

[9]On October 13, 2008, the unprecedented announcement was made that "sizes of the reciprocal currency arrangements (swap lines) between the Federal Reserve and the BoE, ECB; and the SNB will be increased to accommodate whatever quantity of US dollar funding is demanded [at fixed prices]".

banks. The risk of such an approach is that regulated banking becomes increasingly risky and more difficult to regulate, given the procyclical and scalable nature of shadow banking activities.
- The other polar approach is to separate and isolate shadow banking entities and activities more clearly from traditional banks, such that they can be left relatively unregulated and such that the moral hazard and potential misuse of the public safety net can be avoided. The risk of this approach is that it may be ineffective.

In practice, regulatory reforms will include elements of both polar approaches. The EU regulatory response to the crisis in general and shadow banking in particular has been internationally coordinated through the G20 and the FSB. At the end of 2011, the FSB initiated several workstreams aimed at identifying the key risks of the shadow banking system. These workstreams focus on the following policy concerns:

- Limiting spill-overs between shadow banking entities and regulated banks;
- Reducing the vulnerability of money market funds to runs;
- Identifying and controlling the systemic risks from new and unregulated shadow banking entities;
- Assessing and aligning incentives associated with securitization activities;
- Dampening the risks and procyclicality associated with securities lending and repo.

The Commission has been very active in addressing the above policy concerns. The shadow banking regulatory agenda of the Commission has been set out in a Communication (European Commission, 2013a), which emphasizes amongst others the following initiatives:

- **Requirements imposed on banks in their dealings with the shadow banking system have been reinforced.** Subsequent Capital Requirement Directive (CRD) revisions have implemented Basel I, II, and III international agreements and introduced a 5% risk retention by the originator or sponsor of the securitized assets, increased capital requirements for re-securitizations, and strengthened prudential requirements for support given to securitization vehicles. The Capital requirements Regulation and CRD 4 require banks to address the counterparty risk generated by OTC derivative transactions with shadow banking entities (credit value adjustments or CVA), which is expected to lead to reduced bank transactions with unregulated entities, and introduces liquidity requirements for the first time. In parallel, accounting requirements regarding transparency (consolidation and disclosure) have been strengthened through IASB IFRS 7, 10, 11, and 12 provisions revisions;

- **Requirements imposed on insurance companies in their dealings with the shadow banking system have been reinforced** (through the Solvency 2 Directive, which is comparable in approach to CRD).
- **Securitization arrangements have been strengthened.** The Commission has welcomed IOSCO and other recommendations to increase transparency and standardization of disclosure. Initiatives led by the ECB and Bank of England on collateral and labelling initiatives taken by industry are meant to allow supervisors to better monitor risks and make it possible for investors to better analyze risks.
- **A harmonized framework for alternative investment funds managers has been introduced.** The Alternative Investment Fund Managers Directive (AIFMD) presents harmonized rules to register and properly supervise hedge funds, private equity and real-estate funds, with particular attention to their use of leverage and counterparty exposures. Requirements on risk retention by these alternative investment funds are similar to those in CRD 2 and Solvency 2.
- **A framework for risk transfer instruments has been introduced.** The Regulation on OTC Derivatives, central counterparties, and trade repositories, known as European Market Infrastructure Regulation (EMIR), aims to put in place an improved regulatory regime for derivatives trading. EMIR requires the central clearing of all standardized derivative contracts, as well as margin calls for non-standardized contracts. This allows that information relating to all European transactions on derivative products is stored in a trade repository, accessible to all relevant supervisory authorities.
- **An enhanced framework for rating agencies has been introduced.** The Regulations on CRAs (CRA 1, CRA 2, and CRA 3) aim to reduce the overreliance on external ratings, improve the quality of ratings, improve transparency, increase the accountability and make CRAs civilly liable for their ratings, thereby reducing conflicts of interest.
- **An enhanced framework for MMFs and UCITs has been introduced.** The Regulation on MMFs is meant to increase the stability and robustness

of MMFs by strengthening the quality and liquidity of the asset portfolios held by these funds and by establishing appropriate capital buffers; The review of the Undertakings for Collective Investment in Transferable Securities (UCITS) Directive focuses on the use of SFTs to ensure that the liquidity of these funds does not get impaired;

- **Transparency has been increased:** Transparency is increased through new initiatives regarding (i) the collection and exchange of data (ESRB working groups), (ii) developing central trade repositories for derivatives (phased in as of beginning of 2014), (iii) the revision of the Markets in Financial Instruments Directive (MiFID) which increases the transparency of bonds, structured products, and derivative instruments, (iv) the implementation of the Legal Entity Identifier (LEI) which will help to monitor all financial actors on a cross-border basis, and (v) the need to increase transparency about SFTs.

Concluding Remarks

Although important advances have been made over the past years, more conceptual and empirical work is needed in the years to come to take full account of the systemic issues raised by shadow banking.[10] The EU regulatory response to the shadow banking sector should be grounded in a full understanding of the dynamics that drove its rapid growth, the social utility of its intermediating activities, the risks they create, and the extent to which these risks amplify and increase the natural procyclicality of the financial system beyond sustainability. In this respect, several

[10]One example is systemic stability concerns in the area of SFTs. The Financial Collateral Directive lacks clarity on the operational processes that should be followed where collateral takers decide to reuse securities collateral given using a security interest. Client asset protection is a key feature of the MiFID. Currently under revision, it requires the investor's consent for the intermediary's use of its assets, investors can be left unprotected where an intermediary uses a title transfer to use the investor's securities. In essence, the legal framework governing how securities are held and used is currently left to Member States' law. It is composed of a patchwork of national laws. Nevertheless, each of these instruments has a different limited personal and material scope. Together, these measures cover only some of the aspects relevant to how securities are used by financial markets and leave some important gaps and inconsistencies in the regulatory framework, in particular in relation to shadow banking activities.

important policy questions need to be addressed in the area of shadow banking:

- What is the role of regulated European banks in the different shadow banking activities? Was the crisis in the shadow banking system a crisis of the regulated banking system? Have regulators misjudged the evolution of financial risks within the regulated banking system and allowed large banks to become immersed in shadow banking activities with insufficient capital, liquidity, or supervisory oversight?
- Should we isolate banking from shadow banking or regulate shadow banking? Should we expand the boundaries of regulatory oversight, and does that imply that the scope of public safety nets need to be expanded, or not?
- Will regulation itself spur growth of new shadow markets and activities?
- Is the excessive procyclicality of shadow banking activities sufficiently curtailed and, if not, how should it be done?
- Are regulated European banks still excessively reliant on short-term funding from shadow banks?
- Is disclosure to market participants adequate for them to assess risks?
- How much non-bank credit intermediation is desirable?

None of the above policy questions are straightforward, and some of them touch on fundamental issues like the creation of private money and the implications of a fractional banking system (Turner, 2012a; 2012b; Mehrling *et al.*, 2012). The final answers given to these questions and subsequent policy initiatives will have an important impact on the stability of the modern financial system.

References

Acharya, V. and P. Schnabl (2009). Do Global Banks Spread Global Imbalances? The Case of Asset-backed Commercial Paper during the Financial Crisis of 2007–2009. Paper presented at the 12th Jacques Polak Annual research Conference, Washington, IMF.

Acharya, V., T. Cooley, M. Richardson and I. Walter (2010a). Manufacturing Tail Risk: A Perspective on the Financial Crisis of 2007–2009. *Foundations and Trends in Finance*, Vol. 4, No. 4, pp. 247–325.

Acharya, V., P. Schnabl and G. Suarez (2010b). Securitisation without Risk Transfer. *NBER WP* 15730.

Adrian, T. and A. Ashcraft (2012a). Shadow Banking Regulation. *FRB NY Staff Report* 559.

Adrian, T. and A. Ashcraft (2012b). Shadow Banking: A Review of the Literature. *FRB NY Staff Report* 580.

Adrian, T., A. Ashcraft and N. Cetorelli (2013). Shadow Bank Monitoring. *FRB NY Staff Report* 638.

Adrian, T. and H. Shin (2010a). Liquidity and Leverage. *Journal of Financial Intermediation*, Vol. 19, No. 3, pp. 418–437.

Adrian, T. and H. Shin (2010b). The Changing Nature of Financial Intermediation and the Financial Crisis of 2007–2009. *Annual Review of Economics*, Vol. 2, pp. 603–618.

Baba, N., R. McCauley and S. Ramaswamy (2009). US Dollar Money Market Funds and Non-US Banks. *BIS Quarterly Review*, March.

Bakk-Simon, K., S. Borgioli, C. Giron, H. Hempell, A. Maddaloni, F. Recine and S. Rosati (2012). Shadow Banking in the Euro Area: An Overview. *ECB Occasional Paper*, Series No. 133, April.

Boot, A. and L. Ratnovski (2013). Banking and Trading. *IMF Working Paper* 238.

Bouveret, A. (2011). An Assessment of the Shadow Banking Sector in Europe. *ESMA Working Paper.*

Boudghene, Y. and S. Maes (2012). Empirical Review of EU Asset Relief Measures in the Period 2008–2012. *European State Aid Law Quarterly*, No. 4.

Brunnermeier, M. and L. Pedersen (2009). Market Liquidity and Funding Liquidity. *Review of Financial Studies*, Vol. 22, No. 6, pp. 2201–2238.

Cetorelli, N. and S. Peristiani (2012). The Role of Banks in Asset Securitization. *FRB NY Economic Policy Review*, Vol. 18, No. 2.

Claessens, S. and L. Ratnovski (2013). What is Shadow Banking. VoxEU column, 23 August. Available at http://www.voxeu.org/article/what-shadow-banking.

Claessens, S., Z. Pozsar, L. Ratnovski, and M. Singh (2012). Shadow Banking: Economics and Policy. *IMF Staff Discussion Note* 12.

Dang, T., G. Gorton and B. Holmström (2009). Opacity and the Optimality of Debt for Liquidity Provision. *Yale/MIT Working Paper.*

Diamond, D. and P. Dybvig (1983). Bank Runs, Deposit Insurance, and Liquidity. *Journal of Political Economy*, Vol. 91, pp. 401–419.

Dive, M., R. Hodge, C. Jones and J. Purchase (2011). Developments in the Global Securities Lending Market. *Bank of England Quarterly Bulletin*, Vol. 51, No. 3, pp. 224–233.

European Commission (2013a). Shadow Banking — Addressing New Sources of Risk in the Financial Sector. Communication from the Commission to the Council and the European Parliament.

European Commission (2013b). Structural Reform in the EU Banking Sector: Motivation, Scope and Consequences. Chapter 3 of the *European Financial Stability and Integration Report 2012*, April.

ESMA (2013). ESMA Report on Trends, Risks, and Vulnerabilities, No. 2, September.

ESRB (2013). Towards a Monitoring Framework for Securities Financing Transactions, March.

Fein, M. (2013). The Shadow Banking Charade. *SSRN Working Paper.*

FSB (2012). Global Shadow Banking Monitoring Report 2012. November.

FSB (2013a). Global Shadow Banking Monitoring Report 2013. November.

FSB (2013b). Policy Framework for Addressing Shadow Banking Risks in Securities Lending and Repos. August.

Gennaioli, N., A. Shleifer and R. Vishny (2011). Neglected Risks, Financial Innovation, and Financial Fragility. *Journal of Financial Economics*, Vol. 4, No. 3, pp. 452–468.

Gorton, G. and A. Metrick (2011). Regulating the Shadow Banking System. *Brookings Paper on Economic Activity*, pp. 261–312.

Gorton, G. and A. Metrick (2012). Securitised Banking and the Run on Repo. *Journal of Financial Economics*, Vol. 104, pp. 425–451.

Greenlaw, D., J. Hatzius, A. Kashyap and H. Shin (2008). Leveraged losses: Lessons from the Mortgage Market Meltdown. *Proceedings of the US Monetary Policy Forum 2008.*

Hahm, J.-H., H. Shin and K. Shin (2012). Non-core Bank Liabilities and Financial Vulnerability. *Journal of Money, Credit and Banking*, Vol. 45, No. 1, pp. 3–36.

Haldane, A. and V. Madouros (2012). The Dog and the Frisbee. Speech at the Federal Reserve Bank of Kansas City's 366th economic policy symposium, The changing policy landscape, Jackson Hole, Wyoming, 31 August.

Keller, J. (2012). The Shadow Banking System: Economic Characteristics and Regulatory Issues. *Financial Stability Review*, National Bank of Belgium.

Mehrling, P., Z. Pozsar, J. Sweeney and D. Neilson (2012). Bagehot was a Shadow Banker: Shadow Banking, Central Banking, and the Future of Global Finance. August 15, INET.

Pozsar, Z. (2011). Institutional Cash Pools and the Triffin Dilemma of the U.S. Banking System. *IMF Working Paper 190.*

Pozsar, Z., T. Adrian, A. Ashcraft and H. Boesky (2013). Shadow Banking. *FRB NY Economic Policy Review* (previously 2010 FRBNY Staff report Nr. 458).

Pozsar, Z. and M. Singh (2011). The Non-bank-bank Nexus and the Shadow Banking System. *IMF Working Paper 289.*

Rajan, R. (2005). Has Financial Development Made the World Riskier? *Proceedings of the Federal Reserve Bank of Kansas City Economics Symposium*, pp. 313–369.

Ratnovski, L. (2013). Competition Policy for Modern Banks. *IMF Working Paper 126.*

Shin, H. (2012). Global Banking Glut and Loan Risk Premium. Mundell-Fleming Lecture, IMF *Economic Review*, Vol. 60, No. 2, pp. 155–192.

Singh, M. (2012). Puts in the Shadow. *IMF Working Paper 229.*

Singh, M. (2013). The Economics of Shadow Banking. Paper prepared for the Reserve Bank of Australia Conference Liquidity and Funding Markets, August 19 and 20.

Stein, J. (2010). Securitisation, Shadow Banking, and Financial Fragility. *Daedalus*, Vol. 139, No. 4.

Stein, J. (2013). The Fire-sales Problem and Securities Financing Transactions. Speech at the Federal Reserve Bank of Chicago and International Monetary Fund Conference, Chicago, Illinois.

Turner, A. (2012a). Shadow Banking and Financial Stability. 14 March Cass Business School Speech.

Turner, A. (2012b). Securitisation, Shadow Banking and the Value of Financial Innovation. Rostov lecture on international affairs, School of Advanced International Studies, Johns Hopkins University, 19 April.

Collateral: Cross-Border Issues

Manmohan Singh*
International Monetary Fund

The collateral intermediation function is likely to become more important over time. This paper looks at a new concept — collateral re-use (or velocity) in the market. Although there is sizable issuance of good collateral, very little reaches the market. We describe how to measure this re-use rate and explain why this metric is increasingly important for policymakers to understand; especially when there is a shortage of collateral and monetary policy is stuck at the zero lower bound. If these conditions continue, cross-border arbitrage will be likely.

Sources of Collateral

For overall financial lubrication, the financial system requires intra-day debits and credits. The cross-border financial markets traditionally use "cash or cash equivalent" collateral (i.e., money or highly liquid securities) in lieu of posting margin. Financial collateral does not have to be rated AAA/AA. As long as the securities (i.e., debt or equity) are liquid, marked-to-market, and part of a legal cross-border master agreement, they can be used as a "cash equivalent". In this way, collateral underpins a wide range of secured funding (mostly by non-bank investors) and hedging (primarily with over-the-counter (OTC) derivatives) transactions. Such financial collateral has not yet been quantified by regulators and is not (yet) part of official sector statistics but is a key component of financial plumbing.

*Manmohan Singh is a senior economist at the International Monetary Fund.

A great deal of short-term financing is generally extended by private agents against financial collateral. The collateral intermediation function is likely to become more important over time. This paper looks at a new concept — collateral re-use in the market. Although there is sizable issuance of good collateral, very little reaches the market. We describe how to measure this re-use rate and why this metric is increasingly important for policymakers to understand especially when there is a shortage of collateral, and money policy is stuck at zero lower bound.

In the global financial system, the non-banks generally allow re-use of their collateral in lieu of other considerations. The key providers of (primary) collateral to the "street" (or large banks/dealers) are: (a) hedge funds; (b) custodians on behalf of pension, insurers, official sector accounts, etc.; and (c) commercial banks that liaise with dealers. Typically, hedge funds are suppliers of collateral while money market funds are users, in that they supply funds to the market in exchange for collateral. Hedge funds via their prime-brokers allow for collateral reuse as a quid pro quo for the leverage/funding they receive from dealers. The other non-bank providers of collateral generally loan collateral for various tenors to optimize their asset management mandates.

The "supply" of pledged collateral is typically received by the central collateral desk of dealers that re-uses the collateral to meet the "demand" from the financial system. Such securities serve as collateral against margin loans, securities borrowing, reverse repo transactions and OTC derivatives. This collateral is secured funding for the dealers and is received in lieu of borrowing and/or other securities given to a client. Major dealers active in the collateral industry include Goldman Sachs, Morgan Stanley, JP Morgan, BoA/Merrill and Citibank in the US. In Europe and elsewhere, important collateral dealers are Deutsche Bank, UBS, Barclays, Credit Suisse, Societe Generale, BNP Paribas, HSBC, Royal Bank of Scotland and Nomura.

Hedge funds

Hedge Funds (HFs) largely finance their positions in two ways — (i) loans made under prime broker agreements with their prime brokers (PBs) and (ii) repurchase agreements (repos), generally with other banks that are not their PBs.

HFs usually pledge their securities as collateral for re-use to their PB in exchange for cash borrowing from the PB (a process also known as rehypothecation). There are limits to the degree of reuse, however. In the US, for example, Regulation T and SEC's Rule 15c3 limit PBs' use of rehypothecated collateral from clients. This means that any excess collateral of a HF cannot be used by the PB in the US — unless explicitly agreed to — and thus remains "locked". Regulation T limits debt to 50%, or a leverage factor of 2. With portfolio margining (i.e., after netting positions), HFs can increase leverage beyond the factor of 2. However, to have more unconstrained leverage, aggressive strategies are booked offshore (e.g., UK).

Typically equity-related strategies like *equity long/short, quant-driven, event driven*, etc., are funded via PBs. HFs also fund their positions by repoing out their collateral with another bank/dealer in the market who may not be their PB. Similarly, *fixed income arbitrage — global macro* strategies that seek higher leverage — is done via repo financing.

How much collateral was sourced from HFs (end-2007 and end-2012)?

First, we calculate the mark-to-market value of collateral with the HF industry (source HFR or CS Hedge Index, or other market sources), or an average when all sources are available. Based on available data, the HF industry's estimates assets under management, or AUM, to be at \$2.0 trillion for end-2007. The consensus estimates for global HF gross leverage for end-2007 was 2.0.[1] Thus mark-to-market collateral (i.e., AUM × gross leverage) was about \$4.0 trillion.

With mark-to-market value of HF collateral at \$4 trillion and a 36% share of relevant strategies that fund via PBs, and adjusting for long/short

Table 1. Hedge fund strategies.

Market share of various hedge fund strategies after leverage 2007 (in percent)							
	Convert arbitrage	Emerging markets	Event driven	Fixed income arbitrage	Global macro	Long/ short equity	Managed futures
Dec-07	3	15	28	6	18	22	8

Source: CS Hedge Index.

[1] We use gross leverage since we want to estimate the total amount of mark-to-market collateral with HFs. See Ang, Gorovvy and van Inwegan, 2010. We also acknowledge the limitations of calculating global leverage for this industry as reflected in the BIS working paper # 260.

ratio (or delta bias), the borrowing from PB was about 4 trillion $\times 0.36 \times 3/5$ or about \$850 billion.[2]

Non-PB funding was about \$750 billion and calculated as follows: 27% relevant strategies (usually fixed income related and executed via repos) $\times$ \$4 trillion or roughly \$900 billion. After adjusting for haircuts in repo (and also for the fact that all repo-ed collateral is not "cashed" or re-used, we get 0.27 $\times$ \$4 trillion minus 250 billion, or approx **\$750 billion** via non-PB sources.

Strategies that do not involve borrowing/leverage

Note, *managed futures* strategy is via cash that goes to an exchange like CME (Chicago Mercantile Exchange), and thus is not a collateral/leverage based strategy; also *emerging markets or distressed strategies* do not generally require leverage via PB or repo via non-PB. Some hedge funds hold AUM in cash. Thus the total PB and non-PB strategies (with leverage) do not entail that all the total AUM $\times$ gross leverage of mark-to-market value of securities (i.e., in our case \$4 trillion) will hit the street.

Thus, the total collateral from HFs that came to the large dealers (and "hit the street") is estimated to have been about \$1.6 trillion as of end-2007, with \$850 billion to have come via PB funding and \$750 billion from repo funding outside the PBs. Similarly arithmetic for 2012 suggests that \$1.8 trillion of collateral from HFs has come to the large dealers. Leverage is lower (and slowly inching after the collapse in 2008/09) in recent years than in 2007; however, AUM with HFs are higher now than as of end-2007 at \$2.4 trillion.

We now look at the other sources of collateral that come to banks — non-HF sources:

Securities lending — another primary source of collateral

Securities lending provides collateralized short-term funding, just like repo. In a repo, there is an outright sale of the securities accompanied by a

[2]Since we show separately the securities that come from custodians we need to be careful about client's "shorts". So if a PB exchanges client's "shorts" with custodians for securities, we avoid the double counting. (i.e., the PBs total pool of collateral maybe higher than \$700 billion estimated here since we will show the shorts via the custodian's pool of collateral that comes to the street).

specific price and date at which the securities will be bought back. On the other hand, securities lending transactions generally have no set end date and no set price. The beneficial owner can recall the shares on loan at any time and the borrower can return the shares at any time. Thus, securities lending transactions are much more flexible than repos and thus are better conducive in covering shorts where the position's profitability relies on exact timing/tenor matching. Furthermore, with respect to legal rights, securities lending is effectively identical to repo; for example, both transactions include full transfer of title. The asset management complex that includes pension, insurers, official sector accounts such as sovereign wealth funds, central banks, is a rich "source" for collateral deposits. The securities they hold are continuously re-invested to maximize returns over their maturity tenor.

We use Risk Management Association (RMA) as the main data source (see Table 2), which includes only primary sources of securities lending from clients such as pension funds, insurers, official sector accounts and some corporate/money funds. RMA's data includes the largest custodians such as BoNY, State Street, JP Morgan etc. [Another data source, Data Explorers shows larger numbers as they include a significant part of the secondary market activity also. A paper by the Bank of England (2011) using Data Explorers states that about $2 trillion of securities were on loan but includes secondary holdings also (i.e., also counts the bank to bank holdings of primary sources).]

The risk aversion due to counterparty risk since Lehman has led many of the pension and insurance funds, official accounts *not* to let go their collateral for incremental returns. These figures are not rebounding as per

Table 2. Securities lending, 2007–2012.

Collateral received from pension funds, insurers, official accounts etc. (US dollar, billions)						
	2007	2008	2009	2010	2011	2012
Securities lending vs. Cash collateral	1209	935	875	818	687	620
Securities lending vs. Non-cash collateral	486	251	270	301	370	378
Total securities lending	1695	1187	1146	1119	1058	998

Source: RMA.

end-2011 financial statements of banks (and anecdotal evidence suggests even more collateral constraints recently).

The decline in the use of cash collateral (as reflected in Table 2 first row) needs some further explanation. As background, the US, regulatory rules that guide the borrowers only permit cash, and certain government securities (US). Hence, the US developed as a cash collateral business where the lending agent lends client assets versus cash and then reinvests the cash according to the client's direction in very short-term reinvestments. Outside the US (e.g., UK) regulatory rules permit certain types of non-cash collateral that are readily available (such as FTSE equities). In the aftermath of Lehman and the liquidity crisis, borrowers in the US were/are borrowing more hard to borrow stocks (specials), and less general collateral; this explains the decline in the table. Non-cash collateral deals (i.e., collateral for collateral) effectively provide the lenders with a hard fee for the deal, and it does not give temporary cash to generate excess returns by creating a short term money market book.

Bank-dealer collateral

Dealers occasionally receive requests from commercial banks, like Rabobank, for collateral swaps. In such a transaction, typically the collateral posted by the commercial bank may need an "upgrade". Discussions with dealers suggest that such requests are generally minimal and thus insignificant relative to the collateral flows from the key clients (hedge funds, pension funds, insurers, official accounts, etc.). We acknowledge such flows in Fig. 1 with a *de minimis*, but do not consider these flows to impact the arithmetic of the results of our paper (i.e., the velocity of pledged collateral). Other sources of collateral are not material since we only considered collateral that has no legal constraints on re-use.

Figure 3 shows the sources of collateral (in the circles), and the overall collateral received by the banks (in the rectangle) for 2007, 2010, 2011, and 2002. The years 2008 and 2009 were in flux with several key banks in the pledged collateral market having disappeared (e.g., Lehman) or merged with other banks (e.g., Bear Stearns, Merrill Lynch). Even for the year 2009, this data has been verified with investor relation group wherever banks were merged/absorbed.

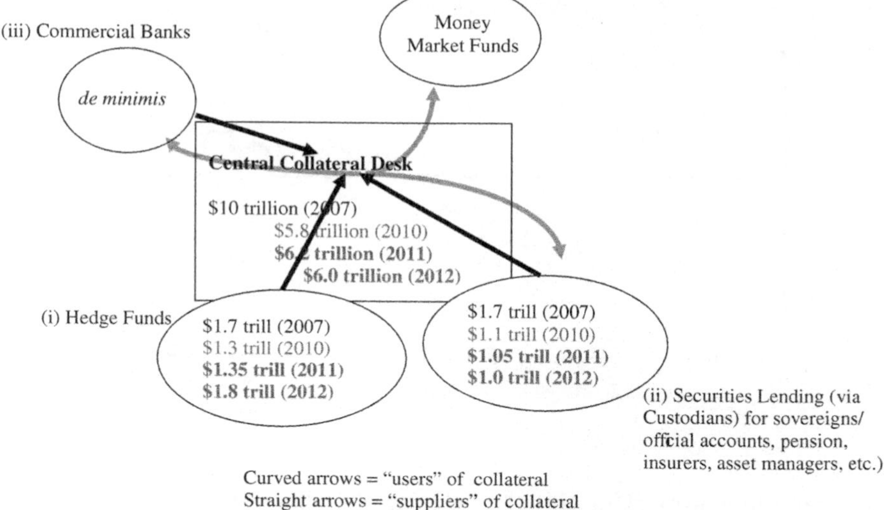

Fig. 1. Sources and uses of collateral — summary (2007, 2010, 2011, and 2012).

Box 1. Augmenting rate of return on security by pledging it for re-use.

The "supply" of pledged collateral comes from non-banks. This is received by the central collateral desk of banks that re-use the collateral to meet the "demand" from other intermediaries — bank or non-bank — in the financial system. This collateral primarily *moves to augment returns* (i.e., return enhancement and not risk transformation). Thus a US Treasury that matures in 30 years and that has a coupon of 4% does not over its lifespan yield 4% to the owner. Aside from the fluctuating market pricing/yield of this security, the return due to re-use in the collateral space will typically provide an extra return to the owner of the security, over its tenor (t_0 to t_{30}). Mathematically, if x is the 30 year US Treasury with 4% coupon, then total returns to the owner if the security is not silo-ed is $\int_0^{30} xdx > 4\%$. The source collateral may include AAA securities like US Treasury bonds, or CCC bonds or equities. Thus this collateral market moves securities that may not be "safe" or AAA/AA as long as the security is liquid and has a market clearing price.

(*Continued*)

Box 1. (*Continued*)

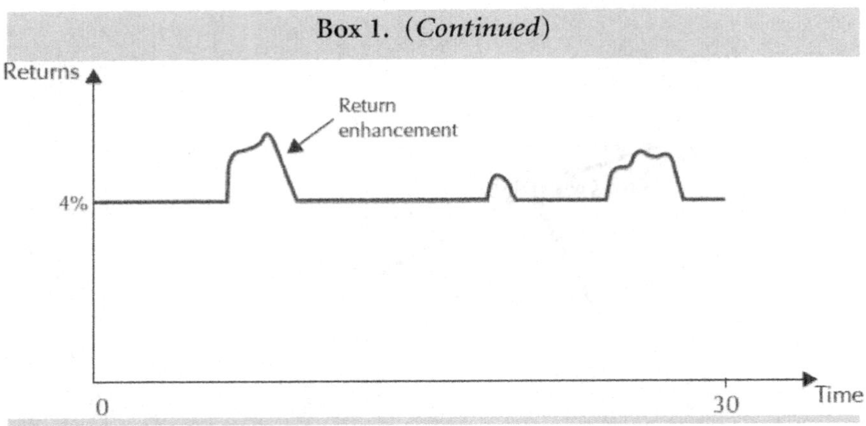

Methodology for Calculating the Velocity of Collateral

Our understanding is that there are 10–15 large banks active in collateral management globally. We may have missed a couple of banks but believe we have picked up over 90% plus of the pledged collateral that is received from primary sources such as HFs, pension funds and insurers, and official accounts.

We then take the total collateral received by the banks as of end-2007 (almost \$10 trillion) and compare it to the primary sources of collateral (the two primary source buckets identified in Fig. 2, namely HFs and Security lenders on behalf of pension, insurers, official accounts, etc.). The ratio of the total collateral received to the primary sources of collateral, is the velocity of collateral due to the intermediation by the dealers.

$$\text{Velocity of collateral} = \frac{\$10 \text{ trillion}}{\$3.3 \text{ trillion}} \text{ or about 3.0.}$$

Collateral sources as of end-2012

Similarly, for 2012, total collateral from primary sources, which could be re-pledged by the large dealers from hedge funds was \$1.8 trillion plus \$1.0 trillion via security lending operations of custodians on behalf of pension

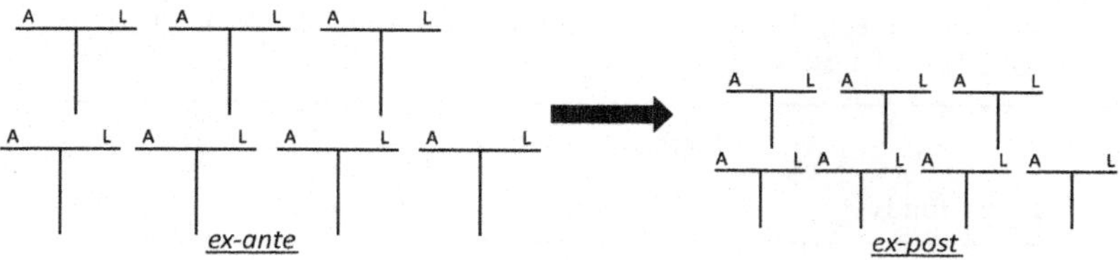

(a) Shrinking of Balance sheets — the first component of deleveraging

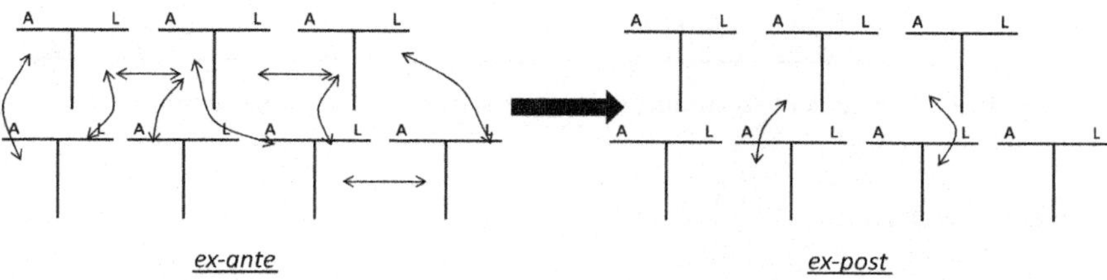

(b) Reduced interconnectedness ("Silo") — the second component of deleveraging

Fig. 2. Deleveraging components — balance sheet and interconnectedness.

funds, insurers, and official sector accounts, for a total of \$2.8 trillion. The total collateral received by the 10–15 large banks was \$6.0 trillion as of end-2012 (still sharply lower than the \$10 trillion peak as of end-2007, but bouncing back from the trough of \$5.0 trillion as of end-2009).

$$\text{Velocity of collateral} = \frac{\$6.0 \text{ trillion}}{\$2.8 \text{ trillion}} \text{ or approximately 2.2.}$$

Table 3 provides a succint summary of the sources of collateral, the total volume received by the large banks and the resultant velocity. The velocity is not an exact metric — it gives an idea of the length of the collateral chains in that year. So the inference is that on average, the collateral chains were longer in 2007 than recently in 2012. The intuition is that counterparty risk before Lehman was minimal but has changed since then (due to some central bank's quantitative easing policies, the ongoing European crisis, etc.). With fewer trusted counterparties in the market owing to elevated counterparty risk, this leads to stranded liquidity pools, incomplete markets, idle collateral and shorter collateral chains, missed trades, and deleveraging.

Table 3. Sources of pledged collateral, velocity, and collateral, 2007 and 2010–2012 (in trillions of USD; velocity in units).

Year	Sources			Volume of secured operations	Velocity
	Hedge funds	Others	Total		
2007	1.7	1.7	3.4	10.0	3.0
2010	1.3	1.1	2.4	5.8	2.4
2011	1.3	1.05	2.35	6.1	2.5
2012	1.8	1.0	2.8	6.0	2.2

Sources: Risk Management Association; and IMF staff estimates. See also Singh (2013).

Collateral Velocity and Deleveraging

Large dealers are incredibly adept at moving the collateral they receive that is pledged for re-use.

The interconnections nexus has become considerably more complex over the past two decades. The re-use rate of collateral — analogous to the concept of the "velocity of money" — indicates the liquidity impact of collateral. A security that is owned by an economic agent and that can be pledged as re-usable collateral leads to chains. Thus, a shortage of acceptable collateral would have a negative cascading impact on lending similar to the impact on the money supply of a reduction in the monetary base. Thus the *first round* impact on the real economy would be from the reduction in the "primary source" collateral pools in the asset management complex (hedge funds, pension and insurers, etc.), due to averseness from counterparty risk, etc.; such collateral remains idle and does not contribute to the completing of markets. The *second round* impact is from shorter "chains" — from constraining the collateral moves, and higher cost of capital resulting from decrease in global financial lubrication.

The first (and more familiar) round involves the shrinking of balance sheets. The other is a reduction in the interconnectedness of the financial system. The reduction in debt (or deleveraging) has two components (see Appendix, last equation). Most recent researchers have focused on shrinking balance sheets (by shedding assets), overlooking this "other" deleveraging resulting from reduced interconnectedness. Yet, as the current crisis unfolds, key actors in the global financial system seem to be "ring fencing" themselves owing to heightened counterparty risk. While "rational" from an individual perspective, this behavior may have unintended consequences for the financial markets. Deleveraging from shrinking of bank balance sheets is not (yet) taking place; however, we still find the financial system imploding as collateral chains shorten (Fig. 2).

Box 2. The 10–15 banks that are at the core for global financial plumbing — A snapshot.

Let the financial system that includes banks, hedge funds, pension funds, insurers, SWFs, etc. be represented by A to Z. Only a handful (say XYZ) can move financial collateral cross border. XYZ also happen to be the large 10–15 banks discussed in this paper. The rest of the financial system from A to W that demand/supply collateral need to connect with each other via XYZ. Entry into this market is not prohibited but extremely expensive/difficult as one needs global footprint and global clients (and the acumen/sophistication to move and price liquid securities very quickly — in seconds sometimes).

For example, a Chilean pension fund may want Indonesian bonds for 6 months, and W (a hedge fund in HK) may be holding these bonds and willing to rent out to A for 6 months for a small fee. But W does not know there is demand from A. Only via XZY, can A connect to W. Since XYZ sits in the middle of the web, they have the ability to optimize in ways that give them an advantage — the Indonesian bonds may come into their possession because they've loaned W money, or because they have a derivative with W, or through a security lending agreement.

Such securities that need to move cross border under a "repo" or "security lending" or related transaction, they need to be legally perfected (and herein legal perfection entails rules such as title transfer, rehypothecation). Similarly for OTC derivative margins, there is ISDA master agreement. For prime-brokerage/HF collateral, similar master agreement that resonates easily between XYZ.

Thus it is not easy for all real economy collateral to be able to move cross border. This market for bilateral pledged collateral is the only true market that prices at mark to market all liquid securities (bonds + equities).

(Continued)

Box 2. (*Continued*)

Given that collateral is in short supply (as reflected by repo rates), either

(1) Velocity of collateral comes back — this is a task that only XYZ can handle in bulk do if more good collateral is sourced through them. However, regulatory proposals like leverage and liquidity ratio may result in balance sheet constraints for XYZ to do collateral transformation. Or, central banks can make balance sheet room for XYZ (as with the recent Feds' reverse repo).

(2) Or, like Reserve Bank of Australia that will use their balance sheet to provide good collateral to meet the increase demand when regulations kick in — this will be market-based. RBA will not issue new debt to meet this demand (unlike proposals in academic circle — Gourinchas/Jeanne, 2013). The ECB type approach also helps but collateral pricing may not be market-based.

The balance sheet shrinking due to "price decline" (i.e., increased haircuts) has been studied extensively — including the recent April 2012 *Global Financial Stability Report* of the IMF and the European Banking Association recapitalization study (2011). Some of the academic literature on this issue spans the work initiated by Geanakoplos (2003).

However, de-leveraging of the financial system due to the shortening of "re-pledging chains" has not (yet) received attention. *This* deleveraging is taking place despite the recent official sector support. This second component of deleveraging is contributing towards the higher credit cost to the real economy. In fact, relative to 2006, the primary indices that measure aggregate borrowing cost are well over 2.5 times in the US and 4 times in the Eurozone (see Fig. 3). This is after adjusting for the central bank rate cuts which have lowered the total cost of borrowing for similar corporates (e.g., in the US, from about 6% in 2006 to about 4% at present). Figure 3 shows that for the past three decades, the cost of borrowing for financials has been below non-financials; however this has changed post-Lehman. Since much of the real economy resorts to banks to borrow (aside from the large industrials), the higher borrowing cost for banks is then passed on the real economy.

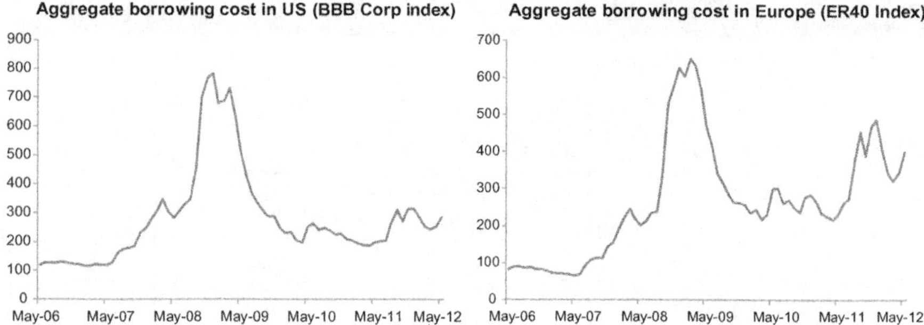

Fig. 3. Average cost of borrowing for the real economy (US and Europe indices).
Source: BoA-ML indices; Barclays Intermediate.

As the "other" deleveraging continues, the financial system remains short of high-grade collateral that can be re-pledged. Recent official sector efforts such as ECB's "flexibility" (and the ELA programs of national central banks in the Eurozone) in accepting "bad" collateral attempts to keep the good/bad collateral ratio in the market *higher* than otherwise. ECB's acceptance of good and bad collateral at non-market price brings Gresham's law into play. But, if such moves become part of the central banker's standard toolkit, the fiscal aspects and risks associated with such policies cannot be ignored. By so doing, the central banks have interposed themselves as risk-taking intermediaries with the potential to bring significant unintended consequences.

Collateral and Cross-Border Issues

Some central banks (Fed, Bank of England) have become large repositories of good collateral as a result of their QE policies. But excess reserves at central banks are not the same thing as good collateral that circulates through the non-bank/bank nexus. As a result of this, the non-bank/bank nexus over time has begun to give way to a new central bank/non-bank nexus that has weakened the market's financial plumbing and increased shadow banking "puts" to compensate for the lack of good collateral (Fig. 4).

Although there are many variants and interpretations of "exit", a key aspect is its impact on the part of the market where non-banks interact with the large dealer banks to determine the price of collateral (the repo rate).

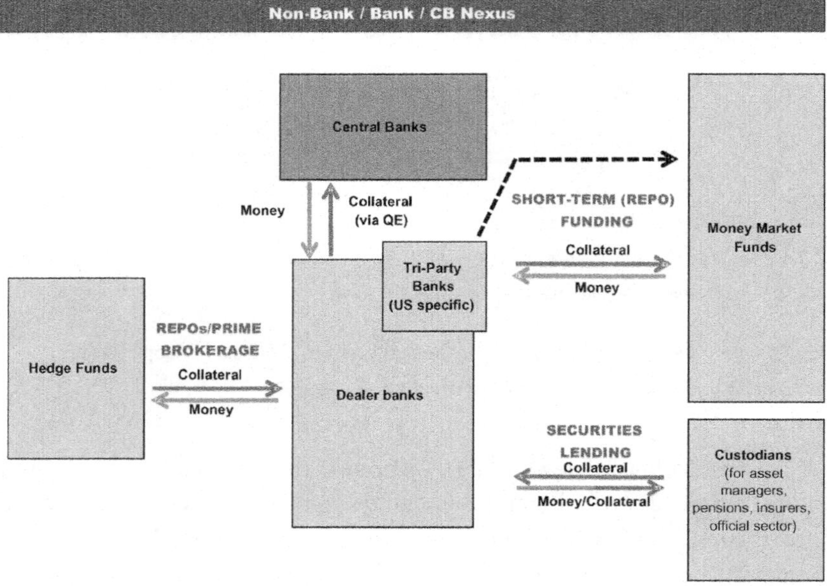

Fig. 4. Collateral and financial plumbing.

Some central banks that have undertaken QE are now holding sizable amounts of high-quality liquid assets (or good collateral) on their balance sheets. Their proposals to unwind that inventory come in part to stem any shortage of good collateral. However, such proposals for unwinding will have implications for this part of the market in a way that may cause major adaptations to take place.

While it is true that sooner or later, these balance sheets will have to unwind — either voluntarily when central banks release collateral and take in money, or involuntarily as the securities held at central banks mature or roll off — unwinding will increase both the (money) interest rate and the (collateral) repo rate.

In the US, the Federal Reserve (Fed) has bought good collateral from non-banks, i.e., not banks (see Carpenter *et al.* (2013)). This has increased bank deposits, (that belong to non-banks via the QE money they got in lieu of collateral sold to Fed). So the effect of QE-type efforts is to convert what had been good collateral into additional bank liabilities (i.e., non-banks deposits at banks). Now, while QE continues, a variant of "QE reversal" may happen simultaneously.

The Fed's fixed allotment reverse repo program inaugurated on September 23, 2013, is the first official attempt to unwind part of its balance sheet. The success of this program will be affected by allocation of balance sheet "space" between banks and non-banks amidst a tighter regulatory environment. Non-banks' "balance sheet space" will be key to any unwinding of collateral. With Basel III regulations at the door (especially the leverage and LCR ratio), the banking system is likely to have limited appetite for increasing balance sheet. Reverse repos would actually reduce total bank balance sheets by the amount of reverse repo the Fed does with eligible non-banks such as MMMF/asset managers.

If we look at collateral chains, at one end there is the MMMF investor — the household and corporate wealth pool (the supplier of money). At the other end, after a couple of loops for transformation, and some haircuts and subordination for extra capital, lies the promise to pay made by the borrower — household (mortgage) or hedge fund. The Fed's reverse repo relieves bank balance sheet constraints but short-circuits the chain. The household and corporate wealth pool is better off; *they get a deposit alternative that is superior to anything available now.* The borrower pool is worse off as money will go directly to the Fed, and will not be transformed into any lending to them.

The truth is that excess reserves do not simply become "good collateral" as the central bank unwinds its balance sheet. This is primarily because collateral with these non-banks via reverse repos *cannot be rehypothecated, or onward re-pledged,* and thus will not contribute to financial lubrication. The reasoning for this is that two clearing banks (JPMorgan and Bank of NY) can only support rehypothecation of securities in the triparty process through what is called GCF (or general collateral), which is an inter-dealer triparty service (i.e., banks) for members of the government securities division of DTCC. If one is not a GCF participant, then they effectively have "read-only" access to their collateral (except in the case of default, for which they have a separate, more manual process to send securities to the customer custodian to facilitate sale).

Only banks are able to rehypothecate collateral received via reverse repos (and increase collateral velocity). Thus, the new non-bank/central bank nexus is good for the non-banks since the collateral counterparty is the central bank. But it is also an extension of the Fed's existing "put" to the shadows of the financial system. This has the chance to further weaken the financial plumbing between bank/non-banks. At least prior to QE, non-banks like MMMFs had to work hard to get a positive return (i.e., higher than bank deposits) by choosing a good counterparty. Going forward, it is likely that MMMFs assets will grow, given the guarantee return from reverse repos (and at odds with proposed regulations — like floating NAV — that try to limit the size of MMMFs). Central banks that have been taking good collateral out of the market for sound macro reasons will not let the ownership of these securities go back to the private market as it will impact the repo rates (via collateral velocity). However, the market needs the collateral services that these securities can offer, which transfers with possession, not ownership (for example, under the proposed reverse repo, non-banks will get ownership but not possession to reuse securities). *Securities in the market's possession have velocity; those at the central bank do not.* There will be a net reduction in the overall financial lubrication if non-banks are the primary conduits for Fed's reverse repo.

Conclusions

Just as water finds its own level, collateral in the market domain generally finds its economic rent when it is pledged for reuse. The past few years since Lehman has seen major central banks take out good collateral from markets and replace it with freshly printed money (except for the ECB which has printed money but taken in bad collateral). Sooner or later, these balance sheets will *unwind* — either voluntarily when central banks will release collateral and take in money, or involuntarily as the securities held at central banks mature or roll-off (see Fig. 5, left-hand side). Analytically, the rate of absorbing money will move the LM curve left. Simultaneously the rate of release of collateral (in lieu of money) will move the IS curve up. So unwind will increase both, the (money) interest rate and the (collateral) repo rate. As both rates move up, policy makers will attempt to keep them close (and not create a wedge between them). This may be another reason

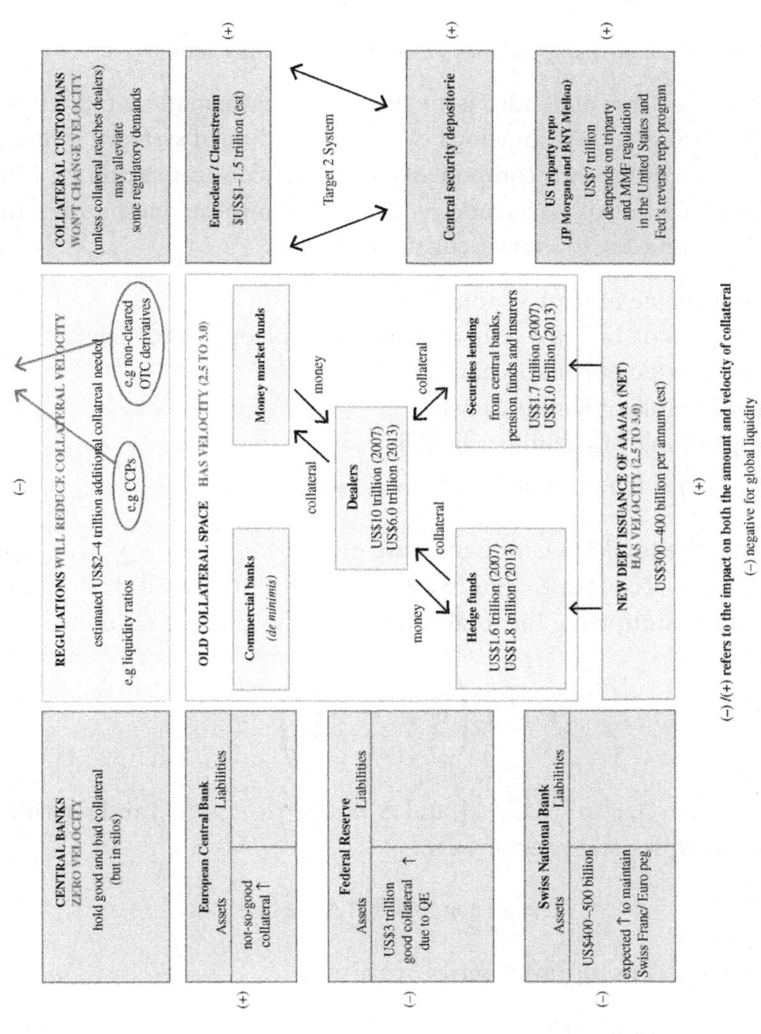

Fig. 5. Central banks and cross-border collateral implications.

why the Fed may want to keep an eye on the repo rate and hence its reverse repo program (while still doing QE).

Appendix

Deleveraging components — balance sheet and interconnectedness

The purpose of this appendix is to provide a mathematical framework developed by Shin (2009) showing how the unwinding of systemic leverage can be separated into two components, i.e., **balance sheet shrinking** (due to haircuts/shedding of assets) and **reduced interconnectedness within the financial system** (due to shorter collateral chains).

x_i = market value of bank i's total liabilities
y_i = market value of bank i's assets that can be pledged as collateral
e_i = market value of bank i's equity
a_i = market value of bank i's assets
π_{ji} = proportion of j's liabilities held by i
$d_i = 1 - \left(\frac{e_i}{a_i}\right)$ is the ratio of debt to total assets

Noting that the total assets of bank i are given by $a_i = y_i + \sum_j x_j\pi_{ji}$ and from a simple accounting identity, it follows that the total debt can be computed by multiplying the totals assets with the leverage ratio:

$$x_i = d_i\left(y_i + \sum_j x_j\pi_{ji}\right)$$

Let $x = [x_1 \dots x_n]$, $y = [y_1 \dots y_n]$, and $\Delta = diag[d_1, \dots, d_n]$ and rewriting the previous equation in vector form:

$$x = y\Delta + x\Pi\Delta$$

Solving for x and using Taylor series expansion,

$$\begin{aligned} x &= y\Delta(I - \Pi\Delta)^{-1} \\ &= y\Delta(I + \Pi\Delta + (\Pi\Delta)^2 + (\Pi\Delta)^3 + \cdots) \end{aligned}$$

The matrix $\Pi\Delta$ is given by[3]

$$\Pi\Delta = \begin{bmatrix} 0 & d_2\pi_{12} & \cdots & d_n\pi_{1n} \\ d_1\pi_{21} & 0 & \cdots & d_n\pi_{2n} \\ \vdots & \vdots & \ddots & \vdots \\ d_1\pi_{n1} & d_2\pi_{n2} & \cdots & 0 \end{bmatrix}$$

The interaction between institutions and the system is elegantly captured by the above matrix notation. While we often talk about systemic leverage and systemic risks, the above matrix notation captures a very subtle issue, i.e., *it makes a distinction between impact of systemic leverage on an institution and impact of the institution on the remaining system.* This distinction between the two concepts is essential to breaking down endogenous systemic leverage into two exogenous variables, which provide additional insight into the economics of building leverage through collateral. The sum of the elements of the ith row of $\Pi\Delta$ represents the net impact of bank i's leverage of the remaining system. The sum of the elements of the ith column represents the net impact of systemic leverage on bank i. Note that the powered matrices $(\Pi\Delta)^t$ indicate the collateral value of the asset in the tth link of the re-pledging chain.

Using the matrix $\Pi\Delta$, the change in deleveraging can be decomposed into two effects: price decline on balance sheet assets, and the decline in the interconnectedness factor, independent of price decline of assets. Assume there is a parameter σ that captures measured risks which affects both the price of marketable assets (y) as well the haircuts (which determines the debt ratios and consequently Δ). Denote $\Delta(\sigma)$ as the diagonal debt ratio matrix, and $y(\sigma)$as the market value of marketable securities as function(s) of σ. [Note: (y) is defined here as price of marketable assets on the balance sheet <u>and</u> off balance sheet (i.e., pledged assets).]

Define:

$$M(\sigma) \equiv \Delta(\sigma)(I - \Pi\Delta(\sigma))^{-1}$$

[3]Note that the sum of the elements of the rows of $\Pi\Delta$ is always strictly less than 1. This means that the infinite Taylor series converges and hence, $I - \Pi\Delta$ has a well-defined inverse.

Suppose $\sigma < \sigma'$, then the decline in debt is given by:

$$x(\sigma) - x(\sigma') = y(\sigma)M(\sigma) - y(\sigma')M(\sigma')$$

Rewrite this as follows:

$$\begin{aligned} x(\sigma) - x(\sigma') &= y(\sigma)M(\sigma) - y(\sigma')M(\sigma) + y(\sigma')M(\sigma) - y(\sigma')M(\sigma') \\ &= \underbrace{(y(\sigma) - y(\sigma'))M(\sigma)}_{\substack{\text{Balance sheet shrinking} \\ \text{(price decline)}}} + \underbrace{y(\sigma')(M(\sigma) - M(\sigma'))}_{\substack{\text{Reduced interconnectedness} \\ \text{(chain shortening)}}} \end{aligned}$$

This identifies two parts: The balance sheet shrinking (via price declines/haircuts on the balance sheet) and the reduced interconnectedness (due to shorter collateral chains). The first has been studied extensively. The second term represents the de-leveraging in the financial system and could be significantly larger than the on balance sheet (first term).

References

Ang, A., S. Gorovyy and G. van Inwegan (2011). Hedge Fund Leverage. *Journal of Financial Economics*, Vol. 102, No. 1, pp. 102–126.

Bank of England, Quarterly (2011). Developments in the Global Securities Lending Market.

Financial Services Authority, UK (various issues). Assessing Possible Sources of Systemic Risk from Hedge Funds.

Geanakopolos, J. (2003). Liquidity, Default and Crashes. *Cowles Foundation Paper* No. 1074.

Shin, H.S. (2009). Collateral Shortage and Debt Capacity. Princeton University (unpublished note).

VII

Public Policy: Where to from Here?

Shadow Banking: Where from Here?

Sarah Breeden*

Bank of England

Introduction

Policymakers' work to date in addressing systemic risks outside the banking system has centered on the key fragilities that were exposed during the recent crisis. A particular focus has been the so-called shadow banking system, which has been defined by the Financial Stability Board (FSB) as credit intermediation occurring wholly or partly outside the regular banking system (and often involving leverage and maturity mismatch). This definition has been used to organize key planks of the international reform agenda, including for securities financing markets, money market funds and other parts of the non-bank financial sector.

The reforms suggested by the FSB are of crucial importance; the Bank of England has long been an active supporter and participant in their development. But a key question is: what systemic risks from outside the banking system might remain once they are enacted, either because they have been out of scope or magnified as a consequence? This short paper focuses on one overarching theme — the transformation of counterparty credit risk into funding liquidity risk, and its possible manifestation as disruption to market liquidity — with some selected examples.

*Head of Division, Markets, Sectors and Interlinkages Division, Financial Stability Directorate, Bank of England. Any views expressed are solely those of the author and cannot be taken to represent those of the Bank of England or the Financial Policy Committee. Grateful thanks go to Mathieu Vital and Lewis Webber for their comments and contributions.

Reliance on Collateral to Reduce Counterparty Credit Risk Creates Liquidity Risk

The recent financial crisis demonstrated that systemic risk can arise when counterparties share common exposures (thereby leading to common sources of vulnerability) and where there are interconnections between participants in the financial system (which can act to propagate and amplify initial shocks). The counterparty credit risk that can arise from interconnections is well understood, as reflected in key parts of the international reform agenda. For example, a number of the most important recommendations involve channeling transactions through the most robust entities, including central counterparties, promoting netting and increasing the use of collateral.

An important aim of such proposals is to prevent cascades of counterparty credit risk rippling through the system and causing wider damage. But such changes do not necessarily eliminate risks. In particular, increased reliance on collateral to reduce counterparty credit risk *creates* funding liquidity risk since changes in collateral requirements, valuations and/or margin rates can automatically trigger larger cash-flows between counterparties than would otherwise have been the case.

To illustrate this point, Fig. 1 shows a stylized network of collateral calls that could arise in the event of sharp movements in market interest rates that caused changes in asset valuations. It is based on data collected as part of a recent exercise undertaken for the Bank of England's Financial Policy Committee to assess the vulnerability of participants in the UK financial system to rises in long-term interest rates and credit spreads. It highlights that the complex web of interconnections amongst participants in the financial system persists today — albeit sometimes in a hidden, contingent form. Looking forward, we might expect contingent funding liquidity risk arising through reliance on collateral to rise.

For example, estimates by the Basel Committee on the Global Financial System (2013) suggested that the increase in collateral supporting OTC derivatives reforms alone might be as high as US$2 trillion. The vast majority of that is likely to involve fixed income securities. If that is the case, a rise in rates of 100 bps could lead to a fall in the aggregate value of that collateral of around 6%, in turn resulting in an aggregate system wide margin

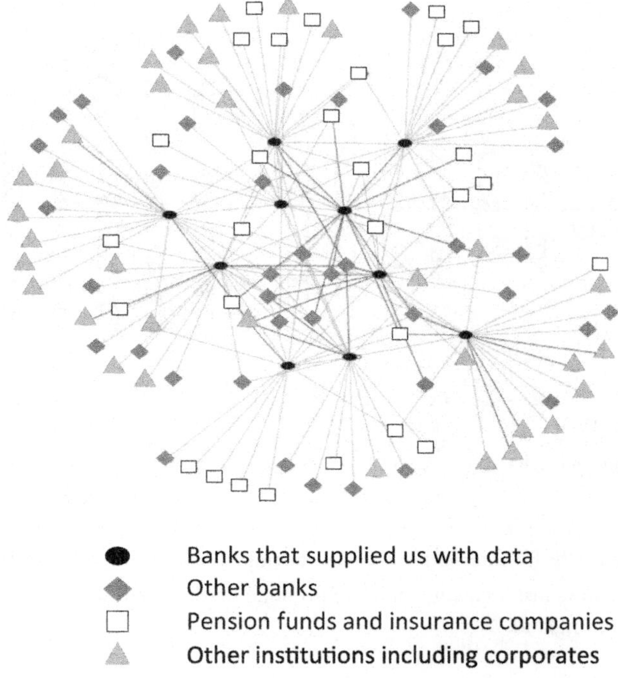

Fig. 1. Connectivity in the UK financial system.
Source: Bank of England.

call of US$120 billion from this channel alone. In net terms, that might not matter much for securities dealers because they might be expected to receive and post collateral in roughly equal size (Fig. 2). But for non-bank entities — all the squares and triangles in Fig. 1 — there may be a possibility that contingent exposure to net collateral calls has been increased by recent reforms.

Complex Financial Networks can Amplify Liquidity Shocks

Funding liquidity shocks can be amplified by interconnections embedded in a complex financial network. For example, Fig. 3 — taken from the FSB Shadow Banking Monitoring Report 2013, and which will be described

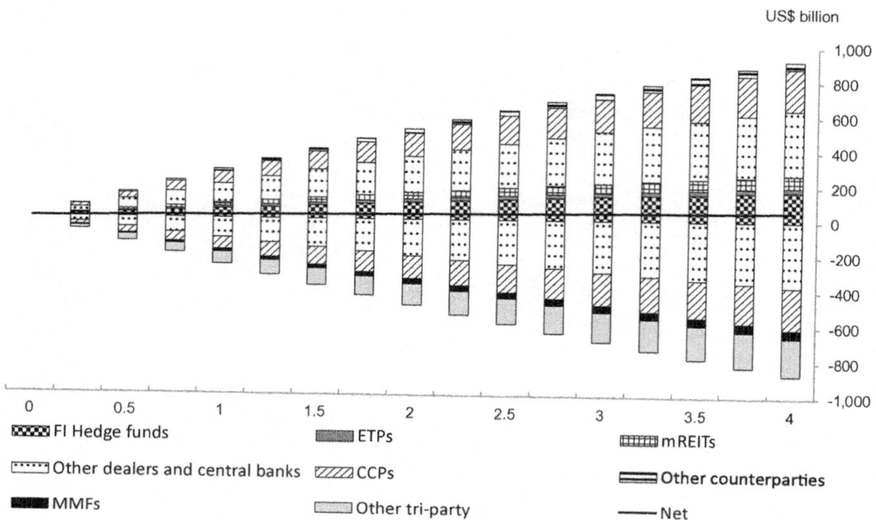

Fig. 2. Margin calls for international dealers against different counterparty types.[a]
Note: [a]x-axis shows instantaneous shock to nominal market interest rates in percent.
Source: Bank of England.

further in a forthcoming Bank of England Financial Stability Paper — shows how chains of collateral re-use and cash reinvestment in repo markets can increase aggregate leverage, even under relatively conservative assumptions. Such leverage is readily translated into funding shocks when collateral values or margin rates change.

Figure 3 assumes a high collateral haircut, of 10%, and that investors reinvest only half of the proceeds from posting collateral in further securities. But even then, a three-investor chain with a couple of cash reinvestments can achieve a leverage multiplier of around two in aggregate, roughly akin to the financial leverage of a typical hedge fund. This analysis is illustrative, but could be interpreted as an analogue for the relationship between an agent lender intermediating between a real-money beneficial owner of securities (like a pension fund) and a prospective securities borrower (like a hedge fund). There is an analogy here with the more familiar banking system money multiplier, only with collateral rather than money being reused, as has been observed in previous work (see, for example, Singh (2011)).

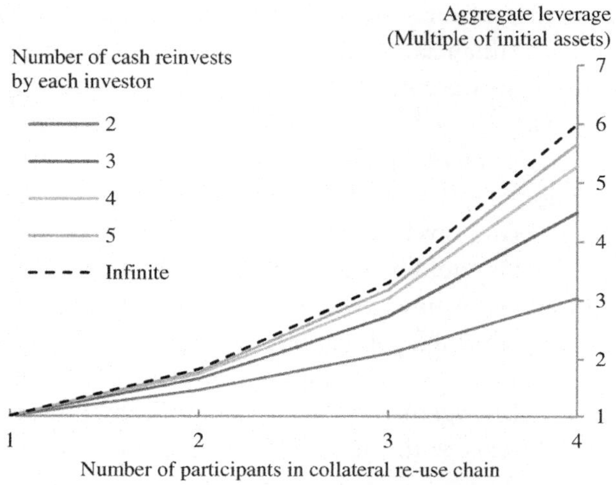

Fig. 3. Illustration of variation of aggregate leverage for different repo chains.[a]

Note: [a]'Aggregate leverage' is defined as the ratio of the total value of collateral held in the chain to the value of the collateral initially posted by the first investor, assuming a collateral haircut of 10% and that each investor chooses to retain 50% of the cash raised from each transaction with their immediate counterparty.

Source: Bank of England.

Potential Impact: Tipping Points in Liquidity

Crystallization of large scale *funding* liquidity risk for non-banks without access to a central bank liquidity backstop has the potential quickly to turn into *market* illiquidity, especially if it necessitates abrupt asset fire sales to meet margin payments. This somewhat akin to the mechanism of Brunnermeier and Pedersen (2009) in which funding liquidity and market liquidity interact.

A particular concern might be that a sudden imbalance between the underlying demand for certain assets and their supply triggers further, abruptly self-fulfilling spirals in market liquidity in which actual and perceived risks of fire sales creates greater uncertainty and falls in asset prices, increasing mark-to-market losses for investor more broadly. Such effects would be exacerbated where initial asset positions were large, common or concentrated, regardless of whether those concentrations arise in specific counterparties or collateral types.

To the extent that reliance on collateral reduces the diversity of responses to shocks within the financial system and creates sudden demand for transactions that are all one way because of margin calls, the system may become more prone to sharp bifurcations in market liquidity. In other words, there may be some environments in which the likelihood of acute disruptions from crystallization of system-wide liquidity risk is low, but where that likelihood suddenly becomes very much larger for only small shifts in underlying conditions. This could be seen as alternative, more sudden analogue of the procyclicality issue described in Gorton and Metrick (2012) in their work on the run on the bilateral repo market.

Figure 4 illustrates how such tipping points in market liquidity can materialize in a stylized agent-based model. Specifically, it shows how market liquidity might vary with the probability that investors switch to the most profitable investment strategy at each instant given a fixed menu of possibilities. Starting from the left-most point where investors' preferred strategies are completely entrenched, aggregate market liquidity initially

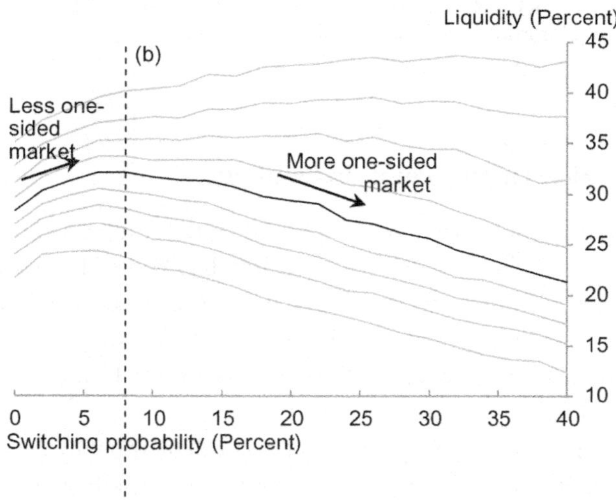

Fig. 4. Tipping points in liquidity.[a]

Notes: [a]Variation in the proportion of desired orders actually transacted ('liquidity') with probability of agents switching to the *ex post* successful investment strategy at each point in time. Dark solid line shows median, light solid lines show other deciles (10th to 90th). [b]Tipping point in liquidity.

Source: Bank of England.

increases as it becomes more likely that investors switch types. This occurs because there are sufficient random transactions in the population as a whole that, by chance, run contrary to those placed by investors following the successful strategy that went previously unfulfilled. But a tipping point is quickly reached, beyond which increases in likelihood that investors switch types reduce liquidity. This occurs because the greater commonality between desired transactions overwhelms the small population of randomly-opposing orders that could fulfill them. It is only a rough analogy, but to the extent that reliance on collateral undermines diversify of behavior among investors in a stressed environment, the outcome might be a financial system that suddenly flips liquidity states from the benign to the systemic.

It is unlikely that firms face private or microprudentially-generated regulatory incentives to consider the broader liquidity risks created through webs of collateral-based transactions that would narrowly be considered 'safe' in the same way as they would consider the counterparty credit risk they would otherwise face absent collateral. And even if investors did face those incentives, transaction chains are likely to make it very difficult for them to assess accurately such risks if they cannot observe the broader financial network. Investors might also expect the authorities to extend extraordinary support measures in such a circumstance if systemically important banks or markets were impacted.

All of this sounds like a systemic risk we should care about.

How should the Authorities Respond?

A useful first step could be to size the contingent funding liquidity risk than may be generated through reliance on collateral — and its possible manifestation as disruption to market liquidity — taking into account the various amplification and adverse feedback effects that might operate, as described above. Stress-testing is already proving a useful approach to risk assessment for banks in a similar regard. It may be useful to mirror this approach when thinking about specific vulnerabilities arising or propagating through key non-bank sectors and markets.

Indeed, this broad approach — of modeling specific vulnerabilities in systemically important financial markets — has already been used by the BIS working group on the macroeconomic effects of OTC derivatives

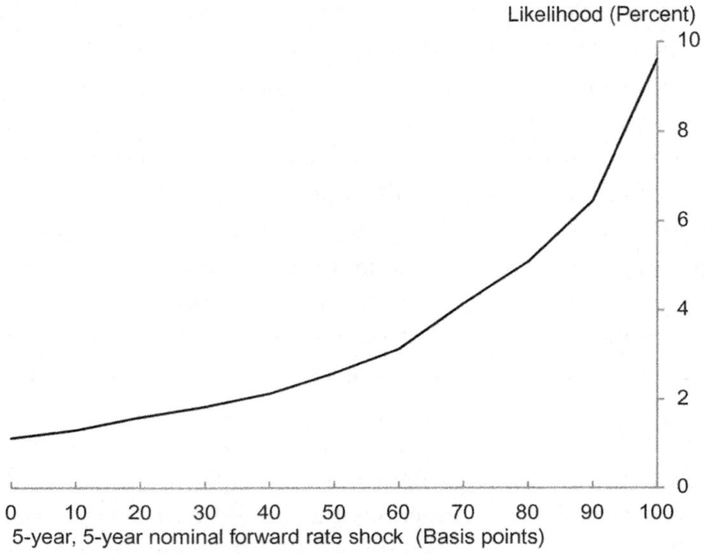

Fig. 5. Upper bound on conditional probability of 'crisis' from OTC derivative markets under alternative common shocks to the UK, the US and euro area forward rates.[a]

Note: [a]'Crisis' defined as a 240 bps increase in PDs for all major securities dealers over three months conditional on common shocks to the UK, the US and euro area medium-term interest rates of at least the size shown on *x*-axis.
Sources: Bloomberg and Bank of England.

reform (Bank for International Settlements, 2013). At its heart, this work recognized that mark-to-market changes in derivative exposures could propagate through the system via changes in CDS-based capital charges, which could feed back on itself via adverse spirals in perceived counterparty credit risk — ultimately leading to some possibility of a crisis. Figure 5 illustrates this effect for different increases in medium-term market interest rates internationally occurring over a three-month window. Depending on the scale of the initial movements, the adverse feedback loop can lead to significant amplifications and probability of crisis.

A useful next step would be to adopt a similar approach to the recent BIS work for modeling the impact of margin calls on liquidity risk and fire-sales throughout the system for broadly. But to perform such analysis, granular, transaction level data are needed to provide a proper understanding of the overall financial market landscape, including regarding common exposures and interconnections. The BIS study did not have such data available. Instead, mathematical techniques were needed to estimate the network of exposures in the financial system, along with assumptions about the extent of netting between dealers. This cannot be satisfactory and it underlines the importance of the less eye-catching data aspects of the international reform agenda. Undoubtedly there is more to do, including in thinking about how public disclosures might help enhance market discipline.

It could also be helpful to design policies that could break, or at least attenuate, adverse feedback mechanisms in the non-bank financial sector and/or systemically important financial markets. For example, minimum collateral haircuts or margin rates — as has been proposed for all derivative and some repo transactions as part of recent FSB work (FSB, 2013) — can in some circumstances impose costs on market participants for transactions that they might otherwise undertake in greater aggregate size, potentially to the benefit of system stability. They represent the market equivalent of prudential capital requirements for banks and may be important for reducing system wide liquidity risk for those counterparties without access to central bank liquidity backstops. Going further, countercyclical haircuts or margin rates could help ensure that counterparties are better equipped to confront the liquidity risk that can arise when macro financial conditions deteriorate and asset values fall.

In some circumstances, reconfiguring the boundary of prudential regulation and access to central bank liquidity backstops may be another option worth considering, particularly where there are concentrations of risk outside the regular banking system. This could be especially important if resilience in segments of the non-bank sector becomes more important to the resilience of the wider financial system.

Conclusion

The regulatory focus on mitigating risks from shadow banking, as defined by the FSB, and the provision of credit outside the banking system has been a necessary response to the crisis. But even once the FSB reforms are enacted, there will be other risks for the authorities to monitor and manage, including system-wide funding liquidity risk arising from reliance on collateral and its potential manifestation as disruptions to market liquidity.

If the authorities are to be successful in mitigating *all* systemic risks from outside the banking system, now may be the time to start broadening our interests along such lines.

References

Bank for International Settlements (2013). Macroeconomic Impact Assessment of OTC Derivatives Regulatory Reform. August.

Basel Committee on the Global Financial System (2013). Asset Encumbrance, Financial Reform and the Demand for Collateral Assets. May.

Brunnermeier, M.K. and L.H. Pedersen (2009). Market Liquidity and Funding Liquidity. *Review of Financial Studies, Society for Financial Studies*, Vol. 22, No. 6, pp. 2201–2238.

Financial Stability Board (2013). Strengthening Oversight and Regulation of Shadow Banking — Policy Framework for Addressing Shadow Banking Risks in Securities Lending and Repos. August.

Gorton, G. and A. Metrick (2012). Securitized Banking and the Run on Repo. *Journal of Financial Economics*, Vol. 104, No. 3, pp. 425–451.

Singh, M. (2011). Velocity of Pledge Collateral: Analysis and Implications. International Monetary Fund, Working Paper, November.

Webber, L., E. Bertalanffy-Fournier and M. Vital (forthcoming). Securities Financing Markets and Financial Stability. Bank of England, Financial Stability paper.

What is Shadow Banking?

Stijn Claessens*

International Monetary Fund

Lev Ratnovski*

International Monetary Fund

There is much confusion about what shadow banking is. Some equate it with securitization, others with non-traditional bank activities, and yet others with non-bank lending. Regardless, most think of shadow banking as activities that can create systemic risk. This paper proposes to describe shadow banking as "*all financial activities, except traditional banking, which require a private or public backstop to operate*". Backstops can come in the form of franchise value of a bank or insurance company, or in the form of a government guarantee. The need for a backstop is in our view a crucial feature of shadow banking, which distinguishes it from the "usual" intermediated capital market activities, such as market-making, broking and underwriting, and related entities, such as custodians, hedge funds, and investment companies.

It has been Very Hard to "Define" Shadow Banking

FSB (2012) describes shadow banking as "credit intermediation involving entities and activities (fully or partially) outside the regular banking system". This is a useful benchmark, and has been much used in writings

*We have benefitted from discussions with numerous colleagues at the IMF and would like to thank them and others for their very useful comments. The views expressed in this paper are those of the authors and do not necessarily represent those of the IMF or IMF policy. An earlier version of the paper was posted at www.voxeu.org/article/what-shadow-banking.

about shadow banking, but the definition has two weaknesses. First, it may cover entities that are not commonly thought of as shadow banking, such as leasing and finance companies, credit-oriented hedge funds, corporate tax vehicles, etc., yet that do also intermediate credit. Second, it describes shadow banking activities as operating primarily outside banks. But in practice, many shadow banking activities, e.g., liquidity puts to securitization SIVs, collateral operations of dealer banks, and repos, are conducted within banks, especially systemic ones (Pozsar and Singh, 2011; Cetorelli and Peristiani, 2012). Both reasons make the description less insightful and less useful from an analytical and operational point of view. More generally, the description does not seem to capture well the activities and entities commonly referred to as shadow banking and that fall between those traditionally intermediated by institutions and those traditionally intermediated by markets (Fig. 1; see Claessens *et al.*, 2012 for a further discussion of shadow banking activities and processes).

"Traditional" intermediation by institutions	Activities commonly referred to as forms of "shadow banking"	"Traditional" intermediation by market entities
Traditional banking (deposit taking and lending) Traditional insurance	***Securitization***, including: tranching of claims, maturity transformation, liquidity "puts" from banks to SIVs, support to par value money funds. ***Collateral services***, primarily through dealer banks, including: supporting the efficient re-use of collateral in repo transactions, for OTC derivatives and in prime brokerage; securities lending. ***Bank wholesale funding arrangement***, including the use of collateral in repos and the operations of the tri-party repo market. ***Deposit-taking and/or lending by non-banks***, including that by insurance companies (e.g., France) and bank-affiliated companies (e.g., India and China).	***In capital markets*:** Hedge funds Investment companies Underwriters Market-makers Custodians Brokers ***In non-bank sector*:** Leasing and finance companies Corporate tax vehicles

Fig. 1. Spectrum of financial activities.

An alternative — "functional" — approach treats shadow banking as a collection of specific intermediation services, as suggested in part by the grouping in the center column in Fig. 1. Each of these services responds to its own demand factors (e.g., demand for safe assets in securitization, the need to efficiently use scarce collateral to support a large volume of secured transactions, the need for collateral in repos for funding, etc.). The functional view should always be the starting point for analysis of any financial service and offers useful insights. It stresses that shadow banking is driven not only by regulatory arbitrage, but also by genuine demand, to which intermediaries respond. This implies that in order to effectively regulate shadow banking, one should consider the demand for its services and — crucially — understand how its services are being provided (Claessens *et al.*, 2012; Cetorelli and Peristiani, 2012; Pozsar *et al.*, 2010; and others in this volume).

The challenge with the functional approach is that it does not tell researchers and policymakers what the essential characteristics of shadow banking are. While one can come up with a list of shadow banking activities today, it is unclear where to look for shadow banking activities and risks that may arise in the future. As shown, among others, by Adrian, Ashcraft, and Cetorelli (2013), the types of shadow banking activities of concern in 2008 are not the same as today. And the functional approach is challenged to distinguish activities that appear on the face similar, yet differ in their systemic risk (e.g., a commitment by a bank to provide credit to a single firm versus liquidity support to many SIVs). Related, most studies focus on the US and say little about shadow banking in other countries where what shadow banking can take on very different forms. In Europe, lending by insurance companies is sometimes called shadow banking. "Wealth management products" offered by banks in China and lending by bank-affiliated finance companies in India are also called shadow banking. It is unclear though how much do these activities have in common with US shadow banking from a functional perspective.

A New Way to Describe Shadow Banking: All Activities that Need a Backstop

To improve on the current approaches and definitions, we propose to describe shadow banking as "*all financial activities, except traditional banking, which require a private or public backstop to operate*". This description captures many of the activities that are commonly referred to as shadow banking today, as shown in Fig. 1. And, in our view, it is likely to capture those activities that may become shadow banking in the future. Indeed some activities that are being mentioned recently as shadow banking, such as the increased use of agency real estate investment trusts (REITs), leveraged finance, and reinsurance in the US (see Adrian, Ashcraft, and Cetorelli, 2013), fall under this definition.

Why Do Shadow Banking Activities Always Need a Backstop?

Shadow banking, just like traditional banking, involves risk — credit, liquidity, and maturity — transformation. This is well accepted by the existing literature, and fits all shadow banking activities listed in Fig. 1. The purpose of risk transformation is to strip assets of "undesirable" risks that certain investors do not wish to bear — as they do not have the competitive advantage, as regulations inhibits the type of risks they can take on, or for any other reason.

Traditional banking transforms risks on a single balance sheet. It uses diversification and the law of large numbers, monitoring, and capital cushions to "convert" risky loans into safe liabilities — bank deposits. Shadow banking transforms risks using different mechanisms, many of which are more akin to those used in capital markets. It aims to distribute the undesirable risks across the financial system ("sell them off" in a diversified way). For example, in securitization, shadow banking strips assets of credit and liquidity risks through tranching and banks providing liquidity puts (Pozsar *et al.*, 2010; Pozsar, 2011; Gennaioli, Shleifer, and Vishny, 2013). Or it facilitates the use of collateral to reduce counterparty exposures in repo markets and for OTC derivatives (Gorton and Metrick, 2012; Acharya and Öncü, 2012; Singh, in this volume).

While shadow banking thus uses many capital markets type tools, it differs from traditional capital markets activities — such as trading stocks and bonds — in that it needs a backstop. This is because, while most undesirable risks can be distributed and diversified away, some residual risks, often rare and systemic ones ("tail risks"), can remain. Examples of such residual risks include systemic liquidity risk in securitization, risks associated with large borrowers' bankruptcy in repos and securities lending, and the systematic component of credit risk in non-bank lending (e.g., for leveraged buyouts). Entities involved in shadow banking need to show that they can absorb these risks so as to minimize the potential exposure of the ultimate claimholders who do not wish to bear them.

Yet shadow banking cannot generate the needed ultimate risk absorption capacity internally. The reason is that shadow banking activities have margins that are low, too low to support a backstop by themselves. To be able to easily distribute risks across the financial system, shadow banking focuses on "hard information" risks, that is, risks that are easy to measure, price and communicate in anonymous markets, e.g., through credit scores and verifiable information. This also means that these services are contestable, and therefore have generally too low margins to generate sufficient capital internally to buffer residual risks. Therefore, shadow banking needs access to a backstop, i.e., a risk absorption capacity external to the shadow banking activity itself.

The backstop for shadow banking also needs to be sufficiently deep for two reasons. First, shadow banking usually operates on large scale to offset significant start-up costs, e.g., of the development of infrastructure, and given the low margins. Second, residual, "tail" risks in shadow banking are often systemic, so can realize *en masse*.

There are two ways to obtain such a backstop externally. One is private — by relying on the franchise value of existing financial institutions. This explains why many shadow banking activities operate within large banks or transfer risks to them (as with liquidity puts in securitization or with backstops for REITs). Another is public — by using explicit or implicit government guarantees. Examples include, besides the general implicit guarantee provided to the small number of "too-big-to-fail" banks active in shadow banking, the Federal Reserve securities lending facility (TSLF) that backstops the collateral intermediation processes, the implicit too-big-to-fail guarantees for tri-party repo clearing banks and other dealer banks (Singh, 2012), the bankruptcy stay exemptions for repos which in effect guarantees the exposure of lenders (Perotti, in this volume), or the implicit, reputational and other guarantees on bank-affiliated products (as widely described in the press regarding so-called "wealth management products" in China) or on liabilities of non-bank finance companies (as noted for India; Acharya *et al.*, 2013).

The Need for a Backstop as a "Litmus Test" for Shadow Banking

Assessing whether an activity requires access to a backstop to operate could be used as the key test of whether it represents shadow banking. For example, the "usual" capital market activities (in the right column of Fig. 1) do not need external risk absorption capacity (because some, like custodian or market-making services, involve no risk transformation, while others, like hedge funds, have high margins and investors that do not seek to avoid specific risks), and so are not shadow banking. Only activities that need a backstop — because they combine risk transformation, low margins and high scale with residual "tail" risks — are systemically-important shadow banking.

Policy Implications

Acknowledging the need for a backstop as a critical feature of shadow banking offers some useful policy implications and guidance for future research and data collection.

- First, it gives direction on where to look for new shadow banking risks: among financial activities that need franchise value or government guarantees to operate. Non-traditional activities of banks or insurance companies are "prime suspects". It is hard to point to the shadow banking-like activities which may give rise to future systemic risk conclusively, but one example could be the liquidity services provided by sponsor banks to exchange traded funds (ETFs), or large-scale commercial bank backstops for leveraged financing and buyouts.
- Second, it explains why shadow banking poses significant prudential and other regulatory challenges. Shadow banking uses backstops to operate; backstops reduce market discipline and thus can enable shadow banking to accumulate (systemic) risks on a large scale. In the absence of market discipline, the one force which can prevent shadow banking from accumulating risks is regulation and supervision, but this is obviously a large task.
- Third, it suggests, when the right questions are asked, that shadow banking is nevertheless almost always within regulatory reach, directly or indirectly. Regulators can control shadow banking by affecting the ability of regulated entities to use their franchise value to support shadow banking

activities, as was done in the aftermath of the crisis by limiting the ability of banks to offer liquidity support to SIVs. Or by managing the (implicit) government guarantees, as is attempted in the US Dodd–Frank Act by limiting the ability to extend the safety net to non-bank activities and entities. Or by general attempts underway to reduce the too-big-to-fail problem.

- Finally, it suggests that the migration of risks from the regulated sector to shadow banking — often suggested as a possible unintended consequence of tighter bank regulation — is a lesser problem than some fear. Shadow banking activities cannot migrate on a large scale to areas of the financial system that do not have access to franchise values or government guarantees. This by itself does not make spotting the activity occurring within the reach of the regulator necessarily easier, but at least it narrows the task. And it provides for a starting point when it comes to measuring the shadow banking system: activities within or closely associated with banks.

References

Acharya, V. and T.S. Öncü (2012). A Proposal for the Resolution of Systemically Important Assets and Liabilities: The Case of the Repo Market. *International Journal of Central Banking*, Vol. 9, No. S1, pp. 291–349.

Acharya, V.V., H. Khandwala and T. Sabri Öncü (2013). The Growth of a Shadow Banking System in Emerging Markets: Evidence from India. *Journal of International Money and Finance*, Vol. 39, pp. 207–230.

Adrian, T., A.B. Ashcraft and N. Cetorelli (2013). Shadow Bank Monitoring. *FRB of New York Staff Report* No. 638.

Cetorelli, N. and S. Peristiani (2012). The Role of Banks in Asset Securitization. *Federal Reserve Bank of New York Economic Policy Review*, Vol. 18, No. 2, pp. 47–64.

Claessens, S., Z. Pozsar, L. Ratnovski and M. Singh (2012). Shadow Banking: Economics and Policy. *IMF Staff Discussion Note* 12/12.

Financial Stability Board (FSB) (2012). Strengthening Oversight and Regulation of Shadow Banking. Consultative Document.

Gennaioli, N., A. Shleifer and R.W. Vishny (2013). A Model of Shadow Banking. *The Journal of Finance*, Vol. 68, No. 4, pp. 1331–1363.

Gorton, G. and A. Metrick (2012). Securitized Banking and the Run on Repo. *Journal of Financial Economics*, Vol. 104, No. 3, pp. 425–451.

Perotti, E. (2014). The Roots of Shadow Banking, in this volume.

Pozsar, Z., T. Adrian, A. Ashcraft and H. Boesky (2010). Shadow Banking. *New York Fed Staff Report No. 458.*

Pozsar, Z. (2011). Institutional Cash Pools and the Triffin Dilemma of the US Banking System. *IMF Working Paper* 11/190.

Pozsar, Z. and M. Singh (2011). The Nonbank–bank Nexus and the Shadow Banking System. *IMF Working Paper* 11/289.

Singh, M. (2012). Puts in the Shadow. *IMF Working Paper* 12/229, Washington, DC.

Singh, M. (2014) Collateral: Cross-Border Issues, in this volume.

Exploring Systemic Risks in European Securities Financing Transactions: First Steps to Close Data Gaps

Joachim Keller*

National Bank of Belgium

Introduction

Securities financing transactions (SFTs), and other instruments involving collateralization, are widely used by banks and other financial institutions and constitute an important part of the financial system. As a funding tool involving maturity and liquidity transformation and leverage, they can be regarded as part of the shadow banking system as defined by the Financial Stability Board (FSB, 2011). SFTs also expose institutions to collateral market risks. In this perspective, they are also relevant if the concern is risk stemming from market-based activities, i.e., the money market funding of capital market lending (Mehrling *et al.*, 2013).

Under normal conditions, SFTs can enhance liquidity in securities markets and money markets and may also contribute to minimising settlement risks. A wide range of market participants, including credit institutions, pension funds, insurance companies, asset managers, broker dealers and investment firms, enter into these transactions to obtain financing, invest cash or borrow specific securities. More recently, financial institutions have sought to use SFTs to source more collateral in order to re-use it to satisfy various contractual and regulatory requirements.

However, SFT markets may also be a source of risks. Clearly, from a macro-prudential perspective it is important to monitor these risks. Yet,

*Advisor at the National Bank of Belgium and Chair of the European Systemic Risk Board's (ESRB) Task Force on SFTs.

it is widely accepted that there are large data gaps that prevent supervisors from monitoring the risks adequately. Policymakers at the global level have published proposals relating to how to monitor such markets, mainly by collecting highly granular data. These proposals are fundamentally justified. There also exists scope for complementary efforts to close data gaps. First of all, some of the proposed solutions require substantial time such that some short-term, low cost efforts are warranted to fill some gaps quickly. In addition, data collections also account for regional circumstances. Specifically, data gaps in SFT markets are arguably much larger in Europe than in the United States.

For these reasons, the ESRB is currently conducting two data collections to address some important data gaps that exist in Europe. Specifically, the ESRB focuses on the two distinct practices of the (re-)use of non-cash collateral by financial institutions and the re-investment of cash collateral by institutions that lend securities on behalf of beneficial owners (agent lenders).

The outline of this paper is as follows: The first section recalls briefly the main risks that may arise from SFTs and reviews the broad dimensions that an effective monitoring scheme must cover. The second section highlights the motivation for the data collections of the ESRB. The ensuing section provides some preliminary high-level results of the ESRB data collection. The last section concludes.

Risks and Monitoring Needs in SFT Markets

This section reviews the main risks and derives on a broad level the implications in terms of monitoring needs.

Main risks in SFT markets

Systemic risks due to fire sales externalities

From a macro-prudential perspective, an important source of risks in collateral markets is due to fire-sale dynamics. Stein (2013a, 2013b) provides a detailed description of such risks; however, it is useful to summarize the main features here in order to motivate the monitoring requirements. A fire sale is a forced sale of an asset at a dislocated price in a situation where the seller is forced by some constraints to sell (see Shleifer and Vishny, 1992,

2011). In financial markets, fire sales dynamics may thus unravel as follows:

1. A lender provides funds to a borrower and receives collateral in turn. If the borrower fails to repay the funds, the lender has the right to sell the collateral and in practice may often do so quickly because he faces financial constraints as well. For example, the financial constraints may be due to short-term financing (which applies to banks, money market funds, but could also apply to asset managers and hedge funds subject to client withdrawal).
2. The sale of the collateral leads to a strong reduction in its asset price and also that of similar collateral. The strong price reduction imposes a negative externality on other market participants and may bring them in distress, forcing them to sell collateral as well. A self-reinforcing process of declining collateral values and forced sales of institutions ensues, reaching a systemic dimension. Although the shocks transmit through collateral prices, the bilateral relationships of financial institutions can matter as contagion channels (interconnectedness).
3. An important condition for collateral prices to fall steeply is the absence of "arbitrageurs" in the market that could buy such assets, putting a floor on collateral prices. Often, such arbitrageurs (asset managers, hedge funds or potentially any financial institutions) are financially constrained as well. Specifically, their financial constraints may be tighter in distressed market conditions.[1]

Risks stemming from the re-investment of non-cash collateral

As described by the FSB (2012), the re-investment of cash collateral gives rise to credit intermediation outside of the banking system. The practice is closely related to collateral markets as the underlying securities lending transaction serves as the source of cash collateral. The re-investment of cash collateral introduces a layer of interest rate risk, credit risk and maturity risk, all of which can exacerbate liquidity problems in times of stress.

This practice is mainly relevant for agent lenders who act on behalf of their clients (who remain the beneficial owners of the collateral) but do not provide indemnifications against losses. As the agent lender retain excess

[1] See Shleifer and Vishny (1992; 1997) for the discussion of LTCM, the prime example of an arbitrageur unable to maintain a contrary market strategy due to financial constraints.

profits but shares losses with the beneficial owners, a conflict of interest may arise which could potentially exacerbate risk-taking by the agent lender.[2] As part of a wide credit intermediation chain, the re-investment of cash collateral can create negative externalities beyond the beneficial owners and agent lenders of the initial transaction. Specifically, the withdrawal of cash collateral may force agent lenders to withdraw their funding of other financial institutions.

Implications in terms of monitoring

The nature of the risks outlined above determines the type of information that supervisors must collect. Clearly, any risk assessment requires highly granular data. However, considering the existing data gaps and to assess the usefulness of first-step data collections, it is useful to recall the broader dimensions along which data is needed.

Interconnectedness and counterparty-level information

Clearly, policymakers must have information on the identity and role of the participants in SFT markets to assess how fire-sales may spread through the financial system. At least, information at the aggregate (sector) level should be monitored to identify aggregate imbalances and to understand the economic drivers behind the role of institutions from various sectors in SFT markets. Better still, information at the institution/transaction level (bilateral exposures) should be collected to assess network structures in SFT markets and to understand how shocks triggered by the failure of an important counterparty but also through a fall in collateral value propagate through the system.

Regarding the re-investment of cash, it is also important for supervisor to have counterparty-level information: First, to "locate" the institutions (agent lenders) that engage in such practices but also, importantly, to understand the linkages (i.e., funding channels) created by the agent lenders' re-investment programs.

[2] Another problem related to information and lack of control on behalf of the client is that the agent lender may reinvest the cash collateral into comingled accounts instead of segregated accounts. Comingled funds are by construction less transparent than separate accounts and this opaqueness could provide an incentive for clients to "run" when markets come under pressure.

Institution-level information

Clearly, to form a macro-prudential perspective it is important to have sufficient information at the entity-level to assess the vulnerability of institutions to shocks and their capacity to transmit shocks. As financial institutions potentially increase their reliance on SFTs and in general on the (re-)use of collateral to run their business, their exposure to collateral market fluctuations (i.e., price and availability of collateral) also increases. As the valuation of low-quality collateral falls, firms would find it more expensive to perform collateral transformation and therefore more difficult to sustain their funding position. For those institution that have significant collateral re-use and collateral transformation activities, any mismatches in the source and use of collateral can also pose liquidity risk, which in turn may exacerbate the risks of fire-sales.

Regarding the re-investment of cash collateral, it is important to assess the risks related to the maturity/liquidity transformation that agent lenders incur when re-investing cash.

Information on collateral and market practices

It is essential to understand the riskiness of collateral as it is the transmission vehicle of shocks in SFT markets. In that respect, supervisors must have information on the collateral used in SFTs and whether specific types of collateral are concentrated at specific institutions or sectors. In addition, overall market practices that have an impact on liquidity and market depth of collateral, such as re-usage practices, should also be monitored by supervisors.

In aggregate terms, the re-use of non-cash collateral may act as a credit multiplier, increasing financial system leverage and pro-cyclicality. In stressed market conditions, market participants may become more sensitive to risk and reluctant to allow re-use of their collateral, putting strains on already tight liquidity conditions (Singh, 2011). As a potentially important factor of how fire-sale risk may materialize, it is thus important to monitor (re-)usage practices of financial institutions.

Policy Efforts to Improve Monitoring of SFT Markets

The presence of significant data gaps in SFT markets is widely acknowledged. Policymakers around the globe are working on proposals for a comprehensive monitoring of SFTs markets, which would allow for a comprehensive monitoring of all relevant risks.

Global proposals for better monitoring

On a global level, the FSB has issued in August 2013 a set of recommendations targeted at improving transparency in SFT markets — that is, collecting "more granular data on securities lending and repo exposures amongst large international financial institutions" (FSB, 2013). The ERSB contributed to the debate by laying out a framework capable of monitoring risks arising from SFT markets (ESRB, 2013). An earlier contribution to address information needs is Adrian *et al.* (2011).

A common theme in all this contributions is the recommendation to collect highly granular level at the transaction level. Collecting such granular information requires substantial efforts and also time until an adequate framework will be established (e.g., trade repositories or improving regulatory reporting). However, some complementary data is also required, such as on the re-use of non-cash collateral and the re-investment of cash by agent lenders.

Scope for a one-off data collection

The ESRB has decided to collect information on two topics on which data is scant, namely the re-investment of cash collateral and the re-use of non-cash collateral. Currently, no monitoring framework for supervisory authorities in the EU exists to identify the build-up of systemic risks stemming from these practices. The ESRB's decision is thus motivated by the recommendations set out in FSB (2013) and ESRB (2013). The two one-off data collections are thus some first steps towards closing the data gaps discussed above. They should be regarded as a "pilot study" which will provide some first results as well as a first step towards the build-up of an effective monitoring framework.

The two data collections have nevertheless a somewhat different character. The collection on the re-investment of cash collateral addresses a well-defined issue and is a response to the FSB recommendation to collect such data. The data collection on non-cash collateral is a first step in an area where information is scant, where the nature of the risks is systemic and where such information could provide useful input for a wider risk monitoring framework. Before presenting some results of these collections, it is useful to provide some more details on the motivation for the data collections.

(Re-)use of non-cash collateral

Information for supervisory authorities is particularly scarce on the (re-)use of non-cash collateral. The lack of information due to the off-balance sheet nature of the re-use of non-cash collateral means that little of the potential risks facing institutions can be understood. Such opaqueness is likely to increase, absent new policy measures, as firms continue to optimize their collateral management in order to reduce funding costs. Specifically, information on the re-use of non-cash collateral is only available for some banks by public disclosure in a non-standardized way and little use has been made so far (Singh (2011) and subsequent papers are a notable exception).

From a macro-prudential perspective, there is also scant information regarding the counterparties of SFT and collateral markets. Available information is mainly at the aggregate market level. The implication is that the degree of interconnectedness and the network structure underlying SFT market is poorly understood.

Re-investment of cash collateral

Information on cash re-investment by agent lenders is only available at the very aggregate level from industry sources. That is, there is information on the volume of securities lending of Euro-denominated securities and the volume of cash collateral as well as some information on how the cash is re-invested. However, there is no information available on the counterparty level.

Collecting data on re-investment of cash collateral from (systemically important) institutions is also in line with the FSB recommendations on data collection.[3]

Data Collection (Re-)Use of Non-Cash Collateral

This section reviews the data collection on the (re-)usage of non-cash collateral and presents some high-level results. The results should be regarded

[3]The recommendations are summarized in a table format in FSB (2013), Annex 6.

as preliminary and more indicative of the scope of insights to be gained. Confidentiality reasons also prevent a detailed reporting of results at this stage.

Set-up

The ESRB collected the data on the (re-)use of collateral by using a set of templates and by addressing them to a sample of relevant European financial institutions.

The template

The set of templates on the re-use of non-cash collateral covers the issue from a double angle: (i) the collateral that the reporting institution receives; and (ii) the collateral that it posts. The templates show the type of collateral received and posted as well as the type of counterparty to whom it is given or from whom it is received. In terms of counterparties, the templates require the reporting institutions to provide collateral in and outflows by counterparty sector but also provide information on their collateral flows with their 15 most important counterparties.

Specifically, the collateral in- and outflows are collected by type of instruments. The instruments include repo and securities lending, but also derivative transactions where an institution receives or posts (for CCP and non-CCP cleared derivatives) collateral. The template also asks for client assets that can be re-used (i.e., re-hypothecation, margin lending) and for collateral posted to cover short sales. The templates also requests information on whether collateral received is eligible for re-use and whether collateral posted is effectively being re-used.

The sample

The templates have been addressed to 38 EU banking institutions. They account for €28.2tn of total assets and represent more than 60% of total assets of the EU banking sector. Essentially, banks have been asked to provide a point-in-time picture of their collateral flows.[4]

[4]Precisely, the reporting periods are end of February 2013 and end of November 2012 to provide at least some information on trends and mitigate potential problems with window dressing or extraordinary conditions that could distort the information on a particular date. Clearly, two points-in-time are not sufficient for an assessment of the temporal evolution of collateral usage practices.

Some First Results

This section sketches some of the preliminary results and highlights how the insights could be used in going forward.[5]

Overall amounts and distribution by instrument and collateral

The institutions receive a total of roughly €4tn of non-cash collateral and post roughly €4.3tn non-cash collateral across all types of instruments. The amounts of inflows and outflows amount to 14.1% and 15.3% of total assets, respectively.

Table 1 shows the volume of collateral received and posted through the various instrument. SFTs, i.e., repo and securities lending, account for roughly 88% of all collateral received and 83% of all collateral posted, which confirms the initial assumption that the majority of collateral flows is associated with SFTs. The key difference between in- and outflows is represented by client assets (which are obviously only inflows) whilst short sales are only associated with collateral outflows (and cash inflows).

The banks are in aggregate net collateral providers. However, at the bank-level, there are significant differences. It can be shown that investment banks are provider of funding (i.e., net collateral takers) while all other banks are net collateral givers, i.e., they use SFTs to fund themselves.

The collateral breakdown shows the type of instruments being posted and received as collateral (Table 2). Perhaps unsurprising given recent

Table 1. Collateral received and posted by instrument (€bn).

Instrument	Collateral received	Collateral posted
(Reverse) Repo	2,800	3,047
Securities lending/borrowing	707	761
Derivatives (collateral received)	140	
Derivatives (non-CCP cleared, collateral posted)		174
Derivatives (CCP cleared, collateral posted)		26
Total client assets	267	
Short sales		259
Other instruments	57	310
Total	**3,971**	**4,576**

Source: ESRB.

[5]If not otherwise indicated, all data is shown for end of February 2013.

Table 2. Collateral received and posted by instrument (€bn).

Collateral	Collateral received	Collateral posted
Government debt	2,602	2,632
Covered bonds	111	180
Debt instruments issued by FIs	305	392
Debt instruments issued by non-FIs	128	120
Asset-backed securities	94	250
Loans	1	206
Equities	605	523
Other	126	274
Total	**3,971**	**4,576**

Source: ESRB.

market turbulences, the majority of collateral is constituted of government debt. Equities and other financial institutions' debt also present significant portions of collateral (both for outflows and inflows). There is evidence of funding of risky assets: the outflow of assets such as loans, ABSs, and debt instruments, is higher than their inflows. The opposite applies to government debt.

Looking more closely at the collateral composition of STFs (Fig. 1), the data reveal the high proportion of government debt used in repos. In securities lending transactions, equities and government debt are widely used. In line with the observation of SFTs as a funding tool, the data provides some evidence on collateral transformation, i.e., the institutions post collateral of lower quality and receive collateral of higher quality.

Re-use of collateral and collateral velocity

Collateral is typically fungible and can be re-used if provided under a transfer-of-title agreement (as opposed to re-hypothecated assets). Table 3 shows the ratio of collateral eligible for re-use to total collateral received. Clearly, the eligibility rate is very high for repo and securities lending transactions which are typically transfer-of-title agreements and give thus full right of use to the receiver. Client assets can be re-used less often (re-hypothecation under client agreements). Because SFTs represent the largest part of collateralized transactions, banks can potentially freely re-use most of their collateral. Overall, it appears that the institutions had difficulties in

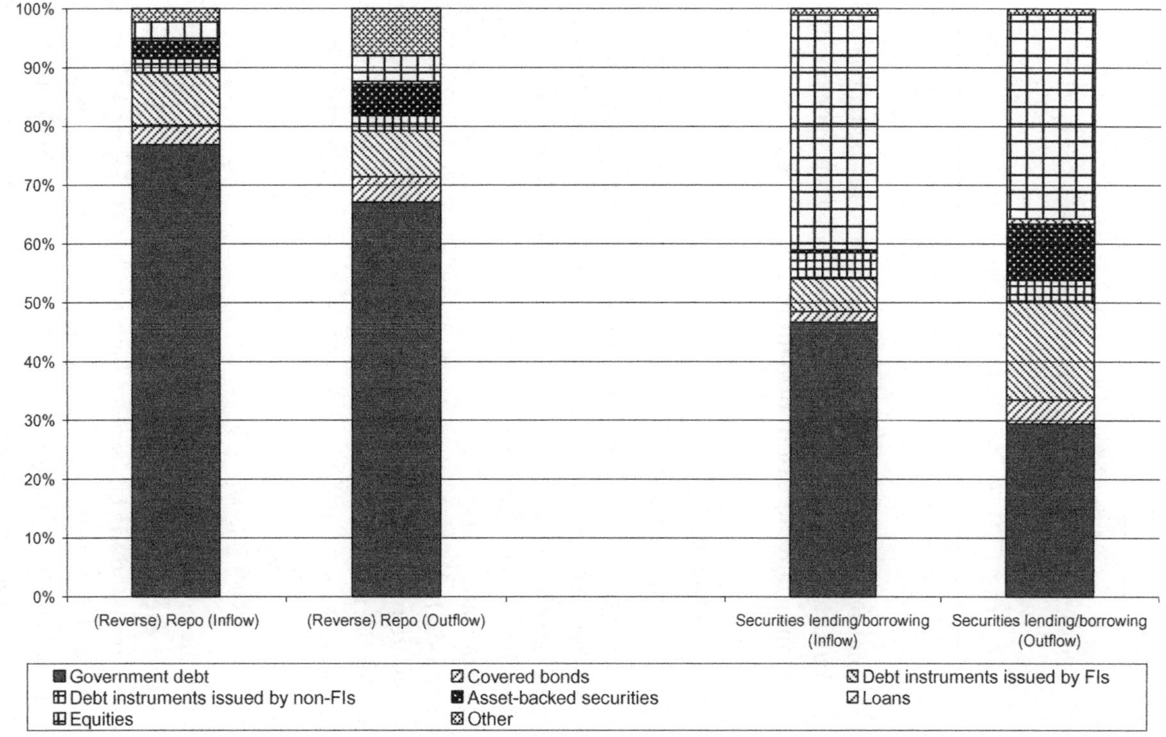

Fig. 1. Collateral in and outflows by collateral assets instrument.

Source: ESRB.

Table 3. Collateral received and posted by instrument (€bn).

Instrument	Total collateral inflow	Collateral inflow eligible for re-use	Eligibility (%)
(Reverse) Repo	2,800	2,754	98%
Securities lending/borrowing	709	699	99%
Derivatives	140	115	82%
Total client assets	267	124	46%
Other instruments	57	36	64%

Source: ESRB.

providing information on the volumes of collateral actually being re-used. This is due to the fungibility of collateral but should in general be possible and it is also an important piece of information.

Institution-level information

Because the data is collected at the bank-level, the identification of institution-level differences is also feasible. Some of the main questions that can be answered with the collected data are the following: How do banks differ in their reliance on collateralized transactions? How do re-usage practices vary across banks? How does the funding profile vary across banks?

Given the information on the banks in the sample (size, geographic location, business model), the analysis of the data will allow to assess whether specific patterns are typical for any classification of banks. It may also provide guidance for the identification of the institutions that could be subject to additional monitoring requirements based on their role in SFT markets.

Interconnectedness and network structure

Figure 2 shows the aggregate collateral flows between the aggregate sample of banks and the various counterparty sectors. Clearly, a large part of collateralized transactions takes place between banks. Central clearing counterparties (CCPS) play an important role as well. In terms of net collateral flows, central banks, money market funds and hedge funds are most important. Central banks and MMFs provide funding to the banking sector and take collateral, while hedge funds are large net providers of collateral to banks.

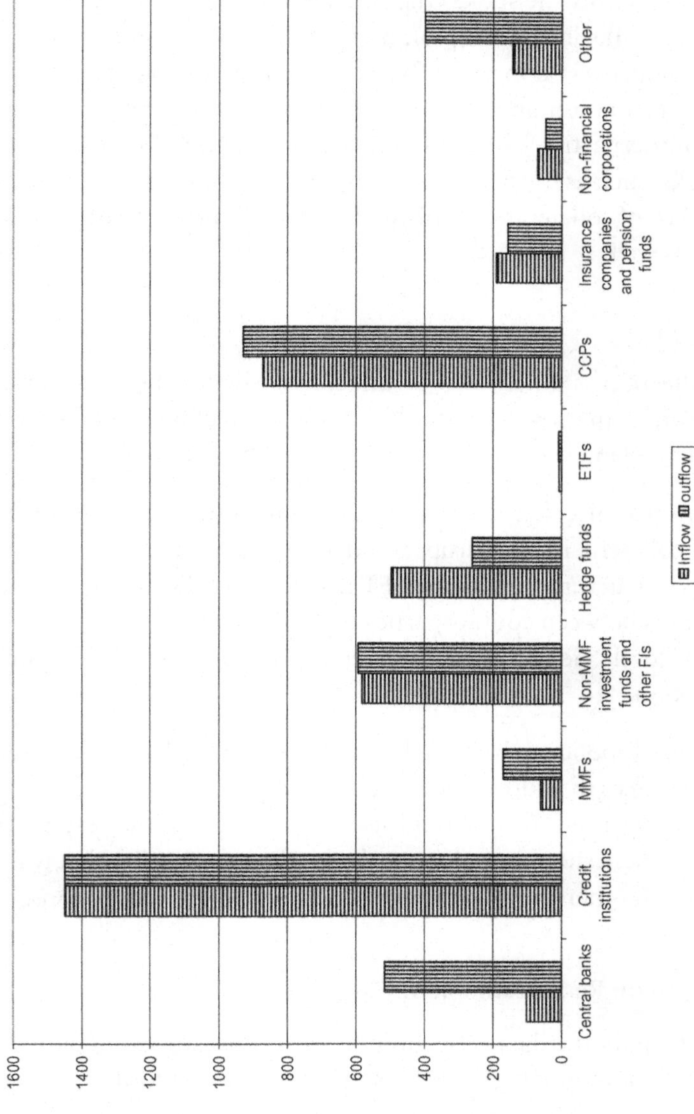

Fig. 2. Collateral in- and outflows of sample institutions by counterparty sector (€bn).

Source: ESRB.

This aggregate picture shows only a high-level view on counterparties. As discussed above, the data collection also asked for the 15 largest counterparties of banks. This data allows to draw the network underlying collateral markets and to identify the spokes (i.e., bilateral transactions) between the nodes (i.e., the banks in the sample). Basically, the data is sufficient to do two steps of an analysis akin to Duffie's (2013) three-step approach. That is, using the information on the most relevant institutions and their most important counterparties. The missing step is then to develop scenarios of possible shocks, such as the failure of an important counterparty or shocks to a specific class of collateral. For this, additional risk-relevant information may be used as well.

The way forward

This data collection is a first step to understand better the risk-relevant factors in collateral markets. Specifically, the data collection should provide some important elements of information in the dimensions:

- The importance of collateral re-use across institutions and the overall velocity of collateral in the European financial systems;
- The network structure underlying SFT markets and the degree of interconnectedness between counterparties (sectors); and
- Some high-level views on collateral transformation and maturity transformation.

In going forward, policymakers could combine this evidence with other information sources to address specific questions.

Some regularly monitoring should also be envisaged. In this respect, the evidence gather here should be compared with the information that will be gathered through other (new) reporting schemes and data collections.

Data Collection on Re-Investment of Cash Collateral

This section reviews the data collection on the re-investment of cash collateral and presents some high-level results. Analogously to the non-cash results, the results should be regarded as preliminary and more indicative of the scope of insights to be gained. Confidentiality reasons also prevent a detailed reporting of results at this stage.

Set-up

The ESRB collected the data on the re-investment of cash collateral by using a set of templates and by addressing them to a sample of relevant European agent lenders.

The template

The set of templates capture the re-investment of cash collateral obtained by agent lenders through their securities lending transactions. Data was collected on total assets (own assets and clients' assets) as well as assets available for securities lending transactions. Focusing on cash re-investment, reporting institutions were asked to provide additional information on the re-investment of the cash collateral in order to assess the aforementioned risks. More precisely, the collected data on securities lending, cash collateral and cash collateral re-investment give us an amount of information sufficient to conduct a preliminary analysis of:

- The assets and collateral posted to the institutions, split by type of clients, which can be subsequently re-invested. It also includes the portion of the securities lending portfolio that is guaranteed by the reporting institution, the collateral received from securities lending and the division into segregated or comingled accounts.
- A maturity breakdown of the cash collateral received, including information on earliest termination maturities, i.e., the earliest possible liquidity outflows and the latest point of time where the received cash has to be paid back.[6]
- The cash collateral re-investment portfolio, with further breakdowns by type of product/transaction, e.g., cash and bank deposits, reverse repos, bonds or loans. It also includes a more detailed breakdown of the asset classes of the securities received through reverse repos; for the products and transactions the liquidation period has been reported, which will allow for an assessment of liquidity and maturity transformation as well as how fast the reporting institution can raise cash in "normal" times.

---

[6]They provide information on the potential maturity and currency mismatches that agent lenders could face when re-investing the cash collateral received when entering into SFTs. Information is required by the type of product in which the cash is further re-invested.

- Potential currency mismatches in the cash collateral received and re-invested.

This collection of firm-level data also gives us the possibility to assess the feasibility of the different types of institutions to provide the relevant data and whether the data collection captures the relevant risks in an efficient manner.

The sample

The templates have been addressed to 15 agent lenders. The data have been collected at two points in time (February 28, 2013 and November 30, 2012) analogously to the non-cash data collection.

Some preliminary results

Market overview and identification of the credit intermediation chain (interconnectedness)

The data collection exercise gathered data from financial institutions reporting around €8tn in total assets available as of February 28, 2013.[7] Around €5.5tn is available for securities lending, while €750bn are actually used for securities lending. The agent lenders receive in aggregate €580bn cash collateral and €284bn non-cash collateral.

Looking into the breakdown by client location of the total assets available, the first key observation that arises is the high degree of interconnectedness between the EU agent lenders surveyed and their non-EU clients (beneficial owners), with 43% of assets stemming from those non-EU beneficial owners (33% are own assets, 24% are EU beneficial owner assets). This shows a potential for significant cross border linkages between EU and non-EU jurisdictions.

Among EU clients, the main beneficial owner types are insurance corporations and pension funds (35%), followed by other asset managers (such as non-ETF UCITS) (32%), "Other investment funds and other financial intermediaries" (16%), and ETFs (9%).

[7] All subsequent numbers used in the report are based on data reported as of February 2013, unless otherwise indicated.

The collateral received from securities lending transactions amounts to €864.4bn, including €283.9bn in non-cash collateral and €580.5bn in cash (67.2%). Cash collateral dominates especially in the case of the agent lenders' own securities on loan (87.6%), and to a lesser extent for non-EU clients (66.2%).

This evidence seems to differ from information available from industry sources ("Markit magazine"), which typically shows a low proportion of cash collateral for Euro-denominated securities. Markit data shows that 25% of EU securities on loan were collateralized with cash and 75% with non-cash, globally (there is no split available by location of agent lenders from Markit).[8]

A very significant portion of the cash collateral is reinvested (€543.8bn), equivalent to 97.9% of the cash collateral received. As shown in Fig. 3, of the €543.8bn reinvested, a large part goes into reverse repos (66%), followed by debt (credit institutions 11.4%, governments 7.2%, and non-financial issuers 2.6%), ABS (5.1%) and cash and bank deposits (4.4%). This suggests that re-investment of cash can increase interconnectedness between financial institutions through increased exposure to other market participants.[9]

Institution-level information on risks

As discussed above, risks related to maturity transformation may arise from the re-investment of cash collateral. It may be useful to distinguish between liquidation risk and maturity risks in the analysis of the data.

— Liquidation risk: The majority of cash collateral received is at open maturity (€304bn), i.e., the collateral can be requested to be returned

[8]It is worth noting that a portion of the cash collateral received is in segregated accounts (€212.9bn or 36.7% of total cash collateral received), and this portion is especially large for non-EU clients. This reduces contagion risks as agent lenders are legally not allowed to use these segregated funds to back investments or face losses outside of the account.

[9]These findings show much higher re-investment in reverse repos than indicated in the Risk Management Association (RMA) survey, which shows reverse repos represent 40% of USD cash and 50% of EUR cash collateral received. However, the data available in the RMA survey is not as detailed as what would be required for monitoring purposes both in terms of granularity (e.g., asset classes) and coverage (e.g., EU market participants). Note that the RMA survey only focuses on the 15 largest US investment banks.

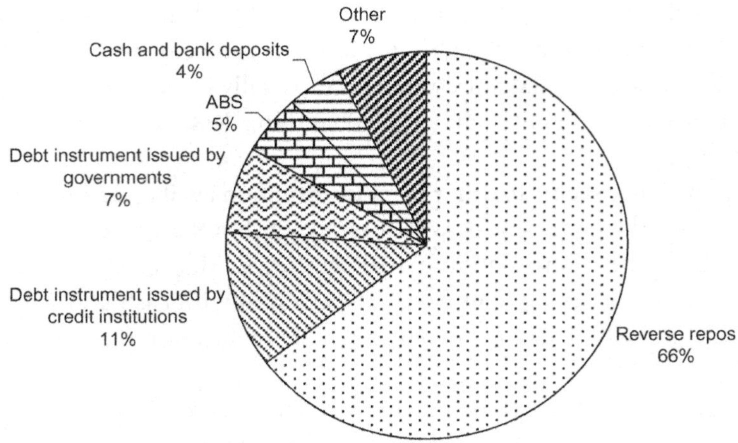

Fig. 3. Cash collateral re-investment by instrument.
Source: ESRB.

at any point in time by one of the counterparty after the order. This implies that securities lending cannot be seen as a stable source of funding by financial institutions, as evidenced during the financial crisis by AIG.[10] This picture is confirmed by Markit data, showing that approximately 70% of securities lending transactions using cash as collateral are at open maturity. On the other hand, cash collateral is overwhelmingly reinvested at term maturity (€496.6bn, see Fig. 4).

This difference can be regarded as "liquidation risk", i.e., the potential inability of an agent lender to liquidate assets in time to return the cash collateral at any point in time to the entity that borrowed the security, due to the cash being reinvested in term transactions.

On the other hand, this risk is mitigated by the fact that most of the open maturity cash collateral received seems to include early termination clauses. Indeed, €259.3bn of the cash collateral (out of a total €563.3bn) received is at term maturity, and agent lenders report that a total €551.7bn include an earliest termination provision. However, a large majority (€384.5bn or

[10]AIG used securities lending as "a mechanism for raising cash to support a yield-enhancement re-investment strategy with no collateral market purpose, and such use was subject to the same run risk as exists in repo markets" (Keane, 2013).

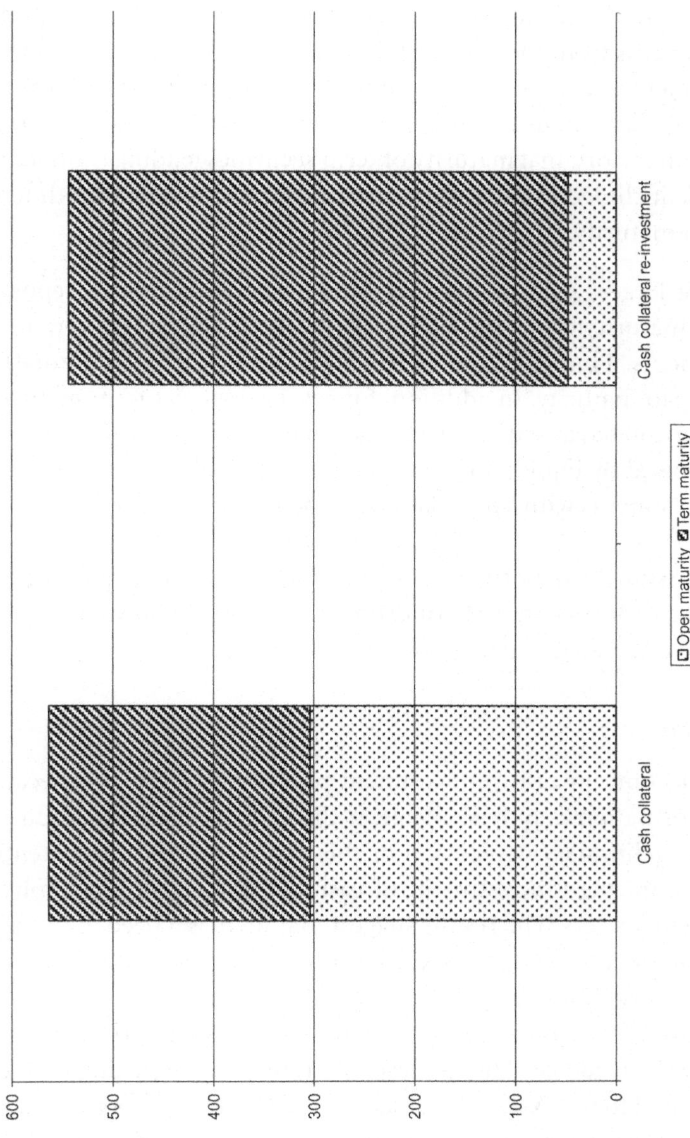

Fig. 4. Maturity (open or term) of cash collateral (underlying securities lending transaction) and of cash collateral re-investment (€bn).

Source: ESRB.

69.7%) of these provisions are very short-term, stipulating that the cash collateral might be requested within the same day of the order.

> Maturity risk: The second type of risk, closely associated to the liquidation risk, stems from the expected liquidation period of cash collateral re-investments. A significant amount of the cash collateral reinvested (€179.8bn) has a liquidation period greater than 30 days, i.e., much longer than the original maturity of term securities lending transaction or what is included in the earliest termination provision of both term and open maturity transactions (Fig. 5).

While the largest part of the investment goes into reverse repos, it appears that maturity transformation risks might be concentrated in non-repo instruments. First, €47.3bn in reverse repos (13.4% of the total) is invested at open maturity. In addition, for reverse repos at term maturity, the largest portion has an expected liquidation period of one day (€134.7bn or 38%), followed by liquidation period between 1 and 30 days (€97.1bn) and by re-investments with a liquidation period longer than 30 days €73bn (20.7%).

In comparison, the majority of non-repo instruments have an expected liquidation of 30 days or more (€106.8bn or 55.6%), and only half of that amount has a one-day maturity (€44.2bn or 23.1%).

The way forward

The data collection on cash re-investment provides new insights because currently information is only available at the aggregate level by industry sources. The preliminary conclusion of this analysis is that the potential risks arising from the re-investment of cash collateral may also apply to European agent lenders. The results suggest that there is a need for regular data collection of cash collateral received from securities lending transactions and how it is reinvested.

In terms of information collected, there is scope for improvements of the template. For instance, a higher level of granularity regarding non-EU clients is required to fully assess the risks facing EU agent lenders. Similarly, information on the counterparties of reverse repo transaction should be collected. To measure the amount of maturity transformation that is taking place and any associated maturity risk or mismatch, more granularity

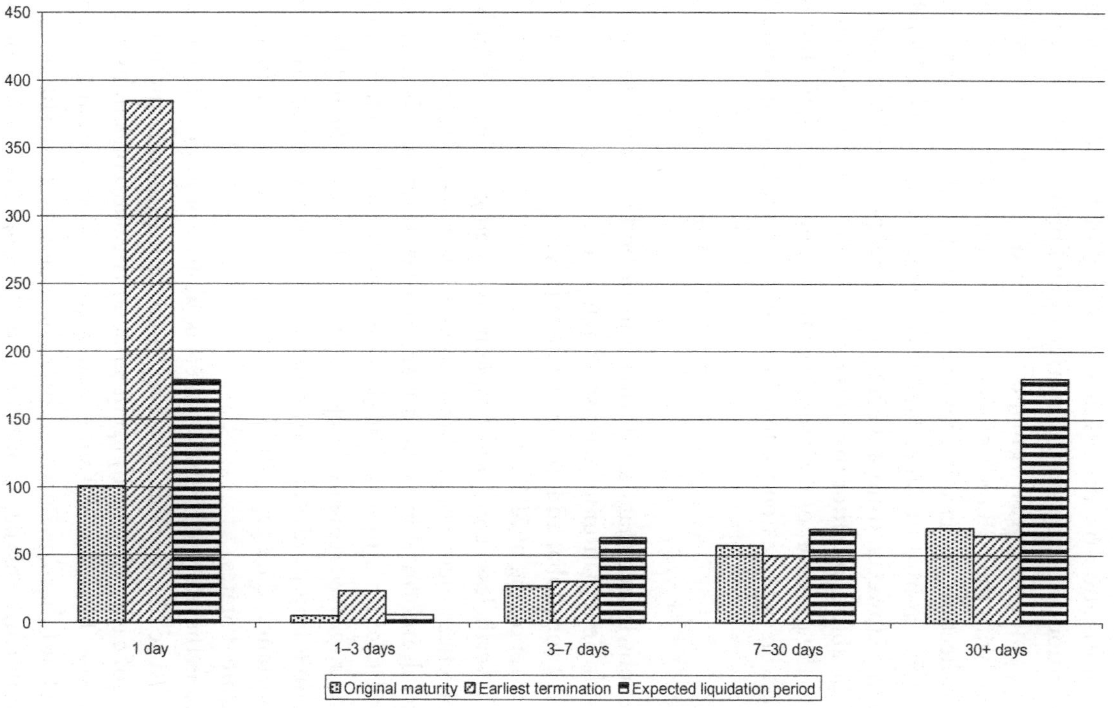

Fig. 5. Original maturity and earliest termination provision of securities lending transactions, and expected liquidation period of re-investments (€bn).

Source: ESRB.

(i.e., at the individual transaction or investment level, and greater detail on expected liquidation period especially as regards periods longer than 30 days in order to calculate weighted average maturity and liquidity). In addition, information on the residual maturity of the cash collateral received in addition to the original maturity should provide much greater clarity as to the amounts at risk. A mapping of the observed data gaps and areas of opacity with the FSB recommendations is warranted.

The data collection exercise is primarily targeted at agent lenders and other lenders who re-invest cash collateral obtained from securities lending transactions. However, from a macro-prudential perspective it can be important to be able to monitor the risks outlined above and also to detect any changes in the practices of cash re-investment. Therefore, in the future this data collection can be extended to other institutions than agent lenders.

Concluding Remarks

It is widely acknowledged that the information currently available to supervisors is not sufficient to monitor the risks that may arise from SFT markets. Policymakers at the global and local level have issued proposals for much more granular reporting of SFTs.

There is nevertheless scope for complementary efforts. First, in order to monitor practices such as the re-investment of cash collateral or the re-use of collateral, information beyond transaction-related data is needed. Second, it will take time to implement large-scale projects such as trade repositories or improved regulatory reporting. Any data that help to fill gaps in the short run is thus needed. Lastly, data gaps vary across jurisdiction. In Europe, for instance, data gaps on SFT markets are arguably much larger than in the United States.

The ESRB is therefore currently undertaking two one-off data collections on the re-use of non-cash collateral by credit institutions and on the re-investment of cash collateral by agent lenders. The data collections fulfill a double purpose: First, they fill some data gaps and improve supervisors' information about these practices. Second, they serve as "pilot studies" for a regular monitoring. This paper presents some preliminary findings of the data collections; a conclusion on how such regular monitoring should be designed is still premature. However, the first results suggest the usefulness of the information gathered.

The data on the re-use of non-cash collateral will provide useful insights in the network structure of collateral markets and cross-sector linkages. Such information could be used as input for macro-prudential risk analysis, in combination with additional risk-relevant information. In addition, the assessment of re-usage practices and the velocity of collateral, as well as high-level evidence on collateral and maturity transformation should provide relevant information for macro-prudential supervision.

The cash re-investment data collection reveals interesting information on the role of individual institutions, the agent lenders. This is a major step as only aggregate information is available currently to supervisors. The collection also provides insights on the risks that agent lenders take. The data collection may thus serve as a template for a regular monitoring.

References

Adrian, T., B. Begalle, A. Copeland and A. Martin (2011). Repo and Securities Lending. *Federal Reserve Bank of New York Staff Reports*, No. 529, December.

Duffie, D. (2013). Systemic Risk Exposures: A 10-by-10-by-10 Approach. In *Risk Topography: Systemic Risk and Macro Modeling*, M.K. Brunnermeier and A. Krishnamurthy (eds.). Chicago: University of Chicago Press.

European Systemic Risk Board (2013). Towards a Monitoring Framework for Securities Financing Transactions. *Occasional Paper* No. 2, March.

Financial Stability Board (2011). Shadow Banking: Scoping the Issues. April.

Financial Stability Board (2012). Securities Lending and Repos: Market Overview and Financial Stability Issues. April.

Financial Stability Board (2013). Strengthening Oversight and Regulation of Shadow Banking: Policy Framework for Addressing Shadow Banking Risks in Securities Lending and Repos. August.

Keane, F. (2013). Securities Loans Collateralized by Cash: Re-investment Risk, Run Risk and Incentive Issues. *Current Issues in Economics and Finance*, Vol. 19, No. 3, Federal Reserve Bank of New York.

Mehrling, P., Z. Pozsar, J. Sweeney and D.H. Neilson (2013). Bagehot was a Shadow Banker: Shadow Banking, Central Banking, and the Future of Global Finance. December.

Singh, M. (2011). Velocity of Pledged Collateral: Analysis and Implications. *IMF Working Paper* 11/256.

Shleifer, A. and R.W. Vishny (1992). Liquidation Values and Debt Capacity: A Market Equilibrium Approach. *Journal of Finance*, Vol. 47, No. 4, pp. 1343–1366.

Shleifer, A. and R.W. Vishny (1997). The Limits of Arbitrage. *Journal of Finance*, Vol. 52, No. 1, pp. 35–55.

Shleifer, A. and R.W. Vishny (2011). Fire Sales in Finance and Macroeconomics. *Journal of Economic Perspectives*, Vol. 25, No. 1, pp. 29–48.

Stein, J.C. (2013a). The Fire-sales Problem and Securities Financing Transactions. Speech at the Workshop on "Fire Sales" as a Driver of Systemic Risk in Tri-Party Repo and Other Secured Funding Markets. Federal Reserve Bank of New York, New York City, October.

Stein, J.C. (2013b). The Fire-Sales Problem and Securities Financing Transactions. IMF and Federal Reserve Bank of Chicago Conference "Shadow Banking Within and Across Borders", November.

Index

CPSIA information can be obtained at www.ICGtesting.com
Printed in the USA
BVOW09*0345090115

382579BV00004B/6/P